TRANSITION AND SCHOOL-BASED SERVICES

Transition and School-Based Services

Interdisciplinary Perspectives for Enhancing the Transition Process

Edited by
Sharon H. deFur
James R. Patton

An International Publisher

8700 Shoal Creek Boulevard
Austin, Texas 78757-6897
800/897-3202   Fax 800/397-7633
Order online at http://www.proedinc.com

© 1999 by PRO-ED, Inc.
8700 Shoal Creek Boulevard
Austin, Texas 78757-6897
800/897-3202   Fax 800/397-7633
Order online at http://www.proedinc.com   *# 40135305*

Publisher's Note: The Division on Career Development and Transition of the Council For Exceptional Children (CEC) will receive all royalties from sales of this book.

Library of Congress Cataloging-in-Publication Data

Transition and school-based services : interdisciplinary perspectives
  for enhancing the transition process / edited by Sharon DeFur, James
  R. Patton.
    p. cm.
  Includes bibliographical references and indexes.
  ISBN 0-89079-806-0 (softcover : alk. paper)
  1. Handicapped students—Services for—United States.
2. Handicapped students—Counseling of—United States. 3. Life
skills—Study and teaching (Secondary)—United States. 4. School-to
-work transition—United States. 5. Special education—United
States. I. DeFur, Sharon. II. Patton, James R.
LC4031.T72 1999
371.9'0473—dc21   98-47362
                                         CIP
This book is designed in Goudy.

Production Director: Alan Grimes
Production Coordinator: Dolly Fisk Jackson
Managing Editor: Chris Olson
Art Director: Thomas Barkley
Designer: Jason Crosier
Print Buyer: Alicia Woods
Preproduction Coordinator: Chris Anne Worsham
Staff Copyeditor: Martin Wilson
Publishing Assistant: John Means Cooper

Printed in the United States of America   FEB 2 9 2000

1   2   3   4   5   6   7   8   9   10   03   02   01   00   99

CONTENTS

Preface

The beginning of wisdom is to call things by their right name.

—Chinese proverb

Much has been written about the interdisciplinary nature of transition planning and service provision, but the primary focus has been on the transition services at the point of exiting school. The importance of working with vocational education, adult services, higher education, and community organizations cannot be overstated. Admittedly, postschool transition services remain underdeveloped and deserve ongoing attention.

This book, however, urges professionals who work with secondary students with disabilities to look at a different set of interdisciplinary team players and to consider what these potential team members bring to the in-school transition planning and services provision process. The Division on Career Development and Transition (DCDT) of the Council for Exceptional Children conceived this book as a result of increasing conversations with school-based providers who taught us the interrelationship of the fields described herein. The contributing authors to this book represent pioneers in their respective fields who are charting new ways of thinking about the way that their respective professions interface with one another.

DCDT identified increasing linkages with other professionals as one strategy to provide best practice information to professionals who provide transition-related services to children and youth with disabilities. What we realized were the multiple creative possibilities that emerge when such partnerships are formed. In reading this book, the special educator will discover partnerships they had not considered previously, the administrator will recognize staffing resources to accomplish school as well as student goals, and the school-based service provider will identify a place on the transition planning team that, perhaps, they had never considered.

In this book, special educators will find out how pupil personnel service and related service providers can offer specialized student and family support toward acquiring transition skills while still in school. Also, the authors offer ideas to address critical transition issues. For example, dropping out of school remains a national crisis for students with disabilities; administrators and teachers proclaim behavior challenges of students with disabilities to be major barriers to instruction; every state has raised expectations for all students, adding increased demands for appropriate accommodations; and families speak of the lack of socialization in and outside of school for their children. Furthermore, transition planning and service provision must begin early and there is now a legislative mandate to begin identifying transition service needs by age 14 and to consider the transition-related service needs of students. The need for Individual Education Program (IEP) transition planning teams to look holistically at students and their families emerges as central to successful postschool outcomes. This book calls for all professionals who work with secondary-aged students to come out of their professional isolation and work together to solve the complex issues facing students with disabilities and their families.

We believe that effective interdisciplinary work begins when we learn about one another's fields and perspectives. We are hopeful that this book offers you insight into your colleagues' professions and their role in transition planning and services. Together we can help youth and young adults create better futures for themselves.

S. H. deFur
J. R. Patton

Contributors

Steve Brannan, EdD
Portland State University
Foot of Southeast Spokane
    Street, #31
Portland, OR 97202

Gary M. Clark, EdD
Department of Special
    Education
3001 Dole Building
University of Kansas
Lawrence, KS 66045

Ann W. Cox, PhD, RN
Virginia Institute for Devel-
    opmental Disabilities
301 West Franklin Street
Richmond, VA 23220

Sharon H. deFur, EdD
College of William & Mary
School of Education
P.O. Box 8795
Williamsburg, VA 23187

Sherrilyn K. Fisher, PhD
I.R.M.C
600 Minnesota Avenue
Kansas City, KS 66101

Priscilla Harvell, MA
California State Depart-
    ment of Education
Diagnostic Center North-
    ern California
39100 Gallaudet Drive
Fremont, CA 94538

**Katherine J. Inge, PhD,
    OTR**
Virginia Commonwealth
    University—RRTC
P. O. Box 2011
Richmond, VA 23284

P. David Kurtz, PhD
University of Georgia
School of Social Work
212 Tucker Hall
Athens, GA 30604

Pamela J. Leconte, PhD
George Washington Uni-
    versity
2134 G Street NW
Washington, DC 20052

Edward M. Levinson, PhD
Indiana University of Penn-
    sylvania
Department of Educational
    & School Psychology
242 Stouffer Hall
Indiana, PA 15705

Martha Markward, PhD
University of Georgia
School of Social Work
212 Tucker Hall
Athens, GA 30604

James R. Patton, EdD
PRO-ED, Inc.
8700 Shoal Creek
    Boulevard
Austin, TX 78757

Jeanne B. Repetto, PhD
University of Florida
Department of Special
    Education
G 315 Norman Hall
Gainesville, FL 32611

**Kathleen J. Sawin, DNS,
    RN**
Virginia Commonwealth
    University
School of Nursing
Box 980567
Richmond, VA 23298

Jayne Shepherd, MS, OTR
Virginia Commonwealth
    University
Box 980008, MCV Station
Richmond, VA 23298

**Katherine O. Synatschk,
    PhD**
Austin Independent
    School District
1111 West 6th Street
Austin, TX 78703

Kristine Wiest Webb, PhD
University of Florida
Department of Special
    Education
G 315 Norman Hall
Gainesville, FL 32611

PART

I

FOUNDATIONS

CHAPTER

BASIC CONCEPTS OF THE TRANSITION PROCESS

James R. Patton

We thought that it would be beneficial to begin this book with a short chapter that highlights some of the major factors that should be considered in relation to transition practices. Although the following principles have been generated with students who have special needs in mind, they actually apply to all students.

The movement from high school to young adult life is a drastic transition for everyone. The idea of assessing needs, planning for these needs, and acting on these plans is sound practice. However, a mandate to implement such a process exists only for students who are eligible for special education and other necessary related services. A movement is afoot to expand this idea to include a larger range of students—all secondary-age students.

Successful Adult Functioning

To understand the importance of good transition planning, it is useful to consider the outcomes associated with successful functioning in adulthood, which is the ultimate goal of transition planning efforts. The diagram presented in Figure 1.1 depicts a simple conceptualization of the transition implications of adulthood. A brief explanation of the model, starting at the far right, follows.

In this model the ultimate outcome for which all professional efforts should be directed is to help create lives which are characterized by personal fulfillment. This concept relates closely to the notion of quality of life, as discussed by Halpern (1993). While the literature is replete with different definitions of

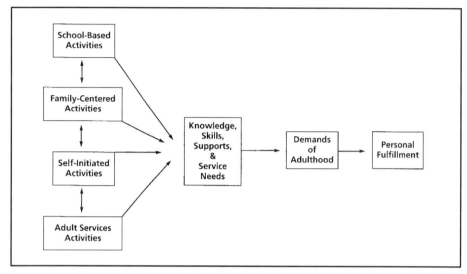

Figure 1.1. Adulthood implications of the transition process. *Note.* From *Transition From School to Young Adulthood: Basic Concepts and Recommended Practices* (p. 5), by J. R. Patton and C. Dunn, 1998, Austin, TX: PRO-ED. Copyright 1998 by PRO-ED, Inc. Reprinted with permission.

quality of life, Halpern suggests that quality of life—or personal fulfillment—relates to three elements: happiness (transient state of affect); satisfaction (feelings and behavior patterns associated with different adult roles); and sense of general well-being (enduring sense of satisfaction with one's life). All that professionals do with students should be guided by the overriding theme of enhancing their quality of life by imparting the means for them to be personally fulfilled.

To enjoy some sense of personal fulfillment, an individual must be reasonably successful in meeting the challenges of everyday life, whether at work, at home, in school, or in the community. Various references (Brolin, 1993; Cronin & Patton, 1993) provide listings of the major demands encountered in adulthood. People who feel that they are personally fulfilled do not always deal successfully with the day-to-day issues that arise in their lives; however, they are more likely to handle them successfully most of the time.

How does one become competent to deal with the daily challenges of life? Three factors are essential. First, an individual must have knowledge of an array of facts, procedures, and events which are part of her or his postschool environments. Second, the individuals needs to acquire specific skills that will be necessary in the assortment of settings in which the person must function. Third, the person must identify, access, and use a host of supports or services which will be of great assistance in dealing with everyday events.

It is possible to think of the individual supports and services as related or as part of a continuum. Luckasson et al. (1992) suggest that services are "a subset of supports or . . . a type of support" (p. 144). A slight distinction is used in this book. *Supports* involve a variety of resources, including other people (e.g., family, friends, co-workers) or technology (e.g., assistive devices), whereas *services* are either generic (i.e., available to all in the community, such as community mental health services) or specialized (i.e., services for which one usually has to be determined eligible under some set of criteria, such as vocational rehabilitation or personal care attendants). The point is that everybody uses supports and services throughout life and the idea of seeking such support is a natural part of life.

As can be seen n Figure 1.1, four entities share the responsibility for preparing students for adulthood. These four elements—school, family, the student, and adult services—are intricately involved in the transition process. Ideally, efforts to prepare students for dealing with the everyday challenges of adulthood begin early in school as a part of the ongoing education of students. This proactive approach to transition can be considered transition education (Clark & Kolstoe, 1995). Transition efforts which begin around age 14 are more reactive in nature and are limited to a more restricted timeframe (i.e., the amount of time a student remains in school).

It is important to recognize that the process whereby students are taught the knowledge and skills as well as linked to the supports and services they will need later on is a shared responsibility. While schools operate under the mandate of federal regulations and should take the lead in this effort, the family, the student, and other service providers also play critical roles. In reality, however, nonschool players might not contribute substantially to the overall process. When this is the case, school-based personnel will likely need to play a much more critical role.

Guiding Principles of the Transition Process

Certain principles can be gleaned from the professional literature on transition as well from ongoing practice, as reported by those who are involved in the transition process on a day-to-day basis. The following list is adapted from the book *Transition from School to Young Adulthood: Basic Concepts and Recommended Practices* (Patton & Dunn, 1998). These fundamental principles permeate the remaining chapters in this book.

▶ **1. Transition efforts should start early.**

This point has been emphasized in various forums by a number of different professionals. One example of support for starting early is shown in the position statement on the definition of transition that was developed by the Division on Career Development and Transition of the Council for Exceptional Children (Halpern, 1994). The definition of transition, as embedded within this position statement, states that "the foundation for transition should be laid during the elementary and middle school years" (p. 250). Changes to the regulations governing the transition process, as spelled out in the 1997 reauthorization of the Individuals with Disabilities Education Act (IDEA), underscore the importance of starting the actual planning process at an earlier age.

Without question, it is preferable to consider the transition process from a proactive rather than a reactive perspective. Certain precursors of the knowledge and skills needed in adulthood can be started at the preschool level. Most can be addressed prior to the time when transition needs are assessed at the age of 14. What is needed is a systematic K–12 transition education program which has a strong base at the elementary level (Clark, Carlson, Fisher, Cook, & D'Alonzo, 1991).

Families should be informed of the transition process early on. They can be provided information that they need to consider as their son or daughter moves through school. Moreover, as many families have come to learn, some transition-related activities must be initiated early to ensure a seamless transition to postschool settings (e.g., getting a student's name on a waiting list for a community living setting).

▶ **2. Planning must be comprehensive.**

The main message associated with this principle is that a range of adult outcome areas should be evaluated when a needs assessment is conducted. If a strong proactive transition education program is in place, then fewer areas of need are likely to be identified. Nevertheless, a comprehensive look at each student must be performed, and dismissal of some transition planning areas should not be done solely as a function of the student's disability. Comprehensive transition planning must include attention to the following dimensions: employment, further education/training, daily living (including money management and personal management), leisure activities, community participation, health (physical, emotional, and spiritual), self-determination/self-advocacy, communication, interpersonal relationships/social skills, and transportation/mobility.

For instance, certain aspects of the transitional needs of certain youth, particularly those with learning disabilities, may be overlooked because of the misconception that these students do not have needs in some areas (e.g., daily living). The data on functional abilities depicted in Table 1.1 suggests that a number of young adults with learning disabilities need to acquire basic functional skills along with other community living skills. This table does not address some of the more spe-

Table 1.1
Functional Abilities, By Disability Category

Disability Category	Percentage of Youth with Parents Reporting:		
	High* Self-Care Skills	High† Functional Mental Skills	High‡ Community-Living Skills
All conditions	86.4	56.9	61.4
Learning disabled	95.5	66.0	74.2
Emotionally disturbed	94.1	65.3	66.9
Speech impaired	91.8	68.9	67.3
Mentally retarded	67.4	32.8	29.4
Visually impaired	51.6	31.8	41.2
Deaf	83.4	44.3	43.4
Hard of hearing	92.3	60.7	45.8
Orthopedically impaired	42.3	50.5	32.5
Other health impaired	65.3	57.3	41.2
Multiply handicapped	34.5	12.8	21.3
Deaf/blind	21.0	6.8	13.2

Note. Adapted from *The Transition Experiences of Young People with Disabilities: A Summary of Findings from the National Longitudinal Transition Study of Special Education Students,* by M. Wagner, J. Blackorby, R. Cameto, K. Hebbeler, and L. Newman, 1993, Menlo Park, CA: SRI International.

*Skills include dressing oneself, feeding oneself, and getting around outside the home. Scale ranges from 3 to 12. High is 12.

†Skills include counting change, reading common signs, telling time on an analog clock, and looking up telephone numbers and using the phone. Scale ranges from 4 to 16. High is 15 or 16.

‡Skills include using public transportation, buying clothes, arranging a trip out of town, and using community resources, such as a swimming pool or library. Scale ranges from 4 to 16. High is 15 or 16.

cific transition needs that these students need to have (e.g., study skills deficits) in order to be successful in settings like postsecondary education.

▶ 3. The planning process must balance what is ideal with what is possible.

It is easy to recommend that transition services should be comprehensive and suggest that a great amount of effort be put into the transition process for each student. While this recommendation is sound and the accompanying suggestion warranted, the realities of serving large numbers of students must be taken into consideration. The practices associated with sound transition planning practice must be acceptable to those who have to carry them out. This concept, known as *treatment acceptability*, is important to appreciate when developing transition services, if professionals want such services implemented.

Recommended practices need to be immediately useful to school-based staff and they cannot be too time demanding. Some transition specialists have extremely large caseloads and they are not able to conduct in-depth assessments on every student. Techniques and methodologies are needed that provide as much information as possible within a reasonable amount of time and with a reasonable amount of effort. The appropriate use of information that already exists on students, along with the efficient and effective utilization of other school-based personnel, can contribute to making the task of designing comprehensive transition plans easier.

▶ **4. Student empowerment is essential.**

The literature on transition regularly stresses the importance of preparing students to be active, contributing participants in their transition planning process. They should be because it is their lives which are being discussed and about which decisions are being made. The physical presence of students at their transition planning meeting is not sufficient; they should be the driving force behind this process and the meeting. Of course, this will not always be possible, as a small number of students may not be capable of directing their transition planning process. However, far too few capable students are active contributors.

In recent years, a number of curricular materials focused on teaching students how to become active players in the planning process have become commercially available. Two notable examples of this type of material are *NEXT S.T.E.P.: Student Transition and Educational Planning* (Halpern et al., 1997) and *ChoiceMaker Self-Determination Curriculum: Self-Directed IEP* (Martin, Huber Marshall, Maxson, & Jerman, 1996).

▶ **5. Family involvement is crucial.**

Families play a key role in the shared responsibility for preparing their children for dealing successfully with the challenges of life. Moreover, for most young adults with disabilities, it is their parents or guardians who become their service coordinators during their young adult lives. For these reasons, it is imperative that parents and guardians become informed, skilled, and active in the transition process. Clark and Patton (1997) suggest that, in addition to determining the preferences and interests of students, it is valuable to do the same with families.

Transition professionals must not become disillusioned by the fact that a substantial number of parents and guardians will either choose not to assume the important role discussed above or will be ineffective in this role. During the time the student is still in school, it is possible and necessary for school-based personnel to take responsibility for certain critical activities for which the families should share responsibility. After students exit the school system, they and their families are very often on their own, without the supports they have previously had available.

One idea that comes from the practices associated with early intervention services is to conduct transition planning activities such as those used in the development of the Individual Family Service Plan (IFSP). One of the components of the IFSP is information on the family's strengths and needs. This information is used to assist in the development of services that will benefit the young child. Similarly, it may be useful to assess a family's strengths and needs when generating transition plans, particularly when determining who should be responsible for carrying out crucial transition planning activities, such as making contacts with needed adult service providers.

Transition personnel must respect family values. It is important to recognize that families will base their requests, opinions, and comments on their own community or cultural values, practices, and traditions. Their perspectives must be respected, even when in conflict with those of school-based personnel.

▶ 6. The transition planning process must be sensitive to diversity.

There is no question that the transition process is affected by the changing demography in this country (Patton, Cronin, & Jairrels, 1997). Heightened awareness of cultural diversity has emerged in recent years, and clearly, sensitivity to specific cultural distinctions must be taken into account. However, cultural diversity is only one type of diversity that must be addressed. Other important dimensions include race, ethnicity, religious beliefs, gender, and sexual orientation. Although all of these elements are worthy of attention, specific considerations are not always obvious. For instance, gender issues, as they relate to the transition process, may be so subtle that they are overlooked. For example, it is quite likely that female students may be limited in their exposure to various vocational options such as plumbing. Female students should be afforded a wide range of choices that are not limited to gender-specific stereotypes.

▶ 7. Everyone uses supports and services.

As the John Cougar Mellencamp song suggests, "everyone needs a hand to hold on to." All people, as Condeluci (1995) notes, are interdependent beings. It is very natural for people to use natural supports that exist in their everyday environments. People ask co-workers for rides to work when their cars are in for repair. People drop off their children at their grandparents house when they need to be away from home. People pay folks to cut their grass, pick up their garbage, clean their clothes. People use community services regularly. Interestingly, few people find anything wrong with using a myriad of supports and services.

With this in mind, it is essential that specialists convey to youth with special needs that the use of supports and services is acceptable and often essential. Transition personnel need to teach these individuals when and how to use the array of natural supports and services available to them in the settings in which they live, work, and play. Transition personnel must also be careful not to create situations where students are overly and unnecessarily reliant on supports.

▶ **8. Community-based activities are important.**

Most students with disabilities will prosper from experiences that are provided in real-life contexts. These students are more likely to acquire the knowledge and skills they will need to function in community settings if they have opportunities to learn and practice in these actual settings.

Community-based assessment and community-based instruction are strongly recommended for determining a student's needs and providing meaningful learning. One of the strongest reasons for delivering instruction in community settings is that many individuals with disabilities have difficulty generalizing the skills they have learned in the classroom to community settings (Dunn & Rabren, 1997). Community-based instruction can occur at all levels of schooling; however, it is most often utilized at the secondary level.

▶ **9. Interagency commitment, cooperation, and coordination must be strengthened.**

Adult service providers are key players in the transition process. Most adult services, such as vocational rehabilitation, mental health, human services, and postsecondary education institutions, whether public or private, are responsible for a wide range of services, with transition not being one of their major charges. However, to enhance the overall effectiveness of the transition planning process, adult service providers must be involved. As a result, efforts must be ongoing to improve the coordination of various agencies and school-based transition services.

▶ **10. Timing is crucial if certain linkages are to be made and a seamless transition to life after high school is to be achieved.**

Changes associated with the reauthorization of IDEA provide a strong message that the timing associated with the transition planning process is critical. A statement of transition needs is now required by age 14 for all identified students. This requirement improves the chances that appropriate plans will be developed and that requisite activities will be performed.

The overall goal is for the student to move from school to all subsequent settings without difficulty and without the interruption of services that will be needed (i.e., seamless transition). Only when the timing is right will transition personnel be able to accomplish this goal.

▶ **11. Transition planning process should be considered a capacity-building activity.**

Considering the transition needs of students is by definition a deficit-oriented process. While this cannot be totally ignored, the process should promote the recognition of the student's strengths as well as weaknesses. A thorough needs assessment should determine both areas of concern and areas where the individual shows competence and proficiency. Transition staff need to consider both aspects of the student's profile. The multiple dimensions that should be examined, if a comprehension transition process is invoked, provide a suitable framework for looking at the strengths of the student.

▶ **12. Ranking of transition needs must occur.**

Some youth will display an extensive list of needs. Whereas the identification of these needs is extremely important, the issue of which needs should be addressed first arises. If the student is likely to exit school in the near future, a ranking of the student's needs must be completed. This ranking can be based on a number of factors, such as which areas are most critical for successful adult functioning, or which areas the individual will encounter first. The priority that will be chosen should be determined by the student when appropriate.

▶ **13. Transition planning is beneficial to all students.**

Comprehensive transition planning makes sense for all students in school. In reality, most students leave school underprepared for many of the challenges of young adulthood. Even those students who go to well-respected schools, who grew up in the most loving and nurturing families, and who display conceptual and practical intelligence, are very likely to go to college or enter the workforce without the knowledge and skills to deal successfully with various demands of everyday life.

To date, systematic transition planning is only required for students who are eligible for services under IDEA. However, rumblings are beginning to be heard in other quarters. The National Association of Secondary School Principals (NASSP) (1996), in their document entitled *Breaking Ranks: Changing an American Institution*, espouses the idea of individual planning: "Each student will have a *Personal Plan for Progress* to ensure that the high school takes individual needs into consideration" (p. 11).

NASSP recognizes the need for transition planning as well, and recommends that activities begin during high school and address postschool issues.

By the time a student reaches the halfway point in high school, the *Personal Plan for Progress* should start emphasizing a transition plan to direct the student's curricular goals toward whatever it is that the young person wants to do after earning a diploma. Even a dropout will have a progress plan so that the youngster leaves with a blueprint for making as good use as possible of the immediate future and perhaps for returning to formal education. (p. 18)

The principles highlighted in this chapter serve as major benchmarks by which transition services should be evaluated. As mentioned, these topics will resurface throughout the chapters in this book. This list is by no means complete, as other important points and guiding principles could have been included. Its intent is to be a vehicle for focusing attention during the ensuing discussions on transition provided by authorities who represent a wide array of school-related services. Let the journey begin.

References

Brolin, D. E. (1993). *Life centered career education: A competency-based approach* (4th ed.). Reston, VA: The Council for Exceptional Children.

Clark, G. M., & Kolstoe, O. P. (1995). *Career development and transition education for adolescents with disabilities* (2nd ed.). Needham Heights, MA: Allyn & Bacon.

Clark, G. M., Carlson, B. C., Fisher, S., Cook, J. D., & D'Alonzo, B. J. (1991). Career development for students with disabilities in elementary schools: A position statement of the Division on Career Development. *Career Development for Exceptional Individuals, 14,* 109–120.

Clark, G. M., & Patton, J. R. (1997). *Transition Planning Inventory.* Austin, TX: PRO-ED.

Condeluci, A. (1995). Interdependence: The route to community (2nd ed.). Winter Park, FL: GR Press.

Cronin, M. E., & Patton, J. R. (1993). *Life skills instruction for all students with special needs: A practical guide for integrating real-life content into the curriculum.* Austin, TX: PRO-ED.

Dunn, C., & Rabren, K. (1997). Preparation practices. In P. Browning (Ed.), *Transition in action for youth and young adults with disabilities* (pp. 173–204). Montgomery, AL: Wells Printing.

Halpern, A. S. (1993). Quality of life as a conceptual framework for evaluating transition outcomes. *Exceptional Children, 59,* 486–498.

Halpern, A. S. (1994). The transition of youth with disabilities to adult life: A position statement of the Division on Career Development and Transition, The Council for Exceptional Children. *Career Development for Exceptional Individuals, 17,* 115–124.

Halptern, A. S., Herr, C. M., Wolf, N. K., Doren, B., Johnson, M. D., Lawson, J. D. (1997). *NEXT S.T.E.P.: Student transition and educational planning.* Austin, TX: PRO-ED.

Luckasson, R., Coulter, D. L., Polloway, E. A., Reiss, S., Shalock, R. L., Snell, M. E., Spitalnik, D. M., & Stark, J. A. (1992). *Mental retardation: Definition, classification, and systems of supports* (9th ed.). Washington, DC: American Association on Mental Retardation.

Martin, J. E., & Huber Marshall, L. H. (1996). *Choicemaker self-determination curriculum: Self-directed IEP.* Longmont, CO: Sopris West.

National Association of Secondary School Principals. (1996). *Breaking ranks: Changing an American institution*. Reston, VA: Author.

Patton, J. R., Cronin, M. E., & Jairrels, V. (1997). Curricular implications of transition: Life skills instruction as an integral part of transition education. *Remedial and Special Education, 18*, 294–306.

Patton, J. R., & Dunn, C. (1998). Transition from school to young adulthood: Basic concepts and recommended practices. Austin, TX: PRO-ED.

Wagner, M., Blackorby, J., Cameto, R., Hebbeler, K., & Newman, L. (1993). *The transition experiences of young people with disabilities: A summary of findings from the National Longitudinal Transition Study of special education students*. Menlo Park, CA: SRI International.

CHAPTER

SPECIAL EDUCATION, TRANSITION, AND SCHOOL-BASED SERVICES: ARE THEY MEANT FOR EACH OTHER?

Sharon H. deFur

Transition refers to a change in status from behaving primarily as a student to assuming emergent adult roles in the community. These roles include employment, participating in post-secondary education, maintaining a home, becoming appropriately involved in the community, and experiencing satisfactory personal and social relationships. The process of enhancing transition involves the participation and coordination of school programs, adult agency services, and natural supports within the community. The foundations for transition should be laid during the elementary and middle school years, guided by the broad concept of career development. Transition planning should begin no later than age 14, and students should be encouraged, to the full extent of their capabilities, to assume a maximum amount of responsibility for such planning (The DCDT Position on Transition, Halpern, 1994).

Upon graduation, youth with disabilities, like their nondisabled peers, want opportunities to live, learn, and work as active members of the adult community. Many of these youth face disability-related challenges in entering postsecondary education, employment, and independent living as young adults. Many face challenges negotiating the secondary education culture and curriculum; many experience academic and social failure, compounded by adolescence; and many choose to disengage from the school community. Special education may help youth and their families in this transition phase, but special educators alone do not have the full range of expertise needed to confront these challenges. School systems include a broad range of actual or potential services, from related specialized services to prevention services, from direct services to consultative services. Existing services can be coordinated across service providers, or new services can be created through cooperative efforts to meet the individual needs of adolescents and young adults with disabilities.

Secondary special educators, as individual education program and individual transition plan case managers, hold a primary responsibility for developing or providing transition services for youth with disabilities. For some, this new role comes naturally and fits with both their training and their philosophy; for many others, the role feels in conflict with the traditional academic focus of secondary special education (Knott, 1997). Transition service policy and philosophy promote a team approach, but originally the transition team focused on adding the adult service provider and the student to the traditional IEP team. Although these team members retain importance in preparing for students' exit from school, research shows that long-range planning or transition planning must begin much earlier than in the final year or two of school (Clark, Carlson, Fisher, Cook, & D'Alonzo, 1991; Morningstar, Turnbull, & Turnbull, 1996; Repetto & Correa, 1996). The transition planning team therefore must develop a focus on in-school services as well as postschool services. Broadening the potential membership of the interdisciplinary school transition team represents a first step in articulating this focus.

In this chapter, the historical and existing relationships of school-based services and secondary special education are examined, focusing on the transition planning process. Special educators are challenged to take a leadership role in coordinating the existing resources within school settings to provide the supports and services students need to experience success that prepares them for effective adult roles.

Historical Overview of Special Education and Transition

Special education law guaranteeing a free appropriate public education has been operative for nearly 25 years. Policy analysts and education researchers continue to examine the impact that this complex legislation has had on the lifelong outcomes for people with disabilities. This law, unlike any other education law, attempts to standardize procedures for addressing the needs of individuals with disabilities and their families, granting them safeguards against those who would relegate these individuals to a second-class status. The law was conceived during an era when government assumed a role of equalizer. The law survived the recent emphasis of decreasing the role of government, and emerged with an amended law that maintains assurance of equal access while adding components of accountability, a current prevailing federal philosophy. Table 2.1 provides an overview of disability-related legislation developed over the past 30 years. This review illustrates the evolution of laws that began with providing access to opportunities to current laws that set standards for programs that promote independence and community integration.

An Era of Equality

In 1975, when then President Ford signed P.L. 94-142, the Education of All Handicapped Children Act (EHA), disability advocates celebrated. In retrospect, this disability civil rights initiative began two decades earlier when the decision over *Brown vs. Board of Education* (1954) transformed the educational system to one where the right to a free and appropriate integrated education became law. Early efforts on behalf of children with disabilities focused on equal opportunity, access, and equity, paralleling efforts occurring with racial integration as well as with the implementation of Title IX, which addressed issues of gender inequality. Consistent with these initiatives, policy makers set about framing legislation that intended to address issues of equality, thus forming the underpinnings for the original EHA.

Furthermore, in creating the EHA, policy makers responded to the testimony of families and advocates that cited barriers that the educational system had in place for serving students with disabilities; the 94th Congress attempted to carry out legislation that would be preventive of recurring inequities. The policy intent behind each EHA requirement reflected a federal attempt to reduce the possibility of discrimination by public education and maximize the possibility for opportunities for educational access. (In the 18th Report to Congress on the Implementation of the Individuals with Disabilities Education Act, the United States Department of Education [USDOE] reported that this country had achieved this primary goal of students with disabilities being offered a free appropriate public education, with 95% of these students now receiving services in regular school buildings [USDOE, 1996].)

In developing this legislation, the concept of an IEP designed to meet the unique needs of a student with a disability emerged; this component recognized

(*Text continues on page 20*)

Table 2.1
Selected Federal Legislation Related to Special Education and Transition Services for Youth with Disabilities

Year	Legislation	Public Law	Transition Implications
1969	Elementary and Secondary Education Amendments	91-230	Title VI of the 1969 amendments established the Education of the Handicapped Act. Title VI added programs to serve children with specific learning disabilities.
1973	Rehabilitation Act	93-112	Section 503 requires employers receiving federal contracts to take affirmative action to recruit, hire, train, and promote individuals with disabilities. Section 504 is considered the first civil rights law protecting the rights of individuals with disabilities. Section 504 statute reads, "No otherwise qualified handicapped individual in the United States shall, solely by reason of his handicap, be excluded from participation in, be denied the benefits of, or be subjected to discrimination under any program or activity receiving Federal financial assistance." This section also includes requirements that 1) individuals with disabilities must have opportunities to participate in or benefit from services equal to those that are provided to other individuals; for example, excluding children or youth with disabilities from any education programs because of their disability violates their civil rights; 2) colleges and postsecondary programs that receive federal funds may not discriminate against applicants on the basis of disability; in addition, these postsecondary institutions must make reasonable accommodations to make it possible for qualified students with disabilities to participate; and 3) all programs must be barrier-free. Programs or institutions that fail to comply with these requirements risk losing all federal funds received by the institution or agency. Benefits of this legislation for youth with disabilities include increased access and support in institutes of higher education and community college.
1975	Education of All Handicapped Children Act (EHA)	94-142	Mandated free, appropriate public education for all children and youth with disabilities, including special education and related services. A written individualized education program (IEP) must be developed and implemented for all children and youth eligible for special education or related services.
1976	Vocational Education Act Amendments	94-482	Extended the provision of vocational education services to disabled individuals of all ages. Secondary and postsecondary programs receive funds, of which a percentage must be spent on special populations. Vocational education plans for youth with disabilities must be coordinated with the youth's IEP. Youth with disabilities participating in vocational education are afforded the same assurances guaranteed by Section 504 and PL 94-142.
1981	Rehabilitation Comprehensive Services and Developmental Disabilities Act of 1978	95-602	This law was interpreted by the Rehabilitation Services Administration to allow persons with severe learning disabilities to receive rehabilitation services.
1982	Job Training Partnership Act (JTPA)	97-300	Established programs to prepare youth and unskilled adults for entry into the labor force and to afford job training to those economically disadvantaged persons, and other persons facing serious barriers to employment. Persons with disabilities are eligible for JTPA training. Youth with disabilities can participate in programs funded under JTPA programs while in secondary school as well as after exiting secondary school.
1983	Education of All Handicapped Children Act Amendments	98-199	Established a new grant authority to fund programs to improve secondary special education and transitional services for youth with disabilities.
1984 and 1986	Rehabilitation Act Amendments	98-221 & 98-506	Increased the emphasis on services to youth with disabilities. In the 1986 amendments to the Rehabilitation Act, the state plan requirements were changed to require states to: (a) plan for individuals who are making the transition from school to work, and (b) reflect how the state rehabilitation agencies will implement the new supported employment program.

Year	Act	Number	Description
1984	Carl D. Perkins Vocational Education Act	98-524	Strengthened provisions and assurances to youth with disabilities, including access to the full range of vocational program offerings in the least restrictive environment and the provision of vocational assessment prior to students entering vocational education.
1990	Carl Perkins Vocational and Applied Technology Education Act	101-392	Significant funding changes were made in this legislation, but the assurances for special populations were maintained and the emphasis on transition support increased. In addition, vocational education is expected to coordinate efforts with vocational rehabilitation as well as special education. This legislation established a technical preparation program (Tech Prep) that begins with two years of preparation in secondary school, followed by two years of training in community college.
1990	Individuals with Disabilities Education Act (IDEA)	101-476	(Formerly Education of All Handicapped Children Act) Defined transition services as follows (§602(a)(19)): a coordinated set of activities for a student, designed within an *outcome-oriented* process, which promotes movement from school to postschool activities, including postsecondary education, vocational training, integrated employment (including supported employment), continuing and adult education, adult services, independent living, and community participation. The coordinated set of activities shall be based upon the individual student's needs, taking into account the student's preferences and interests, and shall include: instruction, community experiences, the development of employment and other postschool adult living objectives, and, when appropriate, acquisition of daily living skills and functional vocational evaluation. In §602(a)(20) a requirement was added that the IEP include a statement of the needed transition services for students beginning no later than age 16 and annually thereafter (and, when determined appropriate for the individual, beginning at age 14 or younger), including, when appropriate, a statement of interagency responsibilities or linkages (or both) before the student leaves the school setting.
1990	Americans with Disabilities Act (ADA)	101-376	Guarantees equal opportunity for persons with disabilities in employment, public accommodations, transportation, state and local government services, and telecommunications.
1992	Rehabilitation Reauthorization Act	102-569	Directs state rehabilitation agencies to address working with youth with disabilities in the state plan. Intention is to reduce service gaps between education and rehabilitative services when these are needed for exiting students. The legislation intends to strengthen the coordination between vocational rehabilitation and the schools, including exchange of information and data, provision of services, and access to rehabilitation services.
1994	School-to-Work Opportunities Act	102-239	Promotes the development of transition programs for all students and echoes the role for agency and community cooperation. Demonstrating cooperation at the federal level, selected funding from the U.S. Department of Education and the U.S. Department of Labor are combined to provide money to establish statewide systems for school-to-work opportunities for all students. In addition to state funds, the Act also provides grants to local *partnerships*, which include broad community representation, including people with disabilities.
1997	Individuals with Disabilities Education Act Amendments	105-17	Added related services to the coordinated set of activities offered to students with disabilities as transition services. It also added the requirement that by age 14, IEP committees address transition goals, including the secondary education course offerings that facilitate achieving postschool transition goals. The Act Amendments clarified that all rights given to parents under IDEA transfer to students who reach the age of majority (18 in most states) and who can give informed consent. It expanded the emphasis on the inclusion of students with disabilities in statewide assessment and required that an alternate assessment be developed for students who do not participate in statewide assessment.

Note. Adapted from "Transition of Youths with Learning Disabilities to Adulthood: The Secondary Education Foundation," by S. deFur and H. Reiff, 1994, in *Adults with Learning Disabilities* (pp. 101–102), by P. J. Gerber and H. B. Reiff (Eds.), Andover, MA: Andover Medical Press.

that students with disabilities require specialized instruction to achieve success in the public school environment. For some students, related services would also be necessary to benefit from special education. The IEP remains the central focus of special education—it is the process and place where decisions are made and special education programs are planned.

Early special education policy framers heard testimony that revealed that decisions about students with disabilities—that is, decisions such as special education classification, education programs, and acceptance into schools—were often made by one person; at times, these decisions went against the will of the parents. The policy framers heard from researchers that better and fairer decisions would be made by a team of people. Thus, the concept of the multidisciplinary team as the context for special education decisions was established. Parents, educators, and support services were to be equal partners in developing students' educational programs.

An Era of Accountability Emerges

Beginning in the 1980s, the atmosphere in Washington, D.C. began changing from a focus on equality to one of accountability and results. In this context, researchers looked at the outcomes of the first generation of students to exit school after having received special education. Both researchers and policy makers were sorely disappointed. Students with disabilities experienced lower rates of employment, lower wages, and lower independence than their peers without disabilities (Fardig, Algozzine, Schwartz, Hensel, & Westling, 1985; Hasazi, Gordon, & Roe, 1985; Mithaug, Horiuchi, & Fanning, 1985). In the 1983 reauthorization of the EHA, secondary special education services were challenged and encouraged to provide educational opportunities that promoted a seamless transition from school to employment by linking students with the appropriate adult service agency (EHA, 1983; Will, 1984); however, no federal requirements accompanied this policy. Some states took proactive steps and mandated school to postschool transition planning, but for the most part, only fragmented efforts occurred.

1990 IDEA Amendments

In 1990, the EHA was amended and renamed the Individuals with Disabilities Education Act (IDEA) (P.L. 101-476). These amendments included a mandate for transition services and planning for all students with disabilities, ages 16 and older; these services were to be addressed in the IEP/ITP of all students, a clear signal that transition services were to be an integral part of every student's special education program. Furthermore, regulations specified that transition services should include the development of employment and other adult living objectives, instruction, and community experiences, unless the IEP/ITP team could justify not providing these services. Students' interests and preferences, which could be best articulated by having the student present at the meeting, influenced transition service decisions. In addition, the local school division was responsible for including adult service providers or other organizations that might provide or pay for such transition services in the meeting. Policy makers moved from a position of articulating legislation that guaranteed equal opportunity to a position of structuring policy designed to produce desired outcomes through specifying the ideas believed to contribute to those outcomes.

IDEA Outcome Findings

Each year since the implementation of EHA, the United States Department of Education (USDOE) has reported to Congress on the status of special education and students with disabilities. Follow-up research conducted within states and localities in the early 1980s sparked the USDOE to commission a National Longitudinal Transition Study that followed the postschool status of students with disabilities who left school between 1988 and 1990. This study, along with other outcome research, formed the basis for USDOE's report on the relationship of secondary school experiences to the early postschool results of youth with disabilities in the 17th Annual Report to Congress on the implementation of the IDEA (1995). The findings are disturbing in some areas and encouraging in others.

Although the increases in the educational levels of individuals with disabilities have been considerable, students with disabilities continue to experience high drop-out rates. Nationally, in 1993, 30% of those students enrolled in grades 9–12 dropped out of school, while another 8% left before entering grade 9. Twenty-eight percent of youth with learning disabilities and 48% of students with emotional disabilities left school before graduating or completing a vocational program. The follow-up data found that students who dropped out of school were less likely to enroll in postsecondary, vocational, or academic programs. In addition, these students faced greater difficulties in finding and keeping employment. Policy and programs that attempted to decrease the likelihood of students dropping out were a natural response to these findings. Clearly, age 16, the required age for initiating transition services, is too late to prevent students from dropping out of school.

Employment outcomes for young adults with disabilities represent a major accountability benchmark for IDEA. Independence and integration into the community share equal importance with employment. In an era where lifelong learning becomes more important each day, postsecondary education also represents an important outcome measurement. The good news is that overall young adults with disabilities are beginning to report improved outcomes in employment and postsecondary education, particularly when compared with older people with disabilities. These rates of employment and participation in education do remain behind those of their peers without disabilities, although for some students, such as those who have learning disabilities, these differences are minimal.

The 17th Annual Report to Congress (USDOE, 1995) reported that three important determinants for employment success (initial rates and wages) for students with disabilities emerge from the research. These determinants include: 1) time spent in regular education; 2) work experience during secondary school; and 3) vocational education during secondary school. Likewise, time spent in regular education correlated with more positive outcomes for living independently and being more fully integrated into the community. This correlation may be related to the inherent competencies of individual students; that is, students who have more academic and social competencies are more likely to receive their primary education in regular education and are more likely to experience success in employment and independent living. However, *successful* interaction with the regular environment plays a major role in promoting positive postschool outcomes for students with disabilities.

Successful interactions in school developed as a theme for postschool success in the 17th Annual Report (USDOE, 1995). For example, community work experiences during secondary school were associated with a lower drop-out rate. Participation in vocational survey courses contributed significantly to the probability of competitive employment, and successfully completing a concentration in a specific vocational area resulted in a much higher rate of yearly pay (USDOE, 1995). On the other hand, many students with disabilities experienced high failure rates in high school, especially in the 9th and 10th grades. Course failure was one of the strongest predictors of dropping out, which leads to a litany of other negative outcomes. The report concluded that successful time in regular education relates to positive results; for those students who fail, the result can be harmful. The report suggested that secondary special education can contribute most to postschool success by creating an environment where students with disabilities experience school success, whatever their placement. The outcome data suggested that secondary regular and special education and related services were failing to create that environment for many students. Policy makers responded by articulating those factors believed to create the framework for success.

1997 Reauthorization of IDEA (P.L. 105-17)

In June of 1997, President Clinton signed new amendments to the IDEA. These amendments made changes that have implications for a new emphasis on transition services as a means to achieve improved outcomes for individuals with disabilities. Access to the general curriculum, clear measurement of student progress, and student participation in statewide accountability testing (standard or nonstandard) combine with clear roles of families and students as partners in the process and illustrate some of the changes of the new law.

The IDEA of 1997 cited findings that suggested that the implementation of IDEA has been hindered both by low expectations and by a lack of attention to research on proven methods of teaching. The findings emphasized the importance of ensuring students' access to the general curriculum to the maximum extent possible; the importance of strengthening the role of parents and ensuring that families have meaningful opportunities to participate in the education of their children; the importance of coordinating with other local educational improvement efforts; and the importance of providing appropriate special education and related services, aids, and supports in the regular classroom. Given these findings, the amendments stated the primary purpose of the IDEA was "to ensure that all children with disabilities have available to them a free appropriate public education that emphasizes special education and related services designed to meet their unique needs and prepare them for employment and independent living" (§1400(d)(1)(A)). For the first time, this legislation specified that the aim of a free appropriate education provided under IDEA is to ultimately *prepare students with disabilities for employment and independent living.* This implies that transition planning should be in the forethought of all special education services.

The outcome accountability focus of the new IDEA forces IEP/ITP teams annually to examine if students are making progress toward their long-term goals. In actuality, each IEP/ITP meeting, beginning in preschool, should consider whether the educational program planned will help the students live and work independently in the community when they leave school.

The IDEA amendments of 1997 made subtle but substantive changes that affected the transition services offered to students with disabilities. These changes included the definition, the age requirement for the initiation of services, inclusion in statewide testing, discipline evaluation and service requirements, inclusion of a regular educator as part of the IEP/ITP team, and transfer of rights to students who reach the age of majority.

Related Services Added to List of Required Transition Services

In Section 1401(30), transition services are defined as a coordinated set of activities for a student with a disability that:

(A) is designed within an outcome-oriented process, which promotes movement from school to post-school activities, including post-secondary education, vocational training, integrated employment (including supported employment), continuing and adult education, adult services, independent living, or community participation;

(B)   is based upon the individual student's needs, taking into account the student's preferences and interests; and

(C)   includes instruction, related services*, community experiences, the development of employment and other postschool adult living objectives, and, when appropriate, acquisition of daily living skills and functional vocational evaluation. (*added with the passage of P.L. 105-17)

In the 1992 Federal Regulations Governing IDEA, transition services were described as special education or related services, yet little has been written about the role of related services in transition. In the 1992 regulations, IEP/ITP teams were directed to justify not providing instruction, community experiences, and the development of employment and other postschool adult living objectives.

In Section 1401(22) of the IDEA Reauthorization in 1997, related services were defined as: transportation, and such developmental, corrective, and other supportive services (including speech–language pathology and audiology services, psychological services, physical and occupational therapy, recreation, including therapeutic recreation, social work services, counseling services, including rehabilitation counseling, orientation and mobility services, and medical services, except that such medical services shall be for diagnostic and evaluation purposes only) as may be required to assist a child with a disability to benefit from special education, and includes the early identification and assessment of disabling conditions in children.

The addition of related services to the list of required transition services suggests that policy makers want IEP/ITP teams to consider the supports that students may need to benefit from the available transition services. This would be consistent with the underlying legislative philosophy of providing students access to the general curriculum and to integrated settings.

Traditionally, secondary students in special education have not been recipients of many related services, with very few students receiving such IEP/ITP services after the age of 16, the age when transition services have been required. The addition of related services as a transition service forces special educators and related service providers to examine whether supports should be provided that would enable a student to access a more integrated work, education, or independent living environment, demonstrate higher skills and abilities, or accomplish objectives leading toward the student's transition goals.

Transition Planning To Begin at Age 14

In the IDEA of 1990, policy makers suggested that transition planning might begin earlier than the age of 16, at least for some students, but left the decision to do so to individual planning teams or to state regulations. The age to start transition planning varied within states and across states. Some argued that students were not ready to make career decisions before age 16; others, like the Division on Career Development and Transition, promoted the concept of career development as one that begins in the primary years and continues throughout life. Nonetheless, the primary focus of the transition initiative for local school divisions and adult services was at school exit, not on long-term planning and preparation.

National school exit data (USDOE, 1995, 1996) show the ongoing crisis of dropping out among students with disabilities. If transition planning and services are to make a difference in this statistic, interventions must occur before the age of 16. At 16, students already have a long history of failure and social disengagement that is difficult to reverse.

In response to the concern regarding the dropout rate and testimony to the importance of beginning transition planning early, the IDEA of 1997 required that transition planning begin by age 14. Specifically, the legislation stated (§1414(d)(1)(A)(vii)):

(I) beginning at age 14, and updated annually, a statement of the transition service needs of the child under the applicable components of the child's IEP that focuses on the child's courses of study (such as participation in advanced placement courses or a vocational education program);

(II) beginning at age 16 (or younger, if determined appropriate by the IEP Team) a statement of needed transition services for the child, including, when appropriate, a statement of the interagency responsibilities or any needed linkages.

Transition at age 16 and beyond forced educators, families, and students to confront the inevitable ending of special education entitlements and to make decisions about how to enter the adult world upon school exit. Contacting adult services and developing relationships with community organizations represented new ground for many special educators. Clearly, these steps have been helpful to students and families and will remain important components of the IEP/ITP process in secondary education. However, the requirement to begin transition planning at age 14 will force schools to look within their own resources to create the supports and programs needed to move toward accomplishing long-range goals.

Secondary education offers a myriad of programs and extracurricular activities to develop students' skills and to address the challenges of adolescence. For example, prevention programs that attempt to address the use of drugs and alcohol or inform students about the risks of sexual activity are common in many secondary schools or within the community. Truancy prevention programs and dropout prevention programs are also found within secondary schools. Mentorships are becoming more common in schools that face social challenges. Law officers are found integrated into many school staffs as schools face an increase in violence and gang activity. Many students with disabilities have characteristics that make them eligible for these programs too, but seldom do IEP/ITP teams and other related school-based programs collaborate. Instead, schools too often offer students fragmented supports, losing sight of a holistic philosophy of student support. If special education is to take advantage of addressing students' transition needs at age 14, it must adopt a holistic approach that focuses on the student. This holistic perspective implies the need to broaden the expertise of the IEP/ITP team.

Students With Disabilities To Participate in Statewide Testing

Historically, children and youth with disabilities participated in statewide testing at a much lower rate than their peers without disabilities. Many systems excluded these students out of concern that the overall school or school division test scores would be lowered. Many standardized tests did not allow for any accommodations that might be needed by a student with a disability. In states where IEP/ITP teams were required to discuss statewide testing, many students were exempted from taking these tests under the auspices of the testing situation being too stressful for them.

People routinely ask what is the consequence of not taking a test when there are no sanctions, barriers, or obvious benefits that result from taking the test. Standardized tests provide an accountability tool for schools, allowing them to prove that their educational program is effective. To exclude a "group" of students from that accountability measure decreases how much accountability a system feels toward that group. Policy makers wanted to make sure that school systems held themselves accountable for student progress and thus added a requirement that children with disabilities be included in general statewide and districtwide assessment, with appropriate accommodations (§1412(a)(17)). Furthermore, states were directed to develop and conduct alternate assessments for students for whom participation in the general state assessment would not be appropriate. States are now required to report participation rates and performance outcomes on state tests to the federal government.

Many students in secondary education must pass a competency test or another measure of skill acquisition to be granted a diploma. Testing accommodations, participation, and decisions about alternate assessments may affect diploma status, school exit, and long-term transition goals. IEP/ITP teams will need to consider these factors as a part of long-term transition planning.

Functional Behavior Assessment Required

Some students with disabilities present behavioral challenges to the school setting because of their disability and their social development. Because behavior problems tend to escalate with the onset of adolescence for all students, middle and secondary school administration and teachers must search for strategies to address the safety and order of schools and classrooms. An increasing number of students face long-term suspensions or expulsions. Long-term suspension and expulsion interrupts student learning when no alternative instruction is available. Long-term suspension and expulsion perpetuate a negative cycle of poor academics and inappropriate behavior in and out of school, and as a result the community suffers. When students return to school, they face social rejection and academic failure and often enter a cycle of truancy and misbehavior. Dropping out of school becomes one alternative for these students.

Behavior issues are transition issues. Most employees, including those with disabilities, who lose their jobs do so because of inappropriate behavior or poor social skills. Furthermore, youth with disabilities represent a significant proportion of incarcerated youth. Behavior problems and success in school are often mutually exclusive; behavior problems in school often correlate with behavior problems in the community.

In the 1997 amendments to IDEA, policy makers included language that directed IEP/ITP teams to examine closely the relationship between a student's behavior and learning. The legislation stated in Section 1414(d)(3)(B)(i) that the IEP/ITP team should consider strategies and positive behavioral interventions to address the behavior of a child whose behavior impedes learning. In addition, the legislation required that a functional behavioral assessment be conducted on students who engage in behavior that constitutes a possible long-term suspension or expulsion, if none currently exists as part of the IEP evaluation.

A functional behavior assessment requires evaluating the student's behavior in the context of his or her disability, determining the behaviors manifested because of the disability, and then identifying those controllable environmental factors that contribute to, or inhibit, the behavior. This allows a determination to be made if the behavior is a manifestation of the disability (required when considering long-term suspension or expulsion) and provides data from which to make changes to the student's IEP or behavior intervention plan, if needed.

The legislation does not specify who will do the "functional behavior assessment," but many school-based service providers offer expertise that could contribute to this assessment. Furthermore, school-based service providers have specialized training that could help in identifying the supports students might need to maintain appropriate behavior or in identifying steps to control the environment where the inappropriate behavior is occurring.

Regular Education Teacher as an IEP/ITP Team Member

Regular educators include those responsible for vocational, fine arts, and physical education, as well as academic instructors. These partners hold primary responsibility for educating most students with disabilities, but they have not always been included as active decision makers regarding students' IEP/ITPs. Few realize the role these teachers hold in influencing transition planning for students with disabilities. IEP/ITP participation promotes this understanding. Likewise, students with disabilities benefit from educational program decisions made in the context of regular education. The IDEA of 1997 emphasizes access to the general curriculum for students with disabilities, along with an expectation of improved student achievement and postsecondary outcomes. Transition planning involves examining the supports needed for youth to be successful in the general secondary curriculum. Special and regular educators must engage in collaborative problem solving with students, families, and school-based service providers to help youths with disabilities achieve higher standards.

Transfer of Rights at Age of Majority

Becoming self-determined—that is, having choice and control in one's life—is a goal for all individuals. Individuals with disabilities' ability to exercise self-determination was limited when barriers to employment, housing, transportation, and the community in general were pervasive. Although all barriers have not been eliminated, people with disabilities have successfully advocated for laws that have made a difference. The transition initiative benefitted from these efforts and recognized that many past policies and practices promoted a culture of dependence rather than interdependence.

In this country, age 18 is considered the age of majority, meaning the age in which a person lawfully receives the rights and responsibilities of an adult. For example, at age 18, one may vote, serve in the military, and give or deny permission for medical treatment or services. Moreover, academic records and access become the right of the individual and not the individual's family, as authorized in the Family Educational Rights and Privacy Act (FERPA). Previously, the IDEA and FERPA seemed to be in conflict with one another, because the IDEA maintained the parent in a decision-making role for students with disabilities, even after the student reached 18 years of age. This created conflict with adult service agency policy regarding permission to serve students, as well as with IEP/ITP decisions being made regarding the student's education after the age of 18.

Section 1414(d)(1)(A)(vii)(III) stated that the IEP must contain, beginning at least one year before the child reaches the age of majority under state law, a statement that the child has been informed of his or her rights under this title, if any, that will transfer to the child on reaching the age of majority under Section 1415(m). Section 1415(m), which discusses the transfer of parental rights at age of majority, states

1. . . . when a child with a disability reaches the age of majority under State law (except for a child with a disability who has been determined to be incompetent under State law)—

   a. the public agency shall provide any notice required by this section to both the individual and the parents;

   b. all other rights accorded to parents under this part transfer to the child;

   c. the agency shall notify the individual and the parents of the transfer of rights; and

   d. all rights accorded to parents under this part transfer to children who are incarcerated in an adult or juvenile Federal, State, or local correctional institution.

2. SPECIAL RULE—If, under State law, a child with a disability who has reached the age of majority under State law, who has not been determined to be incompetent, but who is determined not to have the ability to provide informed consent with respect to the educational program of the child, the State shall establish procedures for appointing the parent of the child, or if the parent is not available, another appropriate individual, to represent the educational interests of the child throughout the period of eligibility of the child under this part.

This change raises many issues for transition teams. How will the team decide that the rights remain with the parent? How will the team mediate when students and parents differ in opinions regarding the student's educational program and placement? How will the team help parents to make this transition step? Who will take a role in each of these steps? Expertise in working with families, mediating conflict, and facilitating decision-making will be critical to support this transfer of roles and responsibilities.

Each change to the IDEA underscores the necessity for redefining the IEP/ITP transition team to include school-based related services where appropriate. Collaborative problem solving, shared roles and responsibilities, shared decision making, and shared vision can transform these new policies into positive outcomes for youth and young adults with disabilities.

Trends in Transition Planning and Services

In preparing youth with disabilities for adult life roles, many transitions must be considered. The Division on Career Development and Transition supports a life skills instruction approach when considering transition planning. According to Clark, Field, Patton, Brolin, and Sitlington (1994), "A life skills instruction approach is a commitment to providing a set of goals, objectives, and instructional activities designed to teach concepts and skills needed to function successfully in life . . . curricular content should emphasize instruction in such areas as personal responsibility, social competence, interpersonal relationships, health (physical and mental), home living, employability, occupational awareness, job skills, recreation and leisure skills, consumer skills, and community participation" (p. 126). According to research conducted by Kohler, DeStefano, Wermuth, Grayson, & McGinty (1994), exemplary transition programs address specific postschool vocational, social, and residential outcomes and develop these through systematic planning that involves the student, parents, and school and adult services personnel. Such programs offer transition services in areas such as counseling, vocational assessment, and academic tutoring, and services are provided cooperatively by educators and community providers.

The legal definition of transition services describes transition outcomes of postsecondary education, vocational training, integrated employment (including supported employment), continuing and adult education, adult services, independent living, or community participation. These outcomes can be classified into three general areas: 1) postschool employment; 2) postschool education; and (3) postschool adult and independent living.

Postschool Employment

Employment outcomes represent one of the most commonly considered areas of transition planning and service provision. In preparing students for employment, the importance of real job experiences before leaving school is documented in follow-up research (Wagner, D'Amico, Marder, Newman, & Blackorby, 1992; Wehman, 1996). Kohler et al. (1994) cited characteristics of an effective secondary education program focused on preparing students for employment; these characteristics included community-referenced curricula focused on career education, academic competencies, employability, and vocational skills. Instruction, including community-based instruction, on-the-job training, and vocational training, would be delivered in integrated settings and in least-restrictive environments. Employment opportunities and services, including job placement and supported employment services, would be routinely addressed during the secondary education period. In a limited study of students with mild disabilities, Karge, Patton, and de la Garza (1992) reported that students with mild disabilities were not receiving the following important transition to employment services and preparation: a) job search skills, including job finding, resume writing, job applications, job interviewing, and preparing essential documents for getting a job; b) job maintenance skills that emphasize job-keeping behaviors (proper dress, time cards, punctuality, getting along with others); c) job-related functional academics; and d) paid jobs in the community before graduation.

Transition programs and services developed since 1990 have emphasized employment preparation and outcomes. In an increasingly technical workplace, young adults with disabilities face even greater challenges for the future, with unskilled labor becoming a concept of the past. Secondary transition programs must prepare students for the challenges as well as identify the supports needed for success. For example, assistive technology offers an avenue for people with disabilities to access high-skill, high-wage jobs. Secondary transition employment programs must consider how assistive technology or other supports and accommodations, might improve the long-term employment outcome for students.

Postschool Education

High schools in the United States emphasize preparing students for college. Indeed, even some middle schools offer high school credit classes. In high school, students take college entrance exams and guidance counselors advise students in taking those courses that will help them gain admittance to college. In the United States, more young adults access postsecondary education than in any other developed country. Many youth with disabilities, particularly students with learning disabilities, anticipate attending a college program. However, many students with disabilities do not succeed in their postsecondary educational experience (Wagner et al., 1992).

In an exemplary transition planning process, school counselors and others are available to inform students and families about the postsecondary options and to help them choose the program and setting that may be the best match (deFur, Getzel, & Trossi, 1996; Karge, et al., 1992; Kohler et al., 1994). Students often fail in postsecondary education settings because they lack necessary academic, functional, and social supports (Scott, 1996). Identifying these needed supports and assisting students and families to access them are important roles of the transition team. Discussion of the demands of the postsecondary education setting and preparing students for those demands are frequently overlooked in transition IEP/ITP discussions.

Postschool Adult and Independent Living

Social and independent living instruction, including community-based instruction, are important components of an exemplary transition program (Kohler et al., 1994; Wehman, 1996). This includes getting around in the community, either independently or through natural supports (Karge et al., 1992; Wehman, 1996). For many students, the transition team needs to help with decision-making in areas such as living arrangements and finances (Wehman, 1996). Perhaps most important to a person's overall quality of life is the transition concern of community integration with a life filled with friends, self-esteem, and having fun (Karge et al., 1992; Wehman, 1996). For educators, this transition area presents the greatest challenge, because few educators have received training in these related areas. The use of support services in the school or community that understand the importance of recreation and leisure opportunities needs to occur more often in transition IEP/ITP meetings.

Collaborative Transition Planning

Transition planning, like IEP planning, often erroneously begins with team members discussing the services the system has to offer. Decisions about services commonly reflect the system's needs (i.e., availability of services), rather than being focused on the student's needs. Time needs to be spent in the process of discernment. Discernment begins by gathering data, asking questions, and exploring options, not by offering solutions or answers. Discernment means relating options to the dreams for that student. Discernment requires reflection. Collaboration fosters a discernment process of transition planning.

Assessment—data gathering—represents a first step in a discernment process and becomes the cornerstone of effective transition services. This data gathering involves assessment of the youth's skills and assessment of the environment (Sitlington, Neubert, Begun, Lombard, & Leconte, 1996). Sitlington et al. (1996) describe roles that special education and school support personnel can hold in providing transition assessment. They suggest that the special educator can play diverse roles, such as gathering informal assessment data, coordinating assessment services, developing student portfolios, and helping students and families understand the assessment results. School guidance and counseling personnel offer skills in a variety of assessment services for students, including occupational interests and vocational abilities of students through formal and informal interest surveys and postassessment counseling. Therapists and other support staff can help identify the need for ongoing support services in postsecondary settings. Collaborative assessment planning offers more opportunities for conducting comprehensive assessments and a higher probability that data will be integrated into the transition education plan.

Transition planning and service provision with a student focus using a discernment approach begins with gathering data about the student. The next step is gathering data about transition options. After that is a step to assess the environment and match the environment with the student data. Then, decisions can be made regarding training and preparation. Finally, the decisions are followed and revised as needed. Throughout this process, the student's long-term goals become the guiding principle on which all other actions are evaluated. Inge and Tilson (1994) describe an individualized placement model for supported employment that follows this process.

Traditionally, in IEP/ITP meetings, the person who will be identified to provide a specific special education service will be chosen based on traditional roles or training. For example, the vocational evaluator provides a vocational evaluation, guidance offers college selection counseling, and special educators provide remedial support. The dilemma arises when a transition service need is identified and no one at the meeting holds that traditional service role. For example, a student may need a community work experience with a possible job coach and no one at the meeting has a job description that matches this need. Thus, the team may believe that the needed services are not available.

In a creative collaborative model, roles may also be held based on individual interest or willingness to try on a new role, particularly when accessibility to specialists is limited. In a collaborative model, the team begins with the student transition goals and need(s). Next the team examines the accommodations, supports, services, or activities to be delivered, and then decides who could facilitate these services or activities.

Ideally, teams look to those members who bring discipline expertise related to the strategy to provide the transition service. In reality, IEP/ITP teams where transition planning occurs have a limited range of interdisciplinary participation (Virginia Department of Education [VaDOE], 1997). Consequently, services may not be provided or needs may go unattended. Often, special educators and families are asked to take on roles for which they may have limited experience.

Alternatively, collaborative teams expand the team composition to provide the service, or teams seek consultants to share or support the team in appropriate service provision. Cross-discipline training (including students and families) broadens individual competence and confidence to take on roles that seem initially beyond one's experience. Logistically, an individual planning team may not include all the potential school-based service providers, but it could include all the expertise of those individuals or a process for finding such expertise, such as consultation.

Transition services should be aimed at preparing appropriate and related supports, as well as helping students develop needed skills. Supports can allow youths with disabilities to work, go to school, and live independently (Steere, Pancsofar, Wood, & Hecimovic, 1990). Adopting the philosophy of developing needed supports means that team members must persist in exploring creative ways to plan for appropriate supports.

Skills for Collaborative Transition Planning

Developing and providing effective transition services for an individual can be a complex task where the skills needed exceed the time or training of any one person. An interdisciplinary team approach, where team members have skills and knowledge about transition issues, and skills in working as a team, provides a formula for creative alternatives (deFur & Taymans, 1995; Stodden & Leake, 1994). To be effective, interdisciplinary teams must share an understanding of the framework of one another's professions, while each individual team member would bring unique discipline expertise to the team (Petrie, 1976). The framework for transition specialists' skills has been suggested by several researchers (Asselin, Todd-Allen, & deFur, 1998; deFur & Taymans, 1995; Kohler, in press). DeFur and Taymans (1995) reported transition practitioners' (special educators, vocational educators, and vocational rehabilitation counselors) ranking of essential transition competency domains for transition specialists (see Table 2.2). The following chapters of this book illustrate that each school-based discipline brings expertise that could enhance the subskills within these domains.

In a study by deFur (1990), transition specialists identified 112 competencies as important to the transition process, and more than half of these were believed to be critical skills. The respondents voiced concerns that one person, even one who was skilled in transition services, would not likely hold all of the competencies. In reality, secondary special educators serve as primary case managers of IEP/ITPs, yet many lack the specific knowledge and skills essential to comprehensive transition planning and services (Foley & Mundschenk, 1997; Knott, 1997). Collaboration skills that tap the range of expertise available within the potential transition team become increasingly important in serving the needs of transition age youths with disabilities.

Cross-Disciplinary Competencies

Competencies of school-based related service providers have potential overlap with some of the competencies identified as important for secondary/transition

Table 2.2
Competency Domains for Transition Services

Rank Order of Transition Specialist Competency Domains

1. Knowledge of agencies and systems change
2. Development and management of individualized plans
3. Working with others in the transition process
4. Vocational assessment and job development
5. Professionalism, advocacy, and legal issues in transition
6. Job training and support
7. Assessment (general)
8. Transition administrative functions
9. Philosophical and historical considerations in transition
10. Career counseling and vocational theory and transition
11. Program evaluation and research
12. Curriculum, instruction, and learning theory (general)

Note. From *A Validation Study of Personnel Preparation Competencies for Transition Specialists in Special Education, Vocational Rehabilitation, and Vocational Education,* by S. deFur, 1990, Ann Arbor, MI: University Microfilms. Copyright 1990 by University Microfilms. Adapted with permission.

special educators in the literature. These competencies include working with families and students, providing support in placing students in community settings, providing specialized instruction and assessment in areas related to transition, and in providing expertise in the area of prevention (deFur, 1990; Foley & Mundschenk, 1997; Gibbs, Perkins, & Repetto, 1997; Kohler, in press).

Empowering Families and Youths

References to the importance of family and student involvement in transition can be found consistently throughout transition research (Miller, La Follette, & Green, 1990; Morningstar, Turnbull, & Turnbull, 1996; Repetto & Correa, 1996; Steere et al., 1990; Wehman, 1996). Parental involvement stands out as a primary indicator of student success in transition programs. Families (including extended family) serve as informal and formal role models for youths with disabilities. Family support and resources influence decision making about the student's goals for education and employment (Morningstar et al., 1996). Yet families continue to report a lack of equal partnership in IEP/ITP and transition planning, particularly families from culturally diverse backgrounds (Getzel, Todd, & deFur, 1997). School social workers, psychologists, school nurses, recreation specialists, and guidance counselors bring unique understandings and skills in working with families in the transition process. The following are competencies that are important in working with families and students:

- Assess and empower the family support system to facilitate the transition of youths and young adults with disabilities.

- Teach self-advocacy skills to families and youths with disabilities.

- Identify and gather information and support resources for youths and families.

- Develop and implement parent education programs to enhance family understanding of their role in transition.

- Apply career education theories and models to the career development of individuals with disabilities and their families.

Supporting Community Experiences

Achieving a good fit between oneself and one's job or avocation contributes both to satisfaction and performance. Often, youths with disabilities fail in vocational training or community placements because the placement decision is based on training or job availability rather than on a good match between the demands of the setting and the skills of the youth. Sometimes, youths fail because the system did not provide the right supports to be successful. Occupational therapists, physical therapists, and assistive technology specialists possess specialized knowledge and skills that could help in these assessment and placement activities. Psychologists or behavior specialists understand the systematic application of behavioral theories to help some youth develop job or community participation skills. Guidance counselors have training in the areas of work adjustment and work behaviors. Tapping some or all these resources may allow the interdisciplinary team to create more successful vocational training or community-based experiences for students. The following are competencies identified as important in providing community participation opportunities for youths with disabilities:

- Design and conduct a variety of functional assessment techniques to ascertain job task and social skills.

- Match the skills and interests of the youth with skills and demands required by the community placement.

- Clearly articulate to prospective employers accurate and realistic information and expectations.

- Identify the modifications within a community or job training environment needed to accommodate the characteristics of a youth or young adult with a disability.

- Provide technical assistance to employers and other community members to enable youths with disabilities to maintain employment and community participation.

- Provide technical assistance to business and industry in integrating programs to employ youths and young adults with disabilities.

- Systematically apply behavioral principles to develop, increase, and maintain an individual's work rate to acceptable levels of performance in the work environment.

- Describe the relationship of specific disability populations to transitional services, employment needs, and vocational training possibilities.

- Describe theories of human behavior and work adjustment in vocational and leisure settings.

Providing Transition Instruction and Assessment

Increasingly, special education personnel preparation programs are offering skill development in specialized instruction and assessment for transition; however, research suggests that most secondary special educators lack the specific competencies or resources for carrying out instruction in transition planning areas (Knott, 1997; Kohler, in press). Consequently, without these skills and without team members that bring these skills, transition planning for many students remains lacking. For example, vocational assessment represents a critical component in transition planning (Sitlington, et al., 1996), but not all schools have vocational evaluators, and nor do all students need a comprehensive vocational evaluation. Besides formal vocational evaluation, vocational assessment data can be gathered by special educators, guidance counselors, psychologists, occupational and physical therapists, assistive technology specialists, and so forth. Collaborative teams provide an opportunity to maximize support resources and individual skills. The following are competencies in specialized instructional and assessment expertise that are important for someone on the transition team to hold:

- Apply various career and guidance counseling approaches to facilitate the vocational, personal, and community adjustment of individuals with disabilities.

- Identify strategies, equipment, and assistive devices for adapting curricula and instructional environments to meet individual learner needs.

- Effectively plan and implement an appropriate functional skill instructional program.

- Provide direct instruction in job-seeking and job-keeping skills.

- Provide direct instruction of independent living skills necessary to successful community placement.

- Use medical/physical information for the purposes of diagnosis and program planning.

- Conduct and interpret transition planning assessments, such as vocational assessment.

- Assess the demands of the community-based placement and recommend modifications or accommodations.

Transition Planning Prevention Strategies

The transition planning team that meets the challenges of secondary education must include expertise that can facilitate decision making that focuses on strategies to prevent school dropout, involvement with gangs or criminal activity, and teenage pregnancy. Confronting these topics may be new to special education IEP/ITP planning and, as with any conflictual topic, will raise the anxieties of the IEP/ITP team. Establishing collaborative relationships between existing prevention programs and special education transition programs will be critical to address these issues (Gibbs, Perkins, & Repetto, 1997). Gibbs et al. (1997) compared a database of promising practices in transition and dropout prevention and concluded the following:

- Transition programs and dropout prevention programs share similar goals.

- Transition and dropout prevention programs need to begin early, even before middle school.

- Programs need to prepare students so they can be successful in community-based training sites.

- Programs should empower students to express their interests and preferences and should help students see the relevance of the curriculum to their future lives.

- Programs should establish partnerships and interagency councils to establish linkages and ensure information sharing.

At present, most secondary special educators do not perceive themselves as highly skilled in transition planning, service development, or in collaborating with community agencies (Foley & Mundschenk, 1997; Knott, 1997). School structure does not readily lend itself to collaborative problem solving, even with school colleagues. Still, the expertise exists across the disciplines serving educational systems; it is the system or structure that must be changed to take advantage of the available resources.

Interdisciplinary Transition Planning and Services

In education, specialists frequently respond to problems with new programs. New programs are resource intensive and often duplicate existing services. This contributes to fragmented efforts at problem solving. Gardner (1989) suggests that no new program should be started without first attempting to link with, or broaden, existing services. Romualdi and Sandoval (1995) promote the development of collaborative partnerships between education and community services to combat the multitude of needs of the children education must serve. The IEP/ITP transition concept of a multidisciplinary team represents the intent to forge such partnerships. However, Romualdi and Sandoval assert that special education multidisciplinary teams have performed primarily as a referral function, focusing on individual deficits rather than on a holistic perspective, thus limiting the opportunities for meaningful consultation. They identify barriers to effective interdisciplinary functioning, including minimal involvement of parents and regular educators and uneven involvement across disciplines. Commitment to problem solving, professional flexibility, and collegiality are considered an essential step in the transformation to a collaborative team.

Transition Teams

Transition teams that include multiple contributors to the process are described as interdisciplinary. Traditionally, training and professions promote a discipline-specific approach to problem solving; that is, people solve problems themselves through the perspective of their own experiences and specific frame of reference. For example, if I am a special educator, I analyze issues from a special education context, whereas a guidance counselor analyzes issues in guidance terms. If I happen to be the parent, my role as parent is my filter. If I happen to be a therapist, it is that lens through which I observe and reflect problems and issues. Solving problems through discipline-specific means may seem efficient, but it may often be flawed and limited by a narrow context. For example, consider that special education teachers may recommend vocational education programs for students without consulting either the student or the vocational teacher (or others who have an interest or expertise in the vocational education of this student). On one hand, the student may get access to instruction in a technical area. However, the student's interests and preferences may not be specifically linked to the course, or the demands of vocational class setting may not match with the student's special education needs. This approach can often result in disappointment, failure, and lost time in an inappropriate program.

IEP/ITP teams are called multidisciplinary teams in the IDEA. Traditionally, members of multidisciplinary teams present their single discipline view to the other members of the team; then the collective information contributes to decisions or recommendations. However, fragmentation of services is a potential risk of multidisciplinary approaches. For example, in transition planning using a multidisciplinary approach with Greg, a student with physical disabilities, the physical therapist presents findings and recommendations regarding Greg's physical disability needs in using public transportation and his daily therapy needs. The psychologist might identify social and self-advocacy skill concerns and recommend counseling services. The job placement specialist finds Greg a job that might be a match with the student's interests and preferences. Information is shared and Greg may get discipline-specific services that do not overlap in time or content. Greg gets services, but little or no attempt is made to relate those services.

To create powerful transition decisions and recommendations, the IEP/ITP team needs to be interdisciplinary or collaborative where many good ideas can be generated through the collective wisdom of a diverse group. In this model, person-centered decisions drive the planning. By collaborating, the team (including Greg) spends time discovering Greg's long-term goals and then establishes the strategies for the upcoming year that promote movement toward those long-term goals. Activities or supports needed to progress toward these goals are outlined. Last, the team identifies who and how these services would be delivered. Perhaps the real issue for Greg is his lack of self-confidence and experience in traveling independently or working. Natural supports in combination with therapy might accomplish Greg's goals faster than discipline-specific service offerings.

The skills and resources of school-based service providers open a new avenue of thinking and offer alternatives for early transition planning and for the time of school exit transition planning. Linking with existing resources will be essential for the current transition planning system if education is to create the environment students with disabilities need to succeed. School-based service providers bring many competencies identified as critical to transition service planning.

Teamwork can be challenging because of the way organizations are designed. Traditionally, service providers, schools, training programs, and so forth have been organized by discipline expertise. Policies and procedures sometimes support separation of resources and activities, and few incentives to work together currently exist. Developing a shared collaborative philosophy provides the framework to eliminate these barriers.

Interdisciplinary transition planning offers an opportunity to ensure that students with disabilities have successful in-school experiences, a critical factor for keeping students in school to complete their education. Such planning has the potential to identify and provide the supports needed. These supports include special education and related services, but traditionally students receive fewer directly related services as they get older. Other school-based services or programs, such as guidance, prevention, and extracurricular activities, are available in middle and high schools, but it is not clear whether these become an integral part of students' individual education/transition planning.

Student Participation

Increasingly, students with disabilities attend or are being involved in their IEP/ITP transition planning, a critical requirement of the law and an important step in developing skills in self-determination. Students are more likely to attend their IEP/ITP transition meeting as they approach graduation than when they first enter high school (VaDOE, 1997). From a positive view, students choose to be involved during the critical transition time, with most of them attending the IEP/ITP meeting just before their senior year. On the other hand, students may not perceive themselves to be critical decision makers in school-based planning during their early high school years. For students of that early high school age who are not connected or who are failing, opportunities to create the needed support system may be being overlooked.

Furthermore, secondary education provides social and leadership skills development through offering a variety of extracurricular activities—sports, clubs, service organizations, music, and drama. These experiences serve to build relationships and connection to the larger community. The things learned in these settings provide young adults with the attitudes, skills, and interests that help them integrate into their community fully. Developmentally, adolescents need opportunities to build relationships and discover their own identities and this occurs more healthily in positively structured settings. In a sample of 1,695 Virginia transition-age students with disabilities, only one third of the students reported involvement in any extracurricular activity (VaDOE, 1997). Of this group, 44% of students with learning disabilities or other health impairments reported extracurricular involvement. Thirty-four percent of students with mental retardation said they were involved in activities. Fewer than one fourth of the students with emotional disabilities (23%) and only 18% of students with severe disabilities reported any extracurricular involvement.

If successful high school social experiences play as high a role in postschool success as high school academic experiences, and there is little reason to doubt that they do not, then these findings elicit a great deal of concern. Schools and communities must take steps to change this picture of disenfranchisement if the expectations to change the level of social integration of people with disabilities are to be realized. Otherwise, adolescents with disabilities will continue to seek alternative ways of feeling validated. Truancy, gangs, and crime occur when teens feel no affiliation with their school or community systems. IEP/ITPs seldom address these complex issues; perhaps it is time to examine the role of school-based services and transition planning as a prevention or intervention resource.

School-Based Service Provider Participation

By law, IEP/ITP teams must include the parent, the teacher, and an administrator, and the student when transition services are being planned. National data show that the participation of therapy-related service providers such as occupational therapy, physical therapy, or speech therapy declines sharply as students enter secondary education (USDOE, 1995). For the most part, transition planning IEP/ITP teams have included the traditional IEP members, with the addition of adult service providers for some students in their last year of school.

A review of the IEP/ITPs of 1,695 transition-age students in Virginia revealed that in general, psychologists, occupational therapists, physical therapists, and other related service providers rarely participate or attend the formal transition planning meeting for students with disabilities (see Table 2.3). Participation rates reflected team members who provided prior input into the transition IEP development or attendance, whereas attendance reflected those who physically attended the meeting. Students with severe disabilities had more participation by related service providers than other students. Likewise, students with sensory or physical impairments as well as speech impairments received more of these services and IEP/ITP participation than students with learning disabilities, emotional disabilities, or other health impairments. Psychologists rarely participated in the IEP/ITP meetings of students with disabilities in secondary education, but if they did, they were more likely to be involved with students who had emotional disabilities and other health impairments (e.g., Attention-Deficit/Hyperactivity Disorder). Overall, guidance counselors participated regularly, but primarily for students with learning or emotional disabilities, and never for students with severe disabilities. Assistive technology was used occasionally for students in regular vocational education (3%), and more often for students in special vocational education settings (14%) (VaDOE, 1997).

Participation in transition IEP/ITP meetings by school-based services parallels historical approaches to secondary special education where support services withdraw as students age (see Table 2.8). This pattern imitates the medical insurance model, in which service is withdrawn when benefit is no longer evidenced. However, this approach overlooks the knowledge and expertise offered by school-based services that could help identify needed supports for individuals in the transition process. The one area that contradicts this trend is the participation of guidance counselors, whose participation increased as students aged. Because many more students with disabilities are seeking access to postsecondary education (more than 50% of students with disabilities in Virginia anticipate

Table 2.3
Rates of Participation in Transition IEP Meetings by Participant

Participants	MR (N = 314)		LD (N = 1004)		ED (N = 191)		OHI (N = 87)		SD (N = 63)		Other (N = 46)		N = 1695 ages 14–22	
	Part.	Attend	Part.	Attend	Part.	Attend	Part.	Attend	Part.	Attend	Part.	Attend	Total Part.	Total Attend
Student	93%	82%	96%	85%	97%	86%	99%	92%	87%	51%	98%	93%	95%	85%
Parent/Family Member	96%	77%	95%	77%	99%	87%	98%	98%	100%	90%	96%	91%	96%	81%
Special Education Teacher	97%	95%	96%	95%	99%	98%	98%	98%	100%	100%	83%	76%	96%	96%
Psychologist	2%	<1%	2%	<1%	13%	1%	8%	6%	2%	2%	11%	2%	4%	1%
Physical Therapist	3%	3%	1%	0%	1%	0%	6%	2%	32%	22%	9%	9%	3%	2%
Occupational Therapist	3%	3%	1%	0%	1%	0%	2%	1%	38%	33%	13%	11%	3%	2%
Speech Pathologist	21%	18%	5%	3%	2%	1%	9%	9%	51%	43%	43%	39%	11%	8%
Guidance Counselor	34%	13%	56%	34%	60%	35%	16%	0%	0%	0%	17%	4%	51%	27%

Note. Adapted from Project UNITE—Transition Services Information, by Virginia Department of Education, 1997, Richmond, VA.
MR = Students with mental retardation; LD = Students with learning disabilities; ED = Students with emotional disabilities; OHI = Students with other health impairments; SD = Students with severe cognitive or multiple disabilities or autism; Other = Students with speech language impairments, visual impairments, hearing impairments, orthopedic impairments, or traumatic brain injury.

Table 2.4

Comparison of Participation: Freshman Year Versus Year Prior to Exit

Participant	Freshman Year		Year Before Graduation	
	Participated	Attended	Participated	Attended
Student	93%	67%	96%	87%
Parent/Family Member	99.5%	87%	92%	70%
Special Education Teacher	98%	98%	95%	92%
Psychologist	5%	<1%	5%	1%
Physical Therapist	10%	9%	3%	1%
Occupational Therapist	10%	8%	3%	1%
Speech Pathologist	29%	24%	6%	4%
Guidance Counselor	34%	17%	50%	28%

Note. Adapted from Project UNITE—Transition Services Information, by Virginia Department of Education, 1997, Richmond, VA.

further education), participation by guidance counselors represents a major resource for transition planning in this area.

It may be possible that school-based personnel have influence in the educational programming for secondary special education students in more subtle ways than through direct participation in IEP/ITP decisions. In a survey of secondary special educators conducted by Foley and Mundschenk (1997), the researchers found that more than half of the respondents reported 1 to 5 interactions with school psychologists (64%) or other related services personnel (55%) each month. The researchers referred to communication of incidental information between special educators and school-based services as supporting professional collaborative efforts, but they concluded that secondary special educators may not frequently engage in collaborative problem solving. In fact, they expressed concern that most of the reported interactions between secondary educators and other school personnel did not seem substantive regarding students' educational programs.

Very few transition IEP/ITPs address services needed for student recreation and leisure. The IEP/ITPs of students with severe disabilities are more likely to address these areas of adult living than the IEP/ITPs for students who have less obvious cognitive limitation. For example, in the Virginia sample, 83% of students with severe disabilities needed group-sponsored recreation services, whereas only 43% of the students with mental retardation identified the need. About 20% of students with sensory or physical impairments identified this need.

Overall, these findings paint a picture of a multidisciplinary approach where one stays within the narrow confines of one's discipline rather than an interdisciplinary approach where expertise sharing becomes the norm. In a multidisciplinary team, people maintain their roles, present their findings, and provide their specific expertise, but little dialogue across disciplines occurs. In an interdisciplinary approach the goal is to share information and to identify overlap in findings and in services. Transition assessment, transition planning, and transition service provision (special education and related services) present natural settings for interdisciplinary planning, problem solving, and service provision. School-based services offer a multitude of skills and expertise in addition to those of the typical special education teacher. Bringing some or all of these skills to the planning table fosters a spirit of cooperation and creative problem solving. Further discussion of how specific disciplines might address transition service needs can be found in the later chapters of this book.

Transforming the Transition IEP/ITP Team

The transition IEP/ITP team that includes targeted representatives from school-based services demands a shift in the traditional paradigm of special education service delivery as well as a shift in the model of related service delivery. The new paradigm requires that each professional be able to step out of his or her "box" and embrace a more holistic approach to service provision. The new paradigm suggests that special educators and related service providers need to examine the supports and instruction that students require to narrow the gap between long-term transition goals, annual goals, and current circumstances. The new paradigm asks special educators and related service providers to be student centered in their planning and service provision. The new paradigm asks for special educators and school-based service providers to come together to share a philosophy and a vision of collaborative services.

How and where does one begin to make this paradigm shift? How does one expand the view of the Transition IEP/ITP Team? What is the role of the special educator in this process? What is the role of the school-based service providers? Of families and students? How does one logistically include all potential players in the process? How does one obtain the commitment and cooperation of other service providers? What are appropriate roles for related services personnel? Adopting a collaborative philosophy and process represents the first step to answering these questions. Table 2.5 illustrates four stages of school services working together.

Networking describes the first step in any collaborative process. Getting to know the frames of reference and expertise available within school-based services seems simple. In reality, secondary special educators have minimal interaction with related service providers. Consequently, they have little opportunity to

Table 2.5
Networking, Coordination, Cooperation, and Collaboration for School-Based Transition Services

Type of Interaction	Example of Activity	Impact on the Student	Impact on the System
Networking refers to the active solicitation and establishment of information and referral sources and the promoting of one's own product.	Service providers attend child study and exchange business cards or information with other professionals and family members. They refer to a service provider (e.g., a student with behavior problems is referred to a psychologist).	Information and referral sources are identified. Student gets referred to another service provider.	Easy to use; no conflict with other disciplines; minimal time commitment; no direct services are provided; service linkages may evolve; no investment in the process.
Coordination refers to the arrangement of services or team member resources to maximize efficiency and possibly effectiveness; interaction is on an as-needed basis.	Guidance counselors schedule truancy counseling services on Day 1; nurse provides pregnancy prevention information on Day 2; social worker meets with student to discuss home concerns on Day 3.	Individual gets services and goes to one discipline per day, but information is not shared. Potential for fragmentation is high.	Communication important; services are provided as planned; no conflict with other disciplines; minimal time commitment; may wrongly assume needs are being met.
Cooperation implies some planning and division of roles; requires the sharing of some information; support is expected by the group; interaction usually around one specific task of definable length; resources may be shared.	Student goals include work experience as a hotel reservationist. Occupational therapist and vocational evaluator assess work demands. Speech therapist provides voice training for answering phones. The assistive technology specialist assesses computer skills and adaptations needed. Special educator coordinates implementation and provides job coach.	Student gets specific services for this event; student gets the benefit of services that are based on expertise of the disciplines.	Responsibilities are shared by multiple school-based players; competencies reflect the summation of individual team member skills.
Collaboration means working side by side, sharing the vision, decisions, leadership, and resources, as well as ownership of the student's concerns and in reaching a successful outcome; it implies a longer lasting relationship with a more clearly defined mission; resource sharing may be unequal. In true collaboration, the outcome is something that could not have been achieved by one person or entity alone.	The collaborative transition planning team includes all appropriate school-based service providers. A team with a student as the focus creates a vision of student goals for five years from now. The team articulates what is positive and possible for the next year. Team collaboratively identifies the supports and special education the student will need to achieve goals. Team members agree to provide or find support needed.	Individual needs drive the services rather than existing programs or systems driving the services; individual gets needed services.	Requires time commitment and trust; requires authority to act outside of the traditional role or programs; challenges bureaucracy; results/outcomes are enhanced. The results of collaboration must be mutually beneficial to all parties involved.

Note. Adapted from "Collaboration as a Prevention Tool for Youths with Disabilities," by S. deFur, 1997, *Preventing School Failure, 41*, pp. 173–178.

explore the potential resources in a collaborative relationship. This book represents a first step in supporting networking among special educators and school-based service providers.

Networked referral to other service providers remains a common transition planning approach, but reliance on networking as a primary means to provide transition services may be faulty. Usually, little or no interaction occurs with the referral source, which reduces accountability. Networking takes an essential first step in collaboration, but alone it will not be sufficient for students with complex transition service needs.

As disciplines develop a better understanding of the transition expertise of other disciplines, coordination of services represents the next logical step in working together on behalf of students. Service coordination prevents duplication of services. To coordinate, people order and arrange services to achieve discipline-specific services for the youth with a disability. However, team members can coordinate transition services with others and not actually engage in true cooperation or collaboration.

As expanded transition planning teams achieve a level of commitment to working together, opportunities to cooperate will emerge when people look for ways to support and complement one another's transition services, and when they share resources. Cooperation requires more personal and resource investment than coordination or networking.

Collaboration starts with networking, coordination, and cooperation. However, true collaboration also requires shared decision making, responsibility, accountability, and trust. Collaboration requires time and energy to develop relationships and agreements around areas such as decision making or roles and responsibilities. Collaboration occurs more readily when the group interacts and all participants display an ownership for successful student outcomes.

Teams that collaborate make better decisions. For example, collaborative teams generate more alternatives, which in turn open more options. In addition, team members are willing to share resources when clear outcomes are identified as being consistent with their mission and values. Collaborative, committed, and proactive transition teams and individuals are a formula for transition success.

Final Thoughts

The raised expectations for improved outcomes for youths with disabilities challenge professionals to examine new ways of creating meaningful learning environments so that these expectations can be achieved. Because of higher standards, it is undeniable that the complexity of serving youth with disabilities increases daily. Professionals are faced with the axiom that says that if they continue to do the same thing again and again, they should not be surprised to get the same results they have always gotten. To improve student outcomes, transition specialists and educators must change the way they do business. Implementing broad-based collaborative transition planning and services offers one change to explore.

Legislation, research, and definite need set a ready stage for a broad-based school team approach to early transition planning, as well as for school exit transition planning. School personnel have existing expertise that when combined can begin to address the complex educational needs of adolescents with disabilities and their families. Limited time and resource commitment creates potential barriers to changing to a truly collaborative and person-centered model. Risk taking and leadership will be required to challenge the existing structure and to explore new ways of service provision for secondary students with disabilities.

This book offers special educators and related service providers insight into each other's frames of reference for transition planning and services, a first step in effective teamwork and communication. The range of expertise described illuminates the potential that exists to improve the quality of student outcomes when people choose to work collaboratively. The challenge remains for professionals to take the necessary steps to develop the relationships and to create the setting that fosters interdisciplinary collaborative transition teams.

References

Asselin, S. B., Todd-Allen, M., & deFur, S. (1998). Transition coordinators: Define yourselves. *Teaching Exceptional Children, 30*, 11–15.

Brown v. Board of Educ., 347 U.S. 483 (1954).

Clark, G. M., Carlson, B. C., Fisher, S., Cook, J. D., & D'Alonzo, B. J. (1991). Career development for students with disabilities in elementary schools: A position statement of the Division on Career Development. *Career Development for Exceptional Individuals, 14*, 109–120.

Clark, G. M., Field, S., Patton, J. R., Brolin, D. E., & Sitlington, P. L. (1994). Life skills instruction: A necessary component for all students with disabilities. A position statement of the Division on Career Development and Transition. *Career Development for Exceptional Individuals, 17*, 125–134.

deFur, S. (1990). *A validation study of personnel preparation competencies for transition specialists in special education, vocational rehabilitation, and vocational education.* Ann Arbor, MI: University Microfilms, Inc.

deFur, S. H. (1997, Summer). Collaboration as a prevention tool for youths with disabilties. *Preventing School Failure, 41*, 173–178.

deFur, S., Getzel, E., & Trossi, K. (1996). Making the postsecondary education match: A role for IEP planning. *Journal of Vocational Rehabilitation, 6*, 231–241.

deFur, S., & Reiff, H. (1994). Transition of youths with learning disabilities to adulthood: The secondary education foundation. In P. Gerber & H. Reiff (Eds.), *Adults with Learning Disabilities* (pp. 99–110). Andover, MA: Andover Medical Press.

deFur, S., & Taymans, J. (1995). Competencies needed for transition specialists in vocational rehabilitation, vocational education, and special education. *Exceptional Children, 62*, 38–51.

Education of All Handicapped Children's Act of 1975, 20 U.S.C. §1400 *et seq.*

Education of All Handicapped Children's Act Amendments of 1983, 20 U.S.C. §1400 *et seq.*

Family Educational Rights and Privacy Act, 20 U.S.C. §1232 *et seq.*

Fardig, D. B., Algozzine, R. F., Schwartz, S. E., Hensel, J. W., & Westling, D. L. (1985). Postsecondary vocational adjustment of rural, mildly handicapped students. *Exceptional Children, 52*, 115–121.

Foley, R. M., & Mundschenk, N. A. (1997). Collaboration activities and competencies of secondary school special educators: A national survey. *Teacher Education and Special Education, 20*, 47–60.

Gardner, S. (1989). Failure by fragmentation. *California Tomorrow*, 19–25.

Getzel, E., Todd, M., & deFur, S. (1997). *Families speak out about transition experiences*. Unpublished manuscript, Virginia Department of Education.

Gibbs, E. H., Perkins, D. A., & Repetto, J. B. (1997). Dropout prevention and exceptional student education transition programs: A study of promising practices. *The Journal of At-Risk Issues, 3*(2), 22–28.

Halpern, A. (1994). The transition from youth to adult life: A position statement of the Division on Career Development and Transition. *Career Development for Exceptional Invduals, 17*, 115–124.

Hasazi, S. B., Gordon, L. R., & Roe, C. A. (1985). Factors associated with the employment status of handicappped youth exiting high school from 1979–1983. *Exceptional Children, 51*, 455–469.

Individuals with Disabilities Education Act of 1990, 20 U.S.C. §1400 *et seq.*

Individuals with Disabilitities Education Act Amendments of 1997, 20 U.S.C. §1400 *et seq.*

Inge, K. J., & Tilson, G.(1994). Supported employment: Issues and applications for individuals with learning disabilities. In P. Gerber and H. Reiff (Eds), *Learning Disabilities in Adulthood* (pp. 179–193). Boston: Andover Medical Publishers.

Karge, B. D., Patton, P L., & de la Garza, B. (1992). Transition services for youth with mild disabilities: Do they exist? *Career Development for Exceptional Individuals, 15*, 47–67.

Knott, L. (1997). *Survey of secondary special educators' knowledge and involvement in transition*. Unpublished doctoral dissertation, Virginia Polytechnic Institute and State University, Blacksburg.

Kohler, P. D. (in press). Implementing a transition perspective of education. In F. Rusch & J. Chadsey (Eds.), *High school and beyond: Transition from school to work*. Belmont, CA: Wadsworth.

Kohler, P. D., DeStefano, L., Wermuth, T. R., Grayson, T. E., & McGinty, S. (1994). An analysis of exemplary transition programs: How and why are they selected? *Career Development for Exceptional Individuals, 17*, 187–201.

Miller, R. J., La Follette, M., & Green, K. (1990). Development and field test of a transition planning procedure: 1985–1988. *Career Development for Exceptional Individuals, 13*, 45–55.

Mithaug, D. E., Horiuchi, C. R., & Fanning, P. R. (1985). A report on the Colorado statewide follow-up survey of special education students. *Exceptional Children, 51*, 397–404.

Morningstar, M. E., Turnbull, A. P., & Turnbull, H. R. (1996). What do students with disabilities tell us about the importance of family involvement in the transiton from school to adult life? *Exceptional Children, 62*, 249–260.

Petrie, H. G. (1976). Do you see what I see? The epistemology of interdisciplinary inquiry. *Journal of Aesthetic Education, 10*(1), 29–43.

Repetto, J., & Correa, V. (1996). Expanding views on transition. *Exceptional Children, 62*, 551–563.

Romualdi, V., & Sandoval, J. (1995). Comprehensive school-linked services: Implications for school psychologists. *Psychology in the Schools, 32*, 306–317.

Scott, S. (1996). Understanding colleges: An overview of college support services and programs available to clients from transition planning through graduation. *Journal of Vocational Rehabilitation*, 6, 217–230.

Sitlington, P. L., Neubert, D. A., Begun, W., Lombard, R. D., & Leconte, P. J. (1996). *Assess for success: Handbook on transition assessment*. Reston, VA: Council for Exceptional Children.

Steere, D., Pancsofar, E., Wood, R., & Hecimovic, H. (1990). Principles of shared responsibility. *Career Development for Exceptional Individuals*, 13, 143–154.

Stodden, R. A., & Leake, D.W. (1994). Getting to the core of transition: A re-assessment of old wine in new bottles. *Career Development for Exceptional Individuals*, 17, 65–76.

U.S. Department of Education. (1995). *To assure the free appropriate public education of all children with disabilities: Seventeenth annual report to Congress on the implementation of the Individuals with Disabilities Education Act*. Washington, DC: Author.

U.S. Department of Education. (1996). *To assure the free appropriate public education of all children with disabilities: Eighteenth annual report to Congress on the implementation of the Individuals with Disabilities Education Act*. Washington, DC: Author.

Virginia Department of Education. (1997). [Project UNITE—Transition Services Information]. Unpublished raw data. Richmond, VA: Author.

Wagner, M., D'Amico, R., Marder, C., Newman, L, & Blackorby, J. (1992). *What happens next? Trends in postschool outcomes of youth with disabilities: The second comprehensive report from the National Longitudinal Transition Study of special education students*. Menlo Park, CA: SRI International.

Wehman, P. (1996). *Life beyond the classroom: Transition services for young people with disabilities* (2nd ed.). Baltimore:. Brookes.

Will, M. (1984). *OSERS programming for the transition of youth with disabilities: Bridges from school to working life*. Washington, DC: U.S. Department of Education.

PART

SPECIFIC DISCIPLINES AND TRANSITION

CHAPTER

SCHOOL PSYCHOLOGY

Edward M. Levinson

James P. Murphy

"People often say that this or that person has not yet found himself. But the self is not something one finds, it is something one creates."

—Thomas Szasz

Establishing Common Frames of Reference

Overview of School Psychology

School psychology has its roots in both clinical psychology and education, and is considered to have begun when Lightner Witmer founded the Orogenic school to study children. Prompted by the testing of military candidates, new legislation, and the educational reform set forth by President John F. Kennedy and others, school psychology emerged as a separate discipline. The role and function of the school psychologist has evolved over the years due to educational reforms, conferences, legislation, new tests and assessment procedures, and federal funding. Of these, perhaps the most important has been federal legislation. The Individuals with Disabilities Education Act of 1997 (IDEA) (P.L. 105-17), and its predecessor, The Education for All Handicapped Children Act of 1975 (EHA) (P.L. 94-142), arguably have had the most significant effect on the current role and function of school psychologists. Currently, four major areas of practice are defined by the National Association of School Psychologists (NASP): psychological and psychoeducational assessment, consultation, direct service, and program planning/evaluation. All of these roles have a common purpose: solving problems at either an individual or systems level.

The following role descriptions are taken, in part, from the NASP Standards for the Provision of School Psychological Services (Thomas & Grimes, 1995).

Psychological and Psychoeducational Assessment

Assessment is a large part of the school psychologist's job, an important aspect of the educational process, and has long been the most common role of school psychologists (Woody, Lavoie, & Epps, 1992). Partially as a result of legislative mandates, school psychologists are most clearly identified with the role of psychological and psychoeducational assessment, and spend the majority of their time involved in this role (Carey, 1995). Most often the assessments conducted by school psychologists are designed to assess a student's eligibilty for special education services, and are at least partially a function of state and federal special education regulations. For years, however, many in school psychology have argued that assessments should have the purpose of identifying and testing the effectiveness of interventions designed to solve academic, social, or behavioral difficulties rather than determining eligibility for special education services (Reschly & Ysseldyke, 1995; Shinn, 1989). The extent to which such a shift in the focus of assessment occurs will partially determine the value of school psychological assessment for transition planning. This will be discussed in more detail in a later section.

School psychologists assess many different aspects of the child, adolescent, or adult as needed, and they use a variety of assessment methods in doing so. Assessments evaluate areas such as personality, emotional status, social skills, intelligence, academic achievement, communication, adaptive behavior, family, environmental, and cultural influences, and vocational development, aptitude, and interests. While the purpose of the assessment theoretically determines the areas to be assessed, in practice, intellectual, academic, adaptive behavior/social skills, and personality assessments are often emphasized by school psychologists, given that assessments focus on special education eligibility. While the other areas listed are sometimes a part of the assessment (depending upon the reason for the assessment), the assessment of vocational development, aptitude, and interests is rarely a part of the assessments conducted by school psychologists, despite their inclusion in NASP standards.

School psychologists are not limited to the use of standardized norm-referenced tests when completing assessments, and they routinely include interviews, observations, and behavioral evaluations as well. In fact, most school psychologists are trained to conduct a multitrait, multimethod, multifactored assessment that incorporates several assessment techniques and assesses multiple traits. Assessments are conducted in a nonbiased manner and in a manner that takes the student's background and culture into consideration. Assessment results are communicated through reports, multidisciplinary team (MDT) meetings, or meetings with parents (Woody et al., 1992). Recommendations for programming are most often included in reports, individual education plans (IEP), or individual family service plans (IFSP).

Consultation

School psychologists consult with school personnel, parents, and outside agencies as necessary in order to help develop and design programs and procedures for the prevention of disorders, to help promote student learning, and to improve the overall educational system. The school psychologist also develops and provides activities to parents and educators that will help them to develop or improve their skills and knowledge in learning, development, and behavior management strategies. The school psychologist is often responsible for providing inservice activities or other forms of training to help parents and teachers. Consultation is an *indirect* service role, and it is this role that the school psychologist assumes when trying to assist others who will be working directly with students.

The goals of consultation are many, varied, and influenced by the specific problem(s), the identity of the client, and the role of the school psychologist in a particular school. Prevention goals focus on providing services to a population in an effort to prevent a disorder or problem behavior from occurring. For example, school psychologists may consult with teachers to assist them in better managing behavior in their classes. Consultation is also designed to change or improve the organization and functioning of the entire school system. Frequently, school psychologists will consult with administrators and assist them in designing programs that target systemic problems, such as absenteeism, substance abuse, or discipline issues.

A considerable body of research exists on consultation in the school psychology literature. Many researchers contend that consultation is a more effective approach to the provision of school psychological service delivery than are other approaches. Advocates of consultation argue that by working with and changing the behavior of parents, teachers, and administrators, a greater number of children can be positively affected than by working with individual students alone (Kratochwill, Elliott, & Rotto, 1995). Hence, the consultation literature in school psychology has explored consultation models, consultant–consultee relationships, overcoming consultee resistant to change, and other areas pertinent to successful school-based consultation.

Direct Service

The direct service role of the school psychologist is closely related to the consultation role, but is distinctive in its own right. While consultation is defined as working with someone (parent, teacher, administrator) who will intervene directly with children, direct service is defined as working directly with the student (Medway, 1985). Direct service involves activities like counseling, behavior management, social skills training, tutoring, and so on. The direct service role consists of three aspects as defined by NASP standards. First, school psychologists provide services to help individuals and groups function more effectively. Second, they design programs to deal directly with clients to improve cognitive, affective, social, and vocational development. Thirdly, school psychologists involve their clients as much as possible in the process.

Program Planning and Evaluation

School psychologists design programs to meet the needs of individual students. Examples of such programs include suicide prevention programs, substance abuse prevention programs, peer tutoring programs, and crisis intervention programs. They also assist in designing methods to evaluate the effectiveness of programs. Program evaluation consists of three roles: (1) determining the legitimacy of a program's goals and objectives, (2) determining the representativeness of a program's goals and objectives, and (3) determining the appropriateness of goals and objectives (Borich, 1985). The school psychologist is responsible for evaluating students and programs in the school in an effort to make the school a more effective institution, and to improve education in any and all ways possible.

Other Roles

In addition to the roles previously described, school psychologists are sometimes involved in the design and implementation of research studies in the schools. Though this is often a part of evaluating the effectiveness of a program which has previously been implemented, research studies are also designed to test the effectiveness of a program *prior* to implementation and to monitor the effectiveness of an intervention. School psychologist practitioners often collaborate with faculty in school psychology training programs when conducting research. Additionally, like other school personnel, school psychologists are sometimes asked to assume administrative responsibilities which entail supervision of other staff. Finally, school psychologists sometimes function as supervisors of other psychologists and related staff members.

Actual Roles Versus Desired Roles

The roles described above are the roles proposed by NASP and are those that school psychologists are trained to perform. Largely as a result of legislative mandates and special education regulations, school psychologists spend a majority of their time conducting assessments and often have little time to function in other roles (Levinson, 1990). Levinson (1990) found that nearly one quarter of school psychologists in Pennsylvania reported spending 61 to 80% of their time in assessment; however, only 3% reported that they wanted to spend that much time in assessment. Nationally, data suggest that school psychologists spend approximately 50% of their time in assessment, though they prefer to spend approximately half of their time involved in this (Carey, 1995). School psychologists consistently report that they spend more time in assessment than they would like; and less time than they would like in consultation, counseling, and research (Carey, 1995; Levinson, 1990).

Training of School Psychologists

Currently, the training and entry-level requirements for the profession vary somewhat from state to state, though most states require a minimum of a master's degree plus 30 additional graduate credits. Approximately 21% of school psychologists have a 30-hour master's degree, 56% have a 60-hour master's degree (specialist degree), and 23% have a doctoral degree (Wilson & Reschly, 1996). Though training programs must undergo certification or accreditation by their state departments of education (or other appropriate certification/accreditation body), and individuals wishing to practice as school psychologists must submit their credentials to this body for approval, increasingly states are accepting NASP's Nationally Certified School Psychologist (NCSP) credential for certification. The NCSP is based upon NASP standards for program approval, requires successful completion of a knowledge-based exam, and requires evidence of continuing professional development for renewal.

School psychology training programs are accredited by NASP at the specialist level and at the doctoral level. Specialist-level programs require a minimum of three years of full-time study (at least 60 semester hours) and a supervised internship for one academic year lasting at least 1,200 hours (a minimum of 600 hours must be in the schools). Doctoral-level programs require a minimum of four years of full-time study (at least 90 semester hours) and an internship experience of 1,500 hours. The domains included in school psychology training programs are: (1) psychological foundations, including biological bases of behavior, human learning, social and cultural bases of behavior, child and adolescent development, and individual differences; (2) educational foundations, including instructional design, and the organization and operation of schools; (3) interventions/problem solving, including assessment, both individual and group counseling and behavior management, consultation, and systems change; (4) statistics and research methodologies, including research and evaluation methods, statistics, and measurement; and (5) professional school psychology, including history and foundations of school psychology, legal and ethical issues, professional issues and standards, alternative methods for the delivery of school psychological services, emergent technologies, and roles and functions of school psychologists.

Practica experiences are a vital part of the school psychologist's training and allow students to practice their skills in a supervised setting prior to and in preparation for the internship experience. These practica can be laboratory or field based and must include opportunities to become oriented with the educational process, as well as practice in assessment and intervention. Practica most often occur in university-based clinics or public schools, and must occur before the internship experience.

The internship is the culminating experience in the school psychologist's training and occurs at or near the end of the training program. The internship occurs on a full-time basis for one academic year or part-time for two consecutive academic years. The internship must adhere to a written plan and give the student opportunities to practice a variety of services to a varying range of clients. The student must have the opportunity to work with diverse clients, with a range of problems, and in different settings. The student intern provides a number of services, including assessment, counseling, behavior management, and consultation; however, the experience is not limited to these services. The intern is entitled to at least two hours of direct supervision per week from a certified school psychologist, and is awarded appropriate academic credit for successfully completing the internship.

Future Training and Practice

Recently, NASP released *School Psychology: A Blueprint for Training and Practice II* (Ysseldyke, Dawson, Lehr, Reschly, Reynolds, & Telzrow, 1997), a document that was designed to further define and modify the domains of practice necessary to improve services to children, educators, and families as the profession of school psychology enters the 21st century. This document identifies ten domains of school psychology leadership and function in the schools. These domains are listed and described in Table 3.1. Several of these domains have particular relevance to the future involvement of school psychologists in transition. Though these will be discussed in more detail later in this chapter, the domains of *socialization and*

Table 3.1
Future Domains of School Psychology Leadership and Function in the Schools

Data-Based Decision Making and Accountability: School psychologists must be able to define current problem areas, strengths and needs (at the individual, group, and systems level) through assessment, and measure the effects of decisions that result from the problem-solving process.

Interpersonal Communication, Collaboration, and Consultation: School psychologists must have the ability to listen well, participate in discussions, convey information, and work with others at an individual, group, and systems level.

Effective Instruction and Development of Cognitive/Academic Skills: School psychologists must be able to develop challenging but achievable cognitive and academic goals for all students, provide information about ways in which students can achieve these goals, and monitor student progress toward these goals.

Socialization and Development of Life Competencies: School psychologists must be able to develop challenging but achievable behavioral, affective, or adaptive goals for all students, provide information about ways in which students can achieve these goals, and monitor student progress towards these goals.

Student Diversity in Development and Learning: School psychologists must be aware of, appreciate, and work with individuals and groups with a variety of strengths and needs from a variety of racial, cultural, ethnic, experiential, and linguistic backgrounds.

School Structure, Organization, and Climate: School psychologists must have the ability to understand the school as a system, and work with individuals and groups to facilitate structure and policies that create and maintain schools as safe, caring, and inviting places for members of the school community.

Prevention, Wellness Promotion, and Crisis Intervention: School psychologists must have knowledge of child development and psychopathology in order to develop and implement prevention and intervention programs for students with a wide range of needs and disorders.

Home/School/Community Collaboration: School psychologists must have knowledge of family influences that affect students' wellness, learning, and achievement, and they must be able to form partnerships between parents, educators, and the community.

Research and Program Evaluation: School psychologists must know current literature on various aspects of education and child development, be able to translate research into practice, and understand research design and statistics in sufficient depth to conduct investigations relevant to their own work.

Legal, Ethical Practice and Professional Development: School psychologists must take responsibility for developing as professionals, and they must practice in ways which meet all appropriate ethical, professional, and legal standards to enhance the quality of services and to protect the rights of all parties.

Note. Adapted from *School Psychology: A Blueprint for Training and Practice II*, by J. Ysseldyke, P. Dawson, C. Lehr, D. Reschley, M. Reynolds, and C. Telzrow, 1997. Bethesda, MD: National Association of School Psychologists.

development of life competencies, home/school/community collaboration, and *research and program evaluation* may be especially critical to transition planning.

Overview of School Psychology and Transition

In the last fifteen years, much has been written relative to the school psychologist's involvement in vocational programming, most commonly in regard to the provision of vocational assessment services (Levinson, 1993). That five major publications of the National Association of School Psychologists (*Best Practices in School Psychology I, II, III, Children's Needs: Psychological Perspectives, Children's Needs: Development, Problems and Alternatives*) each include a chapter relevant to career development (Levinson, 1987a; Levinson & Brandt, 1997), vocational assessment (Anderson, Hohenshil, Buckland-Heer, & Levinson, 1990; Hohenshil, Levinson, & Buckland-Heer, 1985; Levinson, 1995b), and transition (Levinson, 1995a; Levinson & McKee, 1990) attests to the significance of the topic for the profession.

Historically, psychologists have always been interested in the relationship between psychology and work, and several emminent psychologists have written extensively about this relationship. Freud (1962) considered love and work to be the two major areas of human endeavor, and proposed that an individual's self worth was intimately related to work. Erikson (1968) proposed that work contributed to one's identity, and believed that it was a particularly important contributor to development during adolescence. Bruner (1974) believed that neuroses among young people were more likely to involve choices about work and preparation for work than they were to involve sex. Jung (1960) contended that individuals in their natural state would not work, and that work was enculturated through civilization.

Despite psychology's longstanding interest in work, the school psychologist's involvement in vocational aspects of practice can be traced to Hohenshil (1984), who is widely considered to be the "father of vocational school psychology." Hohenshil noted that a 1973 computer search of the literature failed to identify a single article specifically dealing with roles for school psychologists in vocational programming. Judging from the paucity of the literature, Hummel and Hohenshil (1974) concluded that the career development of public school students was an area of human endeavor which had escaped the attention of school psychologists. Largely due to the work of Hohenshil and his colleagues, the mid 1970s and 1980s witnessed an increase in the number of programs presented at state and national school psychology conferences on the topic, as well as an increase in the number of published articles and journals devoted to vocational school psychology. In 1977, the President of NASP appointed a national commission to study the school psychologist's role in career and vocational education. The ensuing report recommended that school psychology should expand its services in vocational and career education programs, and that a specialty area in vocational school psychology should be established to expand psychological services to adolescents and adults, and to provide training to school psychologists who wished to upgrade their skills in the vocational aspects of practice. Following through on this recommendation, the NASP Delegate Assembly finally recognized vocational school psychology as the first *official* specialty area in the profession, and established the National Committee on Vocational School Psychology. This committee now functions as a NASP special interest group which has previously been active in sponsoring cost-free workshops on vocational assessment and programming at school psychology conferences, and providing school psychologists with reference materials relative to vocational practice in the schools. Though highly active in the late 1970s and 1980s, this committee has been relatively inactive in recent years.

NASP provided considerable early support for vocational school psychology, and in fact, incorporated both vocational assessment and intervention practices into its *Standards for the Provision of School Psychological Services* (Thomas & Grimes, 1995). These standards, which encompass the areas of assessment, consultation, and direct services, are defined as follows (Thomas & Grimes, 1995):

1. *Assessment:* "Psychological and psychoeducational assessments include evaluation, as appropriate, of the areas of . . . career and vocational development, aptitude, and interests."

2. *Consultation:* "School psychologists provide skill enhancement activities (such as . . . vocational development) to school personnel, parents, and others in the community, regarding issues of human learning, development and behavior."

3. *Direct Service:* "School psychologists design direct service programs to enhance cognitive, affective, social, and vocational development."

Despite such standards, one might still question whether school psychologists and those who influence the role of school psychologists (e.g., principals, supervisors) are supportive of school psychologists being involved in vocational assessment and transition practices. Early research provided some tentative answers to this question. In a survey of school superintendents, school psychologists, and school psychology trainers in Virginia, Murray (1975) found that administering, scoring, and interpreting vocational interest surveys for individual child study and making recommendations for placement of children in vocational classes were both activities in which school psychologists should be involved. Pfeffer (1978), in a survey of individuals in leadership positions with NASP, found that a majority of the respondents viewed career counseling and development as an area in which school psychologists should participate.

Despite this early support for the school psychologist's involvement in vocational activities, more recent data indicate that school psychologists are interested in, but not particularly involved in, vocational aspects of practice. Shepard and Hohenshil (1983) surveyed 218 practicing school psychologists and found that 75% of the respondents applied 3% or less of their time to vocational responsibilities. They also found that 91% felt unprepared to provide effective vocational services. However, these same respondents attached great importance to these activities, despite their noninvolvement (significant differences were found between ratings of importance and involvement). Levinson (1988), in a study of Pennsylvania school psychologists, found that 66% had no involvement in vocational assessment, 61% had no involvement in vocational counseling, 59% had not consulted with vocational instructors, and 87% had no involvement in vocational program development. Similarly, Carey (1995), in a national study of school psychologists, found that less than 1% of time was spent in vocational assessment.

More recently, Staab (1996) surveyed a randomly selected sample of 602 school psychologists working at the secondary level to determine a) the functions they performed in the area of transition planning, b) the importance they attached to transition planning, and c) the barriers they perceived to exist that prevented them from participating in transition planning activities. Analysis of the 278 useable questionnaires that were returned indicated that school psychologists were interested in transition planning activities, perceived these activities to be important, but generally felt unprepared to perform the activities listed. Other than transition functions listed under the category of assessment, school psychologists did not describe the transition activities listed by Staab as being "regularly" or "routinely" performed. Only two transition activities were described as activities that school psychologists "definitely should" perform: "explain test results to students so that they understand their strengths/needs, and modifications/adaptations needed for successful transition planning and programming," and "completing triennial evaluations to help meet transition planning needs." Approximately half of the school psychologists surveyed indicated that school psychology skills were "underutilized" in the transition process, and 81.7% of them indicated that performance of the transition activities listed were "somewhat important," "important," or "very important." School psychologists listed time constraints and caseloads as barriers to transition planning involvement. While recent data may be lacking about the exact amount of time school psychologists spend in transition activities, it seems safe to assume that the vast majority of school psychologists have little regular involvement in these activities, and those that do spend only a small amount of time engaged in such activities.

Existing Challenges for School Psychologists

What are the reasons for the school psychologist's limited involvement in transition activities? Studies conducted by Shepard and Hohenshil (1983), Levinson (1988), Levinson (1990), and Staab (1996) provide some tentative answers to this question. Clearly, most school psychologists have had limited training in transition assessment and programming (despite some NASP-sponsored activities), and hence may be reluctant to involve themselves in this aspect of practice. Despite inclusion in NASP standards, rarely is training in vocational assessment and transition included in school psychology training programs. School psychologists likely to have had some training in this area are school psychologists who have previously been trained as guidance counselors, or those who have purposefully sought out training via professional development seminars or workshops (Levinson, 1988).

Secondly, role restrictions and time constraints typically associated with school psychologist roles often discourage or prevent school psychologists from becoming involved in activities outside of that which would be considered "traditional" service delivery (e.g., testing of students for special education placement). Many school psychologists are under pressure from special education administrators (some of whom supervise school psychologists) to complete evaluations of students referred for special education placement. Often, there is a backlog of referrals, and districts find themselves out of compliance with the mandated timelines for completing these evaluations. Any activity that takes time away from completing such evaluations is often subject to excessive resistance. Relatedly, resistance often comes from other professionals who perceive transition planning as their role and not the school psychologist's role. Territoriality and turf battles often discourage school psychologists from involving themselves in these activities. To be fair, however, it is often school psychologists themselves who perceive these activities to be outside of their realm of responsibility and more appropriately performed by other professionals. This may be particularly true of school psychologists who work at the elementary and middle school levels, who do not view transition from a K–12 career development perspective, and simply believe that transition is something that is done in high schools.

Third, despite the assumption that traditional school psychological assessment data has a great deal of relevance for transition planning, there is only limited empirical evidence at the present time to support vocational interpretation of this data. Consequently, translating traditional school psychological asssessment data into transition recommendations is not easily done. This is especially true with the type of assessment data that school psychologists typically gather to assess a student's eligibility for special education placement. Such assessments traditionally rely upon the use of standardized norm-referenced assessment instruments such as tests of intelligence and academic achievement, the results of which are not easily translated into instructional recommendations of any kind.

Lastly, many existing vocational assessment instruments are time consuming to administer and lack acceptable psychometric characteristics. For these reasons, school psychologists may shy away from learning and using these instruments.

It is clear that given the traditional school psychologist practitioner role, if school psychologists are to become involved in transition planning it will most likely be through the assessment role. School psychologists must be provided with a means to gather data relevant to transition planning, in a time and cost-efficient fashion, using methodology with a strong empirical and theoretical basis and acceptable psychometric characteristics. The methodology used must be easily integrated into traditional school psychological theory and practice so as not to elicit resistance from other personnel. The methodology also must yield data which is easily and justifiably translated into transition-related recommendations. For these reasons, school psychologists should use *The Self Directed Search* (SDS) (Holland, 1985b) at the secondary school level (Levinson, 1990). The means by which the SDS can be used will be discussed in the next section.

In order for school psychologists to become significantly involved in transition activities, several important changes need to occur. First, their knowledge and skills in this area must be upgraded. Despite NASP standards which incorporate vocational/career assessment, vocational/career counseling, vocational/career consultation, and vocational/career program development, there is little evidence that accreditation of training programs is at all contingent on *any* of these skills being taught to preservice school psychologists. Thus, few if any school psychologists who graduate from NASP-approved school psychology programs have been adequately prepared to provide the vocational and transition related activities that NASP itself includes in its standards.

School psychologists at least need to become more informed about career development theory and its application in assessment, counseling, consultation, and program development. School psychologists need to understand transition from a K–12 career development perspective and recognize that there is an important role for them to play in the process, regardless of whether they work at an elementary, middle, or secondary school level. From an assessment perspective, school psychologists need to become more informed about interest and aptitude assessment, as well as other more experientially-based vocational assessment techniques, such as work sampling, situational assessment, and simulated work experiences. Additionally, school psychologists need to become better acquainted with the vocational relevance of the assessment data they currently gather. While some experts will argue that intelligence and academic achievement test data have only minimal relevance to transition planning, personality assessment data has tremendous relevance and is an integral aspect of most theories of career development. School psychologists need to learn how to gather and use such data in a manner that easily translates into transition-related recommendations. Perhaps most importantly, however, school psychologists need to become more familiar with functional assessment, dynamic assessment, curriculum-based assessment, and community-referenced assessment procedures in order to increase the practical relevance and value of the assessment data they gather. Sole reliance on standardized norm-referenced assessment instruments will continue to limit the usefulness of school psychological assessment data for vocational and transition planning.

Without massive special education reform, however, it is unlikely that school psychologists will be able to escape the prison of testing for special education eligibility, testing that often monopolizes their time and inevitably requires use of standardized norm-referenced assessment instruments. Fortunately, there is some evidence that such reform is occurring. In states such as Pennsylvania, Iowa, and Minnesota for example, students experiencing difficulty in regular education are not immediately referred for special education eligibility testing (such referrals immediately initiate a timeline mandated by federal and state special education regulations that is increasingly difficult to meet as referrals build up). Instead, these students are referred to an intervention assistance team (names of teams vary from state to state), which utilizes a problem-solving model designed to generate interventions that have the goal of accommodating student difficulties within regular education. Assessment, within the context of such a problem-solving model, is designed to identify interventions and to test their effectiveness. As a consequence, curriculum-based assessment, dynamic assessment, and functional assessment procedures are increasingly used within the context of such a model. As problem solving within regular education supplants special education referrals as a means of reacting to student difficulties, and as states begin to emphasize noncategorical special education systems and inclusion of students with disabilities in regular education, school psychologists may find increased opportunities to use assessment procedures other than standardized norm-referenced instruments and more time to engage in activities other than assessment.

Finally, if school psychologists are to increase their involvement in transition-related activities, the profession as a whole must demonstrate greater commitment to the area. While tacit acceptance of the importance of transition-related activities is reflected in NASP standards for practice, that school psychologists can graduate from NASP accredited programs with virtually *no* training in the area suggests a lack of true commitment. Historically, school psychologists have worked with students who have disabilities and in the shadow of special education. The high unemployment and underemployment rates and the elevated dropout rates which exist among this population of students clearly suggest that traditional service delivery has not resulted in desirable outcomes and that a change in focus is needed. School psychologists must assume some responsibility for the dismal postschool outcomes of the students with whom they work, and they must commit themselves to change. Inclusion of the "socialization and development of life competencies" domain by Ysseldyke et al. (1997) in NASP's *Blueprint for Training and Practice II* seems to be one step toward such a change in focus. If school psychologists increasingly devote effort to improving student acquisition of social skills and life competencies such as conflict resolution, decision making, and problem solving (as advocated by Ysseldyke et al., 1997), their work will greatly assist transition efforts.

A Bold Vision for the Future: Roles for School Psychologists

Currently, a variety of professionals may assume major responsibility for the development and implementation of transition programs. Although no agreement currently exists as to who should assume this major responsibility, a number of "vocational specialist" or "transition specialist" training programs do exist. The competencies acquired in these programs clearly overlap with the knowledge and skills possessed by school psychologists. In their study of the competencies taught in 13 university "transition specialist" training programs across the country, Baker, Geiger, and deFur (1988) found that general knowledge of learning theory (particularly behavioral theory) and assessment were areas in which an extensive amount of training was concentrated. Both Baker, Geiger, and deFur (1988) and Marinelli, Tunic, and LeConte (1988) agree that adolescent psychology is a frequently omitted but important area in the training of such specialists. Clearly, the school psychologist's expertise in assessment, learning and behavior theory, and adolescent psychology may be most applicable to their involvement in transition programming.

Moreover, vocational assessment is one aspect of a comprehensive transition assessment and the Vocational Evaluation and Work Adjustment Association's (VEWAA) definition of vocational assessment actually incorporates a psychological component (VEWAA, 1975). Thus, if this definition is used as a conceptual basis by those developing school-based vocational assessment and transition programs, involvement of the school psychologist (the only school-based professional capable of providing a "psychological component") becomes a necessity. The following discussion of roles that school psychologists may assume in transition planning is organized according to the major areas of service delivery identified by NASP.

Psychological and Psychoeducational Assessment

From an assessment perspective, school psychologists have much to contribute to transition planning. It is a well-accepted notion that intelligence test data, academic achievement test data, personality assessment data, and adaptive behavior/social skills data all have some relevance for transition programming. Because school psychologists routinely gather much of this data as part of assessments for special education eligibility, one might argue that if school psychologists do nothing more than what they are currently doing they are capable of contributing valuable data to the transition planning process. Validity coefficients of cognitive ability tests for predicting job performance, for example, are impressive, especially when such tests are supplemented with additional predictors like work samples, personality measures, employment interviews, job knowledge, and job-tryout procedures (Wagner, 1997). Because of the relationship between intelligence measures and vocational aptitude measures (Heinlein, 1987; Miller, 1978; Watkins, 1980), intelligence test data may be used to assist in determining the degree to which an individual may attain success in a given vocational setting (Faas & D'Alonzo, 1990; Hartzell & Compton, 1984; Webster, 1974). Given the relationship between IQ and both educational attainment and educational status (Jencks et al., 1979), intelligence test data can be used to assess a student's potential to successfully pursue postsecondary education and the occupations which require such training (Morris & Levinson, 1993). The relationship between academic achievement and vocational outcomes (Ansley & Forsyth, 1983; Biller, 1987; Schill, McCartin, & Meyer, 1985; Wolf, 1983; Zurawell & Das, 1982) suggests that academic achievement test data can be used in a similar fashion.

Likewise, research has indicated that personality assessment data can be used to assess the appropriateness of specific occupations for individual students and can predict both job satisfaction and job performance (Holland, 1985a). Because people most often lose jobs because of affective or social deficiencies rather than technical incompetence, adaptive behavior and social skills data can assist in identifying areas which need to be targeted for intervention prior to job or residential placement. Moreover, because affective or social deficiencies will negatively impact the community functioning of individuals with disabilities and may also limit their social and recreational opportunities, the assessment of personality is especially important.

Whereas assessments of intelligence, academic achievement, adaptive behavior/social skills, and personality are often included in comprehensive school psychological evaluations, other areas relevant to transition planning are not. Depending upon the roles assumed by other transition planning team members, school psychologists may need to alter their assessment strategies somewhat in order to emphasize these additional areas. For example, school psychologists might choose to incorporate measures of vocational interests, aptitudes, and career maturity (via interviews, observations, and paper–pencil tests) into their assessments. School psychologists may also need to incorporate an evaluation of functional living skills into their assessments. An instrument such as the *Social and Prevocational Information Battery* (Halpern, Raffeld, Irvin, & Link, 1975), for example, would provide school psychologists with functional skills assessment data which could be utilized in transition programming.

In particular, the SDS (Holland, 1985b) has been recommended as an instrument that might be particularly useful to school psychologists (Levinson, 1990, 1993) because it adequately addresses many of the issues that may be inhibiting school psychologists from becoming involved in vocational assessment. Generally considered to be an interest inventory, the SDS is based partly upon a theory of personality, is time and cost efficient to use, possesses acceptable psychometric properties, and yields data which are easily translatable into transition-related recommendations (Levinson, 1990, 1993). SDS data can be integrated with other psychoeducational assessment data in generating these recommendations. For example, intelligence and academic achievement test data can assist in determining the likelihood that a student would be successful in pursuing a career that requires postsecondary education. This data might also be helpful in determining the level within a given occupational area to which a student might successfully aspire. Using the SDS, school psychologists can identify occupational areas consistent with a particular student's personality. By comparing the results to vocational training programs available, local jobs available, and college majors, school psychologists generate useful recommendations. For a case study illustrating the inclusion of a transition component in a school psychological evaluation (using transition relevant instruments other than the SDS), readers are referred to Levinson (1987b).

Though standardized norm-referenced assessment data may be useful for identifying some general transition-related goals and objectives, they are not as useful for identifying other specific goals or, perhaps more importantly, identifying instructional recommendations or accommodations which may be necessary in order for these goals and objectives to be met. Hence, school psychologists need to increasingly use other assessment methodologies (e.g., curriculum-based assessment, dynamic assessment, and functional assessment) in order to identify instructional strategies and techniques that may be effective for a particular student. Because of the recent revisions made to the IDEA, school psychologists may be increasingly asked to conduct functional behavioral assessments that will provide data that will have clear relevance for transition planning. Additionally, revisions to the IDEA also afford school psychologists an opportunity to expand the assessment techniques they employ when completing triennial reevaluations. As a consequence, school psychologists may be able to increasingly use situational assessment and other strategies that allow behavior to be assessed in natural environments. Such assessments will increase the specificity and usefulness of the recommendations school psychologists make. Additionally, changes in the requirements of triennial reevaluations may also reduce school psychologist testing requirements, referral backlogs, and excessive caseloads, thereby allowing them to involve themselves in transition activities other than assessment. If reform in special education continues, assessment techniques used by school psychologists will increasingly involve gathering information in natural environments with direct measures of behavior that can be used to identify and define problems, establish and test interventions, monitor progress, and evaluate outcomes (Reschly & Ysseldyke, 1995). Such an assessment focus, which is advocated by Ysseldyke et al. (1997) in A *Blueprint for Training and Practice II*, will dramatically increase the usefulness of school psychological assessment data for transition planning.

Consultation

The school psychologists' knowledge of learning and behavior theory and of adolescent psychology may allow them to serve as effective consultants to teachers (regular, special education, vocational education), rehabilitation counselors, job coaches, and employers relative to the conditions under which optimum learning and performance might be facilitated. Because a large amount of the training pertinent to transition may occur outside of the school in job, community, or residential settings, school psychologists will have to prepare themselves to provide consultative services in settings other than the office or classroom. In particular, school psychologists can assist other professionals in establishing and monitoring behavior management programs. As a consultant, the school psychologist may also function as a liason among parents, the transition planning team, community service agencies, and employers. Their knowledge of consultation theory and practice, in combination with their understanding of group dynamics, may allow school psychologists to act as effective group facilitators by increasing cooperation and coordination among team members, and by over-coming resistance to intervention implementation.

Direct Service

From a direct service perspective, the school psychologist may assist in transition programming by implementing social skills training programs or behavior man-agement programs designed to facilitate acquisition of those skills necessary for successful transition. Such programs may be most effective when implemented within residential, community, or employment settings. Though knowledgeable in counseling, school psychologists' lack of training in career development hin-ders them from providing vocational counseling to students. With additional training, however, it is possible that school psychologists could eventually assume such a role. School psychologists might also conduct inservice workshops on the use of assessment data in transition planning and on basic issues in ado-lescent psychology or learning theory.

School psychologists will probably find themselves working directly with parents of students with disabilities as a function of their role on the transition planning team. Because many school psychologists are knowledgeable about family dynamics and issues that affect family–school collaboration, they may be particularly effective at providing parent training or short-term family counsel-ing aimed at enlisting parental support for and involvement in the implementa-tion of transition plans. Ysseldyke et al's. (1997) "home/school/community col-laboration" domain suggests that school psychologists should study and be knowledgeable about family influences on cognitive, motivational, and social characteristics. These factors will influence student performance, family involvement in education, ways to promote partnerships between parents and educators to improve outcomes for students, and cultural issues that impact home–school collaboration. Because family involvement in transition planning has been identified as a key characteristic of effective transition programs, the extent to which this domain guides school psychology training and practice in the future may greatly affect the school psychologist's usefulness in transition.

Program Planning and Evaluation

There is a need to evaluate the effectiveness of the various programs designed to facilitate acquisition of the skills necessary for successful transition. The degree to which local school and community-based services are successful in facilitating the successful transition of students from school to work and community must be evaluated as well. The school psychologist's understanding of research and program evaluation may allow them to effectively assist in the planning and implementation of such evaluation programs. Similarly, school psychologists can design research to assess the effectiveness of interventions which have been implemented with particular students and the extent to which students are progressing in their acquisition of the skills necessary for successful transition. Currently, however, school psychologists may not be as familiar with single-subject research design as they may need to be in order to effectively monitor intervention effectiveness. Because this methodology is an essential part of a problem solving's orientation to assessment, it is included in Ysseldyke et al.'s (1997) *A Blueprint for Training and Practice II*. Thus, it is increasingly likely that school psychologists will become familiar with this methodology in the near future.

The development and implementation of vocational assessment and transition programs involves the selection, use, and interpretation of assessment instruments. In the past, those professionals entrusted with these responsibilities have had limited training in psychology and have often been ill-prepared to deal with the psychometric and measurement issues that development and implementation of an assessment program requires (Egerman & Gilbert, 1969; Murphy & Ursprung, 1983). In contrast, school psychologists today are well trained in assessment methodology and knowledgeable about psychometric and measurement issues. Consequently, involvement of school psychologists in the establishment and implementation of assessment programs can reduce the risk of inappropriate selection, use, and interpretation of assessment instruments, and can increase the validity of the overall transition assessment process.

Final Thoughts

In summary, research has indicated that school psychologists are interested but relatively uninvolved in transition activities at the present time. Factors such as lack of training, lack of time, lack of familiarity with career development theory, and the psychometric inadequacy of many vocational assessment instruments have hindered school psychologist involvement in transition activities. Moreover, their focus on assessing students for special education eligibility and their reliance on published, standardized norm-referenced assessment instruments have also limited their involvement and usefulness. With the dawning of special education reform and a shift to a problem-solving model of service delivery, school psychologists may become increasingly valuable in transition planning activities. To conclude the chapter, the following passages offer a brief scenario that describes the role a school psychologist might perform relative to transition planning.

A school psychologist was asked to complete a triennial special education reevaluation on Joe, a student with a learning disability. Joe had been identified as having a reading disability in the 4th grade. He had previously been reevaluated in the 7th grade. After reviewing both cumulative and confidential files, the school psychologist noted that Joe had consistently demonstrated above-average intelligence, but slightly below-average academic achievement, particularly in those areas that emphasize reading. Previous evaluations had suggested Joe to be reasonably creative and adept at performing tasks that required abstract visual reasoning. However, he was said to be shy and had some difficulty getting along with others. Given the consistent findings of the two previous intellectual and academic assessments, the school psychologist chose not to conduct another intellectual or academic (other than reading) assessment. Instead, he began by interviewing Joe. In the interview, the school psychologist asked Joe about his postschool plans (he wanted to go to college and major in art, but his parents did not think he could and wanted him to work in the family's hardware store), his social relationships and leisure interests (he had one close friend, did not participate much in school activities, and preferred solitary leisure activities like drawing and playing guitar), his independent living skills (he could do everything on his own but his parents "babied" him), and his previous work experiences (he had done some lawn cutting and had worked in the family hardware store). Next, the school psychologist interviewed Joe's parents and addressed these same areas. Joe's parents indicated that they did not think Joe could be successful in college because he could not read, and they expected him to work in the family hardware store and live at home upon graduation. They confirmed that Joe was shy, had few friends, and preferred solitary activities. They added that, based on their observation of him cutting lawns and working in the hardware store, his work habits were not particularly well developed. Interviews with Joe's teachers confirmed what the school psychologist had previously learned about Joe. To further assess work habits, the school psychologist conducted a structured observation at the hardware store where Joe worked on weekends, contacted families for whom Joe cut lawns, and interviewed Joe's teachers. Based upon the information gathered, the school psychologist chose to conduct an assessment of social skills (Joe, his parents, and his teachers all completed a social skills questionnaire). Additionally, the school psychologist assessed Joe's reading using both standardized norm-referenced tests and informal techniques using Joe's textbooks. The school psychologist used dynamic assessment and informal techniques to assess the extent to which Joe's comprehension of material could be improved through the use of different strategies. Joe's ability to make vocational decisions on his own was assessed through the use of a career maturity measure. Joe's vocational interests were assessed through an interview and his use of a paper–pencil inventory appropriate for his reading level. Given Joe's level of intelligence and his interest in attending college, the psychologist attempted to identify college majors that conformed to his identified interests. Lastly, the psychologist used a transition planning inventory to rule out other areas of concern.

In the transition planning meeting that followed the school psychologist's assessment, the school psychologist presented the results of his assessment. He indicated that Joe had the potential to successfully pursue postsecondary education, particularly in high interest areas like art, drafting, advertising, graphic arts, video communications, and related areas. However, shyness (and an inability to advocate for himself), social skills and work habit deficits, reading difficulties, and parental expectations were issues that might impede a successful transition. The school psychologist recommended that Joe participate in a social skills training program that the school psychologist conducted (to improve areas of deficit and to teach advocacy skills which would be necessary for success in any postsecondary educational setting). The psychologist recommended that Joe continue to explore occupational areas of interest by interviewing and shadowing professionals in these areas, and by reviewing the educational requirements for entry into these fields. The school psychologist also recommended that Joe and his parents become familiar with the services offered to students with disabilities at local colleges. The school psychologist also volunteered to enter into a short-term counseling relationship with Joe and his parents to address parental expectations and post-high-school aspirations. While the school psychologist offered recommendations that would assist Joe in better comprehending reading material, he offered to further assess the effectiveness of each of these techniques by teaching each to Joe and by monitoring the effectiveness of each using single-subject research design methodology.

References

Anderson, W. T., Hohenshil, T. H., Buckland-Heer, K., & Levinson, E. M. (1990). Best practices in vocational assessment of students with disabilities. In A. Thomas & J. Grimes (Eds.), *Best practices in school psychology–II* (pp. 787–798). Washington, DC: NASP.

Ansley, T. N., & Forsyth, R. A. (1983). Relationship of elementary and secondary school achievement test scores to college performance. *Educational and Psychological Measurement, 43* (4), 1103–1112.

Baker, B. C., Geiger, W. L., & deFur, S. (1988, November). *Competencies for transition personnel.* Paper presented at the Mid-East Regional Conference of the Career Development Division of the Council for Exceptional Children, White Sulphur Springs, WV.

Biller, E. F. (1987). Career decision making for adolescents and young adults with learning disabilities: Theory, research and practice. Springfield, IL: Charles C. Thomas.

Borich, G. (1985). Traditional and emerging concepts in program evaluation. In J. R. Bergan (Ed.), *School psychology in contemporary society: An introduction* (pp. 394–420). Columbus, OH: Merrill.

Bruner, J. (1974). Continuity of learning. *The School Psychology Digest, 3,* 20–25.

Carey, K. (1995). *A national study of the role and function of the school psychologist.* Paper presented at the annual meeting of the National Association of School Psychologists, Chicago, IL.

Egerman, K., & Gilbert, J. L. (1969). The work evaluator. *Journal of Rehabilitation, 35*(3), 12–14.

Erickson, E. H. (1968). *Identity: Youth and crises.* New York: Norton.

Faas, L. A., & D'Alonzo, B. (1990). WAIS–R scores as predictors of employment success and failure among adults with learning disabilities. *Journal of Learning Disabilities, 23,* 311–316.

Freud, S. (1962). *Civilization and its discontents.* (J. Strachey, Ed. & trans.). New York: Norton.

Halpern, A. S., Raffeld, P., Irvin, L. K., & Link, R. (1975). *Social and prevocational information battery.* Monterey, CA: Publishers Test Service.

Hartzell, H. E., & Compton, C. (1984). Learning disability: 10-year follow-up. *Pediatrics, 74,* 1058–1064.

Heinlein, W. E. (1987). *Clinical utility of the Wechsler scales in psychological evaluations to estimate vocational aptitude.* Unpublished doctoral dissertation, Virginia Polytechnic Institute and State University, Blacksburg, VA.

Hohenshil, T. H. (1984). The vocational aspects of school psychology: 1974–1984. *School Psychology Review, 13*(4) 503–509.

Hohenshil, T. H., Levinson, E. M., & Buckland-Heer, K. (1985). Best practices in vocational assessment for handicapped students. In J. Grimes & A. Thomas (Eds.), *Best Practices in School Psychology* (pp. 215–228). Washington, DC: NASP.

Holland, J. L. (1985a). *A theory of vocational personalities and work environments.* Englewood Cliffs, N.J.: Prentice-Hall.

Holland, J. L. (1985b). *The self directed search professional manual: 1985 edition.* Odessa, FL: Psychological Assessment Resources.

Hummel, D. L., & Hohenshil, T. H. (1974). The psychological foundations of career education: Potential roles for school psychologists. *School Psychology Digest, 3,* 4–10.

Jencks, C., Bartlett, S., Corcoran, M., Crouse, J., Eaglesfield, D., Jackson, G., McCelland, K., Mueser, P., Olneck, M., Schwartz, J., Ward, S., & Williams, J. (1979). *Who gets ahead? The determinants of economic success in America.* New York: Basic Books.

Jung, C. (1960). *The collected works of C. G. Jung.* New York: Bollinger Foundation, Princeton University Press.

Kratochwill, T. R., Elliott, S. N., & Rotto, P. C. (1995). School-based behavioral consultation. In A. Thomas & J. Grimes (Eds.), *Best practices in school psychology III* (pp. 519–538). Washington, DC: NASP.

Levinson, E. M. (1987a). Children and career development. In A. Thomas & J. Grimes (Eds.), *Children's needs: Psychological perspectives* (pp. 73–82). Washington, DC: NASP.

Levinson, E. M. (1987b). Incorporating a vocational component into a school psychological evaluation: A case example. *Psychology in the Schools, 24*(3), 254–264.

Levinson, E. M. (1988). Correlates of vocational practice among school psychologists. *Psychology in the Schools, 25*(3), 297–305.

Levinson, E. M. (1990). Actual/Desired role functioning, perceived control over role functioning, and job satisfaction among school psychologists. *Psychology in the Schools, 27*(1), 64–74.

Levinson, E. M. (1993). *Transdisciplinary vocational assessment: Issues in school-based programs.* Brandon, VT: Clinical Psychology Publishing.

Levinson, E. M. (1995a). Transition services. In A. Thomas & J. Grimes (Eds.), *Best practices in school psychology III* (pp. 909–916). Washington, DC: NASP.

Levinson, E. M. (1995b). Vocational assessment in the schools. In A. Thomas & J. Grimes (Eds.), *Best practices in school psychology III* (pp. 741–752). Washington, DC: NASP.

Levinson, E. M., & Brandt, J. (1997). Career development. In G. Bear, K. Minke, & A. Thomas (Eds.), *Children's needs II: Development, problems and alternatives* (pp. 533–545). Washington, DC: NASP.

Levinson, E. M., & McKee, L. M. (1990). Best practices in transitional services. In A. Thomas & J. Grimes (Eds.), *Best practices in school psychology II* (pp. 743–756). Washington, DC: NASP.

Marinelli, R. P., Tunic, R. H., & Leconte, P. (1988, November). *Vocational evaluation education: Regional programs.* Paper presented at the Mid-East Regional Conference of the Career Development Division of the Council for Exceptional Children, White Sulphur Springs, WV.

Medway, F. (1985). Direct therapeutic intervention in school psychology. In J.R. Bergan (Ed.), *School psychology in contemporary society: An introduction.* Columbus, OH: Merrill.

Miller, J. T. (1978). A study of WISC subtest scores as predictors of GATB occupational aptitude patterns for EMH students in a high school occupational orientation course. *Dissertation Abstracts International, 38,* (12-A), 7272.

Morris, T., & Levinson, E. M. (1993). Intelligence and occupational/vocational adjustment: A literature review. *Journal of Counseling and Development, 73*(5), 503–514.

Murphy, S. T., & Ursprung, A. (1983). The politics of vocational evaluation: A qualitative study. *Rehabilitation Literature, 44*(1–2), 2–12.

Murray, P. (1975). *An analysis of the role of the school psychologist in the Commonwealth of Virginia.* Unpublished doctoral dissertation, Virginia Polytechnic Institute and State University, Blacksburg, VA.

Pfeffer, R. (1978). *Proposed functions for school psychologists in career education.* Unpublished doctoral dissertation, Virginia Polytechnic Institute and State University, Blacksburg, VA.

Reschly, D., & Ysseldyke, J. (1995). School psychology paradigm shift. In A. Thomas & J. Grimes (Eds.), *Best practices in school psychology III* (pp. 17–32). Washington, DC: NASP

Schill, W. J., McCartin, R., & Meyer, K. (1985). Youth employment: Its relationship to academic and family variables. *Journal of Vocational Behavior, 26,* 155–163.

Shepard, J. W., & Hohenshil, T.H. (1983). National survey of career development functions of practicing school psychologists. *Psychology in the Schools, 20*(4), 445–449.

Shinn, M. (1989). *Curriculum-based measurement: Assessing special children.* New York: Guilford Press.

Staab, M. J. (1996). The role of the school psychologist in transition planning (Doctoral dissertation, University of Kansas, Lawrence, 1996). *Dissertation Abstracts International, 58,* 281.

Thomas, A., & Grimes, J. (1995). *Best practices in school psychology III.* Washington, DC: NASP.

Vocational Evaluation and Work Adjustment Association. (1975). Vocational evaluation final report [special issue]. *Vocational Evaluation and Work Adjustment Bulletin, 8.*

Wagner, R. K. (1997). Intelligence, training, and employment. *American Psychologist, 52*(10), 1059–1069.

Watkins, N. W. (1980). Intellectual and special aptitudes of tenth grade educable mentally retarded students. *Education and Training of the Mentally Retarded, 15,* 139–142.

Webster, R. E. (1974). Predictive applicability of the WAIS with psychiatric patients in a vocational rehabilitation setting. *Journal of Community Psychology, 2*(2), 141–144.

Wilson, M. S., & Reschly, D. J. (1996). Assessment in school psychology training and practice. *School Psychology Review, 25*(1), 9–23.

Wolf, J. C. (1983). Tests of general educational development as a predictor of 2-year college academic performance. *Measurement and Evaluation in Guidance, 16*(1), 4–12.

Woody, R. H., Lavoie, J. C., & Epps, S. (1992). *School psychology: A developmental and social systems approach.* Needham Heights, MA: Allyn & Bacon.

Ysseldyke, J., Dawson, P., Lehr, C., Reschley, D. J., Reynolds, M., & Telzrow, C. (1997). *School psychology: A Blueprint for training and practice II.* Bethesda, MD: NASP.

Zurawell, J. M., & Das, J. P. (1982). Cognitive performance and success in automotives training. *Mental Retardation Bulletin, 10*(2,3), 61–68.

CHAPTER

SPEECH AND LANGUAGE SERVICES

Priscilla Harvell

"Change can be frightening. The challenge for all of us is to remain open to change."

—D. Hunter (1994-95)

Want Ad
1960
Position: Public School Speech Therapist. Union School District seeks full-time speech therapist. Knowledgeable in diagnosis and remediation of communication disorders. Able to work independently. Contact:
Linda in Personnel Department.

Classifieds
2000
Position: Speech–Language Pathologist. F/T position, Union School District. *Skills required:* Functional assessment/intervention strategies, understand/participate in the transition planning process, develop/implement creative services, ability to work collaboratively with transdisciplinary team. Able to communicate with students/families from diverse backgrounds. Knowledgeable in augmentative/alternative communication techniques. Great salary and benefits. Contact: Human Resources.

Resiliency is a term often applied to the act of survival. To be resilient is to be flexible and adaptable in order to maintain existence in the face of change and stress. The above job advertisements for a speech pathologist demonstrate the evolving changes found in education and, more specifically, in the field of speech pathology. The urgency for change is apparent as the 21st century approaches. In such an urban, industrial, and technological society, it is imperative that the profession of speech pathology continue to meet the needs of society. To do so requires change.

Demographic changes point to not only the migration of the rural to urban life, but also to the growing diversity of students. With increasing cultural and linguistic diversity, the country's education has become a challenge for all educators. No longer can professionals be satisfied with a one-dimensional perspective on how they educate or teach. For speech pathologists, this change not only affects assessment procedures but also affects the type of intervention strategies employed and the arenas where interventions will be taught.

Within the past 10 years, the evolution of education laws has focused on the student and meeting the demands of society and the workforce. If speech pathologists are to facilitate movement to meet these needs, the movement must come from both academic learning and the development of skills learned from day-to-day living. This bridging between school, community, and workplace is critical in preparing students for tomorrow's workforce. The California High School Task Force (1992) recognized this need when they stated: "Now, high schools must enter the next stage of improvement activities and shift to an outcome-based approach to meet the challenges of an information-and-knowledge-based, global society in the twenty-first century" (p. 5).

How will this impact the speech and language pathologist (SLP)? As educators, SLPs must transform or else become dinosaurs in the 21st century. This transformation will require SLPs to approach their role with four concepts in mind: (1) autonomy, (2) social competency, (3) purpose and future, and (4) problem solving (see Figure 4.1). If SLPs focus on creating such a resilient view, there is no doubt that the needs of the students and the workforce will be competently addressed.

When looking at the autonomy of the SLP, it is important to understand the role language plays in education. Eggleston (1997) found that "Eighty-five to ninety percent of school-aged children that do manifest learning disabilities have their basic deficits in language and reading" (p. 9). Language plays a major role in all school subjects, including reading, math, history, geography, and even art. Many educators assume that students master normal language development by the middle grades. Much of the mastery of skills is emphasized in written language abilities. In later grades, more complex language is expected, including increased vocabulary, ability to construct more complex sentence structures, and

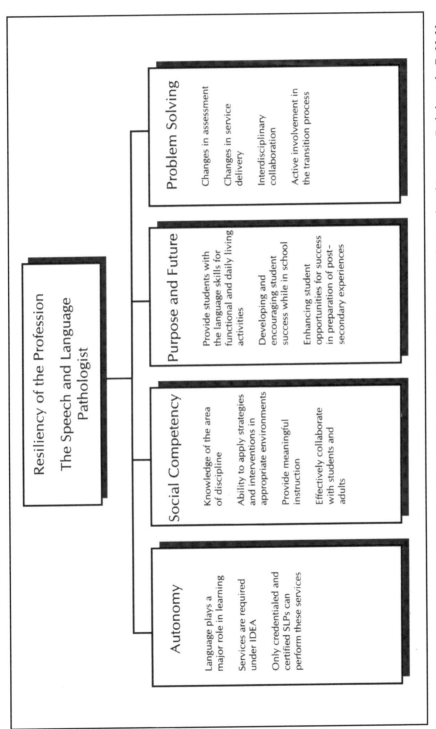

Figure 4.1. Four components of resiliency. *Note.* Adapted from *Resiliency of the Profession: The Speech and Language Pathologist,* by R. H. Hatter, 1996, Fremont, CA: California Department of Education, Diagnostic Center North.

fluency in different kinds of language for different situations. All of this is assumed if a student follows the normal path of development. If this is not the case, then educators may have a student who demonstrates one or more of the following: developmental delays, hearing problems, muscular disorders, and speech/language and other related problems. If these areas are not addressed, then a student will experience difficulty in the school setting and, eventually, in adult life.

Services of SLPs in the school setting are required according to the Individuals with Disabilities Education Act of 1997 (IDEA) (P.L. 105-17). This requirement provides SLPs autonomy, because their services can only be performed by someone with speech and language certification. In addition, social competencies are a required expectation of the SLP. Social competencies are defined by one's knowledge of the area of discipline and by one's ability to apply strategies and interventions in appropriate environments, provide meaningful instruction, and to effectively collaborate with students and adults. If SLPs do not demonstrate the above qualities, then the profession is in jeopardy. The implications for the secondary student mean SLPs play a role in facilitating the student's movement from secondary to postsecondary activities. With this in mind, questions arise: (1) What is the SLP's purpose and impact on students' futures; and (2) Is the SLP willing to problem solve?

Before examining new or modified delivery models, it is critical to discuss and understand the meanings of communication and language disorders.

An Overview of Communication and Language Disorders

Terminology

Communication

The *Random House College Dictionary* defines *communication* as "the imparting or interchange of thoughts, opinions, or information by speech, writing, etc." (1984). Research provides many other definitions of communication (McReynolds, 1990; Owens, 1990). Communication is described as the ability to receive, process, and comprehend ideas, thoughts, and feelings through both verbal and nonverbal means. Language is the ability to comprehend and use spoken, written, and other symbol systems. If one were to simplify the definition, effective and successful communication becomes apparent by the speaker's ability to receive and deliver information so that the listener receives and understands the message.

Normal Language Development

When discussing normal language development, definitions typically refer to four areas: phonology, syntax, semantics, and pragmatics (Nippold, 1993; Scott & Stokes, 1995; Wesson, Otis-Wilborn, Hasbrouck, & Tindal, 1993). Phonology refers to articulation and the phonetic/phonologic parts of speech. Syntax is the grammatical structure and complexity of language. Semantics involves the meaning of language at the word (vocabulary) and sentence (relationships between word combinations) levels. According to Bloom and Lahey (1978), meaning is derived from combinations and their relationships in forming sentences. Pragmatics refers to the functional use of language and presents difficulty for many adolescents with communication disorders. One such difficulty such adolescents face is in using socially appropriate communication (verbal or nonverbal). Bloom and Lahey (1978) discuss the importance of three major components of language: form (syntax/morphology), use (pragmatics), and content (thoughts/ideas/semantics). These parameters of normal language development are the areas by which speech pathologists compare children who have language disorders. Although diverse, these language areas are interrelated. People communicate in their own unique way by listening, speaking, reading, writing, and through body language and vocal inflections.

Communication and Language Disorders

The American Speech-Language-Hearing Association's (ASHA) Ad Hoc Committee on Service Delivery in the Schools provided a statement of guidance (not to be interpreted as official standards) on definitions of communication disorders and variations (ASHA, 1993a). The official statement of the committee reads:

> A communication disorder is an impairment in the ability to receive, send, process, and comprehend concepts or verbal, nonverbal and graphic symbol systems. A communication disorder may be evident in the processes of hearing, language, and/or speech. A communication disorder may range in severity from mild to profound. It may be developmental or acquired. Individuals may demonstrate one or any combination of communication disorders. A communication disorder may result in a primary disability or it may be secondary to other disabilities. (p. 40)

Figure 4.2 provides a graphic of the subdisorders of communication disorders and communication variations.

The ASHA Ad Hoc Committee on Service Delivery in the Schools defines each subdisorder listed in Figure 4.2. However, for clarity purposes, the term *central auditory processing disorder* refers to deficits in the information processing of

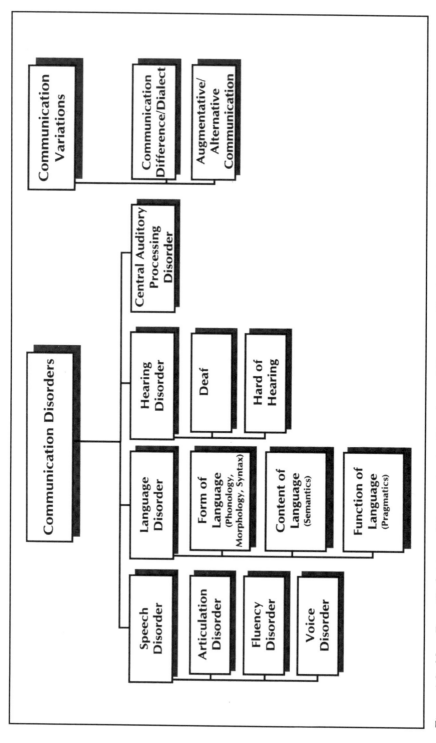

Figure 4.2. *Note.* From "Definitions of Communication Disorders and Variations," by the American Speech-Language-Hearing Association, 1993. *Asha, 35*(10), pp. 40–41. Copyright 1993 by ASHA. Adapted with permission.

audible signals (sounds) not due to impaired peripheral hearing sensitivity or intellectual development (ASHA, 1993a).

Bashir (1989) stated, "Language disorders are chronic and may persist across the lifetime of the individual. The symptoms, manifestations, effects, and severity of the problem change over time . . . as a consequence of context, content, and learning task" (p. 181). This refutes the assumption of some educators who believe students develop all language skills by middle grades. Owens (1995) stated that language disorders apply to a

> . . . heterogeneous group of developmental and/or acquired disorders . . . principally characterized by deficits and/or immaturities in the use of spoken or written language for comprehension and/or production purposes that may involve the form, content, and/or function of language in any combination. (p. 22)

Students with communication disorders such as those described above may experience some or all of the following challenges as they move through the educational system: feelings of failure, low self-esteem, poor academic and social success, high dropout rate, and so on. These challenges will hinder or prevent a student from effectively preparing for adult life. For example, when communication disorders impede academic or vocational training, a student may experience difficulty securing or maintaining employment (U.S. Department of Labor, 1991b). These students pose challenges to the SLP who plays a vital role in that student's road to a quality adult life.

In addition to communication disorders, communication variations are discussed in the literature as well. ASHA describes two such variations: augmentative/alternative communication (AAC) and communication difference/dialect (see Figure 4.2). AAC refers to any communication method that extends the normal methods of impaired speech (e.g., communication book board, mechanical or electronic device, or laptop). Huer (1997) also discusses the importance of culture in AAC practices. The second variation described in Figure 4.2, communication difference/dialect, is discussed by several authors (ASHA, 1993a; Cheng, 1994; Iglesias, 1994; Taylor, 1990; Taylor & Payne, 1994). Other authors discuss how communication difference/dialect of one's culture flavors the choice of words, meanings, and concepts when one is engaged in conversation (Patton & Westby, 1992). The critical point to remember is that understanding communication variations is important because children learn and use language based on interpersonal, societal, and cultural contexts of their environment that are often quite different from the mainstream culture's expectations. This level of understanding regarding communication variations ties in with the purposes of the speech pathology profession (see Figure 4.1).

Language disorders and communication variations are common among school-age students. Although this knowledge is not new, it is important to establish how students with language disorders compare with students who have other disabilities.

Student Profile

Students from the ages 6 to 21 with communication disorders make up the second largest group of disabled individuals (22.2%) in the United States (U.S. Department of Education, 1994). Many of these students have average or above average intellectual ability, are served in regular education classes (85.5%), and graduate from high school (43.9%) (U.S. Department of Education, 1994). Wagner and Shaver (1989) found that secondary students with speech impairments were dismissed at the rate of 18% (three times the rate of students in any other category).

The National Longitudinal Transition Study (NLTS) of Special Education Students (Wagner, Blackorby, Cameto, Hebbeler, & Newman, 1993) provides numerous points of interest regarding students within various disability categories:

- Students with speech impairments had a mean IQ of 80.8, whereas all disabled students had a mean IQ of 79.3.

- Speech-impaired high school graduates earned the following types of credits/units: academic, 60.1%; vocational, 19.8%; life skills, 4.9%; and other, 15.2%.

- Thirty-two percent of speech-impaired students participated in work experience programs, compared with 38.8% for students of all disability conditions.

- Of students with speech impairments, 47.9% to 51.6% received speech/language services from their schools in grades 9 through 12.

- Students with learning disabilities in grades 9 through 12 received fewer SLP services each year. The study showed that students with learning disabilities experienced various levels of language disorders.

- Speech-impaired students in grades 9 through 12 received some help from tutors, readers, or interpreters from their school, ranging from 6.2% in 9th grade to 23.3% in 12th grade; however, only a minority received that service from or through their schools.

- Speech-impaired students earned the following GPAs: regular education classes, 2.6; special education, 2.6.

- 73.3% of students with speech impairments graduated, 1.9% aged out, and 24.8% dropped out or were suspended or expelled (compared to 38% of students from all disabilities categories). These graduation statistics represent a disproportionate share when compared to the high school general population.

According to the same study, postsecondary school outcomes (three to five years after high school) for students with speech impairments were varied:

- Of those individuals who dropped out of high school, 6.8% obtained a school diploma or equivalency certificate (GED) about 3 to 5 years later.

- Some students (5.6%) attended an equivalency program but never obtained a diploma or certificate.

- Some students (19.8%) never attended an equivalency program.

- Twenty-five percent attended two years of college, compared to 11.5% of all students with disabilities.

- Students with speech impairments (less than two years out of secondary school) earned an average of $4.00 per hour, and three to five years out of secondary school they earned an average of $5.25 per hour.

- Of students who had been out of school for three to five years, 54.6% frequently interacted with friends and family members socially (other than those persons with whom they lived).

- Students with speech impairments were either married or living with someone (6.5% less than two years after school; 18% three to five years later).

- The arrest rate was 23% for those youths who had been out of school three to five years. This figure increases 5.2% for youths who had been out of school for less than two years.

The study indicated that students with disabilities whose parents expected them to be successful and were actively involved in their schooling often experienced more success (e.g., employment, postsecondary activities, recreation/leisure goal accomplishments). The authors stressed the importance of the association between a student's school experiences and later transition outcomes. The transition planning process is critical for all students with disabilities. The transition from high school to postsecondary education, employment, and other adult living activities is well represented and discussed in the literature (Michaels, 1994). Thus, one would expect the process that moves students from school to adulthood to occur with greater success. However, literature focusing specifically on communication disorders is limited in its discussion of postsecondary expectations for students (e.g., work, higher education, etc.) and the role the SLP plays in this process.

Speech and Language Pathologist Profile

Who are SLPs and what role do they play? Much of the literature in the field attempts to answer this question (Matthews, 1990; Nation & Aram, 1977; Plummer, Greenstate, Montgomery, Sakata, & Thies, 1987). These authors and others refer to the SLP as a professional educated in the study of human communication, its development, and its disorders. SLPs provide services in public and private schools, as well as in a variety of other settings, such as hospitals, private practice, clinics, colleges, and universities. SLPs hold either a master's or doctoral degree, the Certificate of Clinical Competence (CCC) of the American Speech-Language-Hearing Association, and a state license where one is required. Whatever the setting, the SLP is expected to adhere to a Code of Ethics set forth by ASHA. This Code of Ethics (see Appendix 4.A) describes four Principles of Ethics statements and rules that expand on each principle. SLPs serve more than 2 million school-age children and many of the half-million preschoolers eligible for speech–language services (ASHA, 1993b).

The SLP is the professional primarily responsible for the speech–language program for students with communication disorders. Services include evaluating all students with suspected or identified communication/language disorders, and developing, managing, and coordinating the speech–language program. Traditionally, the role of the SLP in the schools has been as a service provider who worked autonomous of, rather than collaboratively with, other staff. The SLP's approach to assessment, diagnosis, and intervention has focused primarily on the student's speech and language competence, deficiencies, and remediation.

SLPs are encouraged to use a variety or combination of service delivery models (see Table 4.1). However, services are typically provided in a "pull-out" delivery model, in which students are seen individually or in small group sessions in the "speech room" (ASHA, 1993a; ASHA, 1995; Harvell, 1997). Some SLPs also choose to provide speech and language services within a designated space ("push-in") in the classroom. Many SLPs still provide services using these delivery models. However, best practices now dictate the employment of other service delivery options, such as in community and workplace settings. For example, in the community the SLP could identify and design vocabulary, phrases, and scripts to use in social contexts. At job sites, the SLP could meet with supervisors or employers to discuss the communication needs of the student.

As stated throughout the literature, when the needs of the student change, so must the delivery model. Delivery models may consist of a combination of models previously mentioned. SLPs should never limit themselves to one model

Table 4.1
Service Delivery Model Variations

1. **Pull-out:** SLP provides services to individuals/groups in speech room.
2. **Classroom (push-in):** Services provided within the classroom; team teaching by SLP and regular or special education teacher.
3. **Self-contained:** Typically taught by SLP responsible for core curriculum and language intervention strategies.
4. **Consultation:** SLP, regular or special education teacher, and parents work together to facilitate students' communication and learning.

Note. From "Definitions of Communication Disorders and Variations," by ASHA, 1993, *Asha*, 35(10), pp. 40–41. Copyright 1993 by ASHA. Adapted with permission.

exclusively during any intervention program. In order for students to be successful in school, Prelock, Miller, and Reed (1995) suggest the need for students to achieve curriculum goals that are dependent on effective communication skills. A student's ability to use effective communication is equally important in the community and workplace setting (e.g., listening, following and giving directions, and knowing how to engage in conversation with different people, such as a coworker, a boss, a doctor, a clerk). Additional alternative service delivery options can be used in the community and workplace settings. However, for any delivery model to be effective, emphasis should be placed on forming partnerships with parents, educators, and related professionals (Ferguson, 1992; Secord & Wiig, 1990).

Beyond providing direct services, the SLP has other required responsibilities (ASHA, 1993a; ASHA, 1995). Examples of other duties may include providing screenings and comprehensive diagnostic evaluations, writing reports, developing individualized education programs (IEPs) or contributing to writing of individual transition plans (ITPs), conferencing with parents and teachers, planning or providing in-service training, mentoring, supervising support personnel (paraprofessionals), serving as members of Student Study Teams, and a number of other school responsibilities. These responsibilities are not all inclusive but offer an abbreviated description of many typical SLP duties. Many SLPs express concern for the many "hats" they are expected to wear and the limited amount of time available to work with their caseloads and also accomplish various other duties.

SLPs who provide services in the public school setting face many variables that affect their caseloads, including the number of service contact hours, funding issues, caseload size/composition, and caseload guidelines. Based on data collected on caseloads, certified SLPs working in schools reported an average monthly caseload of 52 students (ASHA, 1993b). The data also reported that

68% of "typical" caseloads were composed of individuals 6–17 years of age. A total of 50.9% of caseloads were made up of individuals with moderate impairments, 26.5% with mild impairments, and 22.6% with severe impairments. Typical caseloads presented 59.8% of students with childhood language disorders and 41.9% with articulation disorders.

The variables described above have a major impact on the amount of time SLPs are available for direct or indirect services to students, particularly at secondary schools. These are the settings where meaningful intervention strategies are still desperately needed that provide older students with the tools to address the communication demands encountered at school, in the community, and in the workplace.

Communication continues to be a key factor in the transition of students to adulthood. Therefore, it is only logical that SLPs become a part of the transition planning process for students preparing for postsecondary activities. As SLPs expand upon their resiliency, they prepare themselves and their students for learning that can be applied to future environments.

This chapter will focus on SLPs in the public schools who are working with older students within secondary school settings, and will also focus on their important role in the transition process. The information presented is applicable, with appropriate modifications, to all people with speech–language disorders, whatever their cognitive, emotional, or physical disability.

Current Practices in Speech and Language Pathology and Transition

National trends, such as Goals 2000, focus on the preparation and transition of students from school to successful adult life. The Education for All Handicapped Children Act of 1975 (EHA) (P.L. 92-142) required the provision of "related services," including speech therapy services, to students with disabilities. Such services are provided when it is determined that a student requires these services to benefit educationally. Amendments to the EHA in 1990 and 1997 were discussed earlier in Chapter 1. Not only did these changes result in the renaming of special education laws—from the EHA to the Individuals with Disabilities Education Act (IDEA)—but emphasis focused on increased involvement of both students and parents, and the access to core curriculum for all students with disabilities. The ultimate aim is preparation of students with disabilities, ages 14 and older, for employment and adult living.

Transition is a life span process that evolves over time and highlights those critical steps which shape one's development. For high school students, transition means focusing on those activities that promote movement from school to postschool activities, including the following:

- Helping students and families think about life after high school and the goals to prepare these students;

- Helping stakeholders design a high school plan of action that includes the students' interests, preferences, needs, and abilities;

- Assisting in connecting students and families with the appropriate services needed after high school; and

- Enhancing students' opportunities for success once they leave school.

The IDEA transition services requirements focus on communication, collaboration, and coordination of plans, programs, services, supports, and resources (Storm, DeStefano, & O'Leary, 1996). Without this focus, the student's best interest and vision may not be adequately addressed. Therefore, school personnel become instrumental in supporting this process. Does the SLP have a role within these coordinated sets of activities? The answer is a resounding yes.

The SLP, as a member of the school team, plays a pivotal role in providing those transition strategies needed by special education students with communication disorders. Many SLPs at the secondary level are frequently unaware of the importance of their role in the vocational/transition preparation of the students they serve. They continue to focus their assessment and intervention on strategies that may not reflect the interests, preferences, needs, and communication abilities of their student population.

SLPs aware of the IDEA's transition amendments for students 14 to 22 continue to question how the services they provide can help students move from school to postsecondary settings. One of the concepts of resiliency is the ability to problem solve. As professionals, SLPs will need to problem solve and redefine their role at the secondary level. Certainly, the SLP's role varies from school district to school district. However, availability and expertise will determine specific duties SLPs deliver in the area of vocational/transition services to students.

SLPs are also faced with older students who exhibit subtle speech and language impairments and who do not wish to attend speech therapy. These students are often overlooked or "slip through the cracks" for transition services in the school setting. These students are often described as having negative attitudes when they are encouraged to attend speech therapy. Aune and Friehe (1996) stated that many times "students' passive role in special services systems may account for the often reported negative attitudes that students hold with respect to special services as they make the transition into post-secondary education" (p. 11). The negative attitude referred to here may arise from the SLP's lack of creative, meaningful, outcome-oriented intervention activities for students with impaired speech, language, or cognitive skills. For example, in the following case of Roberto, his speech therapist failed to integrate Roberto's interest as a driving force of his therapy goals and to interactively involve him in planning his future.

 # ROBERTO

Roberto is a 16-year-old male with a history of language and learning disabilities. He is in the 10th grade at ABC Union High School. Roberto currently spends half of his school day in a resource class for Math, English, and History. He does not perform academically without assistance. Interacting with his peers is age appropriate, although he has no "real" friends. However, Roberto is guarded and described as shy with adults. Behavior is not a serious problem.

Poor communication skills present daily challenges. Roberto has difficulty with verbal expression and following more than two consecutive oral directions. Both of his parents speak Spanish and a limited amount of English. Roberto is proficient in neither English nor Spanish. However, he appears to be more comfortable with Spanish when talking with peers. He attends "speech therapy" twice a week for articulation and language development. Specific goals are the remediation of the phonemes /s/ and /z/ and noun and verb agreement (e.g., books are, a book is). Services are provided one to one in the "speech room." The speech therapist indicates Roberto's lack of interest to improve his speech and language skills and says he "could do better if he tried harder." Attendance in the speech program is a serious problem, and Roberto needs constant reminders of his scheduled "speech time."

Roberto loves music and, according to his resource specialist teacher, "hangs out" at the music store (often cutting class to do so). He has shared with the speech therapist his desire to work in the local music store. To date, no transition plan has been initiated for Roberto, and involvement in the Vocational Education Program has not been suggested by school staff.

The intent of the IDEA is that individuals with communication disorders, like any other disability, qualify for transition services. This is important to note because the ability to communicate and how one communicates (verbal or nonverbal) not only affects one's daily life, but has many vocational implications as well. Potential vocational impacts may involve difficulty using the telephone (understanding messages), writing reports, catching on to social cues, and interpreting information from and to others. These are only a few examples and are not meant to reflect an exhaustive list of potential impacts.

For a student with a communication disorder who is transitioning into postsecondary settings, providing adequate time for planning is critical. The IDEA recognizes that transition goals are long-range and require planning, preparation, and a shared responsibility between many individuals and agencies. The IDEA recognizes that SLPs must teach students skills and strategies to enable them to cope with the communication demands of everyday life and become life-long learners. Therefore, students with communication disorders should be actively involved in evaluating their instruction and instructional approaches (i.e., whether specific strategies are working). This involvement and direct feedback allows SLPs to modify and improve their ability to meet the changing needs of their students.

Review of Communication Models

Current literature is limited in its discussion of programs, practices, and approaches that reflect the important role of the SLP in the area of transition issues with older students. However, three models, which expand on best practices in preparing students for life during and after high school and also include the services of SLPs in various school settings, will be briefly discussed. These models are (1) Prototype Service Delivery Model, (2) Providers, Activities, and Contexts (PACs), and (3) Communication Skills/Instrumental Enrichment Program (see Table 4.2).

Summary of Current Practices

Important commonalities exist between the three models in Table 4.2. First, each model encourages collaboration between other individuals involved with the student. Second, the models clearly focus on the needs of the student being served. Third, each student is an active and interactive participant. Fourth, parents are an integral part of their child's communication program and always have a clear role. Finally, each model promotes self-determination, which is important in developing responsible individuals who have the ability to function successfully in society.

Research discusses other collaborative models (Bland & Prelock, 1996; Coufal, 1993; Lunday, 1996; Nelson, 1989, 1993). One such model involves the student with a communication disorder in an inclusive education program (Brucker, 1994; Inclusive Education Programs, 1997; Polansky, 1994). However, if students (ages 14 and older) are a part of an inclusion program, each must have an IEP that includes a transition component or language that identifies a customized career path and supports. Table 4.3 provides sample goals and activities conveying how transition services language (TSL) in curriculum content areas might look in IEPs written by the SLP. The table also suggests how transition services language might appear in the IEP of two students with different special education histories. Such a document may require collaborative efforts between the SLP and the classroom teacher.

It is important to remember that in any service delivery model, the role the SLP assumes in assessment or intervention may not be clearly defined.

Table 4.2
Review of Communication Models

Model	Rationale	Purpose	Process	Findings
Prototype Service Delivery Model (Larson, 1997; Larson & McKinley, 1987)	Adolescent focus Youth at risk Make unrealistic career choices Some type of language disorder Not prepared for further education or world of work	Help adolescent to develop employable skills for "Workforce 2000" Develop speech and language programs in settings where adolescents are taught (e.g., secondary schools, detention centers)	SLP collaborates in academic and environmental settings SLP provides direct/indirect services Model identifies six major components to facilitate process: information dissemination, identification, assessment program, planning, intervention, and follow-up Proposes changes to existing models Intervention process focuses on the functional use of language/pragmatics in the natural environment	Students select SLP classes as an elective SLPs see students five days per week for a semester Marginal students help more involved students
Providers, Activities, and Contexts (PACs) (Blosser & Kratcoski, 1997)	Changes in demographic and economic trends require service delivery options Need for team decision making Consider combination of providers, activities, and contexts (PACs) to meet the specific needs of youth with communication disorder	Framework for service delivery model to meet needs of individuals with communication disorders Focus on essential characteristics of good service delivery Have a creative and flexible service delivery with options to meet the needs and interests of individual Discuss relevancy and clarity of treatment plan as it relates to PACs	Collaborative process involving student, family, educators, service providers, and so on. Establish planning teams Define each team member's specific role and activities related to student's needs, preferences, and abilities	SLP must select best service delivery model that meets funcational communication needs of student In-service training is needed with initiation of different service delivery approach Need to facilitate both student buy-in and the successful employment of the approach
Communication Skills Instrumental Enrichment Program (Feuerstein, 1979; Utsumi, personal communication, December 1996)	Address communication issues facing adolescents in today's world	Produce active, self-motivated learners who have learning strategies to solve academic or real-life problems Provide adolescents who have poor oral and interpersonal communication skills, and who are at-risk of school failure, with skills to mediate their environment	Provide an elective communication class Enrollment based upon teacher referral established by SLP Program has two components: (a) communication skills, and (b) Instrumental Enrichment (a cognitive curriculum)	Students learn to effectively cope through communication in school and community environments Students improve ability to understand and express thoughts, feelings, and emotions clearly

Additionally, does one service model, one role of the SLP, or one setting carry more weight than another? This debate should not impede the expansion, development, and implementation of effective, successful, outcome-oriented treatment programs. Therefore, SLPs must select service delivery models that best meet the functional (practical and applied) communication needs of their

Table 4.3
IEP Transition Services Language

Transition Service Language (TSL)	Content Area	IEP Goal Example	Sample Activities
Instruction	English/Language Arts, Writing, Math	Tommy will identify appropriate vocabulary for completing his résumé (education, work experience, interests).	Select vocabulary from sample résumé or job application; explore interests.
		Johnny will recognize and identify sequence of events on a daily picture schedule.	Choose and act upon activity from a picture schedule.
Community Experiences	English/Language Arts, Writing, Social Science, Health	Tommy will identify and access community and employment resources.	Obtain and complete job application.
		Johnny will walk to an off-campus site and follow safety and traffic guidelines.	Use the vocabulary and concepts for travel and safety issues.
Employment/Postschool Adult Living	English/Language Arts, Social Science	Tommy will participate in a prearranged job interview	Develop language communication scripts appropriate for job interviews; role play mock interview; discussions.
		Johnny will use public transportation with supervision to a work site.	Practice social greeting, vocabulary of transportation.
Daily living skills and functional evaluation	Family life, Health, English/Language Arts	Tommy will appropriately interpret body language/social cues of peers and adults in his community.	Situational role-playing, mock interviews, school office, and so forth.
		Johnny will maintain personal hygiene.	Referral to daily schedule; develop checklist of daily hygiene responsibilities.

students. Flowers (1984) identifies good service delivery as having the following characteristics: effectiveness, coordination of services, uninterrupted participation of all involved parties, and efficient use of all resources. Therefore, services rendered should specifically be coordinated with students, family, and other professionals; reflect the needs, preferences, and interests of the student; occur in naturalistic settings as often as possible; use meaningful and relevant content; and involve real conversational partners (e.g., peers, teachers, co-workers, employers). Effective and ongoing assessment approaches need to occur prior to such success.

Assessment

The literature discusses various assessment approaches (Beck, 1996; Wilson, Blackmon, Hall, & Elcholtz, 1991). For older students with a communication disorder, approaches should highlight not only the needs of the student but also the events, situations, and people within their environment (Hixson, 1993). For the SLP serving secondary-age students with a communication disorder, issues of transition and assessment must be in concert. The SLP must obtain details through effective assessment approaches. It is important to ascertain how a student's communication challenges might interfere with tasks and environmental demands that influence his or her ability to function in both academic and real-life situations. McCue et al. (1994) discuss optimal assessment as useful to the extent that results supply information of how an individual functions within the natural environment when faced with work, education, training, and the demands of independent living. SLPs must ask themselves specific questions relating to the meaningfulness and intent of any assessment conducted with students at the secondary-school level. They should address the following questions in an assessment: (1) What is the purpose of the assessment?; (2) Do the assessment tools appropriately address the student's needs, interests, and abilities?; and (3) Are transition issues a determining factor in methods used to gather information? These questions are hardly inclusive but can be considered a catalyst to SLPs in terms of assessment and its functional purpose. SLPs should keep in mind that any assessment that is not meaningful or functional is of little benefit in the planning and delivery of service. Functional versus formal-based assessments are likely to provide more accurate information regarding a student's ability to function in school, workplace, and community (leisure and social) settings. Best practices involving functional assessments are discussed in the literature (Larson, 1997; McCue et al., 1994).

A functional assessment involves specific behaviors that are observable and measurable and that occur in environments relevant to a student's vocational goals (Halpern & Fuhrer, 1984). The challenge of a functional assessment for the SLP becomes one of not only identifying a student's language or communication strengths and weaknesses, but also understanding the demands and conditions of the environment in which the student anticipates functioning. The need for the SLP to understand the supports and accommodations the student with a language disorder needs in the academic or work setting is paramount in any assessment. The SLP should ask, "How do I obtain functional assessment data that gives me a total picture of a student (i.e., communication abilities, strengths, limitations, interests, vision, etc.)?" Unfortunately, despite increased discussion of the need for more functional assessment approaches in the secondary settings, many SLPs continue to use traditional assessment tools. McCue et al. (1994) discuss a framework for functional assessment that includes assessing students across the following seven domains: executive skills, attention, learning and memory, language and communication, sensory/perceptual/spatial abilities, motor skills, and social/emotional functioning. They discuss each domain using six procedural categories that describe how to go about the assessment in these areas. Table 4.4 displays the six categories with a description of the communication domain.

Although the McCue et al. (1994) model focuses on individuals (age 18 and older) with cognitive disabilities, the components are readily modifiable to students (age 14 and older) with language disorders. The authors suggest this

Table 4.4
Functional Assessment Model: Communication Domain

Six Procedural Categories	How To Gather Information
Existing Information	History of speech/language performance found in school/medical records.
Interview	How the student communicates, processes information, follows directions, attends, etc.; information obtained from the student and others familiar with his or her performance.
Incidental Observation	Observing communication failures and social contacts during formal testing, breaks, on-job sites.
Questionnaires	Formal tools administered to students and by others familiar with their skills.
Testing	Traditional/nontraditional measures administered and interpreted by the SLP.
Simulation and Naturalistic Observations	Communication skills: planning, processing, awareness of failures; pragmatic skills obtained through conversations, various communication tasks.

Note. From *Functional Assessment of Individuals with Cognitive Disabilities: A Desk Reference for Rehabilitation* (pp. 32–33), by M. McCue, S. Chase, C. Dowdy, M. Pramuka, J. Petrick, S. Aitken, and P. Fabry, 1994, Pittsburgh, PA: Center for Applied Neuropsychology. Copyright 1994 by Center for Applied Neuropsychology. Adapted with permission.

framework as a means to gather and integrate information into planning and implementation, with the understanding that the domains themselves are not exclusive and that functional problems may have more than one cause.

A benefit of functional assessment is the required involvement of the student in the process of information gathering. Through this process, the student develops a level of understanding, ownership, and self-analysis of his or her strengths and limitations related to personal preferences, abilities, and needs that lead to positive adult outcomes. Many SLPs encounter students who have set unrealistic goals. However, analyzing their choices through a functional assessment process allows for a more situational/naturalistic evaluation rather than relying solely on traditional testing procedures. Many parents also make unrealistic goals for their older adolescent, and therefore such an assessment process offers opportunities for collaboration in evaluation, intervention, and effective planning for the future.

In addition to assessing the traditional areas of communication disorders discussed at the beginning of this chapter, it is important for the SLP to consider the following questions and the relationship to transition issues:

1. How will the information be used to initiate and modify a student's language intervention program?

2. Is the assessment information solely for the SLP or other team members?

3. Is the information shared with students in such a way that they may begin to become more proficient in compensatory and problem-solving skills?

4. What are the anticipated outcomes of assessment for the student with a language disorder?

5. Is the assessment to identify and select student options, weigh the advantages/disadvantages for selecting those options, and consider all possible outcomes in making decisions?

These evaluative questions address and ensure, in an ongoing fashion, the meaningfulness and purpose of assessment. Meaningful assessment establishes a framework for meaningful intervention.

Intervention

In order to fully prepare the student with a communication disorder for success in today's working climate, intervention strategies need to be meaningful. What role can the SLP play to supply students with the knowledge, skills, and preparation needed to find meaningful, rewarding jobs that also lead to fulfilling lives?

In 1991, the U.S. Department of Labor and the Secretary's Commission on Achieving Necessary Skills (SCANS) published a report entitled *What Work Requires of Schools: A SCANS Report for America 2000*. The SCANS report examined the demands of the workplace and whether today's students were being adequately prepared to meet those demands. SCANS outlined a framework of competencies, skills, and qualities that must be integrated into the context of the job field or area of further education that the student desires. This framework emphasized three areas: (1) basic skills, such as reading, writing, math, listening, and speaking; (2) thinking skills, such as creativity, making decisions, problem solving, knowing how to learn and reason; and (3) personal qualities, such as responsibility, self-esteem, sociability, self-management, integrity, and honesty. One critical point, noted by SCANS, was for learning objectives to be effective and successful. To meet such SCANS criteria, part of learning/integration needs to occur within real environments. SLPs cannot continue to insist that students first learn in sterile environments and then expect them to apply those skills and strategies to actual work and living situations. The SLP plays a valuable part in helping the student with a communication disorder establish links between secondary education and employment discussed in the SCANS report. SLPs can accomplish this by establishing effective and meaningful intervention strategies for and with students that cover those areas of the SCANS framework.

The purpose of developing intervention strategies for students with communication disorders is to encourage greater independence that allows them to shift their *locus of control*. Locus of control is a concept developed and advanced upon by Rotter (1966) from social learning theory. Rosenthal (1996) cites Rotter's description of locus of control as the "tendency of people to attribute the control of events to factors either internal or external to themselves." If individuals believe that the outcomes of their actions are related to personal characteristics (e.g., effort), then they have an internal locus of control. However, those who believe that the outcomes of their actions are related to outside factors (e.g., fate, peers) have an external locus of control. These individuals tend to blame others for their fate and rely on others to take care of their needs. For example, the student who says, "It wasn't my fault because nobody told me," is one who relies on external controls. All too often, the student with a communication disorder tends to rely on others and tends to exhibit an external locus of control.

Rosenthal (1996) reported that locus of control is only one of three aspects of personal control beliefs that seem important. The other two are self-efficacy and perceptions of control. With these perspectives in mind, the SLP should consider whether the outcomes will influence the student's locus of control from one of external to internal. For older students, this shift is critical and important.

Existing Challenges

One theme consistently expressed in the literature and in various local and national surveys was the lack of adequate time to provide effective services, collaborations, and so on (ASHA, 1995; Harvell, 1997; Sowers & Powers, 1991). Many SLPs in secondary school settings also carry caseloads at the elementary school levels. Therefore, the amount of time available to students is always an issue. SLPs report the following additional barriers to successful intervention service delivery with secondary student populations who have mild to moderate communication disorders (Harvell, 1997):

- Time
- Caseloads too large
- Limited curriculum knowledge
- Location
- Administrative restrictions
- Resistance by other SLPs
- Lack of student motivation
- Fear of change
- Lack of appropriate skills
- Burn-out

The literature offers suggestions and models that allow SLPs to effectively use their limited time availability (Larson & McKinley, 1987; Lyon & Lyon, 1980). Some solutions or strategies include the following: in-servicing administrators, teachers (regular/special); team teaching; collaborating with agency staff personnel; professional growth (eliminate fear/resistance of SLPs); problem solving; parent involvement; and believing that all students want and can learn to succeed. Larson (1997) and Elksnin and Capilouto (1994) mention the additional barriers of limited district financial resources, scheduling, and planning time. These are issues that must be negotiated with school and district administrators toward compromise to prevent the consequences of student failure. If SLPs do not address these issues, they will find themselves spending more money in public assistance or incarceration rather than graduating at-risk youth with disabilities.

Program Needs

What do SLPs need to address to achieve effective assessment and intervention strategies with students who have a communication disorder at the secondary level? To answer this, one has to explore changes (paradigm shifts) concerning functional versus traditional assessment, intervention, and collaboration within these two areas.

Paramount to any discussion of change and its implication to the SLP is the need to embrace those changes that will influence the quality of life for students with a communication disorder. Although many SLPs say change has occurred in their approaches to service delivery, assessment, and intervention, changes are not evident in actual observation of practices. Changes require application (not just lip service) of various recommendations described in the literature regarding service delivery, meaningful assessment and intervention strategies, interdisciplinary collaboration, and active involvement in the transition process. Change requires the SLP to become an active member of the transdisciplinary team in order to understand and participate in the transition process. The importance and inclusion of the SLP as part of an educational team that includes the student, SLP, teacher, psychologist, and other professionals should never be overlooked (Zarrella, 1995). In reviewing literature and field observations, one can still see parents or guardians and their concerns for their adolescents omitted from the collaborative process. This collaborative challenge requires educators to be creative in designing and implementing meaningful services. Doing so will provide opportunities for networking with other vocational professionals or agency persons. Traditionally, most professionals have a poor understanding of others' roles, and collaboration is hindered (Larson 1997; Larson & McKinley, 1987). Mutual understanding of professional roles should be the norm, not the exception.

Change will also require SLPs to engage in meaningful and creative therapy to hold the attention and motivation of their student population. To provide meaningful assessment and intervention, the SLP should be in concert with the student's interests, preferences, needs, and communication abilities. With such information, the SLP can engage the student in transition activities such as completing job applications, role-playing interviews, and developing and exploring job and community-specific vocabulary. The SLP should engage the student with a communication disorder in real-life situational activities rather than provide a "traditional" withdrawal-based style of intervention (Blosser & Kratcoski, 1997; McCue et al., 1994; U.S. Department of Labor, 1991b). Only then will the student be able to make the necessary associations and understand the connections between instruction and community and vocational settings.

Activities and Programs Related to Transition Not Presently Clearly Coordinated

SLPs are not the only professionals facing change. A review of recent psychological reports (annual and triennial) finds that little, if any, focus is placed on transition issues. Psychologists, like SLPs, need to interpret assessment results in functional terms rather than in percentiles or scaled scores. Reports must be written that correlate cognitive results to transition issues, and which focus on the student's ability to function as a successful adult. For example, cognitive tests might imply a student's ability or inability to organize, problem solve, or evaluate a situation. With this information, the psychologist, in collaboration with the SLP (when appropriate), can explore the task demands and the cognitive implications.

If one purpose of assessment is to assist in identifying student needs and services, then school psychologists must adopt a life-span approach to assessment (Anderson, Hohenshil, Buckland-Heer, & Levinson, 1990). This means that during the elementary school years, assessments should focus on cognitive abilities, learning deficits, and strengths. However, during the secondary school years (age 14 and older), assessments need to refocus and concentrate more on preparation for transition needs. If assessments are written reflecting life-span needs, instead of solely for the purpose of determining eligibility, they become instruments that are meaningful for schools, students, and families.

As stated, psychologists, like SLPs, will need to make this paradigm shift in how they view their role. Generally, the same assessment instruments can be used, but the interpretations need to be broadened to include vocational and transitional issues. Consideration should be given to providing assessments where students' strengths and limitations are correlated to the demands of career choices. This will result in an invaluable process that could empower students and their families in making informed choices and decisions.

Both SLPs and school psychologists can support this empowerment by facilitating student choices and decision-making rights. The concepts of self-determination and self-advocacy are an evolving trend in the field of education. The SLP can support this development by assisting the student in creating a Student Action Plan (see Figure 4.3). For example, while guiding the students through their Student Action Plan, the SLP not only works on the vocabulary of academics and future employment goals, but also helps the student move closer to achieving an internal locus of control. A Student Action Plan for transition planning allows the SLP to include career education as part of the intervention and remedial strategies, as well as allows the SLP to generate IEP/ITP goals. Another component of the Student Action Plan is allowance of sufficient time for completion of each goal. This requires commitment from the student, the SLP, and others involved in the student planning.

The Student Action Plan is a vehicle that allows the student and the SLP to collaborate with each other, other specialists, and parents. Using such a plan allows the student to identify a goal and the steps involved in accomplishing the goal. Assistance by the SLP or other specialists enables the student to explore personal strengths, obstacles, steps toward goals, needed supports, and anticipated outcomes. Embedded in the process are opportunities for the student to make realistic choices and, ultimately, informed decisions. The process allows the students to look at any obstacles and what accommodations may be needed in school, community, or the workplace. This process places the SLP in a unique

Student Action Plan

Name: Roberto	School: ABC Union High School			Grade: 10
Goal: To work in a music store				
Strengths	Obstacles	Steps to Goal	Supports Needed	Outcomes
1. Likes music and singing.	doesn't know basics regarding finding a job not signed up for chorus	explore want ads interview store owner investigate requirements of chorus class sign up for class	SLP counselor music teacher parent	questions developed with SLP, practiced with others; interviewed store owner after setting appointment enrolled in chorus
2. Very social; friendly with peers; good behavior	does not always understand what is heard or read forgetful not good with words	ask for clarification, repetition write things down practice asking questions; learn work-related vocabulary	SLP, counselor, music teacher, using note pad/recorder, parent, and so on.	developed vocabulary useful in store environment vocabulary words used in context with peers during mock/actual interview
3. Good with hands	impulsive; does not wait for directions	needs to learn to wait before acting job shadow at music store	SLP, vocational specialist, teacher, parent	talked with SLP vocational specialist and parent to discuss job shadowing at the music store

Figure 4.3. Example of Student Action Plan for SLP intervention and collaboration with other persons involved with Roberto.

role to guide students with a communication disorder through a discussion of their disability and its implications in adult life. In reference to the student. Roberto, whose case was discussed earlier in this chapter, the SLP using a student action plan can assist Roberto with his interest in working in a music store. This process will allow the SLP to facilitate Roberto's language development in practicing interviewing techniques and general inquiry skills. This becomes the process in which the SLP can begin to bridge school learning (speech development) with skills necessary for daily living (world of work).

The literature addresses the importance of students' understanding and ability to explain the nature of their disability as they learn self-determination and self-advocacy strategies (Kupper, 1995). This results in improved student self-advocacy and empowerment in IEP/ITP meetings, job interviews, and with interpersonal relationships. An additional attribute is the creation or extension of the collaboration between the classroom teacher (regular or special education), SLP, parent, and other stakeholders important to the student's success. This process is not instantaneous, but rather evolves over a period of time.

A Bold Vision for the Future

Future Challenges

In her presidential address at the 1994 ASHA Convention, Jeri Logemann stated, "In the last 20 years, we have not greatly expanded our models of service delivery or focused our research on the best forms of service delivery for particular disorders, age groups, settings, and so forth" (Logemann, 1994). It is imperative for the field of speech and language communication to implement alternative service delivery models that address appropriate needs of students with language disorders. SLPs must embrace the national legislation (IDEA) that addresses transition services for students of age 14 and older. Expanding horizons is necessary for the SLP and others in the field of speech and language communication to broaden their options to make connections beyond the confines of the "therapy room" into the community and workplace. This must become part of the collaborative process of preparing students with communication disorders for adult life.

In addressing resiliency issues for SLPs, the process of problem solving becomes a pivotal point to survival. To determine the direction the field should travel to reach the 21st century, specific questions will need to be addressed. The first question is *What will be needed in the field of communication disorders?* First of all, there will need to be a paradigm shift. The literature and many professionals in the field discuss change. However, few are willing to actually embrace what is needed to produce change. All too often, professionals mention barriers (e.g., time, caseloads) as problems without exploring and providing solutions to overcome such barriers. Secondly, professionals need to address the idea of transition for the student with a communication disorder that relates to the student's personal preferences, interests, and communicative abilities. They need to help students determine if their goal or vision is realistic, and then help customize instruction to the individual level and needs of the student. All too often, professionals view students as having a passive rather than an active role in planning for their future. The goal becomes one of facilitating a process in which students learn to generate their own plan of action. Thirdly, approaches to assessment and intervention strategies should promote self-advocacy, self-determination, and meaningful, appropriate communication in various settings. Self-determined students become part of the problem-solving and decision-making process crucial to establishing appropriate goals and expectations (Martin & Marshall, 1993; Wehmeyer, 1992). Finally, there is a need for the profession to develop a more proactive role in the area of transition. SLPs will be responsible for identifying their role in the process, understanding the key roles of various disciplines (e.g., psychologists, vocational specialists, care providers, etc.), and collaborating with other disciplines and agency staffpersons.

The second question is *Whose responsibility is it to facilitate the move forward?* As noted previously, the literature discusses shifting students with disabilities away from personal dependence toward personal autonomy, changing the locus of control. Therefore, it will be necessary for the profession to determine its own locus of responsibility. Will they allow other disciplines to dictate their future vision, or will they position themselves as the pacesetters for the future? State and national organizations, such as the California Speech-Hearing Association (CSHA) and ASHA, can serve as catalysts that move the profession forward. One important role these organizations can play is supporting the SLP in the public school setting. ASHA has already approved a strategic plan for SLP assistants. Other state organizations like CSHA have introduced and approved similar legislation, such as Assembly Bill 205. According to Cammarata (1997), professionals need to "have members of [their] profession on school boards across the country, not simply [as] a matter of protecting the students of the system, but to establish value of the specialty [SLPs] in the public consciousness" (p. 16). These organizations are advocates for change. They need to promote communication programs in the high schools that address or include the needs of those students with communication disorders. Language problems do not disappear with age. Professionals need to expand service delivery options both inside and outside the high school setting (e.g., collaborative, team building, community, and job sites). Promoting interagency interaction between the SLP and community colleges, service agencies, and so on, is essential to their effectiveness.

It is important that SLPs advocate those services for older students in the public school systems that will prepare them for the future. This includes supporting interdisciplinary workshops and seminars for students and parents or caregivers on such subjects as the IDEA transition amendments and the older student with communication disorders. The professional organizations must advocate for the continued understanding and improvement of programs using appropriate assessment and intervention of communication differences or variations of students and families. Finally, if the professional organizations are to maintain and amplify their effectiveness to survive in the 21st century, it will be critical for future SLPs to prepare to adapt to the needs of the populations they will be serving. These areas will need continual attention so that the profession continues to set its own standards.

Teacher Preparation Programs

The teacher preparation programs in communication sciences and disorders traditionally have focused on the study of disability categories (phonology, fluency, language) and the intervention methodology to "fix" such impairments. However, future SLP professionals who will serve the older student in secondary schools will need new knowledge and skills to meet the changing needs of today's students and their educational programs. As these new professionals take their places in the changing world of education, they will need to know how to communicate and collaborate with other personnel to provide improved services to students with communication disorders. Preparing SLP students for these changes requires teacher preparation programs to revamp their systems as they guide these new professionals into the field. A recent analysis of SLP preparation programs reveals that the curriculums need to stress intervention strategies to meet the diverse needs of students in the secondary school settings who are preparing for Workforce 2000.

Another component of this analysis identifies the need to recruit and retain high quality students who represent diverse backgrounds (students or families of color, students with communication differences, etc.) to legitimately offer experiences to the changing populations. In addition, programming needs require the merging of regular and special education curriculums, continuing training in a student-centered planning, and encouraging student involvement in collaborative problem solving. Approaches to service delivery models that include assessment of and intervention in community and workplace settings will need to be expanded upon or established.

Systems change is not easy. However, the paradigm has begun to shift. Potential public school SLPs need to take a more proactive role in understanding the dynamics that create changes within academic systems, including reviewing literature, updating skills/knowledge of best practices, collaborating with other disciplines for more effective problem solving, making decisions, and familiarizing themselves with transition laws. Some of the challenges that SLPs face in the system process include taking a stance, being flexible, and participating in cross-discipline service delivery. New SLP students who accept these challenges will receive personal empowerment. In doing so, SLPs can make a difference in the 21st century.

Final Thoughts

In recent years, the field of communication disorders has experienced substantial changes. These changes are a direct result of demographic, sociologic, economic, and legislative trends that have occurred at state and national levels (Logemann, 1994; Montgomery & Herer, 1994). The role of the SLP has evolved and must continue to do so because the needs of students with communication disorders in secondary settings continue to change and expand as the 20th century draws to a close. The everyday impact of communication disorders on learning, living, and vocational issues continues to be evident as students with communication disorders make the transition from school to adult life. Consequently, it is critical that the field of speech and language communication continues to plan, expand, and clearly define the role of the SLP in the secondary schools. Resiliency will be a key factor as both students and SLPs embark upon this journey into the future.

> *"Change can be frightening. The challenge for all of us is to remain open to change, always keeping in the forefront, the needs of students . . . and their families. In order to realize our vision we will have to dust off our grass roots organizing manuals and get busy. We must work together, using our best collaborative and problem solving skills. Creativity and unity will bring about effective and positive change for the students and families we serve. The time is now; if not, it may be never. Before we lose too much, we must get involved. NOW is the time for action."*

—(Hunter, 1994-95)

Acknowledgments

I would like to acknowledge my family and colleagues who provided encouragement and contributed ideas, editing, and other support throughout the development of this chapter. A special thank you to Renee A. Hatter, who was there every step of the way with her brilliance and support.

Appendix 4.A
Code of Ethics
January 1, 1994
American Speech-Language-Hearing
Association

Preamble

The preservation of the highest standards of integrity and ethical principles is vital to the responsible discharge of obligations in the professions of speech-language pathology and audiology. This Code of Ethics sets forth the fundamental principles and rules considered essential to this purpose.

Every individual who is (a) a member of the American Speech-Language-Hearing Association, whether certified or not, (b) a nonmember holding the Certificate of Clinical Competence from the Association, (c) an applicant for membership or certification, or (d) a Clinical Fellow seeking to fulfill standards for certification shall abide by this Code of Ethics.

Any action that violates the spirit and purpose of this Code shall be considered unethical. Failure to specify any particiular responsibility or practice in this Code of Ethics shall not be construed as denial of the existence of such responsibilities or practices.

The fundamentals of ethical conduct are described by Principles of Ethics and by Rules of Ethics as they relate to responsibility to persons served, to the public, and to the professions of speech-language pathology and audiology.

Principles of Ethics, aspirational and inspirational in nature, form the underlying moral basis for the Code of Ethics. Individuals shall observe these principles as affirmative obligations under all conditions of professional activity.

Rules of Ethics are specific statements of minimally acceptable professional conduct or of prohibitions and are applicable to all individuals.

Principle of Ethics I

Individuals shall honor their responsibility to hold paramount the welfare of persons they serve professionally.

Rules of Ethics

    A. Individuals shall provide all services competently.

    B. Individuals shall use every resource, including referral when appropirate, to ensure that high-quality service is provided.

    C. Individuals shall not discriminate in the delivery of professional services on the basis of race or ethnicity, gender, age, religion, national origin, sexual orientation, or disability.

    D. Individuals shall fully inform the persons they serve of the nature and possible effects of services rendered and products dispensed.

    E. Individuals shall evaluate the effectiveness of services rendered and of products dispensed and shall provide services or dispense products only when benefit can reasonably be expected.

    F. Individuals shall not guarantee the results of any treatment or procedure, directly or by implication; however, they may make a reasonable statement of prognosis.

    G. Individuals shall not evaluate or treat speech, language, or hearing disorders solely by correspondence.

    H. Individuals shall maintain adequate records of professional services rendered and products dispensed and shall allow access to these records when appropriately authorized.

    I. Individuals shall not reveal, without authorization, any professional or personal information about the person served professionally, unless required by law to do so, or unless doing so is necessary to protect the welfare of the person or of the community.

    J. Individuals shall not charge for services not rendered, nor shall they misrepresent,[1] in any fashion, services rendered or products dispensed.

    K. Individuals shall use persons in research or as subjects of teaching demonstrations only by their informed consent.

    L. Individuals whose professional services are adversely affected by substance abuse or other health-related conditions shall seek professional assistance and, where appropriate, withdraw from the affected areas of practice.

---

[1] For purposes of this Code of Ethics, misrepresentation includes any untrue statements or statements that are likely to mislead. Misrepresentation also includes the failure to state any information that is material and that ought, in fairness, to be considered.

Principle of Ethics II

Individuals shall honor their responsibility to achieve and maintain the highest level of professional competence.

Rules of Ethics

A. Individuals shall engage in the provision of clinical services only when they hold the appropriate Certificate of Clinical Competence or when they are in the certification process and are supervised by an individual who holds the appropriate Certificate of Clinical Competence.

B. Individuals shall engage in only those aspects of the professions that are within the scope of their competence, considering their level of education, training, and experience.

C. Individuals shall continue their professional development throughout their careers.

D. Individuals shall delegate the provision of clinical services only to persons who are certified or to persons in the education or certification process who are appropriately supervised. The provision of support services may be delegated to persons who are neither certified nor in the certification process only when a certificate holder provides appropriate supervision.

E. Individuals shall prohibit any of their professional staff from providing services that exceed the staff member's competence, considering the staff member's level of education, training, and experience.

F. Individuals shall ensure that all equipment used in the provision of services is in proper working order and is properly calibrated.

Principle of Ethics III

Individuals shall honor their responsibility to the public by promoting public understanding of the professions, by supporting the development of services designed to fulfill the unmet needs of the public, and by providing accurate information in all communications involving any aspect of the professions.

Rules of Ethics

A. Individuals shall not misrepresent their credentials, competence, education, training, or experience.

B. Individuals shall not participate in professional activities that constitute a conflict of interest.

C. Individuals shall not misrepresent diagnostic information, services rendered, or products dispensed or engage in any scheme or artifice to defraud in connection with obtaining payment or reimbursement for such services or products.

D. Individuals' statements to the public shall provide accurate information about the nature and management of communication disorders, about the professions, and about professional services.

E. Individuals' statements to the public—advertising, announcing, and marketing their professional services, reporting research results, and promoting products—shall adhere to prevailing professional standards and shall not contain misrepresentations.

Principle of Ethics IV

Individuals shall honor their responsibilities to the professions and their relationships with colleagues, students, and members of allied professions. Individuals shall uphold the dignity and autonomy of the professions, maintain harmonious interprofessional and intraprofessional relationships, and accept the professions' self-imposed standards.

Rules of Ethics

A. Individuals shall prohibit anyone under their supervision from engaging in any practice that violates the Code of Ethics.

B. Individuals shall not engage in dishonesty, fraud, deceit, misrepresentation, or any form of conduct that adversely reflects on the professions or on the individual's fitness to serve persons professionally.

C. Individuals shall assign credit only to those who have contributed to a publication, presentation, or product. Credit shall be assigned in proportion to the contribution and only with the contributor's consent.

D. Individuals' statements to colleagues about professional services, research results, and products shall adhere to prevailing professional standards and shall contain no misrepresentations.

E. Individuals shall not provide professional services without exercising independent professional judgment, regardless of referral source or prescription.

F. Individuals shall not discriminate in their relationships with colleagues, students, and members of allied professions on the basis of race or ethnicity, gender, age, religion, national origin, sexual orientation, or disability.

G. Individuals who have reason to believe that the Code of Ethics has been violated shall inform the Ethical Practice Board.

H. Individuals shall cooperate fully with the Ethical Practice Board in its investigation and adjudication of matters related to this Code of Ethics.

Note. From *Code of Ethics*, by ASHA, 1994. Copyright 1994 by ASHA. Reprinted with permission.

References

American Speech-Language-Hearing Association. (1993a). Definitions of communication disorders and variations. *Asha, 35*(10), 40–41.

American Speech-Language-Hearing Association. (1993b). Guidelines for caseload size and speech-language service delivery in the schools. *Asha, 35*(10), 33–39.

American Speech-Language-Hearing Association. (1995). *Survey of speech/language pathology services in school-based settings final report executive summary.* Unpublished manuscript. Rockville, MD.

Anderson, W. T., Hohenshil, T. H., Buckland-Heer, K., & Levinson, E. M. (1990). Best practices in vocational assessment of students with disabilities. In A. Thomas & J. Grimes (Eds.), *Best practices in school psychology* (pp. 787–797). Washington, DC: NASP.

Aune, B., & Friehe, M. (1996). Transition to post secondary education: Institutional and individual issues. *Topics in Language Disorders, 16*(3), 11.

Bashir, A. S. (1989). Language intervention and the curriculum. *Seminars in Speech and Language, 10*(3), 181–190.

Beck, A. R. (1996). Language assessment methods for three age groups of children. *Journal of Children's Communication Development, 17*(2), 51–66.

Bland, L. E., & Prelock, P. A. (1996). Effects of collaboration on language performance. *Journal of Children's Communication Development, 17*(2), 31–37.

Bloom, L., & Lahey, M. (1978). *Language development and language disorders.* New York: Wiley.

Blosser, J. L., & Kratcoski, A. (1997). PACS: A framework for determining appropriate service delivery options. *Language, Speech, and Hearing Services in Schools, 28,* 99–107.

Brucker, P. O. (1994). The advantages of inclusion for students with learning disabilities. *Journal of Learning Disabilities, 27*(9), 581–582.

California High School Task Force. (1992). *Second to none: A vision of the new California high school.* Sacramento, CA: California Department of Education.

Cammarata, J. (1997, January 27). The time is now; the job is ours. *Advance for Speech–Language Pathologists and Audiologists, 7,* 4, 16.

Cheng, L. L. (1994). Intervention strategies: A multicultural approach. In K. G. Butler (Ed.), *Cross-cultural perspectives in language assessment and intervention* (pp. 147–154). Gaithersburg, MD: Aspen.

Coufal, K. L. (1993). Collaborative consultation for speech–language pathologists. *Topics in Language Disorders, 14*(1), 1–14.

Education for All Handicapped Children Act of 1975, 20 U.S.C. §1400 *et seq.*

Eggleston, C. (1997, May/June). Did you know? *LDA Newsbriefs, 32*(3), 9.

Elksnin, L. K., & Capilouto, G. J. (1994). Speech–language pathologists' perceptions of integrated service delivery in school settings. *Language, Speech, and Hearing Services in Schools, 25,* 258–267.

Ferguson, M. L. (1992). Implementing collaborative consultation: An introduction. *Language, Speech, and Hearing Services in Schools, 23,* 361–362.

Feuerstein, R. (1979). *The dynamic assessment of retarded performers: The learning assessment potential device, theory, instruments, and techniques.* Chicago, IL: Scott Foresman.

Flowers, R. M. (1984). *Delivery of speech–language and audiology services.* Baltimore: Williams & Wilkins.

Halpern, A. S., & Fuhrer, M. J. (1984). *Functional assessment in rehabilitation.* Baltimore: Brookes.

Harvell, P. (1997). [Survey of public school speech and language pathologists]. Unpublished raw data.

Hatter, R. A. (1996). *Resiliency of the profession: The speech and language pathologist.* Fremont, CA: California Department of Education, Diagnostic Center North.

Hixson, P. K. (1993). An integrated approach to program development. *Topics in Language Disorders, 14*(1), 41-57.

Huer, M. B. (1997, June). Looking through color lenses: Cultural strategies for AAC. *Advance for directors in rehabilitation,* 37–40.

Hunter, D. (1994–95, Winter). Now is the time for action. *Deaf-Blind Perspectives, 2*(2).

Iglesias, A. (1994). Communication in the home and classroom: Match or mismatch? In K. G. Butler (Ed.), *Cross-cultural perspectives in language assessment and intervention* (pp. 15–27). Gaithersburg, MD: Aspen.

Inclusive Education Programs. (1997, July). Tools for inclusion. *LRP Publications, 4*(7), 4.

Individuals with Disabilities Education Act of 1990, 20 U.S.C. §1400 *et seq.*

Individuals with Disabilities Education Act, Amendments of 1997, 20 U.S.C. §1400 *et seq.*

Kupper, L. (Ed.). (1995, December). Helping students develop their IEPs. *National Information Center for Children and Youth with Disabilities Technical Assistance Guide, 2,* 1–3.

Larson, V. L. (1997). *Assessment and intervention strategies for older students with language disorders.* Paper presented at the California Speech and Hearing Association (CSHA) Annual Conference, Palm Springs, CA.

Larson, V. L., & McKinley, N. (1987). *Communication assessment and intervention strategies for adolescents.* Eau Claire, WI: Thinking Publications.

Logemann, J. (1994, November). Creativity plus activism equals a formula for managing change. *Asha, 36,* 27–30.

Lunday, A. M. (1996). A collaborative communication skills program for Job Corps centers. *Topics in Language Disorders, 16*(3), 23–36.

Lyon, S., & Lyon, G. (1980). Team functioning and staff development: A role release approach to providing integrated educational services for severely handicapped students. *Journal of the Association for the Severely Handicapped, 5*(3), 250–263.

Martin, J. E., & Marshall, L. H. (1993). *Self-determination universal transition designs.* Paper prepared for National Institute for Disability Rehabilitation Research's Transition Consensus Validation Process, Center for Educational Research, University of Colorado at Colorado Springs.

Matthews, J. (1990). *The professions of speech–language pathology and audiology: Human communication disorders.* New York: Macmillan.

McCue, M., Chase, S. L., Dowdy, C., Pramuka, M., Petrick, J., Aitken, S., & Fabry, P. (1994). *Functional assessment of individuals with cognitive disabilities: A desk reference for rehabilitation.* Pittsburgh, PA: Center for Applied Neuropsychology.

McReynolds, L. V. (1990). Articulation and phonological disorders. In G. H. Shames & E. H. Wiig (Eds.), *Human communication disorders* (3rd ed.) (pp. 222–265). New York: Macmillan.

Michaels, C. A. (Ed.). (1994). *Transition strategies for persons with learning disabilities.* San Diego, CA: Singular.

Montgomery, J. K., & Herer, G. R. (1994). Future watch: Our schools in the 21st century. *Language, Speech, and Hearing Services in Schools, 25,* 130–135.

Nation, J. E., & Aram, D. M. (1977). *Diagnosis of speech and language disorders.* St. Louis, MO: C. V. Mosby.

Nelson, N. W. (1989). Curriculum-based language assessment and intervention. *Language, Speech, and Hearing Services in the Schools, 21,* 170–184.

Nelson, N. W. (1993). *Childhood language disorders in context: Infancy through adolescence.* New York: Macmillan.

Nippold, M. (1993). Developmental markers in adolescent language: Syntax, semantics, and pragmatics. *Language, Speech, and Hearing Services in Schools, 24,* 21–28.

Owens, R. E. (1990). Development of communication, language, and speech. In G. H. Shames & E. H. Wiig (Eds.), *Human communication disorders* (3rd ed.) (pp. 30–73). New York: Macmillan.

Owens, R. E. (1995). *Language disorders: A functional approach to assessment and intervention* (2nd ed.). Needham Heights, MA: Allyn & Bacon.

Patton, M., & Westby, C. (1992). Ethnography and research: A qualitative view. *Topics in Language Disorders, 12*(3), 15–27.

Plummer, B., Greenstate, J., Montgomery, J., Sakata, K., & Thies, T. (1987, December). Role of the language, speech, and hearing specialist. *California Speech-Language-Hearing Association (CSHA) Newsletter, 13*(3), 6, 15.

Polansky, M. C. (1994). The meaning of inclusion: Is it an option or a mandate? *School Business Affairs, 60*(7), 27–29.

Prelock, P. A., Miller, B. L., & Reed, N. L. (1995). Clinical exchange: Collaborative partnerships in a language in the classroom program. *Language, Speech, and Hearing Services in Schools, 26,* 286–292.

Random House college dictionary (2nd ed.). (1984). New York: Random House.

Rosenthal, G. (1996). The behavior assessment system for children: Locus of control scale. *Child Assessment News, 5*(5), 1–5.

Rotter, J. B. (1966). Generalized expectancies for internal vs. external control of reinforcement. *Psychological Monographs: General and Applied, 80*(1), 1–28.

Scott, C. M., & Stokes, S. L. (1995). Measures of syntax in school-age children and adolescents. *Language, Speech, and Hearing Services in Schools, 26,* 309–319.

Secord, W. A., & Wiig, E. H. (Eds.). (1990). *Best practices in speech–language pathology: Collaborative programs in the schools: Concepts, models, and procedures* (Vol. I). San Antonio, TX: Psychological Corporation.

Sowers, J., & Powers, L. (1991). *Vocational preparation and employment of students with physical and multiple disabilities.* Baltimore: Brookes.

Storm, J., DeStefano, L., & O'Leary, E. (1996). *Individuals With Disabilities Act: Transition Requirements.* Stillwater, OK: Oklahoma State University.

Taylor, O. L. (1990). Language and communication differences. In G. H. Shames & E. H. Wiig (Eds.), *Human communication disorders* (pp. 126–158). New York: Macmillan.

Taylor, O. L., & Payne, K. T. (1994). Culturally valid testing: A proactive approach. In K. G. Butler (Ed.), *Cross-cultural perspectives in language assessment and intervention: A topics in language disorders series* (pp. 93–105). Gaithersburg, MD: Aspen.

U.S. Department of Education. (1994). To assure the free appropriate public education of all children with disabilities. *Sixteenth annual report to Congress on the implementation of the Individuals with Disabilities Education Act.* Washington, DC: Author.

U.S. Department of Labor. (1991a). Secretary's Commission on Achieving Necessary Skills (SCANS) report. *What work requires of schools: A SCANS report for America 2000.* Washington, DC: Author.

U.S. Department of Labor. (1991b). *Training opportunities in Job Corps.* Washington, DC: Author.

Wagner, M., Blackorby, J., Cameto, R., Hebbeler, K., & Newman, L. (1993). *The transition experiences of young people with disabilities: A summary of findings from the National Longitudinal Transition Study of special education students.* Menlo Park, CA: SRI International.

Wagner, M., & Shaver, D. (1989). *SRI International Educational Programs and Achievements of secondary special education students: Findings from the National Longitudinal Transition study.* Paper presented to special education special interest group at American Educational Research Association, San Francisco, CA.

Wehmeyer, M. (1992). Self-determination: Critical skills for outcome-oriented transition services, steps in transition that lead to self-determination. *The Journal for Vocational Special Needs Education, 15,* 3–7.

Wesson, C., Otis-Wilborn, A., Hasbrouck, J., & Tindal, G. (1993). *Linking assessment, curriculum, and instruction of oral and written language: Educating students with mild disabilities.* Denver, CO: Love.

Wilson, K., Blackmon, R., Hall, R., & Elcholtz, G. (1991). Methods of language assessment: A survey of California public school clinicians. *Language, Speech, and Hearing Services in Schools, 22,* 236–241.

Zarrella, S. (Ed.). (1995, October). Transition services benefit youth in education, rehab. *Advance for Speech-language Pathologists and Audiologists, 5.*

CHAPTER

5

OCCUPATIONAL AND PHYSICAL THERAPY

Jayne Shepherd

Katherine J. Inge

Introduction

"The focal point of transition subtly shifts and becomes more defined as the student gets older. In the early stages of transition, the focal point is educating parents on possibilities and considerations. In the early stages with kids, it is giving them the permission to have a life, and to voice their interests, and having the right to say 'this is my life.' It takes tremendous courage to own your life and own who you are . . . that's where I see the whole transition process." Occupational therapist working in transition

—(Dillon, Flexman, & Probeck, 1996)

It takes a tremendous amount of courage for students and professionals to define and develop their roles in the transition process. This chapter suggests possible old and new roles for school-based occupational and physical therapists. First, the history and education of the professions are discussed to give the reader background about the philosophical roots and current training of therapists. Second, the role of the therapist in the transition process is discussed according to research and speculation based on the training and expertise of therapists. Third, the challenges and barriers for therapists participating in transition are discussed, with suggestions to help encourage more involvement of therapy in the transition process. Lastly, a vision for the future of transition planning is presented. The authors hope that this chapter will inspire professionals to include occupational and physical therapy in the transition planning process when appropriate.

Overview of the Professions

Occupational Therapy

Occupational therapy (OT) as a health care profession began in the early 1900s during the era of moral treatment for persons with mental illness. In this era, the treatment of people with mental illness became more optimistic and humanitarian. Occupational therapists helped individuals structure their day through activity. With the onset of World War I, occupational therapists became involved in the rehabilitation of persons with physical as well as psychosocial disabilities. It was during this time that meaningful occupations or activities were used to assist people in obtaining a better state of health (Reed, 1993). OTs began adapting activities and environments so individuals could participate in self-care, work, and leisure tasks. In the 1930s, occupational therapists began to work in pediatric hospitals and specialized schools for children with disabilities. Today, they continue to use occupation and adaptation of the task or environment as main premises to influence the functioning of persons with disabilities.

Focus

Occupational therapy aims to enhance a person's development, increase or restore independence, and prevent disability. Therapy focuses on how a person occupies his or her time to fulfill life roles within various contexts. Self-care, work, school, and play activities are evaluated and used to strengthen the individual's ability to participate meaningfully in his physical, social, and cultural environment (Dunn, Brown, & McGuigan, 1994). To maximize independence, the occupational therapist may adapt the task or environment according to the individual's age and social role. In educational settings, therapists address sensory–motor, cognitive, and psychosocial skills and habits so the student can perform self-care, classroom, work, and play tasks within multiple contexts (e.g., classroom, gym, cafeteria, playground, school grounds, and the community). OTs may address social skills, clothing management, personal hygiene, tool manipulation (e.g., pencil, scissors, rulers, papers, staplers), graphic communication (e.g., handwriting or computer use), mobility, home management, leisure, and vocational skills. Typical occupational therapy evaluation and intervention areas are presented in Table 5.1.

(*Text continues on page 121*)

Table 5.1

Occupational Therapy Evaluation and Intervention Areas

Daily Living or Self-Care Tasks	Typical Activities
Toileting	Gets and uses supplies; manages clothes and position; transfers to toilet; cleans self; uses menstrual and continence equipment (catheters, colostomies, etc.); includes using bathrooms in a variety of settings.
Oral Hygiene	Uses toothbrush and floss; cares for braces; uses orthotics, prosthetics.
· Grooming	Cares for skin, nails, and hair; styles hair; shaves; uses makeup; applies deodorant; cares for eyes and ears.
Bathing or Showering	Gets and uses equipment; soaps, rinses, and dries self; transfers to and from equipment and maintains position.
Dressing	Selects clothes, obtains clothes; puts clothes on; manages fasteners; changes for gym class or work; manages personal devices or prostheses.
Personal Device Care	Maintains (cleans or gets someone else to care for) glasses, prosthetics, orthotics, hearing aids, contact lenses, adaptive equipment, computers and other technological assistive devices, birth control.
Feeding and Eating	Sets up food; uses appropriate utensils and tableware; drinks, sucks, masticates, swallows, coughs, and eats food; manages alternative methods of eating (e.g., tube feeding).
Functional Communication	Communicates needs verbally or nonverbally; uses equipment or systems (e.g., writing equipment, computers, typewriters, telephones, call bells, emergency systems, augmentative communication devices), communication picture boards.
Functional Mobility	Moves from one place or position to another (within environments); transfers to bed, car, bus, toilet, shower, furniture; transports objects; functional ambulation; drives; uses transportation systems (private or public).
Medication Routine	Opens, closes, and obtains correct amount of medication; follows schedule; reports problems.
Socialization	Meets physical and emotional needs; with various contexts, interacts with others in socially appropriate ways (social awareness, presentation, and skills).
Health Maintenance	Follows health procedures (e.g., changing positions; nutrition; exercise); maintains regular appointments with appropriate professionals.
Emergency Response	Prevents threats to health; recognizes hazardous situations; can direct others or take action themselves to prevent situations.
Sexual Expression	Recognizes, communicates, and engages in desired sexual activities; uses birth control.

(continues)

Table 5.1 Continued

Work and Productivity	Typical Activities
Home Management	
Cleaning	Sweeps; mops; dusts; vacuums; cleans tables and other surfaces; empties trash; makes bed; picks up and puts away items.
Meal Preparation and Clean Up	Plans a meal; sets and clears table; gets utensils and food items; opens containers and makes a food item; uses appliances; cleans up (e.g., washes pots and pans and utensils, uses dishwasher); stores food.
Clothing Care	Puts clothes in dirty laundry; sorts; folds; uses appliances (e.g., washing machine, dryer); irons; puts clothes away; mends.
Shopping	Makes shopping list; selects, obtains, and purchases items at drug store, convenience store, grocery store, and others; pays for items correctly.
Money Management	Manages allowance; saves to buy special items; budgets for school, recreation, and other needs; uses bank accounts and other forms of credit.
Household Maintenance	Does yardwork and gardening; washes car; cleans appliances (e.g., heads to video or cassette recorder; refrigerator and oven); makes simple repairs with tools; changes a light bulb.
Safety Precautions	Takes precautions to prevent injuries (potholders; clean up spills); uses appliances correctly around water; has emergency numbers available; can use a fire extinguisher.
Care of Others	
Pet Care	Takes care of pets; provides physical care and nurturance (e.g., feeding, exercise, play).
Child Care	Takes care of siblings or babysits other children; provides nurturance and physical care.
Adult Care	Takes care of adults (e.g., adults who are sick or elderly); provides nurturance and physical care.
Educational Activities	
Learning	Understands learning style and needs; uses multiple sensory experiences if needed; uses adaptations and compensatory techniques as appropriate; asks for modifications when needed.
Student Role	Develops work habits (e.g., organization, time management); manages school tools (e.g., pencils, notebooks, staplers, lockers, books, calculator); expresses needs; completes self care and mobility tasks within school environment; uses adaptations to complete assignments; participates in classroom and school-wide activities; plays on playground; asks for help when necessary.
Higher Education	Researches options; considers accessibility features; considers programming and support service availability (e.g., tutor, special accommodations, assistive technology, personal aide, emergency services available); completes application process; plans realistic schedule.

(continues)

Table 5.1 *Continued*

Work and Productivity	Typical Activities
Vocational Activities	
Vocational Exploration	Explores interests, skills, and possible jobs.
Job Acquisition	Completes application process; interviews; considers factors effecting job hiring.
Job Performance	Performs job effectively; uses time appropriately; has interpersonal skills necessary for job (e.g., self-care skills, social interaction, social awareness) and uses compensatory techniques when needed.

Play or Leisure	Typical Activities
Exploration of Interests	Identifies interests and possible activities; explores assistive devices that make leisure activities possible; determines opportunities for leisure activities.
Participation in Leisure	Participates in leisure activity; works to balance leisure and work activities; obtains, maintains, and uses equipment or materials needed for leisure activity.

Note. Adapted from "Uniform Terminology for Occupational Therapy," by American Occupational Therapy Association (AOTA), 1994, *American Journal of Occupational Therapy, 48*, pp. 1047–1054.

Personnel and Training

There are two levels of training for occupational therapy personnel: the occupational therapist who has at least a bachelor's degree (or may have an entry-level master's degree), and an occupational therapy assistant who completed a certificate or associate degree program. Upon graduation, both therapists and assistants take a certification exam to test entry-level competence as a therapist or an assistant. Therapists can obtain a postprofessional master's degree or a doctoral degree with additional concentration in an area of practice such as pediatrics or school-system therapy. After meeting specific work experience criteria, therapists can apply to take a specialty certification exam in pediatrics. This is an optional credential that therapists can obtain to signify their advanced knowledge in pediatrics.

Occupational therapists are trained to evaluate, treat, and consult with individuals of all ages who may have a physical, psychosocial, or developmental disability. Besides learning a life span approach to development and disability, their education includes biological sciences, behavioral and psychological sciences, normal development, medical conditions, specific occupational therapy techniques, research, and management principles. This biopsychosocial education assists therapists in viewing the person holistically.

Because training focuses on a life span approach, pediatric practice is often seen as a specialty area. Training in school-based therapy is inconsistent among educational programs, and many students may not receive fieldwork experiences in the public schools. For practitioners who obtained degrees before 1975, their formal education about school-based practice may be limited or missing.

There are standards of practice for occupational therapists (American Occupational Therapy Association [AOTA], 1994). These standards recommend guidelines for therapists and are consistent with other documents throughout the profession. Though standards were originally developed for school system practice in 1980 and in early intervention and preschool in 1988, AOTA has rescinded them and has developed generic standards for all areas of practice to help define the roles and responsibilities for therapists.

Physical Therapy

Physical therapy (PT) began during World War I when veterans needed rehabilitation. Physical therapists were called "reconstruction aides," because they used physical modalities (e.g., water, electrical, mechanical agents), exercises, games, and muscle reeducation to rehabilitate veterans (American Physical Therapy Association [APTA], 1997a). The demand for PTs increased in the 1930s and 1940s when the polio epidemic and World War II began. Similar to occupational therapists, it was around this time when physical therapists began to work with children in hospitals and schools (Effgen, 1994). PTs use therapeutic exercise to facilitate the motion, strength, and endurance needed to perform daily activities (APTA, 1997a).

Focus

Physical therapy assists individuals of all ages with disabilities resulting from disease or injury. After assessing the person's strength and ability to move and endure physical activities, therapists plan, design, and implement therapeutic interventions to alleviate or prevent injury or limitations. The goal of physical therapy is to promote fitness, health, and quality of life (APTA, 1997a). In school settings, physical therapists may address the student's ability to 1) move in organized patterns (e.g., gross motor skills), 2) assume and maintain postures, and 3) perform functional mobility tasks (e.g., getting to and from classes, carrying books, climbing stairs, opening doors, using the playground, carrying materials, traveling in the community) (Effgen, 1994).

Personnel and Training

Similar to occupational therapy, there are two entry levels of training for physical therapy personnel: the physical therapist who has a bachelor's degree or an entry-level master's degree, and a physical therapy assistant who has completed a 2-year certificate or an associate degree program. Upon graduation, both therapists and assistants take a national certification exam to test entry-level competence as a therapist or an assistant. Therapists can obtain a postprofessional master's degree or a doctoral degree with an additional concentration in an area of practice such as pediatrics or school system therapy. After working in pediatrics for a specified number of years/hours, physical therapists can obtain an optional credential by taking a specialty certification exam in pediatrics. This credential signifies that therapists have advanced knowledge in pediatrics (APTA, 1998).

Physical therapists also are educated to treat clients across the life span and pediatric practice is often seen as a specialty area. Training in school-based therapy is limited and inconsistent among educational programs, and many students may not receive clinical experiences in the public schools. Many graduates and practitioners, who obtained their degrees before 1975, may have little to no education about school-based practice.

The American Physical Therapy Association (APTA) has developed standards of practice for physical therapy to provide essential skills for delivering quality services (APTA, 1997a, 1997b). These standards cross all areas of practice in physical therapy. Therefore, there are no separate standards of practice for school-based physical therapy. The standards are consistent with the profession's code of ethics and give a foundation to establish physical therapy practice.

Overview of Occupational and Physical Therapy in Transition

Legislation

Students with disabilities were afforded access to a "free and appropriate" public education in 1975 with the Education for All Handicapped Children Act (EHA) (P.L. 94-142). This law also provided for "related services" for every student who required support. The EHA defined related services as "transportation and such developmental, corrective, and other supportive services as are required to assist a child to benefit from special education" and includes occupational and physical therapy (Reg. 300.13, p. 102:53). Therefore, as related service providers, the role of OTs and PTs in the school system is to assist students to participate in and benefit from special education services. This means that a child who is receiving OT or PT in a hospital or an outpatient program may not qualify for these services at school if therapy is not needed to facilitate the student's educational goals. For example, upon testing, Johnny's muscle strength and fine motor coordination are below average for his age. However, Johnny can get around the school, complete self-care tasks adequately, and produce written language adequate for an 8th grader. Therefore, even though Johnny could benefit from therapy, he is not eligible for school-based services because he is able to fulfill his role as a student.

Secondary education and transition services were added to The Education of the Handicapped Act Amendments of 1983 (P.L. 98-199) and were renewed in the 1986 Education of the Handicapped Act Amendments (P.L. 99-457). These amendments authorized funds for research, training, and demonstration projects in the area of transition of learners from school to postsecondary environments. The reauthorization of the amendments in 1990, renamed as the Individuals with Disabilities Education Act (IDEA) (P.L. 101-476), defined "transition services" in the law as follows:

> Transition services means a coordinated set of activities for a student, designed within an outcome oriented process, which promotes movement from school to postschool activities, includes postsecondary education, vocational training, integrated employment (including supported employment), continuing adult education, adult services, independent living, or community participation. The coordinated set of activities shall be based upon the individual student's needs taking into account the student's preferences and interests and shall include instruction, community experiences, development of employment and other postschool adult living objectives, and when appropriate acquisition of daily living skills and functional vocational evaluation (20 U.S.C. §1401 (a)(19), 1990).

Prior to IDEA, transition services had never been defined by law. Although transition had been described within the special education process, it had never been defined in terms of who should participate, when they should participate, and who would provide the services. IDEA mandated transition services for students with disabilities to include community experiences, the development of employment, and other postschool adult living objectives. In addition, an individual transition plan (ITP) had to be developed for each student no later than age 16 and, in some cases, at age 14 or younger. Interagency responsibilities and linkages also had to be included before the student graduated from high school.

The reauthorization of IDEA (P.L. 105-17) was signed into law by President Clinton on June 4, 1997. Related services were further defined to include assisting teachers in identifying and assessing disabling conditions in children. Specifically, the law states that "such medical services shall be for diagnostic and evaluation purposes only, as may be required to assist a child with a disability to benefit from special education, and includes the early identification and assessment of disabling conditions in children (20 U.S.C. §602, 1997). In addition, IDEA of 1997 called for transition planning to begin no later than age 14 and specifically identified related services as personnel who assist in transition planning. Other students who do not qualify for special education services under IDEA (e.g., students who have a physical disability that does not affect education) but who would benefit from transition services, may be eligible for related services under Section 504 of the Rehabilitation Act of 1973.

Current Involvement of School-Based Therapists in Transition Planning

The public schools are second only to hospitals and skilled nursing home facilities as the largest employer of occupational therapists. According to the AOTA 1996 Member Survey, 18% of the occupational therapists employed in the United States work in the public schools (AOTA, 1996). In a 1997 survey of the National Board for Certification in Occupational Therapy (NBCOT), 17% of certified occupational therapy assistants (COTAs) worked in public schools. School-based practice is currently AOTA's largest special interest section. APTA has more than 70,000 members, and APTA membership services estimate that less than 8% of those work in the public schools. This appears to be congruent with a study in Virginia that found that almost twice as many OTs work in the public schools than PTs (Bradley, 1993).

Currently, few occupational therapists are participating in the transition process with students from 14 to 21 years of age, even though their participation has been mandated by law (Brollier, Shepherd, & Markley, 1994; Getzel & deFur, 1997; Inge, 1995). Inge (1995) conducted a national survey of occupational therapists in the public schools to determine the participation and attitudes of therapists related to the transition process. This survey was mailed to 1,000 occupational therapists who were randomly selected from AOTA's direct mail list for school-based practice, which contained 4,000 therapists at the time of the study. Inge had a 76% (755) return rate, with 61.6% (465) of the respondents indicating they did not provide transition services to students from the ages 14 to 22.

Of the 290 respondents who reported that they served these students, the majority indicated that their caseloads consisted primarily of students less than 13 years of age. For instance, the mean number of students served by the respondents in the age group zero to 13 years of age was 33.86, while the mean number in the age group 20 to 22 was less than 1 (.88). Other relevant findings indicated that occupational therapists often did not participate fully in the transition team process (e.g., developing collaborative goals, attending meetings, instructing others, and so forth). For instance, only 15.9% of the respondents replied that they *always attended* meetings for students who were receiving OT services. Moreover, 49.3% of the respondents indicated that they attended ITP/IEP meetings most of the time for students who were receiving OT services, 17.2% attended sometimes, 12.1% attended infrequently, and 5.5% never attended. When asked how they developed ITP/IEP objectives for students who receive OT services, 40% indicated that the OT is expected to write objectives *prior* to the team meeting and these are written on the ITP/IEP.

When therapists were asked if they had time to work with other team members to integrate therapy objectives into the students' daily activities, limited interaction was reported. For instance, respondents were asked how many times per week that they had at least 15 minutes to train other team members to integrate OT techniques into their students' daily activities. Only 5.5% indicated that they had time more than once a week to train other team members to integrate OT techniques into the daily activities of each student. The remaining therapists responded in the following manner: 8.6% never had time to train other team members; 27.2% had time less than once a month; 27.2% had time about once a month; 17.9% had time two to three times a month; and 13.4% had time about once a week.

A recent study of transition services in the Commonwealth of Virginia also indicates that occupational and physical therapists may not be participating in transition planning for students with severe disabilities (Getzel & deFur, 1997). In this study, data was collected on 2,364 students in the public school system from the ages 14 to 21, using a Transition Planning Information Form. A sample of 84 students with significant disabilities was drawn from this data set representing information from the fall of 1994 and spring of 1995 school year. Students were from rural and metropolitan school divisions that had been recipients of one-year transition incentive grants from the five-year Virginia transition systems change project (Project UNITE). As a result, this sample reflects school divisions that have an interest in transition planning and should not be considered representative of all school divisions in the Commonwealth of Virginia.

A review of the Getzel and deFur article reveals the following participation by school system personnel for 84 students' IEP meetings: 93% of the meetings had a special education teacher in attendance, 6% had vocational education teachers, 14% had occupational therapists, 24% had speech therapists, 5% had guidance counselors, and 36% had others that included physical therapists, vision teachers, and other specialized teaching staff. More revealing, however, is the fact that a majority of the students needed specific services, including learning materials modified (66%), assistive technology devices (44%), daily living skills training (85%), and social skills training (75%). In light of these recommendations, the limited participation by therapists seems alarming.

Roles and Functions for Therapists in the Transition Planning Process

Many studies approach the topic of integrating occupational and physical therapy services into the transition process in only a general way. Typically, these articles recommend that related services personnel serve on transition teams and provide training and therapy in community sites, rather than the school building, as students reach transition age. They usually do not discuss the "how to" of the process (Brown, Nisbet, et al., 1983; Everson, 1993; Falvey, 1989; Moon, Inge, Wehman, Brooke, & Barcus, 1990; Wehman, Moon, Everson, Ward, & Barcus, 1988). Several authors have indicated a need for therapists to define and delineate their roles in the public school setting (Brollier, Shepherd, & Markley, 1994; Bundy, 1993, 1997; Colman, 1988; Inge, 1995; Royeen, 1986, 1988). Bundy's study was part of a federal grant to train occupational and physical therapists in school-based practice. Bundy identified four main goal areas for therapists in the public schools. Therapy goals should help students

1. Learn academic subjects;
2. Express knowledge;
3. Fulfill student roles; and
4. Perform self-care and mobility tasks.

Table 5.2 gives a few examples of what activities would be included under each of these areas. These four areas are applicable to students at all ages while they are transitioning from one environment to another. Transitions for students in special education begin when they enter preschool and continue throughout their school career. Therapists think of transition planning throughout a child's school career and are often in and out of the child's life during these times. Transitions from preschool to elementary, elementary to middle school, and middle school to high school are often the building blocks to a student's successful transition from school to work or community living. Therapists often have a longitudinal perspective to bring to the transition process of an adolescent (Lowman, Shepherd, Dillon, Flexman, & Probeck, 1997).

Recently, there have been attempts in the literature to define the occupational therapist's role in the transition process with adolescents (Brollier, Shepherd, & Markley, 1994; Sample, Spencer, & Bean, 1990; Spencer, 1996; Spencer & Sample, 1993). Unfortunately, minimal information or literature can be found on the role of the physical therapist in the transition process except in relation to community-based instruction for students with severe disabilities (Rainforth & York, 1987, 1991; Rainforth, York, & Macdonald, 1992; York, Rainforth, & Dunn, 1990; York, Rainforth, & Giangreco, 1990). Lowman et al.

Table 5.2
Educationally Relevant Goal Areas for Occupational and Physical Therapy in School-Based Practice

1. Learn academic subjects
   - task adaptations (e.g., amount of work; grid paper for mathematics; highlighting tape)
   - environmental adaptations (e.g., structure of sensory, physical, social environments)
   - multiple sensory experiences

2. Express knowledge
   - verbal and nonverbal communication (e.g., how to handle anger; augmentative communication systems; body language)
   - tool manipulation (e.g., pencils, scissors, rulers, papers, staplers, books)
   - graphic communication (e.g., handwriting or computer use)
   - test-taking methods
   - note-taking methods

3. Fulfill the student role
   - socialization
   - classroom and school chores/tasks
   - participate in school, community, and work activities
   - manage and organize school or work materials
   - use appropriate work habits
   - participate in play/leisure activities (e.g., recess, assemblies, extracurricular activities, school sports events)

4. Perform self-care and mobility tasks in and out of the school environment
   - toileting
   - dressing
   - grooming
   - homemaking
   - personal device maintenance and use
   - medication and health maintenance routines
   - functional mobility (e.g., ambulation, climbing stairs, transfers, carrying items, driving, public and private transportation)

Note. Adapted from "Preparing Occupational Therapy Students to Practice in Schools," in A. Bundy, 1997, *School System Special Interest Section Newsletter, 4*(2), pp. 1–2.

(1997) conducted a cross-case qualitative study between three teams of teachers and occupational therapists who provided transition services. This study investigated the role of the occupational therapist in transition planning, and the interpersonal dynamics and factors that influence the collaboration between teachers and therapists. Responses indicated that successful transition planning occurred when therapists and teachers understood each other's roles, used best practices from the literature, shared a common approach to transition planning, and used effective communication strategies. In this study, occupational therapists identified six main roles for the therapist:

1. Support the teacher
2. Educate students, staff, and parents
3. Teach functional skills to students
4. Visit job sites
5. Make modifications in the classroom or on the job site
6. Provide a holistic perspective to the team

In separate interviews, teachers valued the similar roles identified by the occupational therapists. From this study, one therapist said the following:

> I find myself being the lead miner with the light on the hat, shedding light on a bigger picture. So much of [the IEP process] is tunnel vision, looking at what is wrong [with a student]. My role involves shedding light on what the possibilities can be . . . looking at quality of life, what gives meaning to a person, not focusing on deficits. (Field notes)

In the Inge (1995) study, occupational therapists identified similar roles for themselves in the transition process. First, 90.7% responded that therapists should focus on functional skills (e.g., home management, grocery shopping, self-care, preparing meals, etc.) for transition age students. Second, 99% of the respondents felt that OTs should provide consultation, job-site modifications, and assistive technology devices to students on job sites. Third, 93.8% of those responding indicated that occupational therapists should evaluate students in the community to identify assistive technology needs as part of transition planning.

Occupational and physical therapists may become involved in evaluation, service planning, or delivery of services for transition (Spencer, 1996). Like all team members, the therapist's main goal is to promote the adolescent student's self-advocacy role so that the student may achieve his or her own identified goals and dreams (deFur & Taymans, 1995; Sample et al., 1990; Szymanski, 1994). Both OTs and PTs teach functional tasks, evaluate the environment, adapt tasks, use assistive technology, educate others, and promote self-advocacy, prevention and health maintenance. In addition, occupational therapists assist the team in developing the student's interpersonal and social skills (AOTA, 1991b). Some specific examples of how therapists may work in transition are given in Tables 5.3 and 5.4 and in the following passages. Table 5.3 describes possible roles for the occupational therapist and Table 5.4 describes possible roles for the physical therapist in transition.

Table 5.3
Possible Roles for the Occupational Therapist in the Evaluation, Service Planning, or Delivery of Transition Services

1. Teach functional tasks related to temporal aspects (age, maturation, ability/disability, and life stage).
   a. activities of daily living
      - self-care (e.g., dressing, feeding, hygiene, toileting)
      - communication
      - socialization
      - mobility within home, school, and community
   b. home management (e.g., cooking, cleaning, money management)
   c. work and health habits
   d. work skills
   e. leisure

2. Evaluate environmental supports and barriers and recommend adaptations if needed.
   a. Physical characteristics
      - accessibility (e.g., terrain, furniture, objects)
      - sensory stimulation (e.g., tactile, visual or auditory cues or distractions)
      - types of objects, tools, equipment
      - temporal cues (e.g., watches with alarms; toothpaste left out on the countertop)
   b. Social characteristics
      - activities (e.g., individual or group)
      - people
      - role expectations
   c. Cultural characteristics
      - customs, expectations
      - values
      - beliefs

3. Adapt tasks.
   a. change the physical characteristics of the task (e.g., sit instead of stand)
   b. change the social characteristics of the task (e.g., increase or decrease the number of people involved)
   c. change the demands (e.g., do part of task; checklists)
   d. work simplification (e.g., get all items together before shower; reorganize kitchen so able to find objects)
   e. use instructional techniques (e.g., task analysis, forward and backwards chaining, partial participation, positive supports, systematic instruction, natural cues)
   f. teach compensatory techniques

4. Adapt materials or recommend assistive technology.
   a. increase or decrease the size, shape, length, or sensory characteristics of materials and objects being used
   b. adaptive aids (e.g., button hook, reacher, lap board, talking watch, book holder, memory aids, talking calculators)
   c. switches, computers, appliances, augmentative communication devices, telephones, wheelchairs, environmental control units, positioning devices, alerting systems

(continues)

Table 5.3 *Continued*

5. Develop interpersonal and social skills to support participation in the school, community, home, or work environment.
   a. awareness of interests
   b. stress management
   c. time management
   d. self management/coping techniques
   e. leisure activities to promote socialization and develop friendships
   f. assertiveness training
   g. decision-making and problem-solving skills

6. Educate others and learn from others in the home, classroom, community, or workplace.
   a. student training
   b. family training
   c. staff training
   d. peer training

7. Promote self-advocacy, prevention, and health maintenance.
   a. legal rights and responsibilities
   b. disability and health awareness
   c. talk to others about disability and needs
   d. promote habits to maintain health (e.g., hygiene, medications, pressure reliefs, birth control, equipment maintenance, etc.)

Teach Functional Tasks

Occupational and physical therapists assist students in developing, remediating, or compensating for skills that support participation in the school, community, leisure, home, or work environments. Physical therapists often evaluate and develop a student's strength, endurance, and movement patterns so they are able to assume and maintain postures while moving and participating in different environments. As they help a student develop these physical skills, the occupational therapist teaches specific techniques and adaptations to perform activities of daily living (e.g., dressing, feeding, hygiene, toileting, communication, mobility), home management (e.g., cooking, cleaning, money management), work and health habits, work skills, and leisure tasks. One example of how therapists are involved in the academic environment is given in the case of Tim.

 Tim

Tim transitioned to high school and found that he was extremely disorganized while taking notes in six different classes. The teachers were frustrated and asked for suggestions. The PT and OT observed Tim and determined he walked great distances

Table 5.4

Possible Roles for the Physical Therapist in the Evaluation,
Service Planning, or Delivery of Transition Services

1. *Develop or compensate for skills that support participation in the school, community, or work environment.*

   a. strength
   b. endurance
   c. movement patterns
   d. assume and maintain postures

2. *Improve the student's mobility within the home, school, work, and the community setting.*

   a. ambulation
   b. wheelchair mobility
   c. climbing stairs
   d. opening doors
   e. transfers
   f. carrying items
   g. public and private transportation

3. *Promote self-advocacy, prevention, and health maintenance.*

   a. exercise
   b. nutrition
   c. body mechanics/positioning
   d. disability knowledge and precautions
   e. legal rights

4. *Adapt tasks and environments so the student can participate.*

   a. accessibility
   b. position of student and activity
   c. job site analysis

5. *Recommend or adapt assistive technology*

   a. mobility aids (e.g., walkers, canes, wheelchairs, standing tables)
   b. computer access and positioning
   c. augmentative communication device
   d. exercise equipment
   e. accessibility

6. *Educate others and consult in the home, classroom, community, or workplace*

   a. student training
   b. family training
   c. staff training
   d. peer training

between classes, was in a different style chair for each class, and was required to write a considerable amount of information and manage numerous books and class handouts. It was also noted that Tim rarely talked to anyone else.

The physical therapist suggested an exercise program for physical education at home to build up his strength for walking and carrying books, and a designated seat in each class with a large desk surface. The occupational therapist suggested a change in locker location (so Tim could get to and from his locker in the allotted time given to him); a variety of organizational strategies (e.g., backpack divided into sections for pencils, books, glasses, keys; separate clipboards for each class; color codes on books, clipboards; locker shelves for morning and afternoon classes; schedules and to-do lists available; and a talking watch with a timer to remind him to go to class); and a peer buddy to help write down homework and to do things with. A lightweight laptop word processor was suggested if the writing continued to be too taxing for Tim.

By learning these strategies in high school, Tim may incorporate them into routines and habits that assist him when he goes to college. The strategies also begin to teach him how to advocate for his learning style and needs. Other examples of how therapists work on functional tasks are given throughout the next sections that talk about therapy's role in transition.

Evaluate Environmental Supports and Barriers
and Recommend Adaptations if Needed

Occupational therapy's unique contribution to the transition process is to evaluate the context in which activities occur (Spencer, 1996). Dunn, Brown, and McGuigan (1994) developed a model to evaluate the context in occupational therapy which includes temporal and environmental aspects. Temporal aspects relate to the student's age, maturation level, ability and disability status, phase in the family life cycle, and the timing of completing tasks. Environmental aspects include the physical, social, and cultural environments where tasks occur. The objects, furniture, terrain, animals, and sensory aspects within the physical environment may support or impede a student's performance of a task. Social characteristics of the environment such as friends, family members, number of people, type of activity, and role expectations, as well as the cultural aspects (e.g., values, beliefs, customs), are also evaluated to help plan intervention. By considering the contextual aspects in a systematic way, occupational therapists often bring a wealth of information to the team to help plan intervention strategies.

Physical therapists evaluate accessibility issues within the physical environment and make recommendations for change as well (Effgen, 1994; Rainforth et al., 1992). While evaluating the student's mobility, the therapist evaluates what surfaces the student can negotiate. The therapist also determines the type of mobility aid (e.g., wheelchair, cane, walker, or crutches) that is most appropriate. As a student moves throughout various environments, therapists evaluate the physical environment for barriers or supports such as stairs, railings, doors, sitting surfaces, furniture, terrain, and spaces available. The PT often recommends exercises, adapted activities, or assistive devices to help the student move within various environments. The following case scenario of Lisa demonstrates how OT and PT may assist a student on a community outing to the hairdresser.

 ## Lisa

Lisa was going on a community outing to the hairdresser. She was extremely sensitive to noise and had never had her hair washed at a salon. In the planning meeting for this outing, the OT suggested that the teacher and PT choose to go to the hairdresser at a less busy time (to decrease the noise level) and suggested bringing ear plugs in case the salon got busy or the water bothered Lisa's ears during hair washing.

The PT accompanied the student and the teacher on the community outing, and instructed them and the hairdresser on how to transfer Lisa into the salon chair. They found that the chair next to the wall was best, because Lisa could use the wall to help support her when transferring. There were also fewer distractions on that side. While the PT was on the community outing, Lisa needed to use the bathroom. The PT demonstrated how Lisa could use her walker as "grab bars" if she put the walker over the top of the toilet and sat on the toilet backwards. The hairdresser was thrilled because she had an elderly client with the same problem. At the same time, the teacher learned how to structure this task and similar tasks for Lisa in future community outings.

Adapt Tasks

After evaluating the environment, therapists often recommend adaptations to make tasks easier to complete. They may adapt the task itself by changing the physical demands of the task (e.g., sitting instead of standing while dressing) or by changing the demands of the task (e.g., do part of the task, or use the railing while ascending the steps; use a quilt instead of a fitted bedspread). Like other team members, they use instructional techniques such as task analysis, forward and backwards chaining, partial participation, positive supports, systematic instruction, and natural cues to improve the student's performance (Brollier, Shepherd, & Markley, 1994; Shepherd, Procter, & Coley, 1996). Occupational therapists focus on the routines and habits of individuals and may suggest work simplification techniques (e.g., get all items together before showering; keep cleaning supplies in each bathroom instead of carrying them). OTs consider the social and cultural expectations of the environment prior to suggesting adaptations of the task. The case of Cory is an example of adapting a home management task.

Cory

Cory was 15 and wanted to come home by himself after school. Mom was afraid that he would fall when going up the steps to the front door or when he was getting a snack. The PT determined that Cory could get into the house safely by going through the back door because there were no steps to negotiate. The OT suggested placing a pump dispenser filled with water, a glass, and a snack (e.g., fruit or something in a container Cory could open) on the kitchen table so Cory could get a drink and snack by himself. The family telephone was programmed with Mom or Dad's work number and emergency phone numbers. A poster was placed on the wall to remind Cory to lock the door and call Mom or Dad once he was home.

Adapt Materials or Recommend Assistive Technology

Therapists often use or recommend low or high technology to support student performance (Inge & Shepherd, 1995; Struck, 1996). Occupational therapists may make simple adaptations to materials, such as increasing or decreasing the size, shape, length, or sensory characteristics of the materials or objects being used. For example, by placing tubular foam on a pen, a student with below average motor coordination could now grasp and hold the pen while filling out the order form at work. By placing fluorescent glue on the radio on-off button, a student could now find the button with the additional visual and tactile cues. Occupational therapists may recommend adaptive aids (e.g., button hook, reacher, lapboard, talking watch, telephone button enlarger, book holder, splints) to assist in activities of daily living or high-tech environmental control units. If students need assistance in managing bowel and bladder care or other health maintenance activities, OTs consult with nurses on procedures being used and the selection of adaptive aids (e.g., catherization mirrors, positioning devices, medicine containers and schedule; menstrual equipment). PTs may recommend mobility aids (e.g., walkers, canes, wheelchairs, standing tables), orthotics, or exercise equipment, and consult with students and family members about their preferences.

Depending on the expertise of other team members, therapists may be involved in an assistive technology evaluation and intervention program. They may assist in designing, constructing, and fitting adaptive equipment (Inge & Shepherd, 1995; Shepherd et al., 1997; York & Rainforth, 1991). PTs and OTs are part of the team to provide input on computer and augmentative communication device access and positioning, switches, appliances, and wheelchairs. Along with special educators, occupational therapists use their knowledge about perceptual and cognitive skills to consider software possibilities (Struck, 1996).

Wehman, Wood, Everson, Goodwyn, & Conley (1988) suggested that therapists can play an important role in the transition process by providing valuable input for analyzing what a student can do physically, and then modifying functional daily activities by designing, fabricating, or prescribing simple adaptive equipment for community-based vocational training. Sowers and Powers (1991) stated that occupational therapists should

1. Assist the teacher and vocational staff in conducting job-site and task analyses;

2. Identify and implement job design strategies at the job site;

3. Identify and implement strategies to assist in work-related skills such as eating, drinking, and using the bathroom;

4. Provide monthly job site visits to determine additional design and adaptation strategies; and

5. Attend regularly scheduled meetings to review student progress.

Renzaglia, Hutchins, Koterba-Buss, and Strauss (1992) suggested that one of the primary reasons for the limited number of successful employment outcomes for persons with multiple disabilities is the lack of design and fabrication of necessary job or equipment modifications for students to participate in integrated community employment opportunities. Therapists can play a critical role in this design and fabrication process. The following case scenario of Jackie gives an example of therapist involvement in a vocational setting.

Jackie

Jackie was 17 and working in an office word processing three days a week. She began to complain about back and neck pain. The physical therapist did a worksite visit and noticed that her chair was the wrong height and did not support her. She was also using poor body mechanics when reaching for items off the floor. By recommending a different seating system and by educating Jackie, the PT helped Jackie prevent unnecessary injury and taught her how to advocate for her own needs at work. At the same time, the employer learned that this poor seating may affect some of his other employees.

The OT noticed that Jackie had difficulty managing her tools at the desk. The OT simplified the hole punching task by designing a jig to place the papers in and by enlarging the handle of a hole-puncher. He also recommended a headset for the telephone, and specialized software with word prediction to help decrease the number of key strokes needed to complete a typing job. In addition, he noticed that Jackie was isolated from her fellow workers. He suggested a change in desk arrangement to facilitate interaction between workers.

Educate Others and Promote Self-Advocacy, Prevention, and Health Maintenance

Students, family members, staff members, and peers often need information to help them make informed decisions. Sometimes this education is all that is needed for the student to succeed. Many professionals already know or can learn skills from therapists without the therapist being directly involved with the activity. With this in mind, therapists may or may not be involved with a student in all domains of transition planning (Giangreco, 1990). Therapists may ask questions or provide activities to help students and parents think about tasks related to work or community living or issues related to self-advocacy (Spencer, 1996). One therapist eloquently expressed this role:

> An important part of transition is helping parents and kids to see possibilities, focusing on quality of life, what gives meaning. I tell parents that it is O.K. if Johnny falls out of his wheelchair and into the mud when he is camping and that yes, there are accessible camp grounds. In some ways, falling and getting skinned knees is the healthiest thing in the world. Being scared and overcoming. Finding your courage is a powerful and empowering thing. A lot of these kids have been so protected and cared for, that they were unaware of their own inner strengths. They've had to be incredibly strong just for the medical procedures they've gone through." (Dillon, Flexman, & Probeck, 1996, field notes).

By advocating students to try new things or make decisions, team members help students develop the feeling that they can do it themselves. Therapists along with other team members educate students and families about their disability and the precautions and prevention measures they need to consider. Therapists need to teach students how to care for their adaptive aids or other equipment, how to replace it, or how to instruct others in caring for their equipment or their self-care needs. A student with minimal motor movement can direct his own personal attendant or assistant on procedures for performing health care and self-care procedures. Physical therapists often work in conjunction with nurses to teach students about exercise, nutrition, skin integrity, and body mechanics or positioning. Occupational therapists often emphasize typical routines and habits to maintain health, and in conjunction with nurses and physicians, make recommendations about how to manipulate the container or schedule for medications, birth control, or bowel and bladder care. Both therapists assist students in learning how to talk to others about their disability and their needs. Educating students and their families about their legal rights and how to advocate for services is essential, and it is the responsibility of all team members.

As professionals with a medical background, therapists often understand the implications of doing a particular activity or task with students. For example, if

Jason has arthritis and takes a heavy load of classes in the morning, goes to work in the afternoon, and plays drums at night, there may be problems with his energy level and joint integrity. The occupational therapist may recommend a different class schedule with rest periods, suggest methods for Jason to save energy for later in the day (e.g., taking his shower the night before school; organizing items so they are closer to him or where they are used most frequently), and recommend ways to protect his joints (e.g., using adaptive devices such as built-up utensils, reachers, raised commode seats). The physical therapist may work with Jason on an exercise program through adaptive physical education or recommend a community activity such as swimming or walking to build up his strength and endurance for work. In both of these examples, the OT and PT may act as consultants to the student, family, physical education instructor, or teacher. They may see the student once or twice and then the student and others will carry out the program. By asking the student to take responsibility for his health and to advocate for changes, he can participate in a work-study program. Therapists and team members are helping students determine their own life outcomes.

Educating others as a consultant requires many complex skills from therapists, and the awareness to not play the "expert role" (Hanft & Place, 1996). The therapists' skills are only helpful if they understand the context in which the task occurs and who else is available to assist the student in learning a particular task. An example of this is illustrated in the case of Jose.

 Jose

Jose wanted to go with his friends to play putt-putt golf. With the family's permission, the PT had already taught Jose how to direct his friends in getting him and his wheelchair in and out of the car, and how to ascend and descend curbs. With the speech therapist, the OT preprogrammed Jose's augmentative communication device to say social amenities, ask his friends for help, or to do different activities at the golf course. Together, the therapists showed Jose's family and his friends how to use the device.

The OT problem solved with Jose about how he would manipulate his money, and a tax table was placed on the lapboard as an aid when making purchases. Velcro helped to hold a simple folding change purse (with no snaps or zippers) to his lapboard. A velcro strap was placed on his lapboard so that Jose could carry his golf club, and the OT made Jose a splint to help hold his golf club in this hand. By giving Jose some options, therapists helped Jose participate in a leisure activity with his friends and advocate for his own needs during this activity.

Assist in Interpersonal and Social Skill Development

Occupational therapists use group activities for students to develop interests, socialize, gain self-esteem, assume responsibilities, and hopefully develop friendships with peers with and without disabilities. By analyzing the social and cultural context of a classroom or job site, the OT may help engineer a change in the environment that places students in proximity to each other or that requires them to share or help each other in a task. Building friendships and natural supports within environments is essential, because most people are interdependent and usually have an intrinsic urge to connect with others. One therapist discusses this need to have friends:

> A lot of these kids don't have friends. They don't know how to handle friends. They've spent the better part of their leisure time working with adults on what is wrong with them. Thus, they don't know what their interests are; they don't have social skills. The kids are so used to relating to adults that they don't know what to do to socialize which is the normal developmental expectation for this age. (Dillon, Flexman, & Probeck, 1996).

Occupational therapists work with teachers, psychologists, and families to help determine the supports students need to socialize with their peers and fellow workers. School psychologists may help develop self-management programs for students, and OTs assist in identifying the students' interests and responses to environmental input. Therapists may work with teachers on group projects or activities that promote interaction with peers. Through leisure activities or community outings, students are given the opportunity to use interpersonal skills to control anger, problem solve, make decisions, manage their time, and employ relaxation techniques or strategies for stressful situations. Parents Jeff and Cindy Strully (1993) reiterated the desperate need for students to develop interpersonal skills and friendships when they said, "It is friendship that will ultimately mean life or death for our daughter. It is her and our only hope for a desirable future and protection from victimization" (p. 223).

Occupational therapists have a good understanding of behavior, psychosocial needs, and leisure pursuits. Therapists work with students, families, therapeutic recreation personnel, teachers, and social workers to identify possible leisure activities that can be linked with social opportunities. When teams are familiar with available leisure activities, community resources, and possible adaptations, interagency service agreements to provide transportation funds, specialized equipment, or personal assistance may be negotiated.

Overlapping Roles of Occupational and Physical Therapists with Other Team Members

Roles for therapists overlap in many areas with other professionals when providing transition services. If therapy is needed, it often is determined by the student's needs, the experience and knowledge level of the therapist and other team members, and the administrative structure of the school or team (Giangreco, 1996). Assessment methods, family instruction, person-centered planning activities, and assistive technology services are often shared by team members. Behavior, augmentative communication or language, functional positioning, mobility, self-care, work, and home management tasks often require a team effort to mutually develop strategies that are successful across a variety of settings (AOTA, 1997). As teams work together, often there is a blending of roles based on the team members' knowledge, interests, and skills.

Existing Challenges for Therapists

A number of barriers to therapists' participating in the transition process for students have been suggested. Some of these include limited training and experience in school-based practice and transition issues, therapist attitudes toward serving older students with disabilities, limited staff resources, and administrator attitudes toward the need for therapy services in the transition process (Inge, 1995; Rainforth, York, & Macdonald, 1992). This section will specifically address a number of these challenges for therapists. A detailed listing of the barriers for therapists working in school transition programs can be found in Table 5.5.

Lack of Understanding of Best Practices in Education and Transition Programs

When working in the school setting, therapists need to be aware of best educational practices for students with disabilities. Some of these best practices are

1. Inclusion of students within the regular classrooms whenever possible;
2. Development of an age-appropriate, community-referenced, and functional curriculum;
3. Community-based training;
4. Systematic instruction;
5. Integrated delivery of related service; and
6. Collaborative teamwork.

Table 5.5

Barriers for Therapists Working in School Transition Programs

Lack of Understanding of Best Practices in Education and Transition Programs
- Inclusion
- Age-appropriate, community-referenced, and functional curriculum
- Community-based training
- Systematic instruction
- Integrated delivery of related service
- Collaborative teamwork
- Student involvement

Lack of Education in the Role of the Therapist in Transition Services
- Focus on therapeutic interventions for students 13 years of age or younger
- Lack of knowledge related to programming for transition age youth
- Limited preservice and inservice training on transition issues
- Developmentally based evaluations
- Provision of consultative versus hands-on therapy and collaboration

Team Dynamics and Administrative Issues
- Team membership for contract therapists
- Development and documentation of team goals versus individual discipline
- Release time to consult and be part of the team
- Isolation which limits problem solving and peer review
- Rigid guidelines for scheduling services
- Large caseloads with multiple schools, teams, and expectations for therapy and transition
- Itinerant travel
- Lack of storage or space for equipment
- Limited to no funding for community training

In addition, preliminary research indicates that applying a combination of systematic instruction with therapeutic interventions results in skill acquisition for students with severe disabilities (Campbell, McInerney, & Cooper, 1984; Giangreco, 1986b). All of these best practices continue to be critical components of the educational program as students with moderate to severe disabilities reach transition age.

For a student of the age 14 or older, best practices in transition planning also include 1) functional, age-appropriate, and community-referenced curriculum, 2) community-based service delivery in natural environments, 3) individual transition planning using a team approach that is future-oriented, 4) collaborative interagency planning and service delivery, 5) integrated adult services within the community, 6) student and parental involvement, and 7) early planning (Everson, 1993; Grigal, Test, Beattie, & Wood, 1997; Kohler, 1993;

Wehman, 1992; Wehman, Moon et al., 1988). In addition, vocational education and training, paid work experiences (Kohler, 1992) and job placement (Wehman, 1993) are also considered to be best practices for transition services.

Unfortunately, some of the literature available to therapists does not present a best practice approach to service delivery. For instance, Mitchell, Rourk, and Schwarz (1989) described a collaborative "model" program that included occupational therapy for transition-age students with moderate mental retardation. However, services included "pre-vocational," nonfunctional tasks that were trained in a simulated workshop setting. In addition, students were required to move through a sequence of training levels prior to inclusion in the school's vocational program. This type of service provision is in direct conflict with the functional, community-based vocational programming approach that has proven successful for students with severe disabilities in achieving employment outcomes (Gaylord-Ross, 1989; Inge & Wehman, 1993; Renzaglia & Hutchins, 1988).

Snell and Browder (1986) indicated that one of the major unresolved research issues for school programs is the determination of the variables influencing the delivery of related services within the community-based instructional model. They further stated that research is needed on including students with severe disabilities who are also physically challenged within the community domain. The extent to which students receive integrated therapy in a community-based instructional model and ultimately obtain successful transition outcomes may be dependent, in part, upon the acceptance by occupational and physical therapists of best practices related to educational programming (Everson & Moon, 1987; Spencer, 1991). Effective preservice and continuing education programs must be developed that will enhance therapists' knowledge and attitudes regarding best educational practices and effective transition programming for students with severe disabilities because of the critical roles therapists can perform in the transition process.

An even greater problem may be that therapists are not providing services to some students with severe disabilities because they feel that the student is too severely disabled to benefit from occupational therapy services (Carr, 1989; Nesbit, 1993). Carr presented the criteria that occupational therapists have used in Louisiana to determine which students with disabilities should receive services. One of the criteria calls for determining whether a student's cognitive scores on standardized tests fall below his or her motor scores. If this is the case, the student is not referred for occupational therapy, because the student would be considered too severely disabled to use the skills learned during therapy in daily activities. Clearly, if this criterion is applied to most students with severe disabilities, it would exclude them from vocational training and employment as a postschool transition outcome.

Fortunately, some therapists are beginning to understand and use best practices in transition programming. Brollier, Shepherd, Becker, and MacDonald (1994) used data triangulation to conduct a qualitative study on transition and occupational therapy in a large suburban Maryland school district. Observations, interviews, and document reviews compared the best practice components identified in the literature to those practices used within this school system. The study found that as students became older (around 4th or 5th grade), the therapy approach changed from 1) standardized evaluations to ecological assessments, 2) developmental tasks to functional, real-life tasks, 3) direct to indirect and consultative service delivery, and 4) academic-based to community-based instruction. Three areas were identified as essential for occupational therapists to address for successful transition programming: self advocacy, independence in toileting, and the ability to access transportation services.

Lack of Education of the Role of the Therapist in Transition Services

As discussed earlier, very few articles have been published on the roles of therapists in the transition process (Brollier, Shepherd, & Markley, 1994). Although occupational therapists could play a significant role in transition planning, many continue to focus primarily on children with developmental disabilities (DuBois, 1993; Inge, 1995; Neistadt, 1987; Warren, 1986). While literature in the special education field for students with severe disabilities focuses on functional, age-appropriate programming (Brown, Branston et al., 1979; Brown, Branston-McLean et al., 1979; Brown et al., 1983; Brown et al., 1991), many therapists continue to adhere to a developmental approach emphasizing prereadiness skills and simulations, while underemphasizing performance in real-life activities (Brollier, Shepherd, & Markley, 1994).

Spencer (1991) compiled a set of educational materials to describe the role of occupational therapists in the transition process. Intended as a training tool for university programs in occupational therapy, the monograph presents a comprehensive functional approach consistent with the best practices in the special education literature. In addition, Spencer and Sample (1993) developed a module in transition planning and occupational therapy service delivery for AOTA's self-study series in school-based practice. Included are case study examples that demonstrate how the occupational therapist can be involved in vocational activities by adapting curriculum, providing adaptive equipment, consulting with teachers, and consulting with community work sites where students with severe disabilities can gain actual work experience.

Spencer (1991) contrasted the traditional concept of occupational therapy and transition planning. The important differences that she outlined include three major issues that seem applicable to PTs as well. First, therapists traditionally have emphasized the identification of problems and ways to fix the problem through short- and long-term goals. The desired outcome is discharge from therapy. This approach is typical of a medical model orientation, where the therapist attempts to identify the cause of problems in order to develop therapeutic interventions. In contrast, transition planning is concerned with student *outcomes* following school. The planning process spans many years, goals may change, ongoing assessment is required, and "problems" are identified as areas that need support rather than as student deficits. Support is provided through hands-on assistance, links with community resources, adaptations and modifications, and so forth. This change in treatment may be foreign to therapists and parents.

Second, in a traditional direct service model, the therapist plans, coordinates, and delivers therapy. Others such as the student, family, and other professionals may provide input, but ultimately decisions regarding therapy are determined by the occupational or physical therapist. This continues to be a topic of debate among many therapists, who feel that they should make the final decisions regarding therapy (Carr, 1989; Nesbit, 1993).

Inge (1995) found in her survey that 41.7% of the respondents believed that the OT or the OT supervisor should make the final decision on whether a student receives OT services in the school system, whereas 54.8% felt that it should be an IEP team decision. However, transition planning must involve the entire team in setting goals (Brollier, Shepherd, & Markley, 1994; Giangreco, 1996; Giangreco, Cloninger, & Iverson, 1993, 1997; Spencer, 1991). The student and the student's family are the central members of the team, and professionals are to advise, contribute, and support the overall team effort. This team effort is the core of the collaborative teaming approach that uses an integrated model of service delivery (Dunn, 1991b; Hanft & Place, 1996).

Finally, therapists traditionally provided services in one setting (e.g., the clinic, school, home). Visits may be made to other settings during therapy but are not of primary focus. Therapy services related to transition take place in all relevant environments as indicated by the transition team and the IEP. This concept of community-based instruction already has been discussed as a best educational practice for students of all ages with moderate to severe disabilities. However, when Inge (1995) asked occupational therapists if they provided services in vocational training sites, job sites, or other community settings, most responded that they did not. For instance, 65.2% replied that they had never provided OT services in a community setting (e.g., a restaurant, a student's home, a grocery store, a bank, etc.); 20% said they had provided OT services less than once a month; and 7.2% replied it had been provided about once a month. Only 7.6% responded that they provided services in a community setting more than one time a month.

DuBois (1993) noted that the concepts central to transition programming may seem foreign to occupational therapists who practice in the school setting, because many have been primarily concerned with preschool or elementary age students. However, "the heavy emphasis on function may serve to bring many occupational therapists back to their philosophical roots" (p. 53). DuBois suggested the following points for occupational therapists to consider when defining their roles in the transition process. These points are applicable to physical therapists as well:

1. Coordinate and conduct highly functional assessments in a variety of environments.

2. Plan and deliver services to promote productive and meaningful adult functioning.

3. Adapt the school or nonschool environment to maximize student performance (p. 53).

More specifically, DuBois stated that therapists who serve adolescents with disabilities must 1) emphasize collaboration, 2) share responsibility for students' goal attainment, 3) use respectful language, eliminating therapy jargon, and 4) emphasize team-generated goals and not individual therapy goals.

Team Dynamics and Integrating Related Services Within the Educational Program

Students with moderate to severe disabilities have a variety of needs that cannot be met by any one professional (Giangreco, 1996; Orelove & Sobsey, 1996). Consequently, a great deal of the literature on designing and implementing programs for students with disabilities focuses on the provision of related services within the educational program (Campbell, 1989a, 1989b; Dunn, 1991a; Orelove & Sobsey, 1996; Rainforth & York, 1987, 1991; Rainforth, York, & Macdonald, 1992; York, Rainforth, & Dunn, 1990; York, Rainforth, & Giangreco, 1990). The strategies for incorporating related services personnel into the educational program have been referred to as the transdisciplinary model, integrated therapy, and collaborative teamwork.

One of the first articles to discuss integrated therapy services (Sternat, Messina, Nietupski, Lyon, & Brown, 1977) based an argument for integrated therapy model on four assumptions: 1) assessment of motor abilities can be best completed in natural environments; 2) clusters of developmental motor skills should be taught through functional activities; 3) therapy must be longitudinal and contextual to be successful; and 4) skills are useful only if they are taught and verified in the environments in which they naturally occur. These assumptions are consistent with the best practices already discussed for educational programming (Brown et al., 1976; Brown, Branston-McLean et al., 1979).

Transdisciplinary Programming

The transdisciplinary teamwork approach emerged based on the understanding that the multiple needs of students with disabilities are interrelated. In order to understand the varied influences on function, team members must share information and skills and assume some of the responsibilities of other team members to deliver services across traditional disciplinary boundaries.

Asselin, Hanley-Maxwell, and Szymanski (1992) suggested that professionals in the school system and community must provide services using a transdisciplinary model for successful transition from school to employment outcomes. The transdisciplinary model consists of a team of individuals from various disciplines, including the teacher, related services personnel (e.g., occupational therapist, physical therapist, speech therapist), and family members. The team works together to evaluate the student's capabilities and needs and designs the student's IEP/ITP as the student nears the time for transition from school to adult services. Implementation of the IEP/ITP requires team members to assume some of the responsibilities of other team members and to deliver services across traditional disciplinary boundaries through consultation. Everson and Moon (1987) also suggested that the use of the transdisciplinary approach is critical during transition planning. They stated that without the appropriate related services, many students with severe disabilities would be unprepared for employment or independent living after graduation.

Transdisciplinary teamwork involves sharing general information, sharing informational skills, and sharing performance competencies (Lyon & Lyon, 1980). Sharing general information requires team members to communicate knowledge about basic procedures or practices. Sharing informational skills involves teaching others to make judgments or decisions such as determining whether a student is correctly positioned in a wheelchair. Sharing performance competencies refers to actually teaching another team member to perform a skill such as training a teacher to implement oral motor procedures for a student during mealtime.

The sharing of performance competencies is often cited as a criticism of the transdisciplinary model by therapists (Orelove & Sobsey, 1996; Rainforth et al., 1992). Some professionals would state that only therapists are qualified to provide related service intervention due to their highly specialized skills and training (Giangreco, 1990). They may agree that it makes sense to deliver intervention during functional activities, yet still contend that therapy should only be delivered by a qualified therapist (Rainforth et al., 1992).

Rainforth et al. (1992) identified two major problems that occur when therapy is delivered only by therapists. First, the therapist assumes that he or she will always be available to teach skills within functional contexts, although this would be impossible throughout a student's day. Second, the therapist assumes that a student's programming needs can be addressed in isolation (e.g., sensorimotor skills taught in isolation from communication). This is simply not true for most students with disabilities.

Service Delivery Models for Related Services

Application of the transdisciplinary model advocates teaching therapy techniques to a variety of professionals (Giangreco, 1986a, 1986b; Orelove & Sobsey, 1996). Therapists release parts of their roles to other team members to allow students to receive frequent and ongoing intervention within educational contexts in absence of the therapist (Rainforth et al., 1992). This concept is called integrated therapy or integrated programming (Campbell, 1987a; Giangreco et al., 1989; Rainforth et al., 1992). Campbell (1987a) defined integrated programming in the following way:

> All [motor] skills must be incorporated into functional curricular domains, rather than trained in isolation . . . from the environmental context in which those skills will be used. Incorporation of essential skills into functional content areas, embedded in activities that are carried out in a variety of environments, provides the context for teaching functional movement skills. (p. 185)

This role release concept is central to the transdisciplinary model and allows students to receive intervention during naturally occurring times of the day. For example, if an OT is working on dressing skills, she works with the student during the times the activity usually occurs (e.g., getting a coat on and off at beginning or end of the day). Since both the OT and the PT are involved in mobility skills, it may be more efficient to have only one therapist involved with some students. At this point, therapists may consult together to assess and design therapy, but only one therapist assumes primary responsibility for assisting the student with movement needs (York, Rainforth, & Giangreco, 1990). Consultation between the occupational and physical therapist, however, needs to continue by scheduling regular meetings (York, Rainforth, & Giangreco, 1990). Later, therapists may instruct the teachers on programming and only see the student on a need basis.

AOTA (1997) has defined a flexible continuum of service delivery to provide services to students with disabilities and no longer supports identifying service delivery methods as mainly direct, monitoring, or consultation on the

IEP/ITP. In reality, therapists often use a variety of service delivery models throughout the year to meet the individual needs of students. The therapist may complete the evaluation, develop the intervention plan to enhance IEP/ITP goals, and provide hands-on intervention services, or the therapist may instruct others to carry out identified procedures as part of the student's daily routine (AOTA, 1997). If teachers or aides are providing many of the services, the IEP must clearly document that this is not an OT service (AOTA, 1997). If an occupational therapy aide is being used to provide supervised, carefully selected activities, the therapist remains responsible for the outcomes of the intervention and must ensure that the individual implementing the procedures can demonstrate them correctly and without cues (AOTA, 1997; Dunn, 1991a; Dunn & Campbell, 1991).

Therapists often act as consultants to school systems, professionals, or students. Consultation is defined by AOTA (1997) as the "sharing of expert knowledge by one team member with another or other team members" and "reflects the collegial nature of the team" (p. 96) to help students and systems achieve goals and objectives. Therapists are using their knowledge to enable another person or the team to develop programs or solve issues. The responsibility for the outcomes rests with the person or team who sought the consultation (Dunn, 1991a, 1991b; Dunn & Campbell, 1991).

Direct or hands-on therapy may still be included within an integrated service model if the goals and objectives are jointly developed and agreed upon by a student's educational team and are part of the educational plan. This therapy is chosen when the student's needs can be met only through specialized therapeutic interventions that cannot be safely provided by others (Dunn, 1991a). Examples of this might be sensory or neurodevelopmental treatment procedures that elicit autonomic nervous system response to help a student perform activities of daily living (e.g., feeding) or participate in a student role. It also may be inappropriate to provide treatment within the classroom (e.g., working on motor skills while in an algebra class) (Effgen, 1994). If therapists choose to deliver isolated services, they must provide justification for these segregated, isolated practices (Dunn, 1991a; Dunn & Campbell, 1991). Dunn and Campbell further state that therapy must take place within natural environments and be incorporated into students' routines as the usual practice rather than the exception. The following therapist agrees with this concept:

> I work with students in the classroom because they need to focus on being in the class because that is their role. Not being pulled out to work on design copying and parquetry blocks. They need to learn how to compensate, take notes, and learn skills that will help them educationally. This is the point of their being in school . . . to acquire skills that will help them educationally,

not to do therapy per se. Isolated therapy doesn't generalize in my experience. (Dillon, Flexman, & Probeck, 1996, field notes)

Collaborative Teamwork

Using a transdisciplinary model, related service personnel and educators function in teams and share the responsibilities for assessment, the development of group instructional goals, and the implementation of instruction and therapy through an integrated model of service delivery (Giangreco et al., 1993; Giangreco, Cloninger, & Iverson, 1997; Orelove & Sobsey, 1996). Several authors have combined the concepts of transdisciplinary programming and the integrated therapy approach and used the terms *collaborative teamwork* (Giangreco, 1996; Rainforth et al., 1992) or *integrated team programming* (Campbell, 1987a, 1987b) to define how teams should function when providing services to students with severe disabilities. Rainforth et al. view transdisciplinary services and integrated therapy as complementary components of the educational program. In other words, transdisciplinary denotes the role release of information and skills among team members that enables them to implement an integrated approach to service provision.

York, Rainforth, and Giangreco (1990) refer to the role release component of the integrated therapy model as *role expansion*. Effective collaborative teamwork requires members to expand their roles rather than relinquish them as is implied with the word *release*. In this process, team members become both teachers and learners by exchanging information and skills in order to develop team intervention programs that can be implemented throughout a student's school day.

If team members agree that the overall goal of instruction is to improve a student's performance in specific natural environments, then they can function collaboratively to develop one set of instructional objectives (Rainforth & York, 1987). In essence, team members function as equals using a consensus decision-making process to plan and implement an integrated educational program for students with disabilities (Dunn & Campbell, 1991; Rainforth et al., 1992). Team assessment of students results in the identification of targeted areas for programming, and integrated methodologies are designed that assist a student to acquire agreed upon functional skills (Campbell, 1987b; Giangreco, 1996; Giangreco et al., 1993).

Giangreco (1996) developed the Vermont Interdependent Services Team Approach (VISTA) to build collaborative teams with support personnel. Through a series of checklists and worksheets, team members set goals and priorities with students and their families. Giangreco suggests that the following criteria be used to determine if related services personnel are needed as part of the IEP/ITP:

1. If the service were not used, could the student participate in the IEP/ITP?

2. Is there any unnecessary or undesirable overlapping of services or are there any contradictions between services?

3. If the therapist is not directly involved, can the services be generalized across settings?

By answering these questions, teams decide on the types of services needed. If the answers to the first two questions are YES, then some services may not be needed. The frequency and amount of related services needed to meet IEP/ITP goals is also determined by the team by evaluating the answer to the third question. Using this approach, therapy objectives become *embedded* within functional activities, rather than listed as separate skills on a student's IEP (Campbell, 1987a, 1987b; Giangreco, 1986a, 1996). The collaborative team "owns" the problems as well as the solutions, and all members take credit for a student's skill acquisition (Dunn, 1991a). The outcomes of collaborative teamwork are that the students have increased opportunities to develop essential skills, and that professional decisions are more likely to be based on functional analyses of behaviors (Dunn, 1991a; Idol, Paolucci-Whitcomb, & Nevin, 1986).

Administrative Issues

Occupational Therapy

As previously stated, many therapists may not work in transition planning since elementary-age students seem to have priority for OT services (Inge, 1995). Additional insight into why therapists may not be serving transition-age youth were found from the comments written on the back of the therapist's questionnaires from the Inge survey. The therapists commented on 1) school policies that set priorities for OT services for students ages 13 or younger; 2) school administrators who did not value OTs' roles in transition; 3) school administrators who refused to expand OT services due to financial constraints; 4) parents who demanded OT services for elementary-age students but rarely for older students; 5) time and staff shortages; and 6) therapists who thought that special educators were addressing transition issues.

Lowman et al. (1997) identified numerous administrative factors that affected transition planning in their qualitative study of three pairs of teachers and occupational therapists. Therapists and teachers felt supported by administrators when they helped define laws and procedures related to transition, were approachable, and allowed teachers and therapists autonomy in developing transition programs. Teachers and therapists desired three changes in administrative support that were similar to comments made in Inge's study. They desired increased training in transition planning, increased funding for transition programs, and flexibility in determining the age of graduation for students in special education.

Lowman et al. (1997) also identified administrative factors that impeded communication between teachers and occupational therapists working in transition services. Some of these factors included (a) heavy caseloads where occupational therapists travel to numerous schools or are members of numerous teams, (b) lack of knowledge about the value of OT services by other professionals, and (c) differing opinions on the scope of transition services. One teacher explained the logistical problems of working with OTs:

> The OTs are in six to seven schools, and we have to share them with so many people. If you only have one student [at that school] it is hard because they are there for that one kid and it's [difficult] to get together. (p. 13)

Factors that assist in the communication between OTs and teachers include: (a) regularly scheduled meetings, (b) time to prepare for IEP/ITP meetings, (c) previous experiences in transition planning, (d) previous experiences working with the same therapist or teacher, and (e) role release for all professionals. Therapists expressed a concern about parents who disputed changes in occupational therapy service delivery (e.g., discontinue or change level of service from direct to consultative services). When these disputes occur, administrators often become part of the decision if occupational or physical therapy services will be provided. Finally, other barriers that may limit participation in collaborative transition planning include the following: lack of time to consult and be part of the team (Lowman et al., 1997); unfamiliarity with the development and documentation of team goals instead of individual goals (Shepherd et al., 1997); and change in service delivery to providing consultative versus direct therapy in the community (Inge, 1995).

Becoming part of a team is difficult if therapists have huge caseloads or if contract therapists are being used to provide services. When contract therapists provide services to public schools, they usually are reimbursed for direct services only and not for time spent in collaboration with other education personnel (Case-Smith & Cable, 1996). If therapists are spending much of their time traveling between schools, they may be unable to attend meetings or community outings. An occupational therapist responded to Inge's (1995) survey:

> I feel that being able, time-wise, to evaluate transition needs in the home, community, and at work site would be very valuable. However, the large

caseload does not allow for this nor do finances in arranging for community trips. (p. 208).

Physical Therapy

It is quite likely that physical therapists may identify the same barriers to serving transition-age youth as the studies by occupational therapists (Inge, 1995; Lowman et al., 1997; Shepherd et al., 1997). In a study by Effgen and Klepper (1994), physical therapists identified areas of discontent for working in educational systems. Though this survey was not directed at providing transition services, many of the problems may affect the delivery of transition services. Frequently mentioned areas of discontent included (a) too much travel, (b) limited peer contact, (c) lack of time for meetings and administrative tasks, (d) limited continuing education opportunities, and (e) lack of an identified work space. After encountering these problems, therapists may decide to change employment, because many other employment opportunities are currently available (APTA, 1997b). Effgen (1994) suggests that school administrators spend time addressing these concerns so that more time is spent on retention of therapists rather than on recruitment, and, thus, therapist shortages can be reduced.

Scheduling-Related Services Using the Integrated Therapy Model

Therapy services need flexibility in scheduling to ensure that students receive services when most needed. Documenting the frequency of services as a certain number of minutes of therapy per month gives therapists this flexibility (AOTA, 1997). Initially, therapists may need to be in the classroom 20 to 30 minutes a week, but after the student progresses, it may be more appropriate to spend a block of therapy time to go on a community outing or work with two or three students within natural environments. Typically, the primary therapist and teacher meet briefly prior to seeing students to review program data and to determine with whom the therapist will work during the scheduled block. Team members keep track of which students are seen to ensure that students receive an appropriate proportion of related services. Block scheduling allows time for team members to meet to discuss details of instructional programs. This could occur before or after school weekly or biweekly, with longer meetings scheduled at least once each month for all team members (Rainforth & York, 1987).

Vision for the Future

Repetto and Correa (1996) described the ideal "seamless transition system" where students are moved smoothly from program to program, school to school, and from school to adult services or work. Students, families, teachers, therapists, and other team members worked collaboratively toward the goals and interests of the student and family. Services were integrated and coordinated. The curriculum was continuous and was updated with best practices. Communication between team members and administrators was excellent, and the IEP/ITP was a working document that professionals and families felt free to change as the need arose.

Functional, Integrated Therapy that Reflects Best Practice for Students with Disabilities

In addition to the ideal "seamless transition system" presented by Repetto and Correa (1996), an ideal vision for best practices for therapists is presented in this chapter. In this vision, therapists involved in all schools and community agencies understand the meaning of transition and their implicit role, and they are appropriately involved in the process. Therapist knowledge and skills are greatly enchanced through interdisciplinary educational opportunities and therapists receive administrative support for involvement in the transition process.

In this ideal vision for the future, occupational and physical therapists are appropriately involved in transition programming for youth with mild to severe disabilities. Therapists plan functional integrated therapy that reflects best practice principles for students with disabilities. These principles can be found in Table 5.6.

In this vision, therapists contribute to an educational program that facilitates learning and assists the student in assuming his or her role while meeting self-care, communication, and mobility needs (Bundy, 1997). Therapists have given up the "fix it" mentality and are identifying the supports that students require to assume adult roles in the community. They move in and out of a student's life when services and supports are needed. They provide a combination of hands-on and consultative services within integrated environments to students with mild to severe disabilities. Occupational therapists address the sensorimotor *and* psychosocial components that allow students to work, play, and take care of themselves within the community.

In this vision therapists are effective consultants who empower students, families, and other professionals to problem solve in a variety of situations and environments (Dunn, 1991b). Discontinuing therapy at any point in the educational process is positive, but it is not a lifelong sentence. It simply means that currently this student does not need therapy services to learn and participate within the current environment. Throughout their school career, when students' transition to new schools and new phases of adolescence, team members who understand the roles and benefits of therapy and therapy services are again consulted, and such services are begun only when needed. Therapists in schools,

Table 5.6
Best Practices for Related Service Provision: A Challenge to Therapists

- *Focus on student outcomes after graduation,* NOT on the problem.
- *Use functional, environmentally referenced assessments,* NOT standardized, isolated tests.
- *Identify needed supports and abilities,* NOT student deficits.
- *Collaborate, advise, and support team efforts and goals,* NOT separate therapy goals.
- *Be a participating team member,* NOT an "invited stranger."
- *Consult, collaboratively share ideas, and teach others.* Do NOT protect knowledge or "turf."
- *Use real life activities,* NOT simulated, prereadiness, or prevocational activities.
- *Provide services in all relevant environments,* NOT just the school environment or the therapy room.
- *Be creative in scheduling to provide more services.* Do NOT limit services due to inflexible schedules.
- *Use task analysis, compensatory strategies, and environmental modifications,* NOT just remedial techniques.
- *Provide integrated therapy within the classroom and community,* NOT isolated therapy.
- *Embed therapeutic activities in everyday routines,* NOT at isolated, unnatural times.
- *Read articles and research from other professions,* NOT just therapy publications.
- *Learn about the educational environment and all the written and unwritten rules.* Do NOT use a traditional medical model.
- *Advocate for therapy's role in transition.* Do NOT avoid this role due to caseload.
- *Seek further education in transition and vocational programming.* Do NOT rely on old practices and philosophy.
- *Collect data to determine successful strategies.* Do NOT assume someone has improved.

outpatient and rehabilitation facilities, work environments, and other community facilities understand the goal of transition programs and work together for the student. They are open to developing a variety of options for students after high school and are reading literature from many fields to provide state-of-the-art intervention for students. Students are self-advocates who understand the interagency networking and may suggest when therapy services are needed or not needed. They participate in jobs, community activities, and higher education, and are satisfied with their choices and decisions. Table 5.7 presents ways therapists can facilitate their role in transition.

Education of Occupational and Physical Therapists in the Transition Process

National Associations

School-based and adult rehabilitation and community therapists who are unaware of the legislation and best practices for transition services need to assume responsibility to improve their competence in this area. Occupational and physical therapy organizations, educators, special education administrators, rehabilitation agencies, and clinicians must collaboratively develop innovative programs to increase clinician competency in providing transition services for youth with disabilities.

AOTA and APTA need to take the initiative to develop more continuing education courses on consultation and transition services for therapists. These educational programs could be offered regionally or through the World Wide Web, and may be given collaboratively with university programs, occupational and physical therapy departments, and other special education agencies (e.g., Council for Exceptional Children, National Association of Special Education Directors) to promote interdisciplinary or transdisciplinary teaming between special education personnel and administrators.

AOTA and APTA may consider devoting one issue of their respective journals (i.e., *American Journal of Occupational Therapy, American Journal of Physical Therapy*) to discussing the research related to occupational and physical therapy and transition services for youth with disabilities. AOTA's *OT Practice* and *The School System Special Interest Section Newsletter* could publish more case studies and other practice tips related to exemplary transition programs. *Pediatric Physical Therapy and Occupational Therapy and Physical Therapy in Pediatrics* could be another place for professionals to publish articles related to transition. The content of articles submitted to OT and PT publications could also be rewritten and shared within educational and vocational publications to assist other professionals in learning the role of therapy in the transition process.

The World Wide Web offers a variety of ways for therapists and special educators to share their knowledge and questions about transition with each other. Many university programs are beginning to offer course work over the Web, statewide systems-change projects on transition have Internet addresses, the U.S. Department of Education has funded projects designed to disseminate information over the Internet to persons interested in transition programs, and many of the national associations have web sites. AOTA, APTA, and occupational and physical therapy university programs should begin to use these resources and to disseminate continuing education information to therapists working in the school systems.

AOTA's Commission on Practice and the APTA need to develop position papers on the role of therapy in transition and vocational programming for youth with disabilities. Similar to other position papers, these documents could encourage best practice by specifically outlining the knowledge and skills necessary to provide comprehensive, outcome-oriented transition programs. AOTA's School System Special Interest Section (SSSIS) may consider developing a network of therapists who are resources on transition services for school-based

Table 5.7
Practical Suggestions to Support the Therapist's Role in Transition.

1. **Education**

   a. Read articles and research from your profession and other professions.
      - Learn about new laws and your stated role.
      - Forward these articles or readings to administrators and other team members.
      - Use the internet; look at major transition centers and their links.
      - Ask parents about their resources.
   b. Consult, collaboratively share ideas, and teach and learn from others.
      - Take a course, read or get feedback from your students, parents, and peers about your consultative skills.
      - Do a self-assessment of your skills and develop strategies to improve skills.
   c. Keep a file about local, state, and national resources. When working with interagencies, ask for brochures and contact information. Ask families about what has been most helpful to them.
   d. Network with community therapists (e.g., rehabilitation, outpatient, technology centers) so you are aware of their services and they understand transition initiatives.
   e. Advocate for therapy's role in transition.
      - Develop a handout of examples of when and how you get involved in transition.
      - Educate teachers and administrators about your role.

2. **Collaboration with Administrators and Other Team Members**

   a. Brainstorm funding sources from parent groups, community groups, and grants.
   b. Develop guidelines for team meetings, communication techniques, and scheduling options.
      - Question if therapy needs to be involved or if other team members may be able to carry out plans (Giangreco, 1996).
      - Use block scheduling (e.g., 2 hours a month, instead of 30 minutes a week).
      - Develop a communication procedure between team members.
      - Reevaluate procedures periodically.
   c. Collect data to determine successful strategies.
   d. Develop a handout notebook for teachers with solutions for common problems encountered on the job or in the community (e.g., positioning principles; accessibility guidelines; transfer techniques; equipment maintenance or use; simple adaptations).
   e. Develop an activity notebook for yourself to remind you of activities and solutions that worked for past students.
   f. Develop an adaptation kit to carry with you when observing students in their natural environments (e.g., sticky back velcro, duct tape, stickers, magic markers, note cards, materials to enlarge or change the mechanical advantage of handles; foam; sewing kit; elastic; clear vinyl page holders).
   g. Elicit assistance from other school personnel, volunteers, or fellow students interested in working with people with disabilities
      - Provide inservices to groups inside and outside of the school.
      - Work with service organizations in the school.

(continues)

Table 5.7 *Continued*

- Ask for parent or grandparent volunteers.
- Co-develop a circle of friends (O'Brien & O'Brien, 1996) for your students approaching transition.
- Determine if peers within the school can get "credits" for working with you during their study halls.
- If you live near a college or university, ask if students need a service learning project or a fieldwork or clinical internship site.

g. Network with other therapists in your district, state, or nation to share ideas.
- E-mail or use chat rooms on the internet.
- Inservice each other.
- Visit sites.
- Consult special interest groups.

h. Share your successes and failures with your students, families, and colleagues.
i. Celebrate successes by special ceremonies or graduation.
- Have a sense of humor.
- Develop rituals.
- Have students share their successes with other students.

therapists. Continuing education programs on transition may be offered as part of the SSSIS continuing education programs at national, regional, and state conferences. In addition, continuing education on how to be an effective consultant may assist therapists in performing their roles in transition programs.

Schools of Higher Education

In higher education, occupational and physical therapy programs are challenged to present more information to students as the scope of practice increases. Even though this information is essential to practice, time is limited, and schools are invested in teaching entry-level therapists to become generalists (AOTA, 1991a). Therefore, in-depth coverage of best practices for transition and vocational services may be minimal unless a faculty member is particularly interested or vested in this subject. If transition services were mentioned within the educational standards for therapy programs, more entry-level therapists would be aware of their role with youth with disabilities. Courses such as Fieldwork I (e.g., directed observation and participation in school, community, and rehabilitation settings for a limited number of hours), Fieldwork II or Clinicals (8 to 12 weeks of daily participation in a setting), independent studies, or specialty practicums within programs related to transition may assist entry-level therapists in learning about best practices in transition.

Updated modules about transition, similar to the Colorado State University Program (Spencer, 1991), could be developed and distributed to occupational therapy and occupational therapy assistant programs in higher education. Universities could use these modules to teach entry-level students, and in collaboration with local therapists, they could develop a trainer model and offer consultation or continuing education programs to regional areas throughout their state.

Bundy (1997) and Hanft and Place (1996) advocate teaching therapists how to be effective consultants in the public schools. Higher education could offer entry-level and advanced graduate courses in school-based practice. This course of study could emphasize the therapist's role with youth with disabilities and how to provide consultative services. Content for these courses requires practical experiences related to how therapists interview, observe, teach, problem solve, and adapt to others (Bundy, 1997). Best practices in transition and vocational programs need to be highlighted with the research and independent study opportunities that are available. Therapists with expertise in transition could provide supervised training for students in a specialized practicum or could supervise fieldwork in school-based therapy. Bundy (1997) advocates that supervised fieldwork provides a variety of experiences and feedback to students, including hands-on intervention, indirect service, and consultation.

Education of Administrators and Special Education Personnel

Administrators in special education and rehabilitation are challenged to find the best way to utilize occupational and physical therapy services in their settings. Table 5.8 provides suggestions for administrators on how to use therapists effectively within transition services.

Environmentally-referenced, age-appropriate evaluations, collaborative team goals, team development, community-based instruction, and integrated related service delivery are all hallmarks of best practice in transition (Asselin, Hanley-Maxwell, & Szymanski, 1992; Giangreco et al., 1993; Rainforth et al., 1992; Spencer, 1991). Administrators need to be creative in finding time to allow therapists to be fully involved in the transition process. If traditional assessments and isolated treatment models are discouraged, and therapists are given the support to provide indirect, consultative services, then more teachers, parents, and students will benefit from the therapists' knowledge. Therapists need a variety of supports to work in educational environments and to be part of transition teams. The following are examples of the supports that could be given to therapists:

1. Assure therapy participation in collaborative transition teams when they are needed.

2. Provide creative and flexible scheduling to allow consultative service delivery with team involvement (Lowman et al., 1996; Rainforth et al., 1992).

Table 5.8
Suggestions to Help Administrators in Special Education and Rehabilitation Utilize Occupational and Physical Therapy in Transition Services

1. Expect and support the use of best practice from the literature.
   - environmentally-referenced, age-appropriate evaluations
   - collaborative team goals, team development
   - community-based instruction
   - integrated related service delivery

2. Update therapist job descriptions to use educationally relevant and integrated treatment that includes school, work, community-based, and home instruction.

3. Provide time and funding for interdisciplinary and transdisciplinary continuing education courses on transition.

4. Utilize existing resources and guidelines about therapy and transition services.

5. Encourage and support research and individual development plans for all therapists working in the schools.

6. Provide mentorship opportunities for new therapists.

7. Provide guidelines on how to develop and document team goals that are outcome-based.

8. Be creative and flexible in finding time to allow therapists to be fully involved in the transition process and the team.
   - Use block scheduling for treatment and team meetings (e.g., see child for 2 hours each month instead of 30 minutes every week).
   - Use variable scheduling within schools and during the week.
   - Negotiate team time for all therapists.
   - Use different "team configurations" so therapists are not working with 30 or 40 different teams.
   - Give consultation time, schedule meeting times, and develop a communication format for all teams (e.g., written notebook, communication log).

9. Fund community-based training and low- and high-technology adaptations.

10. If using contract therapists, provide the time for therapists to become a team member.
    - Use block scheduling
    - limit the number of teams the contract therapist is on
    - expect them to function as a full ITP member

3. Fund community-based training and low- and high-technology adaptations. (Lowman et al., 1997)

4. Provide time and funding for therapists to participate in interdisciplinary and transdisciplinary continuing education courses on transition. (Inge, 1995)

5. Encourage and support research and individual development plans for all therapists working in the schools.

6. Utilize existing resources and guidelines about therapy and transition services) (AOTA, 1997; APTA, 1990, 1997b; Inge, 1995; Spencer, 1991; Spencer & Sample, 1993).

7. Provide mentorship opportunities for new therapists learning about schools and the transition process (Bundy, 1997; Effgen, 1995).

8. Consider a different "team configuration" so therapists are not working with 30 or 40 different teams.

9. Provide guidelines on how to develop and document team goals that are outcome-based (Shepherd et al., 1997).

If administrators need to use contract therapists, they should provide the time for therapists to become team members. Consultation time, scheduled meeting times, and a communication format with fellow professionals are essential and need to be built into the billable hours. Block scheduling and limiting the number of teams the contract therapist is on will assist therapists in performing their jobs better. Contract therapists should be included in continuing education programs related to transition and should be provided with a job description that describes their role in educationally relevant, integrated treatment that includes transition services.

Final Thoughts

Occupational and physical therapists have much to offer students as they prepare for adult living. Occupational therapists can provide assistance in daily living, leisure, and vocational skills evaluation and programming. They also can provide expertise in assessing the environment and in identifying, designing, and fabricating assistive technology and compensatory strategies for independent living and work. Physical therapists can assist in maximizing the physical functioning of students so that they can fully participate in the various daily living, leisure, and vocational environments encountered in adult life. Moreover, physical therapists can assist in the identification of assistive technology needed for independent mobility in adult environments. However, as long as substantial numbers of students are not receiving the benefit of occupational and physical therapy, it seems unlikely that they will fully realize their transition goals.

References

American Occupational Therapy Association. (1991a). *Essentials and guidelines for an accredited educational program for the occupational therapist.* Rockville, MD: Author.

American Occupational Therapy Association. (1991b). Occupational therapy provision for children with learning disabilities and/or mild or moderate perceptual and motor deficits. *American Journal of Occupational Therapy, 45,* 1069–1074.

American Occupational Therapy Association. (1994). Uniform terminology for occupational therapy. *American Journal of Occupational Therapy, 48,* 1047–1054.

American Occupational Therapy Association. (1996). *Member data survey.* Bethesda, MD: Author.

American Occupational Therapy Association. (1997). *Occupational therapy services for children and youth under the Individuals with Disabilities Education Act.* Bethesda, MD: Author.

American Physical Therapy Association. (1990). *Physical therapy practice in educational environments: Policies and guidelines.* Alexandria, VA: Author.

American Physical Therapy Association. (1997a). *A guide to physical therapist practice, part I: A description of patient/client management.* Alexandria, VA: Author.

American Physical Therapy Association. (1997b). *A guide to physical therapist practice, part 2: Preferred practice patterns.* Alexandria, VA: Author.

American Physical Therapy Association. (1998). *Pediatrics: Minimum eligibility requirements for PT specialist certification* [Online]. URL: http://www.apta.org/spec_cert/98ped

Asselin, S. B., Hanley-Maxwell, C., & Szymanski, E. M. (1992). Transdisciplinary personnel preparation. In F. R. Rusch, L. Destefano, J. Chadsey-Rusch, L. A. Phelps, & E. M. Szymanski (Eds.), *Transition from school to adult life: Models, linkages, and policy* (pp. 265–283). Sycamore, IL: Sycamore.

Bradley, D. (1993). *Results of occupational and physical therapy surveys, 1993.* Richmond, VA: Virginia Department of Education.

Brollier, C., Shepherd, J., Becker, B., & MacDonald, H. (1994, December). Transitioning from school to adult life: A qualitative study. *School System Special Interest Section Newsletter, 1*(4), 1–4.

Brollier, C., Shepherd, J., & Markley, K. F. (1994). Transition from school to community living. *American Journal of Occupational Therapy, 48*(4), 346–354.

Brown, L., Branston, M. B., Hamre-Nietupski, S., Pumpian, I., Certo, N., & Gruenewald, L. (1979). A strategy for developing chronological-age-appropriate and functional curricular content for severely handicapped adolescents and young adults. *Journal of Special Education, 13*(1), 81–90.

Brown, L., Branston-McLean, M., Baumgart, D., Vincent, L., Falvey, M., & Schroeder, J. (1979). Utilizing the characteristics of current and subsequent least restrictive environments as factors in the development of curricular content for severely handicapped students. *AAESPH Review, 4*(4), 407–424.

Brown, L., Nisbet, J., Ford, A., Sweet, M., Shiraga, B., York, J., & Loomis, R. (1983). The critical need for nonschool instruction in educational programs for severely handicapped students. *The Journal of the Association for Persons with Severe Handicaps, 8*(3), 71–77.

Brown, L., Schwarz, P., Udvari-Solner, A., Kampschroer, E. F., Johnson, F., Jorgensen, J., & Gruenewald, L. (1991). How much time should students with severe intellectual disabilities spend in regular education classrooms and elsewhere? *Journal of the Association for Persons with Severe Handicaps, 16*(1), 39–47.

Bundy, A. C. (1993). Will I see you in September? A question of educational relevance. *American Journal of Occupational Therapy, 47*(9), 848–850.

Bundy, A. C. (1997). Preparing occupational therapy students to practice in schools. *School System Special Interest Section Newsletter, 4*(2), 1–2.

Campbell, P. H. (1987a). Integrated programming for students with multiple handicaps. In L. Goetz, D. Guess, & K. Stemel-Campbell (Eds.), *Innovative program design for individuals with dual sensory impairments* (pp. 159–188). Baltimore: Brookes.

Campbell, P. H. (1987b). The integrated programming team: An approach for coordinating professionals of various disciplines in programs for students with severe and multiple handicaps. *Journal of the Association for Persons with Severe Handicaps, 12*(2), 107–116.

Campbell, P. H. (1989a). Dysfunction in posture and movement in individuals with profound disabilities: Issues and practices. In F. Brown & D. H. Lehr (Eds.), *Persons with profound disabilities: Issues and practices* (pp. 163–189). Baltimore: Brookes.

Campbell, P. H. (1989b). Integration strategies for students with handicaps. In R. Gaylord-Ross (Ed.), *Integration strategies for students with handicaps* (pp. 53–76). Baltimore: Brookes.

Campbell, P. H., McInerney, W. F., & Cooper, M. A. (1984). Therapeutic programming for students with severe handicaps. *American Journal of Occupational Therapy, 38*(9), 594–602.

Carr, S. H. (1989). Louisiana's criteria of eligibility for occupational therapy services in the public school system. *American Journal of Occupational Therapy, 43*(8), 503–506.

Case-Smith, J., & Cable, J. (1996). Perceptions of occupational therapists regarding service delivery models in school-based practice. *Occupational Therapy Journal of Research, 16*(1), 23–44.

Colman, W. (1988). The evolution of occupational therapy in the public schools: The laws mandating practice. *American Journal of Occupational Therapy, 42*(11), 701–705.

DeFur, S., & Taymans, J. (1995). Competencies needed for transition specialists in vocational rehabilitation, vocational education, and special education. *Exceptional Children, 62*(1), 38–51.

Dillon, M., Flexman, C., & Probeck, E. (1996). *Examining the role of the occupational therapist and the educator in the transition planning process.* Unpublished research project, Virginia Commonwealth University, Richmond.

DuBois, S. A. (1993). Commentary on lesson 10. In C. B. Royeen (Ed.), *American occupational therapy association self study series: Classroom applications for school-based practice* (pp. 53–57). Rockville, MD: AOTA.

Dunn, W. (1991a). Integrated related services. In L. Meyer, C. Peck, & L. Brown (Eds.), *Critical issues in the lives of people with severe disabilities* (pp. 353–377). Baltimore: Brookes.

Dunn, W. (Ed.) (1991b). *Pediatric occupational therapy: Facilitating effective service provision.* Thorofare, NH: Slack.

Dunn, W., Brown, C., & McGuigan, A. (1994). The ecology of human performance: A framework for considering the effect of context. *American Journal of Occupational Therapy, 48,* 595–607.

Dunn, W., & Campbell, P. (1991). Designing pediatric service provision. In W. Dunn (Ed.), *Pediatric occupational therapy: Facilitating effective service provision* (pp. 140–159). Thorofare, NH: Slack.

Education for All Handicapped Children Act of 1975, 20 U.S.C. §1400 *et seq.*

Education of the Handicapped Act Amendments of 1983, 20 U.S.C. §1400 *et seq.*

Education of the Handicapped Act Amendments of 1986, 20 U.S.C. §1400 *et seq.*

Effgen, S. K. (1995). The educational environment. In S. K. Campbell (Ed.), *Physical therapy for children* (pp. 847–872). Philadelphia: Saunders.

Effgen, S. K., & Klepper, S. (1994). Survey of physical therapy practice in educational settings. *Pediatric Physical Therapy, 6,* 15–21.

Everson, J. M. (1993). *Youth with disabilities: Strategies for interagency transition programs.* Stoneham, MA: Butterworth-Heinemann.

Everson, J. M., & Moon, M. S. (1987). Transition services for young adults with severe disabilities: Defining professional and parental roles and responsibilities. *Journal of the Association for Persons with Severe Handicaps, 12*(2), 87–95.

Falvey, M. A. (1989). *Community-based curriculum: Instructional strategies for students with severe handicaps* (2nd ed.). Baltimore: Brookes.

Gaylord-Ross, R. (1989). Vocational integration for persons with handicaps. In R. Gaylord-Ross (Ed.), *Integration strategies for students with handicaps* (pp. 195–211). Baltimore: Brookes.

Getzel, E., & DeFur, S. (1997). Transition planning for students with significant disabilities: Implications for student centered planning. *Focus on Autism and Other Developmental Disabilities, 12*(1), 39–48.

Giangreco, M. F. (1986a). Delivery of therapeutic services in special education programs for learners with severe handicaps. *Physical and Occupational Therapy in Pediatrics, 6*(2), 5–15.

Giangreco, M. F. (1986b). Effects of integrated therapy: A pilot study. *Journal of the Association for Persons with Severe Handicaps. 11*(3), 205–208.

Giangreco, M. F. (1990). Making related services decisions for students with severe disabilities: Roles, criteria, and authority. *Journal of the Association for Persons with Severe Handicaps, 15*(1), 22–31.

Giangreco, M. F. (1996). *Vermont interdependent service team approach: A guide to coordinating educational support services.* Baltimore: Brookes.

Giangreco, M. F., Cloninger, C. J., & Iverson, V. (1993). *Choosing options and accommodations for children: A guide to planning inclusive education.* Baltimore: Brookes.

Giangreco, M. F., Cloninger, C. J., & Iverson, V. (1997). *Choosing options and accommodations for children: A guide to planning inclusive education* (2nd ed). Baltimore: Brookes.

Giangreco, M., York, R., & Rainforth, B. (1989). Providing related services to learners with severe handicaps in educational settings: Pursuing the least restrictive option. *Pediatric Physical Therapy, 1*(2), 55–63.

Grigal, M., Test, D.W., Beattie, J., & Wood, W. M. (1997). An evaluation of transition components of individualized education programs. *Exceptional Children, 63*(3), 357–372.

Hanft, B. E., & Place, P. A. (1996). *The consulting therapist: A guide for OT's and PT's in school.* San Antonio, TX: Therapy Skill Builders.

Idol, L., Paolucci-Whitcomb, P., & Nevin, A. (1986). *Collaborative consultation.* Rockville, MD: Aspen.

Individuals with Disabilities Education Act of 1990, 20 U.S.C. §1400 *et seq.*

Individuals with Disabilities Education Act Amendments of 1997, 20 U.S.C. §1400 *et seq.*

Inge, K. J. (1995). *A national survey of occupational therapists in the public schools: An assessment of current practice, attitudes, and training needs regarding the transition process for students with disabilities.* Unpublished doctoral dissertation, Virginia Commonwealth University, Richmond.

Inge, K. J., & Shepherd, J. (1995). Assistive technology application and strategies for school system personnel. In K. Flippo, K. J. Inge, & J. M. Barcus (Eds.), *Assistive technology: A resource for school, work, and community* (pp. 133–166). Baltimore: Brookes.

Inge, K. J., & Wehman, P. (Eds.) (1993). *Designing community-based vocational programs for students with severe disabilities.* Richmond, VA: Virginia Commonwealth University, Rehabilitation Research and Training Center on Supported Employment.

Kohler, P. D. (1993). Best practices in transition substantiated or implied? *Career Development for Exceptional Individuals, 16*, 107–121.

Lowman, D. K., Shepherd, J., Dillon, M., Flexman, C., & Probeck, E. (1997). *Examining the role of the occupational therapist and the educator in the transition planning process.* Unpublished manuscript in preparation. Virginia Commonwealth University, Richmond.

Lyon, S., & Lyon, G. (1980). Team functioning and staff development: A role release approach to providing integrated educational services for severely handicapped students. *Journal of the Association of the Severely Handicapped, 5*(3), 250–263.

Mitchell, M., Rourk, J. D., & Schwarz, J. (1989). A team approach to vocational services. *American Journal of Occupational Therapy, 43*(6), 378–383.

Moon, M. S., & Inge, K. J. (1993). Vocational preparation and transition. In M. E. Snell (Ed.), *Instruction of students with severe disabilities* (4th ed.) (pp. 556–587). New York: Macmillan.

National Board for Certification of Occupational Therapy. (1997). *National study of occupational therapy practice.* Gaithersburg, MD: Author.

Neistadt, M. E. (1987). An occupational therapy program for adults with developmental disabilities. *American Journal of Occupational Therapy, 41*(7), 433–438.

Nesbit, S. G. (1993). Direct occupational therapy in the school system: When should we terminate? *American Journal of Occupational Therapy, 47*(9), 845–847.

O'Brien, J., & O'Brien, C. (1996). *Members of each other: Building community in company with people with developmental disabilities.* Toronto: Inclusion Press.

Orelove, F. P., & Sobsey, D. (1996). *Educating children with multiple disabilities: A transdisciplinary approach* (3rd ed.). Baltimore: Brookes.

Rainforth, B., & York, J. (1987). Integrating related services in community instruction. *Journal of the Association for Persons with Severe Handicaps, 12*(3), 190–198.

Rainforth, B., & York, J. (1991). Handling and positioning. In F. P. Orelove & D. Sobsey, *Educating children with multiple disabilities: A transdisciplinary approach* (2nd ed.) (pp. 79–117). Baltimore: Brookes.

Rainforth, B., York, J., & Macdonald, C. (1992). *Collaborative teams for students with severe disabilities: Integrating therapy and educational services.* Baltimore: Brookes.

Reed, K. (1993). The beginnings of occupational therapy. In H. L. Hopkins & H. D. Smith (Eds.), *Willard and Spackman's occupational therapy* (8th ed.) (pp. 26–43). Philadelphia: Lippincott.

Rehabilitation Act of 1973, 29 U.S.C. §701 *et seq.*

Renzaglia, A., & Hutchins, M. (1988). A community referenced approach to preparing persons with disabilities for employment. In P. Wehman & M. S. Moon (Eds.), *Vocational rehabilitation and supported employment* (pp. 91–112). Baltimore: Brookes.

Renzaglia, A., Hutchins, M., Koterba-Buss, L., & Strauss, M. (1992). *Action inventory.* Unpublished manuscript, University of Illinois at Urbana–Champaign.

Repetto, J. B., & Correa, V. I. (1996). Expanding views on transition. *Exceptional Children, 62*(6), 51–563.

Royeen, C. B. (1986). Evaluation of school-based occupational therapy programs: Need, strategy, and dissemination. *American Journal of Occupational Therapy, 40*(12), 811–813.

Royeen, C. B. (1988). Occupational therapy in the schools. *American Journal of Occupational Therapy, 42*(11), 697–698.

Sample, P., Spencer, K., & Bean, G. (1990). *Transition planning: Creating a positive future for students with disabilities.* Fort Collins: Office of Transition Services, Department of Occupational Therapy, Colorado State University.

Shepherd, J., Lowman, D., Teitleman, J., Gross, S., Halizak-Eddy, K., & Susong, J. (1997). *Transition: Characteristics, outcomes, and the role of occupational therapist.* Article in preparation for publication from master's research project, Virginia Commonwealth University, Richmond.

Shepherd, J., Procter, S., & Coley, I. (1996). Self-care and adaptations for independent living. In J. Case-Smith, J. A. Allen, & P. Pratt (Eds.), *Occupational therapy for children* (3rd ed.) (pp. 461–503). Baltimore: Mosby.

Snell, M. E., & Browder, D. M. (1986). Community-referenced instruction: Research and issues. *Journal of the Association for Persons with Severe Handicaps, 11*(1), 1–11.

Sowers, J. A., & Powers, L. (1991). *Vocational preparation and employment of students with physical and multiple disabilities.* Baltimore: Brookes.

Spencer, K. C. (1991). *From school to adult life: The role of occupational therapy in the transition process.* Fort Collins, CO: Department of Occupational Therapy, Colorado State University.

Spencer, K. C. (1996). Transition services: From school to adult life. In J. Case-Smith, A. Allen, & P. Pratt (Eds.), *Occupational therapy for children* (3rd ed.) (pp. 808–822). Baltimore: Mosby.

Spencer, K. C., & Sample, P. L. (1993). Classroom applications for school-based practice: Transition planning and services. In C.B. Royeen (Ed.), *American occupational therapy association self study series: Classroom applications for school-based practice* (pp. 6–49). Rockville, MD: AOTA.

Sternat, J., Messina, R., Nietupski, J., Lyon, S., & Brown, L. (1977). Occupational and physical therapy services for severely handicapped students: Toward a naturalized public school service delivery model. In E. Sontag, J. Smith, & N. Certo (Eds.), *Educational programming for the severely and profoundly handicapped* (pp. 263–278). Reston, VA: Council for Exceptional Children.

Struck, M. (1996). Assistive technology in the schools. In J. Hammel (Ed.), *Self-pace clinical course: Technology and occupational therapy: A link to function, module 11.* Bethesda, MD: AOTA

Strully, J., & Strully, C. (1993). That which binds us: Friendships as a safe harbor in a storm. In A. Novak Amado (Ed.), *Friendships and community: Connections between persons with and without developmental disabilities* (pp. 213–225). Baltimore: Brookes.

Szymanski, E. M. (1994). Transition: Life-span and life-space considerations for empowerment. *Exceptional Children, 60*(5), 402–410.

Warren, L. (1986). Nationally speaking: Helping the developmentally disabled adult. *American Journal of Occupational Therapy, 40* (4), 227–229.

Wehman, P. (1992). *Life beyond the classroom: Transition strategies for young people with disabilities.* Baltimore: Brookes.

Wehman, P., Moon, M. S., Everson, J. M., Wood, W., & Barcus, J. M. (1988). *Transition from school to work: New challenges for youth with severe disabilities.* Baltimore: Brookes.

Wehman, P., Wood, W., Everson, J. M., Goodwyn, R., & Conley, S. (1988). *Vocational education for multihandicapped youth with cerebral palsy.* Baltimore: Brookes.

York, J., & Rainforth, B. (1991). Developing instructional adaptations. In F.P. Orelove & D. Sobsey, *Educating children with multiple disabilities: A transdisciplinary approach* (2nd ed.) (pp. 259–295). Baltimore: Brookes.

York, J., Rainforth, B., & Dunn, W. (1990). Training needs of physical and occupational therapists who provide services to children and youth with severe disabilities. In A.P. Kaiser & C.M. McWhorter (Eds.), *Preparing personnel to work with persons with severe disabilities* (pp. 153–180). Baltimore: Brookes.

York, J., Rainforth, B., & Giangreco, M.F. (1990). Transdisciplinary teamwork and integrated therapy: Clarifying the misconceptions. *Pediatric Physical Therapy, 2*(2), 73–79.

CHAPTER

School Nursing

Ann W. Cox

Kathleen J. Sawin

Introduction

This chapter describes the potential role of the school nurse as a transition team member for students with disabilities served through the Individuals with Disabilities Education Act (IDEA). Although health is recognized throughout the educational literature on transition planning (Armstrong, Carr, Houghton, Belanish, & Mascia, 1995; Johnson, 1996; Wehman, 1992), the literature does not identify a systematic role for the school nurse. However, because the role of the school nurse in the IEP and Individual Healthcare Plan (IHP) are articulated, and because the ITP is an extension of the IEP process, it is clear that there is a continued need for the school nurse in IEP/ITP planning. In addition, various roles are delineated in the literature for school nurses working with medically fragile students, students with special health care needs, students with disabilities, and students with chronic conditions. Indeed, one could argue that the nurse's role in the ITP is a critical and practical role that focuses on communication, with the transition also being planned by the health care system.

In order to explore the school nurse's role in the ITP, sections of this chapter have been developed to (a) introduce the reader to the subspecialty of school nursing (history, contemporary role, professional orientation, standards, and roles and responsibilities related to youth with disabilities in the school setting); (b) present the transition literature in nursing, health transition programs for youth with chronic conditions, and its application to the school-based transition process; and (c) espouse the systematic inclusion of a "health component" to the school-based transition plan with active involvement of the school nurse or other community health providers. It is our belief that health planning through involvement or consultation during the transition process will positively affect the attainment of the desired outcome of community integration.

In this chapter, the designation *youth with chronic conditions* is preferred to the designation *youth with disabilities* because it is more inclusive of the mix of students regularly served by the school nurse. The designation *youth with chronic conditions* is intended to be inclusive of students with disabilities who may or may not have other chronic health conditions and who are between the ages of 14 and 21. In addition, youth with chronic conditions typically require individual plans (IEPs, IHPs) to support their full participation in the school and ITPs to assist with preparation and planning related to movement to more adult-oriented activities. Finally, we will most consistently use the term *youth* instead of *adolescent* or *teen* to refer to the population for whom transition planning is provided.

Overview of School Nursing

Brief History of School Nursing

Five major themes can be identified from a review of the history of school health or nursing. Each has had an influence on the practice of school nursing today. First, there is a long history of school nursing that was an outgrowth of the community health movement. At the turn of the century, the first school nurse was assigned to four New York city schools with the greatest attendance problems, which were due, in part, to exclusion for communicable disease and lack of follow-up. Through intensive education programs directed toward school officials, parents, and children and home follow-up, the exclusion rate was reduced from 10,567 to 1,101 in one year (Wold, 1981).

Second, over the ensuing decades, the changing nature of health problems presented in the school has shaped the picture of school nursing. From the beginning, a focus on infectious disease trends yielded an emphasis on preventive services, such as health education or health guidance activities. More recently, changing demographics and new morbidities of children, such as depression, chemical dependency, or adolescent pregnancy, have yielded a different vision of school nursing (Wold, 1981). The most recent challenge is the increase of students with chronic illness and disabilities.

Third, school systems have also experienced changing political priorities and fiscal constraints. These constraints have led some school districts to change their pattern of employing health personnel. Some schools now depend more on unlicensed assistive personnel, with a general reduction of dependence on professional personnel. At the same time, other health policy specialists promoted the delivery of primary care in the school setting, delivered principally by prepared school nurse practitioners with master's degrees. The creation of this new professional was driven, in part, by the unaddressed health needs of many students (Igoe, 1975). Also, advocates for health services for students identified a unique environment from which to provide primary health care services: the school-based or school-linked clinic.

Fourth, legislative action also had an impact on the development of school nursing. The enactment of the Education for All Handicapped Children Act in 1975 (EHA) (P.L. 94-142) and its subsequent reauthorization and amendments have contributed to the development of the school nurse role for students with disabilities. For the first time, school nursing practice emphasized a tertiary prevention component—that of rehabilitation/habilitation. During the 1980s, several national nursing organizations collaboratively issued a position statement on school nurses working with handicapped children (Igoe, 1980). The statement urged nurses to become more involved in activities related to coordination of care, health promotion, safety, and IEP development. This statement was followed by the National Association of State School Nurse Consultants (NASSNC) defining the role of the school nurse in EHA (Igoe, 1994). The 1991 amendments and provisions to the EHA included renaming the act the Individuals with Disabilities Education Act of 1990 (IDEA) (P.L. 101-476) and replacing the term *handicapped* with the term *disability*, as well as a renewed emphasis on preparing students with disabilities for transition to adult life.

Two additional pieces of legislation, Section 504 of the Rehabilitation Act of 1973 and the Americans with Disabilities Act of 1990 (ADA) (P.L. 101-336) also had an impact on school health. Section 504 addressed conditions not covered by IDEA, such as immunodeficiency syndrome, pregnancy with complications, obesity, and drug addiction. In addition, the ADA, with these other two legislative initiatives, expanded opportunities for all students with disabilities and chronic conditions and promoted full inclusion, integration, independent living, and economic social self-sufficiency.

The fifth and final event affecting school nursing was a collaborative initiative convened by the American Federation of Teachers (AFT, 1992) to examine issues related to special health care needs in schools. This task force was convened in response to the dramatic increase in the number of children with special health care needs in schools. Before the 1980s, these children were cared for

in hospitals or long-term care facilities. Federal and state deinstitutionaliza-
tion policies, cost considerations, and advocacy groups have placed these children and youth back in the home and the public schools. The task force's conclusion, detailed in *The Medically Fragile Child in the School Setting* (AFT, 1992),
offered recommendations regarding role delineation for providing special health
care in the school setting. This document was published along with a survey of
state nurse practice acts that described delegation and supervisory practices for
nurses.

What has emerged from these past decades is a school nurse role that is broad
in scope and expectation. The evolution of the role has occurred most recently
during times of competing school system forces that emphasize cost containment
and expanded student needs. The school nurse role today is one that is generalized to address the health promotion and health service needs of all students
within the system, and is specialized in addressing the unique needs of students
with chronic conditions.

School Nursing Today

Today, the specialty of school nursing represents the second largest related services personnel group in the nearly 6,000 public school districts in this country
(Igoe, 1994). The number of school nurses is estimated at 26,000 (Igoe & Speers,
1992). Many state boards of education require certification of school nurses,
including a minimum of a bachelor's degree. However, too many schools have no
certification requirements. School nurses, therefore, constitute a large group of
health providers who represent varying degrees of education (technical training
to master's and doctoral degrees in nursing or related fields), licensure (practical
nurse to registered nurse licensure), and skills (health promotion, health services
management, and primary care).

Current Definition of School Nursing

The NASN defines school nursing as a specialty branch of professional nursing
that (a) seeks to prevent or identify client health or health-related problems
(primary and secondary prevention), and (b) intervenes to modify or remediate
these problems (secondary and tertiary prevention) (Proctor, Lordi, & Zaiger,
1993). School nurses deliver services to students of all ages from birth through
age 21, and serve students, families, and the school community in regular education, in special education, and in other educational arenas. The school nurse
functions in the school as a community health professional, providing and
accessing services for clients, setting professional goals, and participating in
cooperative school and community health planning (Snyder, 1991).

Standards of School Nursing Practice

Standards of practice for school nurses are statements with accompanying measurement criteria that describe a competent level of behavior in the professional role. These measurement criteria include key indicators of nursing practice and reflect the theoretical framework and current knowledge in the field. The organizations representing school nurses have prepared standards for practice, consistent with the specifications established throughout the nursing profession. These organizations are the National Association of School Nurses (NASN), the American Nurses Association (ANA), the National Association of State School Nurse Consultants (NASSNC), the American School Health Association (ASHA), and the American Public Health Association (APHA). Nursing representatives of these organizations recently have formed a National Nurses Coalition for School Health to better coordinate their positions on issues and to serve as a stronger support mechanism for practice (Igoe, 1994). Furthermore, these organizations have presented guidelines for the educational preparation of school nurses—at a minimum, a bachelor's degree in nursing with state nursing licensure.

Standards of school nursing practice were first developed by the American School Health Association (ASHA) in 1974, and joint statements were issued by the ANA, National Education Association (NEA), and ASHA in 1983 (Woodfill & Beyrer, 1991). The most recent, a 1993 publication by the NASN, outlines ten specialty standards of school nursing practice (Proctor, Lordi, & Zaiger, 1993). These standards, which evolved over a 20-year period, reflect the extensive contributions nurses make in schools and have implications for health services and health education for students in regular and special education. According to Proctor et al. (1993), the school nurse:

1. Utilizes a distinct clinical knowledge base for decision making in nursing practice.

2. Uses a systematic approach to problem solving in nursing practice.

3. Contributes to the education of the client with special health needs by assessing the client, planning and providing appropriate nursing care, and evaluating the identified outcomes of care.

4. Uses effective written, verbal, and nonverbal communication skills.

5. Establishes and maintains a comprehensive school health program.

6. Collaborates with other school professionals, parents, and caregivers to meet the health, developmental, and education needs of clients.

7. Collaborates with members of the community in the delivery of health and social services, and utilizes knowledge of community health systems and resources to function as a school and community liaison.

8. Assists students, families, and the school community to achieve optimal levels of wellness through appropriately designed and delivered health education.

9. Contributes to nursing and school health through innovations in practice and participation in research or research-related activities.

10. Identifies, delineates, and clarifies the nursing role, promotes quality of care, pursues continued professional enhancement, and demonstrates professional conduct.

The NASN explains that specific standards for school nurse practice are needed to reach role consensus and scope of practice for contemporary school nursing. In reference to these standards, the NASN (Proctor et al., 1993) promotes three broad roles for contemporary school nursing practice: the role of the generalist clinician, the primary care role, and the management role.

School Health, School Nursing, and Youth with Disabilities

While school health extends to students of all ages and abilities, students with disabilities and special health care needs—students with chronic conditions—require services provided from within five major systems: medical, educational, social service, public health, and the home (Kelly, 1995). Numerous studies have shown the need to improve linkages between these systems, but barriers exist. Each system is isolated from the others geographically, financially, philosophically, and culturally. Other barriers—communication, language, jargon, established patterns—make it difficult to share information. Linkages between health care systems and schools are of particular importance because students spend the majority of their time in the school environment. School nurses provide a bridge among these systems, because they are used to balancing the demands across both the health and education systems.

School nurses have been actively involved with students with chronic conditions, but most consistently within school practice because of the passage of the EHA. *Youth with chronic conditions* is a broad term referring to youth with special health needs who may or may not receive special education services. The number of these students is rapidly increasing. As a point of emphasis, the NASN identified one of its 10 standards of practice specifically related to students with special health care needs (Proctor et al., 1993): "The School Nurse Contributes to the Education of the Client with Special Health Needs by Assessing the Client, Planning and Providing Appropriate Nursing Care, and Evaluating the Identified Outcomes of Care" (p. 27).

The NASN identified 14 indicators from which the school nursing program is judged to meet the intent of the standard. To effectively implement school nursing services for students with special health care needs, the nurse needs contemporary information on (a) common chronic and disabling conditions; (b) national, state, and local laws governing students and programs in special education, chronically ill students, and the rights of those with disabilities; and (c) appropriate judicial decisions including roles and responsibilities of the nurse and other school-based team members (Proctor et al., 1993).

More recently the NASN developed an issue brief outlining the specific roles and responsibilities of the school nurse in relationship to students with disabilities and called for the inclusion of the professional school nurse as a related services provider under the IDEA (NASN, 1996). The NASN defined the role of the school nurse as a member of the multidisciplinary educational team. As part of this team, the school nurse (NASN, 1996):

1. Assists in identifying children who may need special educational or health-related services.

2. Assesses the identified child's sensory and physical health status, in collaboration with the child, parent(s), and health care providers.

3. Develops individual health and emergency care plans.

4. Assists the team in developing an IEP that provides for the required health needs of the child, which enables the student to participate in his or her educational program.

5. Assists the parent(s) and child in identifying and utilizing community resources.

6. Assists the parent(s) and teachers in identifying and removing health related barriers to learning.

7. Provides inservice training for teachers and staff regarding the individual health needs of the child.

8. Provides or supervises assistive personnel to provide specialized health care services in the school setting.

9. Evaluates the effectiveness of the health-related components of the IEP with the child, parent(s), and other team members, and makes revisions to the plan as needed.

The practice of school nursing for students with chronic conditions is accomplished through the development of an Individualized Health Care Plan (IHP), which is either incorporated into the student's IEP/ITP or is a separate document for health services. According to Haas (1993), the term "individualized healthcare plan" (IHP) comes from *The Standards of School Nursing Practice* (ANA, 1983). IHPs are the application and formalization of the nursing process in the school setting and should include information about the student's needs, nursing interventions designed to meet those needs, and a description of how the care supports the education process of the school. School nurses apply the nursing process, a deliberate problem-solving process, as they formulate IHPs or contribute to the formulation of IEP/ITPs. Nursing interventions are systematic and individualized for each student to reach desired outcomes that are agreed upon by the student, family, and team. School nurses view the student holistically and as partners in implementation. The focus of school nursing practice is enhancement of the student's capacity for learning, growing, and developing.

Transition of Youth with Special Health Care Needs from Pediatric to Adult Health Care

At the same time the educational system is working toward transition from school to work, the traditional health care system is focusing on initiatives such as "healthy and ready to work" (Maternal and Child Health Improvement Projects, 1996). Though each system acknowledges the efforts of the other, these transition initiatives are occurring largely within separate parameters of the life of the whole student and their family, not collaboratively.

As outlined by Blum (1995), the transition to adult health care services became an interest to the health care community in 1985 when the National Center for Youth with Disabilities (NCYD) began operating with a goal to improve services for youth through the second decade of life as they transition to adult living, health care, and vocations. Studies documented that the life expectancy of youth with disabilities had increased dramatically in the last 20 years. Today, more than two million young people between the ages of 10 and 18 have some functional limitation due to chronic and disabling conditions. This represents a 100% increase since 1960, when the prevalence was 1.8%; today, it is 3.8% (Blum & Geber, 1992). This means that more than a million young people from the United States with chronic illness or disability will travel the often rocky course to adulthood by the year 2000. Blum (1995) contends that the optimal goal of transition is to provide health care that is seamless, coordinated, developmentally appropriate, psychosocially sound, and comprehensive. In March 1989 Surgeon General C. Everett Koop convened a national conference entitled "Growing Up and Getting Medical Care: Youth with Special Health

Care Needs." This was the first Surgeon General's conference on transition. Subsequently, the Maternal and Child Health Bureau released *Moving On: Transition from Child-Centered to Adult Health Care for Youth with Disabilities* (U.S. Department of Health and Human Services [USDHHS], 1992). The publication contends that youth benefit from transition services that include training in decision-making skills, assertiveness, and self-advocacy, allowing them to be in control of their own health care.

These and other national health transition efforts have contributed to the knowledge about this important time in the life of a young person with chronic illness and disability. For example, there is a higher than average prevalence of depression and suicide attempts among these youth, and the root cause of this is due to the social isolation experienced by many youth with disabilities (Blum, 1995). Moreover, substance abuse rates among persons with disabilities may be twice as high as those for the general population (Edelman, 1995). Blum (1995) summarized some of the elements that facilitate successful health transition:

- Having high expectations makes a difference.

- Having clear, caring, and consistent rules makes a difference.

- Believing a disability need not be a handicap makes a difference.

- Establishing developmentally expanded expectations, starting in early childhood and moving across into adulthood, makes a big difference.

Health transition programs for youth with chronic illness and disability are a relatively recent phenomenon in this country, most programs having been established after 1988.

Recently, the National Center for Youth with Disabilities (1996) completed a survey of adolescent health transition programs in the United States. Through a tiered process of broadly identifying programs and then surveying the identified programs regarding services provided and emphasis, the center identified 277 programs that support the transition of youth with chronic illness or disabilities from pediatric to adult health care, and received detailed information from 129 of these programs. Results indicated that the transition from pediatric to adult health care was being addressed in both formal structured programs, as well as informally on a case-by-case basis. Medical care, health education, case management, and individual planning for transition to an independent lifestyle were three services offered most often. Vocational and career training, along with self-advocacy training, were the two services offered least often. About half of the programs offered family mental health services and group programs. Clearly, health transition programs focus primarily on health care, with services provided in clinics or community agencies and following an acute-care medical model of health care delivery. Few programs include vocational counselors as part of the team. Even fewer actively engage the educational transition process through collaboration.

School Nursing and Transition

In most settings, the nurse works individually with students and their family. However, there are several goals common to the interventions. The nurse focuses on training for competence and responsibility and teaches skills and expectations needed for independence in care of the health condition. Thus, the core transition skills of self-determination or empowerment, self-evaluation, and goal setting are woven throughout the health component of the plan (Halpern, 1995). With the transition plan, the nurse becomes accountable for teaching the student independence in self-care management, particularly in reference to existing or anticipated transition health care issues.

Even though the literature does not specifically address the role of the school nurse in this important transition activity, there is a large body of literature about the role of nursing (a) within a concept of transition, (b) in addressing the needs of youth with disabilities and chronic health conditions, (c) in focusing on the need for transition within the health care delivery system from pediatric to adult health care, and (d) in identifying the role of school nursing with students in special education with IEPs. A brief review of this body of literature is presented in order to form a foundation from which to suggest the need for consideration of health planning as an essential component of a workable transition plan for youth with disabilities

Transitions: A Central Concept in Nursing

Meleis (1975) proposed that transition is a central concept to the discipline of nursing. A recent review of nursing literature from 1986 to 1992 (Schumacher & Meleis, 1994) reinforces the claim of the centrality of transitions to nursing practice. These authors identified four categories of transitions addressed in the nursing literature: developmental, situational, health–illness, and organizational. In addition, analysis revealed several universal commonalities of both the transition process and outcome. Although there was diversity in the transitions reviewed, the author identified several important process factors ("universal properties") which influenced the quality of the transition experience and the consequence of the transition: (a) the meaning of the transition and the likely effect on one's life; (b) the expectations held by the participants; (c) the level of knowledge/skill of the person; (d) the environment in which the transition takes place; (e) the level of planning for the transition; and (f) the emotional and physical well-being of the participant.

Congruent with the educational literature, this review found that the successful achievement of a transition can be powerful and gives the participant an enhanced sense of subjective well-being, role mastery, and well-being of relationships. Achievement of transition then increases the participants' confidence and mastery (Younger, 1991) and builds skill for future challenges. These authors argued that managing transitions is the "essence" of nursing practice. At the very least, the review documents the nurse's experience in working with and enhancing skills to manage transitions. A professional with such skills can be a valuable resource in transition planning.

Specific Contributions of Nursing to Transition Plans

Developing age-appropriate condition self-management skills starts at the entry of the child in the school system. Thus, the nurse may have worked closely with the child and family throughout the years preceding the development of a transition plan. Commonly the nurse focuses on (Igoe, 1994; Johnson, 1996; Magyary & Brandt, 1996; Meeropol, 1991; Peterson, Rauen, Brown, & Cole, 1994; Proctor et al., 1993):

1. self-care skills needed to manage the specific health condition and maintain stability, including decision making and autonomy skills;

2. coordination and communication with other health care providers working with the family;

3. sexuality, which includes sexuality education, integrating the impact of the condition, abuse prevention, pregnancy prevention, issues in access to reproductive health, and responsible decision making;

4. prevention of secondary conditions;

5. psychological adaptation to condition;

6. nutrition;

7. substance abuse; and

8. attendant or personal care provider training.

Self-Care Skills Management

Developing self-care skills needed to manage one's chronic health condition is a lifelong process that may be accelerated at the time of transition planning. Issues can range from self-dressing to bowel and bladder care, and focus on the prevention of secondary conditions and management of existing conditions. For example, students with select neurological conditions can have major issues with health of their skin. Students who develop pressure-related skin problems may need to stay at home or be hospitalized for weeks to heal a skin sore once it has developed (Russell, Reinbold, & Maltby, 1996). Unresponsive bowel, bladder, and skin issues are major health problems that may cause students with spinal cord injury in a college setting to either severely curtail class attendance or drop out of school altogether (Sawin, 1983).

Studies of youth with chronic conditions have identified that problem solving and autonomy skills are related to positive health outcomes (Blum, Resnick, Nelson, & St. Germaine, 1991; Johnson, 1996; Sawin & Marshall, 1992). Interestingly, many students with disabilities have limited experience making the basic decisions of adolescence (Johnson, 1996; Sawin & Metzger, 1996). Students need to build skills in decisions about the health care condition, but must first have extensive experience making life decisions (e.g., what clothes to purchase, how to wear one's hair, what to do with one's friends, or how to budget). Without these basic decision-making skills, choosing between two options for bladder care, deciding to try a new sitting system, or determining that the use of a wheelchair is a positive functional choice for across campus mobility seems overwhelming. The school nurse understands the expected outcomes and has well-developed interventions that support their achievement. For example, teens with spina bifida need to achieve multiple functional outcomes. By planning nursing intervention systematically, the desired outcomes drive the intervention process as illustrated in Table 6.1. Further, several checklists have been developed to frame discussions around assessing self-care and promoting health function for youth with spina bifida. Table 6.2 provides a simple means by which to organize self-assessment questions by functional health components for youth with spina bifida or cerebral palsy. Figure 6.1 further delineates self-care competency in the management of one's health for youth with spina bifida. These checklists illustrate the typical domains of health assessment that provide data utilized by nurses promoting self-care and health-related decision making.

Coordination and Communication

Another major contribution of the school nurse is coordination and communication with other health care providers working with the family. The focus of these activities is ensuring that the student has a health care home and coordinating care between settings. Adequate insurance coverage becomes an issue, particularly as the time for transition approaches, presenting a challenge to coordination. The parallel systems of transition in the school and health care community contribute to miscommunication with the student and family around health care issues. While this challenge will be discussed more fully later

Table 6.1

Expected Outcomes and Nursing Interventions for Adolescents with Spina Bifida

Expected Outcomes	Nursing Interventions
The adolescent displays appropriate growth and development	Facilitate the adolescent's continuation of regular visits to his or her primary physician. Continue to monitor the adolescent's neurosurgical, urological, and orthopedic care. Seek gynecological evaluation for girls and genetic counseling for both sexes. Provide age-appropriate information about sexual issues, precautions, birth control, and abuse issues.
The adolescent is free of secondary disability.	Ensure the adolescent's active participation in his or her skin care program, including pressure relief exercises, daily inspection, and early identification of breakdown. Teach the adolescent how to manage his or her weight by adjusting diet and exercise. Teach the adolescent to maintain equipment such as braces or wheelchair to prevent injury. Have the adolescent make routine appointments with his or her primary physician, neurosurgeon, urologist, and orthopedist. Teach the adolescent to identify products in home, school, hospital clinic, and community that contain latex.
The adolescent participates in his or her self-care.	Teach the adolescent to manage his or her bowel and bladder programs. Help the adolescent participate in self-care (bathing; shampooing; dressing self, including selecting clothes) to the degree possible. Ensure that the adolescent can list the names of his or her physicians and that he or she knows how to contact them. Ensure that the adolescent administers his or her medications as prescribed.
The adolescent displays appropriate educational development.	Encourage the adolescent to be actively involved in his or her appropriate placement in a school or a vocational center. Evaluate vocational rehabilitation as indicated. Ensure that the adolescent experiences practical living skills in such areas as finances, transportation, meal preparation, and preparation for emergencies. Enroll the adolescent in driver's education as appropriate. Contact resources for assistance as needed (e.g., ITPs).

Note. From "Spina Bifida: The Transition Into Adulthood Begins in Infancy," by P. M. Peterson, K. K. Rauen, J. Brown, & J. Cole, 1994, *Rehabilitation Nursing, 19*(4), 235–237. Copyright 1994 by *Rehabilitation Nursing.* Adapted with permission.

Table 6.2
A Checklist for Health

Health Factor	Concerns
Urinary function	Am I dry?
Exercise	Do I get enough?
Bowel function	Am I in control?
Neurologic function	Is there noticeable change?
Intimacy and friends	Do I have?
Orthopedic function	How is my strength?
	How are my limbs?
	How straight is my back?
Body weight	Is it proportional to my height?
Skin	How are my feet, legs, and bottom?
Eating	Do I control fat and eat enough fiber?
Sex	Am I interested?
Mobility	Am I able to get around?
Mental health	Am I happy?
	Do I like myself?
Health care	When is my next appointment?
	Can I get an appointment?
	Can I get it paid for?
Growth and development	Am I reaching my potential?

Note. From "A Framework for Promoting the Health of People with Disabilities, by D. L. Patrick, M. Richardson, H. E. Starks, & M. A. Rose, 1994. In D. Lollar, *Preventing Secondary Conditions Assoicated with Spina Bifida or Cerebral Palsy* (pp. 3–16), Washington, DC: Spina Bifida Association of America. Adapted with permission.

in this chapter, it is important to note that the school nurse is identified as a key player in facilitating communication among these community-based transition programs. Although several school-based team members assume a coordinating role depending on the primary issues of concern, the school nurse often is the best prepared team member to pull it all together and communicate with the student's health care system transition team, if there is one. The school nurse has the background needed in the physical, psychosocial, and family issues of disability and chronic illness.

In addition, the school nurse can play a prominent role in preparing all students to be informed health consumers in schools and the larger health care system. Students with chronic conditions have a particular need for these skills, which can be obtained in school-based health education programs aimed at developing responsible consumers of health care. One such program, Health-PACT, developed at the University of Colorado Office of School Health, is a prototype consumer-oriented, health education program for youth that prepares

Checklist for Assessing Key Self-Care Health Management Competencies

	Behavioral Outcome			
Task	Is Independent	Needs Assistance	Is Dependent	Comments
Multispecialty Healthcare Team				
• Knows name of primary physician	☐	☐	☐	_____
• Knows office phone number of primary physician	☐	☐	☐	_____
• Knows neurosurgeon's name	☐	☐	☐	_____
• Knows office phone number of neuro-surgeon	☐	☐	☐	_____
• Knows location of neurosurgeon's office or clinic	☐	☐	☐	_____
• Knows urologist's name	☐	☐	☐	_____
• Knows urologist's office phone number	☐	☐	☐	_____
• Knows location of urologist's office or clinic	☐	☐	☐	_____
• Knows name of orthopedist	☐	☐	☐	_____
• Knows orthopedist's office phone number	☐	☐	☐	_____
• Knows how to obtain nursing care	☐	☐	☐	_____
• Knows how to obtain nutritional services	☐	☐	☐	_____
• Knows how to obtain physical therapy/ occupational therapy services	☐	☐	☐	_____
• Appropriately verbalizes intent to seek health care (for problems and for health maintenance)	☐	☐	☐	_____
• Knows how to pay for health care	☐	☐	☐	_____
Medications				
• Can list current medications	☐	☐	☐	_____
• Knows dose of each medication	☐	☐	☐	_____
• Knows when to take each medication	☐	☐	☐	_____
• Administers medication to self	☐	☐	☐	_____
• Knows effects and side effects of each medication	☐	☐	☐	_____
• Knows how to obtain refills	☐	☐	☐	_____
• Knows pharmacy's phone number	☐	☐	☐	_____
• Knows pharmacy's location	☐	☐	☐	_____
• Knows how to pay for medication	☐	☐	☐	_____
Intermittent Self-Catheterization				
• Knows what supplies are needed (e.g., catheter of correct size)	☐	☐	☐	_____
• Knows how to order supplies	☐	☐	☐	_____
• Knows how to pay for supplies	☐	☐	☐	_____
• Knows how often to catheterize self	☐	☐	☐	_____
• Catheterizes self appropriately	☐	☐	☐	_____
• Knows signs and symptoms of urinary tract infection	☐	☐	☐	_____
• States accurately what to do if a urinary tract infection occurs	☐	☐	☐	_____

Figure 6.1. *Note.* From "Spina Bifida: The Transition Into Adulthood Begins in Infancy," by P. M. Peterson, K. K. Rauen, J. Brown, & J. Cole, 1994, *Rehabilitation Nursing, 19*(4), 235–237. Copyright 1994 by *Rehabilitation Nursing*. Reprinted with permission.

students to communicate with health professionals and actively participate in their care. Further, such a program prepares providers for shared decision making (Igoe, 1994).

Sexuality

A nurse's contribution to the development of healthy sexuality often starts with a focus on the physical changes of puberty altered by some conditions (Blum, 1994), and includes sexual education integrating the impact of the condition, abuse prevention, pregnancy prevention, issues in access to reproductive health care, and responsible decision making. Youth, particularly females in this population, are at high risk for sexual and substance abuse (Lollar, 1994 ; Nosek, 1995; Sobsey, 1994). These youth need to learn (a) survival assertiveness skills; (b) the specific issues of their condition for birth control, pregnancy, and parenthood; (c) abuse prevention strategies; and (d) effective sexuality communication. It is important, for example, for students with spina bifida who have a very high incidence of latex allergy to avoid latex condoms. Women with spinal cord injury may not be good candidates for oral contraceptives. Depro-provera has specific indications for some students (Blum, 1997; Sawin, 1998). There may be neurological effects of spinal cord injury, spina bifida, or muscular dystrophy for males or muscular skeletal effects on sexuality for persons with juvenile rheumatoid arthritis.

Even though youth with chronic conditions are sexual beings and have desires and interests similar to their peers, often society treats them as asexual. This can have disastrous consequences for youth, leading them to a number of scenarios, including lack of sexual education to feeling they have to prove their sexuality with risky behavior. Interestingly, parents of youth with chronic conditions who completed a national survey identified that 24 to 34% of the school dropouts for women with sensory conditions (vision and hearing) were because of pregnancy or childbearing issues (USDHHS, 1992). Thus, sexuality issues can be major threats to the transition plan if they are overlooked (Blum, 1997; Sawin, 1998; Spencer, Fife, & Rabinovich, 1995; Suris, Resnick, Cassuto, & Blum, 1996).

Prevention of Secondary Conditions

Another focus of the health component of transition planning is the prevention of "secondary disabilities." Secondary disabilities are the preventable physical, emotional, and social consequences that occur secondary to incomplete or ineffective treatment of the original or primary health condition. A "state of the science" conference was recently initiated by the U.S. Department of Health and Social Services, the Centers for Disease Control, and two volunteer organizations, the United Cerebral Palsy Association and the Spina Bifida Association of America. This cooperative effort addressed the wide range of secondary conditions that occur for youth with disabilities when appropriate prevention efforts are not factored into care, particularly the transition to independent living as a young adult. A model for accentuating preventive strategies in high-risk populations was developed, and strategies to prevent secondary conditions (ranging from mobility, pain, and spasticity to reproductive issues and adjustment concerns) were shared. The conference proceedings delineated a proactive approach toward developing a state of well-being for young adults. This monograph (Lollar, 1994) should be required reading for all students, families, and professionals on IEP/ITP teams for youth with cerebral palsy and spina bifida.

The prevention of secondary disabilities needs to be a major theme of each transition plan. The subsequent skills and information needed to achieve the prevention of secondary disabilities are appropriate to include in the plan. While the specifics of prevention differ with each student's condition, the concept is applicable for all students eligible for IEP/ITPs (Farley, Vines, McCluer, Stefans, & Hunter, 1994).

The last four areas of school nurse focus—psychological adaptation to the condition, nutrition, substance abuse, and training of personal care providers—are more likely to be shared with other school-based transition team members and will be addressed later in the chapter. Several of these areas are appropriate for the total population of students with whom the school nurse works. It is important at every opportunity to reinforce to the student and family that youth with chronic conditions are more alike than different from their peers. Students with chronic conditions need to be integrated with their peers for interventions to be useful and they need to have health education information available that is specific to their health condition.

Impact of Cognition, Timing, and Transition Site

Cognition plays a major role in the IEP/ITP and its health related activities. A self-sufficiency orientation assumes cognition necessary to carry out the activities. If cognition is impaired, families or advocates will need to have increased participation in the planning and implementation of the plan. However, once the student reaches 18 years of age, parents have no legal right to access medical information. Although students can sign a release so that providers can share medical information with parents, family and health care members need to discuss the need to establish guardianship if legal access is felt necessary.

The point in time when the nurse intervenes is influenced by both cognition and content. For example, Spencer et al. (1995) propose a sequence for the introduction of transition-relevant information for youth with arthritis based on developmental age and content in Table 6.3. In dealing with adolescents with arthritis, it is inappropriate to provide initial information on responsible sexual behavior or pregnancy risk at 18 years of age if they are cognitively ready as early as 12 years of age; the introduction of such information to an adolescent who is cognitively and developmentally challenged may need to begin at a later chronologic age.

In addition, Cappelli, MacDonald, and McGrath (1989) developed a tool to measure readiness for transition. These authors found that the readiness questionnaire was a better predictor of successful transition than a student's age. Specifically, the questions *Do you take your medicines without someone having to remind you?* and *When you are not feeling well, who usually phones the clinic or doc-*

Table 6.3
Suggested Guidelines for Transition Program Discussions

Age 12 Years and Older: Adolescent Sexuality

Responsible sexual behavior
Risks of pregnancy
Referrals for counseling

Age 14 Years and Older: Vocation

Career ideas and goals
Related educational needs
Vocational counseling
Summer jobs
Community programs

Age 15 Years and Older: Education

Link between education and rewarding careers
Educational goals
Financing of education
Scholarships and loans

Age 18 Years and Older: Adult Medical Home

Need to eventually transition to adult medical care. Specific transition needs: male or female doctor, urban or suburban clinic, and insurance
Special referrals: need to start early to secure adult medical homes for adolescents with severe disabilities
Possibility that medical transition efforts may not be initially successful

Note. Adapted from "The School Experience of Children with Arthritis: Coping in the 1990s and Transition into Adulthood," by C. Spencer, R. Fife, & C. Rabinovich, 1995, *Pediatric Clinics of North America*, 42(5), pp. 1285–1298. Copyright 1995 by *Pediatric Clinics of North America*. Adapted with permission.

tor? were more helpful than knowledge questions in predicting readiness.

Another factor is the type of transition that the student has chosen. If the student with a disability is transitioning to a college setting, a number of options may be available. At a minimum, the student and family need to ask basic questions regarding the school. The outline by HEATH (Edelman, 1995) found in Table 6.4 and resources from the PACER program are helpful in this assessment. Some universities have preenrollment programs for students with severe disabilities, especially those who will need attendant care (Sawin, 1983). The focus of the nurse in these assessments is evaluation of both the attendant care needs of the student, and more importantly, the student's independent ability to teach others to provide the care needed. Each student must determine if they should move health care to either the college health care center or a local speciality provider.

Similarly, if a team is planning a transition to a structured living situation, health care transition needs should be evaluated. The issues to be addressed here include both the school's and the youth's other care provider's plans for transition. Depending on the student's personal care providers, an existing plan can be continued or a new one can be developed.

Students who transition to work have the most immediate need to establish a health care plan. Insurance is a major problem for these students. One study reported that 25% of young adults are uninsured and that adolescents with disabilities have a similar pattern (McManus, Newacheck, & Greaney, 1990). If the student has a high health care risk, this lack of insurance may be a major barrier to full independent living (Johnson, 1996). Students may become eligible for Medicaid and Supplemental Security Income (SSI); however, employment that raises their income above the eligibility criteria will terminate such benefits.

In summary, the school nurse can have a critical role in transition planning. In many interdisciplinary transition teams, each discipline assumes leadership for designing certain elements of the intervention plan and integrating them with the other members of the team. The school nurse's leadership is critical in designing the plan for the development of skills and curriculum to manage the health condition and in coordinating between the school and the larger health care community. The school nurse also takes a systems approach, working with other primarily pediatric oriented professionals to develop either unique health services for students who are transitioning or to educate existing adult services. In addition, a focus for many students with less visible conditions may be to identify needs for primary health care, prevent secondary disabilities, and assist the student with finding a health care home. The nurse, in addition to the other members of the transition team, participates in monitoring and intervenes when appropriate in other areas, including psychological adjustment to the condition, substance abuse prevention, and nutrition counseling.

Table 6.4
Chronic Illness, Postsecondary Health-Related Transition Plan Questions

1. Medical and Health Needs of the Young Adult
   - Will there be a need to develop a plan for health care transition?
   - What factors would be included in the health component of the transition plan?
   - When should the health transition process be initiated?

2. Chronic Illness Impact
   - How does the chronic illness affect the youth's educational process?
   - How does the chronic illness affect this student's living environment?
   - How does the chronic illness affect activities of daily living?

3. Disclosure
   - In applying to colleges or other postsecondary training institutions, should the individual disclose the chronic illness? To whom? When?
   - What laws are in place to protect the rights of people with disabilities? How do they relate to young adults with chronic illnesses?
   - After acceptance, to whom, under what circumstances, and when should disclosure be made?

4. Accommodations
   - What types of accommodations are currently in place in high school and in the living environment?
   - What accommodations or modifications will need to be in place educationally or environmentally to increase independence?
   - What accommodations are postsecondary educational institutions required by law to provide?
   - If this student needs additional accommodations or modifications, who pays for them?
   - How can the student assess the ability of the postsecondary institution and the surrounding community to meet his or her needs?

5. Locating Resources
   - When should financial, medical, and support service resources begin?
   - Who can assist at the postsecondary site?
   - Whose responsibility is it?

Note. Adapted from "Maximizing Success: Transition Planning for Education after High School for Young Adults with Chronic Illness," by A. Edelman, 1995, *Information from HEATH, 15*(1), p. 3. Copyright 1995 by HEATH Resource Center. Adapted with permission.

Evaluation of Nursing's Impact

A few research projects have examined the impact of systematic nursing activities on health or adaptation outcomes in youth with chronic conditions. Two are notable, one in the school setting and one in the health care setting. Magyary and Brandt (1996) developed and evaluated a school-based self-management program for youth with chronic health conditions. The intervention involved peer groups, cognitive-behavioral intervention, and parent support groups. The evaluation showed that youth in the intervention group had improved self-responsibility with higher therapeutic adherence. While the youth-reported intervention effects did begin to fade after several months, the parent report remained significant. A study carried out in the health care setting also demonstrated the potential impact of skilled nursing care. Pless et al. (1994) examined the impact of a year-long nursing support intervention for youth with a wide variety of chronic conditions and their families. The intervention consisted of an integrated biomedical and psychosocial approach aimed at the family as a unit. The major aim was to foster family coping and independence. After collecting base-line data, a year-long program with ongoing availability of coordinated care by a nurse with a bachelor's degree was instituted. Nurses kept detailed diaries of the content of the family and youth contact. Thematic evaluation revealed focus on both skill development and family and youth support. When compared with the control group, the intervention group had improved adjustment and were less dependent, anxious, and depressed. This effect was the most positive for the 8- to 16-year-old age group. Both of these studies give evidence of the potential of a well-prepared school nurse as a member of transitions teams.

Existing Challenges to Heath Care Transitions

Variability in Preparation and Availability of School Nurses

There are four major challenges that influence school nursing's optimal contribution to transition planning. The first is the previously addressed variability in the preparation and availability of nurses in the school. Although national standards do exist, there are no national or even dominant state models of school health services. Further, the services provided through recently developed school health clinics have not clearly addressed the needs of students with disabilities. Although several authors propose that school-based clinics may become more central to the transition of students, especially for those who are in special education school programs until they are 21 years old (Igoe, 1994; Johnson, 1996), the development of mandated school-based health programs is unlikely. Thus, the availability and the impact of the nurse on school programs has become a local issue. Demonstrating the effect of school nursing's involvement with students with chronic conditions through development of model programs is essential to convince the local administration of the need for such services. This makes ongoing demonstration projects with well-designed evaluation components a critical priority for the discipline. The remaining challenges involve (a) coordination with transition programs in the health care system, (b) overlaps with other disciplines on the school-based transition team, and (c) the role of multiple agencies in state initiatives and programs involved in transition.

Transition Programs in the Health Care System

A major challenge for the discipline is the need for coordination among two largely distinct and different systems addressing the transition of youth with chronic conditions. Table 6.5 summarizes several health care transition models, but because all models assume primary placement in the health care system, none are appropriate for a school-based transition model. The model that has the best fit, the transition coordination model, is the one least prevalent in the health care community at this time (NCYD, 1996). Transition programs based in the health care system vary not only by model type but also by the services offered. In addition, transition programs are housed in various units in the health care system, some in pediatric subspecialty clinics, some in adolescent programs, and some in general pediatric clinics. These transition programs in the health care system do focus on:

- providing developmentally appropriate services;
- acknowledging to the young person that he or she has achieved a new stage of development; and
- offering an environment where adult vocational, social, sexual, physical, and emotional health care can be met.

As described previously, key components of successful transition identified by these health care system programs include: (a) having high expectations; (b) having clear, caring, and consistent rules; (c) believing a disability need not be a handicap; and (d) establishing developmentally expanded expectations, starting in early childhood and moving across into adulthood (Blum, 1995).

The most frequent professionals involved in health care system transition programs are nurses (66%) and subspecialist physicians (61%) (NCYD, 1996). The role of the nurse in these programs varies but most often focuses on coordinating care within the health care system. Other team members include social workers, primary care physicians, and nurse practitioners. Professionals seen by referral or consultation include dieticians, physical therapists, occupational therapists, educators, psychologists, respiratory therapists, and vocational counselors (NCYD, 1996).

Table 6.5
Models for Transition Programs in the Health Care System

Disease-Focused Model:

Provides services based on the management and care of needs of a specific disability or chronic condition.

Adolescent-Focused Model:

Provides coordination of the subspecialist team and adolescent health specialists who may or may not be physicians.

Primary Care Model:

Relies on the family physician or general practitioner to coordinate care among consulting pediatric subspecialists, internists, and others.

Transition Coordination Model:

Provides a multidisciplinary team to assess transition needs and referrals to community service providers.

Note. From *Transitions from Child to Adult Health Care Services: A National Survey,* by National Center for Youth with Disabilities, 1996, Minneapolis, MN: NCYD. Copyright 1996 by the Institute for Health and Disability in the Department of Pediatrics, Division of General Pediatrics and Adolescent Health at the University of Minnesota. Reprinted with permission.

Interventions developed in the community-based health care system can be useful to the school nurse in meeting the needs of the school-based transition plan. Two such programs aim toward teaching autonomy skills. Physicians and nurse practitioners at the University of Virginia developed an autonomy project based around an "interpretive interview" and "teaching physical" that focuses on teaching youth about the impact of their condition (Hostler, Gressard, Hassler, & Linden, 1989). Evaluation indicated that students achieved significant gains in knowledge and autonomy with this interactive approach. A second approach was developed by the Spina Bifida Association of Kentucky's Transition to Independence Project. This project developed a series of workbooks for youth and their parents that focused on the youth making more decisions and taking charge. Evaluation methods are in process, but the program curriculum is well-developed and could be useful for the development of school-based systematic transition programs (Denniston & Enlow, 1995; Hardin, 1995a, 1995b).

The major challenge presented by these parallel systems is one of communication and coordination of activities and priorities. The focus of the health care system is to prepare youth for transition to a new mode of health care while acknowledging the other parallel transitions in school, vocational, and social environments. The goal is successful management of the health condition and related life issues. In the school setting the priorities are different. The priority is education for life and inclusion in community life. Health care issues are pertinent only if they affect the primary education component. It is highly likely that personnel in each system are unaware of the transition planning occurring in the other areas. If the health care transition program involves educational specialists, or if school nursing personnel are involved in the wider community, collaboration is more likely to occur.

Optimal outcomes occur when the school nurse is in close communication with the community-based health transition program and the goals and interventions for condition management are coordinated with the school-based transition plan. The school nurse can be an effective "boundary spanner" between these parallel health and education systems (Igoe, 1994). Indeed, when this occurs, a multiplicative effect is achieved.

Overlaps with Other Disciplines

The third challenge for nurses on school-based transition teams is the perceived role overlap with other team members. Transitions skill assessment in health care parallels similar assessments made by special education, recreational counseling, therapy, and other transition staff. All team members are assessing problem solving, assertiveness skills, and long-range planning. Practically, these team members focus on what skills are in place, what is "missing," and how to address the "missing pieces." However, while the basic process might be similar when applied to specific situations, the skills may need to be adapted. All decision making or assertiveness is context based. While it is excellent to learn the theory and general principles and even practice the skills, the specific application activities may not translate to use in a health specific area. For instance, whereas finding an apartment may take problem-solving skills or holding a merchant accountable for defective merchandise may demand assertiveness skills that might offer the student foundational information for solving a wide variety of problems, these skills do not automatically transfer to solving issues regarding the student's health condition. Because all problem solving is context based, there needs to be experience in solving potential health care dilemmas. Examples of the issues that students face can be found in the following case situations.

Case Situations

- You are a 16-year-old young woman with a spinal cord injury (or spina bifida) and you have just discovered you have a small red skin problem on your "sitting surface." You have a Stage I skin ulcer. You know that if it goes to Stage II it means you will have to stay home from school or work for weeks. However, you do not want to miss the fun of the homecoming football game and dance, nor do you want to look like a nerd if you have to use a big cushion for sitting. What do you do?
- You are a male who weighs 180 pounds and uses a power chair. What would you do if you arrived at a party and there was no accessible entrance or, worse yet, no accessible bathroom?
- You take a medication for spasticity, a condition due to cerebral palsy. You are going to the senior prom and you anticipate drinking and going to the all night after-prom party. You plan to double the amount of your medication to prevent problems related to this anticipated behavior. What problems might this cause?
- You are a 17-year-old female with epilepsy. You know the traditional advice is not to drink with your condition. However, you make it clear that you plan to anyway. You are on the birth control pill for an ovarian cyst and you are considering having sex with your boyfriend. You have a learning disability but are functioning well in school. What health problems can you expect?

Transition counseling needs to take place with team members who have the knowledge to provide information to the novice decision maker. For example, young women with epilepsy are at high risk to have a child with a congenital condition if their pregnancy is unplanned and the medication type or dose is toxic. In addition, drinking, sleep deprivation, and menstrual cycle changes can be related to break through seizures. It is important for youth to know that drinking is not recommended. However, if these young people choose to drink, they need to control the other variables that can put them at further risk. For example, one might choose not to stay out all night because sleep deprivation is associated with additional seizures. Females on some birth control pills can expect an interaction effect with their seizure medication and experience a decrease in birth control effectiveness (Santilli, 1996). Thus, youth with epilepsy who are sleep deprived, drinking, and on birth control pills are at the highest risk for complications associated with this health condition and its management. These students need to understand how to decrease their risks by applying accurate knowledge. All youth with epilepsy who drink need to have a sober friend with them who knows how to handle seizures, and the student in question certainly should not drive. If a student with epilepsy is going to be sexually active, a visit to her physician to discuss the impact of current medications on any unintended pregnancy should be recommended.

Since half of all pregnancies in the United States are unintentional, all women of childbearing age need to be on a multivitamin with folic acid in order to reduce the incidence of infants born with neural tube difficulties. Women with spina bifida, epilepsy, and diabetes, however, have an increased risk of this complication, and thus it would be especially important to include a multivitamin in the daily schedule of all female youth with these conditions. Further, students frequently have questions about the interaction of their medication with speed and marijuana. Even if answers are not available for their specific condition, a plan with the biggest safety net needs to be developed.

Role confusion and overlap on the school-based team can occur with occupational therapists, physical therapists, and the school counselor. Each may be involved with the student and bring unique perspectives. Each assesses and trains for competence and may address common areas such as sexuality, prevention of secondary disability, and some health care management. Working together they are more likely to solve complex problems.

 ## Case Situation: David

David, an 18-year-old, was finishing his senior year in high school. He had a high spinal cord injury and was unable to care for himself. He worked with his school-based transition team and the professionals at the college he was investigating. Issues for him included the length of the college day putting him at risk for skin and urinary problems; a history of skin breakdown and concern regarding ability to safely be in his wheelchair all day; management of his urinary incontinence due to neurogenic bladder; independent eating skills; attendant care training; academic load requirements; and need for financial support. David was intelligent and employment with education was seen as highly likely. The OT worked with the adaptive cafeteria needs; the PT's assessment documented a need for a reclining wheelchair to provide unassisted pressure relief during the day; and the nurse, with consultation from a rehabilitation engineer, problem solved his urological management. The latter arrangements called for a sip-and-puff system with the control tube threaded up through the student's shirt pocket. This system allowed the student to independently empty his urinary leg bag. Throughout, the vocational counselor addressed issues that would make current education and future work a success. Working together, the complex and integrated needs of the student were identified and solutions created.

All of the assessment and counseling interactions, both formal and informal, need to focus on training for competence and on the autonomy and responsibility skills likely to make that successful (Blum, 1995). To be successful, this approach cannot wait until the transition team is created but must be the focus for the student from the first contact with the educational team.

Another overlap area for school nurses with other school-based transition team members includes working with parents. The health components of the transition plan need to involve the parent. Some parents with children with special health care needs can be hypervigilant. Others can aggressively seek independence. An example from a current study that explores the experience of high school youth with epilepsy and their parents illustrates these differing parental approaches (Sawin, Pellock, & Metzger, 1998). Both families had 16-year-old students in fairly good control. The first family's philosophy was: "We let him do everything a kid his age normally does—although with preplanning and discussions with us. Then if there are consequences, we deal with them." The second family indicated that they replaced their son's peer group with the family because they wanted him to have the experiences but did not want to burden others with the responsibility. Thus, rather than keeping the youth home or letting him go skiing with others, they made it a family activity. Family activities are to be encouraged in all forms, but if they routinely take the place of peer activities, especially because of the condition, they lead to parental dependence or rebellion. Learning how to let go is an important skill for parents in all transitions. This family skill of "letting go" needs to be addressed early in the transition plan with parenting involvement and choice. However, letting go when it incorporates an unpredictable health condition needs condition-specific skill building. Parents need to be comfortable that their children can problem solve a predictable, condition-specific crisis in order to incrementally let go.

Sexuality is another area where transition counseling by the nurse may overlap with counseling by other team members. As discussed previously, all humans have the ability to develop sexuality. This concept is not to be confused with sexual activity. Youth and young adults with specific conditions are at high risk for abuse, may have complicated pregnancy prevention needs, or may need specific counseling due to their condition. Although these issues may be addressed by the student's private health care provider or other transition team members, it is more likely that they will not be discussed at all (Blum, 1991; Blum, 1997; Nosek et al., 1994; Sawin, 1998). Sexuality is a basic component of a full life and needs to be addressed in each transition plan. The nurse is one of the best qualified professionals on the school-based team to address this need. However, the team member with the primary relationship with the student may, at times, be a more effective choice. In those instances, the school nurse can be a valuable consultant, providing both content and strategies for addressing this area.

Nurses also can address mental health and substance abuse issues for students in transition. Typically, the nurse provides case finding, education, coordination, and follow-up monitoring. School nurses have an advantage of being a "legitimate confidential professional" that students can access for a variety of physical issues (Cox & Shannon, 1997). They are aware that students with less visible health conditions are often the ones with the most distress (Blum, 1995; NCYD, 1993). With their knowledge of the growth and development tasks of youth, nurses are aware of both the youths' needs for control of some aspect of their condition and the effectiveness of anger channeled in purposeful endeavors. Thus, the school nurse is a team member who can focus on the prevention of mental health issues for this population by structuring in as much control as possible for youth in their health regimes, by screening students for mental health issues, and by working with the school-based transition team to foster positive coping skills.

Mental health issues often surface during physical care. For example, in a discussion of a student's continuing problems with arthritis that were not being well controlled by medication, the nurse asked, "Have you ever made yourself throw up." A year-long history of frequent bulimia was discovered. The student responded, "No one ever asked me that question before." In addition to case finding and coordinating, the nurse may function as a co-leader with psychology or social work staff in groups for youth dealing with specific conditions. School systems fortunate enough to have an Advanced Practice Nurse with a master's degree in mental health nursing can provide the same counseling services as social workers and other comparably trained professionals.

Nutrition issues, common in youth generally, are frequent in youth with chronic conditions and need systematic evaluation. Decreased mobility may mean decreased calorie needs, but not decreased needs for specific nutrients. Skin breakdown may require increased protein intake. A chronic condition complicated by bulimia or anorexia can put the youth at risk for a wide number of negative health and education outcomes. If needed, a consulting nutritionist is usually available through state programs aimed at children with special needs and may be helpful in addressing specific issues.

Thus, whereas the nurse might be involved with a wide range of transition team members and each may be working on similar issues with the outcome goals of self-responsibility, self-determination, and self-evaluation, the contribution of the health component cannot be overlooked. To do so may endanger the plan and limit a student's options. Schools that do not have a nurse capable of providing this service need to explore options to build this component into needed IEP/ITP teams.

The Impact of State Initiatives and Programs

The last challenge faced by nurses in school-based teams is coordination with other state agencies. A recent national study indicated that multiple agencies in each state are addressing transition issues for youth, and each have their perceptions of the barriers that keep transition programs from being successful (NCYD, 1993). The findings of this study included the following:

- All survey participants considered insufficient transition planning the most important factor limiting successful transition.

- Participants identified significant gaps across programs in the availability of individual transition planning.

- Most psychosocial services were provided by fewer than 1 in 5 states.

- Even though 97% of all directors saw a need for interagency efforts to meet the needs of these adolescents, only 64% of programs actually participated in any interagency agreements, programs, or activities.

- States with an adolescent health coordinator had significantly higher levels of services, especially psychosocial services, for this population when compared with states that had no such position.

- A significant number of program directors look to departments of education to provide services, even in areas where the education system seems an inappropriate choice for such services.

All programs surveyed were in agreement that the most important factor was lack of transition planning. Nurses, along with all members of the ITP team, need to be aware of the specific programs available within their own state. They also need to participate in the full use and coordination with the various agencies of those services needed by the youth in their schools. One program aiming at increasing collaboration between state agencies is the DASH program at the Center for Disease Control and Prevention. This grant program has funded projects in Florida, West Virginia, and Wisconsin that build linkages between state agencies. Florida's legislature has shown particular foresight, calling for comprehensive services available in the schools. Their "full service schools" integrate education with medical, social, and human services on school grounds or in easily accessible services (Igoe, 1994).

It is interesting to note that in the 1993 survey by the National Center for Youth with Disabilities, a significant number of health-related transition program directors looked to departments of education to provide services, even in areas where the education system has been reluctant in the past. Specifically, the following percentages of the participants felt that these services for youth with chronic conditions should be the responsibility of a state's Department of Education:

- Health education—60%
- Sexuality/family life education—59%

- Provision of health services in schools—47%
- School health clinics—44%
- Transition to adult health care—14%

Even though several of these are not traditional services offered in the school setting to this population, the increase in school-based clinics or youth services centers that are school linked signal growing pressure for education to comprehensively address an increasing number of health issues. Having school nurses and other health professionals prepared to participate in the care of youth, particularly in developing IEP/ITPs, will be critical if this integrated vision is implemented.

New Vision for the Future

Although new paradigms of supports have emerged in the field of developmental disabilities, youths who are exiting the secondary education system are finding that the services needed to support their desire to be productive, contributing, and self-sufficient adults in the community are ill-coordinated and clearly fragmented (Bradley, Ashbaugh, & Blaney, 1994). The addition of transition assessment and planning to the IDEA in 1990 has supported the development of structures and policies to bridge the gap between school-based and adult-based service in the larger community. These new transition models, however, often do not address the health care issues affecting youths and young adults with disabilities (Betz, 1996), except perhaps in the mental health area (Wehman, 1992).

Likewise, the health care system has become concerned about the transition of youths with chronic conditions to adult health care services and has begun to develop models based on similar desired outcomes: choice and control, self-advocacy, and community integration. Health-related transition programs for youths with chronic conditions is a relatively recent phenomenon in this country, with most programs having been established after 1988 and located within the health care delivery system. However, these two systems of services for children and youth with disabilities—education and health—seem to be working toward similar goals in isolation of each other. Should the bold vision for the future recognize that these parallel streams of transition activity have much to contribute collectively to the individual outcomes espoused by both? Should professionals propose broader interagency collaboration and consultation in an effort to refine these models or even develop new ones? The answers are obviously "yes" to both of these challenges, yet professionals struggle to articulate exactly how to achieve the vision. Herein lies the problem. While professionals struggle to articulate specifics, they find themselves speaking in generalities. This is because students with chronic conditions are unique, educational and health care systems vary, school nurses and other educational personnel have varying levels of expertise, and communities differ. Therefore, the vision for the future is simply that the health component—healthy decision making, prevention of secondary disability, and health services—become an essential area that is addressed by school-based transition teams.

Clearly, the vision for the future of school-based transition team services and supports must be centered around the needs and desires of the individual students and their families. Transition planning, acknowledged by those participating in it as an essential process, must begin early enough to allow for incremental skill building in order to achieve the desired outcomes of community integration, meaningful work, and maximal interdependence and interdependence in adult life. Meaningful attention to health throughout the school-based transition process is necessary in terms of maintaining and optimizing health services, preventing secondary disabling conditions, and promoting healthy decision making.

One account of the interrelationship between health and success in community life was aptly stated by A. Bergman (1991) in response to conference recommendations addressing access to health care of youth and adults with developmental disabilities:

> We say that there won't be discrimination in employment because of the ADA. But if I am not assured adequate, accessible health care in my community, then I might miss too many days of work and then I will lose my job. Then the employer has grounds to fire. Not because of my disability, not because of discrimination, but because of continued absenteeism. So we don't get protection for absenteeism, and we don't want protection for absenteeism. We want rewards for participation and contribution, but we have to have that comprehensive health care system to do it. (p. 43)

Indeed, all good intentions on behalf of appropriate planning for transition could be undercut if health care issues are not addressed.

Not all youth with disabilities have obvious or compelling chronic health issues. However, according to a survey reported by the American Council on Education (Edelman, 1995), more than one-third of new full-time college freshmen with disabilities have chronic illnesses. If this is true for those who have already moved into postsecondary education, one would have to conclude that many youth with disabilities in secondary education also have ongoing chronic health issues. There are many team members who can and do contribute to aspects of health within the schools, in the health care system, and in the larger community. An often overlooked resource, however, is the school nurse.

So, where does one begin creating this vision of school-based transition planning that includes a health component? Perhaps it is best to begin with the end in mind, by asking what are the important components of adult life that youth with chronic conditions must navigate, and what information and skills are needed to navigate safely? It becomes quite clear that the maintenance and the enhancement of one's health clearly is one of these components. This affects many other important areas, just as they affect health.

It would seem obvious that youth with chronic conditions who have an IEP/ITP should have a health service component in the plan. Within this health service component, one should specify an assessment of healthy decision making, any health care procedures required by the student, any medications that the student requires, and an outline of any emergency procedures to be followed if there is a health complication (Nelson, 1991). Plans are incomplete without consideration of and planning for the provision of required health care services at school and after graduation. IEP/ITPs, therefore, should include appropriate health care and wellness information objectives. Second, health and wellness education programs in the school curriculum must be made available for all youth, including those with disabilities and chronic conditions. All youth with chronic conditions need preventive health services that address substance abuse, sexual abuse, and mental health. The literature suggests that youth with disabilities are particularly vulnerable to these new morbidities of the 1990s (Blum, 1995; Edelman, 1995; Sobsey, 1994; USDHHS, 1992). Third, all students with disabilities need a "health care home" for the ongoing provision of primary care. Furthermore, steps need to be taken to identify an adult-focused, adequately prepared, primary health care provider. Ongoing collaboration with the community health care system is a must. Finally, development of problem solving, assertiveness, and skills to use the health care system effectively are essential outcomes for the health component of the transition process.

To achieve these goals, the following recommendations are suggested:

• Address the health needs of youth with chronic conditions throughout the school-based transition process. Usually health care is assumed to be the responsibility of the family or the residential setting if the youth or young adult lives out of the family home. Too often professionals forget that the individual needs to be in control of health care decisions to the maximum extent possible. Preparation needs to begin early and extend throughout the transition planning process. Emphasis should be on decision making, prevention of secondary disabilities, and health service management.

- Include an adequately prepared school nurse who has developed an individual health care plan along with the student and family, and who has participated in IEP/ITP development in order to provide a link between the school, family, and community health care system. The baccalaureate level school nurse with experience and through staff development can contribute to the attainment of the integration of the health component within the IEP/ITP. If unavailable or not adequately prepared, consultation can be sought through the health care system or from other members of the school-based transition team. The point is that the right person, not just *any* person, is necessary. The identification of a knowledgeable health care provider will depend on the staff that the school has available. If the school nurse role is actually being filled by a health aide, obviously one will need to look elsewhere for the expertise required.

- Identify a person in the school to implement the health component objectives in the IEP/ITP in concert with the team, the student, the family, and the health transition program. The person will need (a) to be able to integrate the physical and emotional needs of the student, (b) to view each health encounter as an opportunity to further health knowledge and decision making, and (c) to collaborate with the student's community health care providers and family. This does not need to be the school nurse, particularly if the nurse is not regularly available. It will require that the individual consult with the school nurse or other health provider on the implementation. If this individual is the school nurse, this person should hold a baccalaureate degree and nursing license as a minimal requirement. Certification in school nursing is desirable. In some cases, one may need the skills of an advanced practice specialty nurse practitioner.

- Advocate that the baccalaureate prepared school nurse with certification in school nursing be recognized as a related services provider within IDEA legislation. The complex needs of students with chronic conditions and disabilities, their increasing number, and the movement of school-based clinics to more comprehensive services all speak to the need for a well-prepared health care professional involved in IEP/ITPs. Unfortunately, with the demands on school systems, this is just one of a number of pressing issues. Inclusion of the school nurse as a related service provider will correct an oversight in the original legislation and provide the team with the expertise needed to create an IEP and ultimately an ITP with the appropriate health care issues addressed.

If educational transition teams continue to overlook the health care issues affecting adolescents and young adults with chronic conditions, they risk compromising the intended outcomes of the transition planning process: employment, community integration, and self-sufficiency. For the most part, the generic health care needs of youths with disabilities are not significantly different from the rest of the population. However, chronic health status can be a barrier that is difficult to overcome in implementing an effective transition plan. Youths with chronic conditions may not be covered by their parents' health insurance policies unless they remain dependent on their families and are incapable of self-sustaining employment. The prevailing view and the overriding consideration must continue to be to bring about full integration of persons with developmental disabilities through access to the community health care system, just as full integration is the goal in public education, employment, and other endeavors. The adequately prepared school nurse is an asset as a member of the school-based transition team as it incorporates the health component during the transition process.

Appendix 6.A
Resources for Youth
and Their Families

Organizations and Associations

Spina Bifida Association of Kentucky. 982 Eastern Parkway, Box 18, Louisville, KY 40217-1566, (502) 637-7363. The following guidebooks have been produced from the Spina Bifida Association of Kentucky's Transition to Independence Project:

> *Becoming the Me I Want to Be: A Guide for Youth with Spina Bifida and Their Parents*, P. Hardin, 1995.

> *Building Skills: A Guide for Parents and Professionals Working with Youth People Who Have Spina Bifida*, by P. Hardin, 1995.

> *Making Choices: A Journal Workbook for Teens and Young Adults with Spina Bifida that Provides Opportunities for Making Choices About Their Lives*, by S. Denniston and C. Enlow, 1995.

HEATH Resource Center. One Dupont Circle, Suite 800, Washington, DC 20036-1193, 1-800-544-3284. The HEATH Resource center is a program funded by the U.S. Department of Education and houses the National Clearinghouse on Postsecondary Education for Individuals with Disabilities. The clearinghouse collects and disseminates information nationally about disability issues in postsecondary education, including educational support services, policies, and procedures related to educating or training people with disabilities after they have left high school.

The PACER (Parents Advocacy Collaborative for Educational Rights) Center. This center has compiled a practical workbook to prepare the student to participate as a productive member in his or her own IEP/ITP meeting:

> *Information for Parents of High School Students with Disabilities in Transition to Adult Life*: PACER.

Many other transition materials are available through PACER. The center has an extensive catalog that may be helpful to families. For information call 1-800-848-4912.

Other Publications

The following are additional resources available for youth and their families:

Easy for You To Say: Question and Answers for Teens Living with Chronic Illness or Disability, by M. Kaufman, Toronto, Canada: Key Porter Books.

No Pity: People with Disabilities Forging a New Civil Rights Movement, by J. H. Shapiro, 1993, New York: Times Books.

Taking Charge: Teenagers Talk About Life and Physical Disability, by K. H. Kreigsman, E. L. Zaslow, and M. A. D'Zmura-Rechsteiner, 1992, Bethesda, MD: Woodbine House. (Available from the American Spina Bifida Association. This is a much acclaimed primer for older school-age and teenage patients.)

Transitioning Youth from Pediatric to Adult Health Care by Taking Responsibility for Adolescent Health Care (TRAC). Vancouver: British Columbia's Children's Hospital. (Available from the BC Children's Hospital, 4480 Oak Street, Room 22D20, Vancouver, BC V6H 3V4, Canada.)

References

American Federation of Teachers. (1992). *The medically fragile child in the school setting.* Washington, DC: Author.

American Nurses Association. (1983). *Standards of school nursing practice.* Kansas City, MO: American Nurses Publishing.

Armstrong, N. T., Carr, T.S., Houghton, J., Belanish, J., & Mascia, J. (1995). Supporting medical and health concerns of young adults who are deaf–blind. In J. Everson (Ed.), *Supporting young adults who are deaf–blind in their communities* (pp. 43–66). Baltimore: Brookes.

Bergman, A. (1991). From recommendations to policy. In E. Eklunds (Ed.), *Health care for youth and adults with developmental disabilities: Policies and partnerships* (pp. 42–44). Silver Spring, MD: American Association of University Affiliated Programs.

Betz, C. L. (1996). A systems approach to adolescent transitions: An opportunity for nurses. *Journal of Pediatric Nursing, 11*(5), 271–272.

Blum, R. W. (1991). Overview of transition issues for youth with disabilities. *Pediatrician, 18,* 101–104.

Blum, R.W. (1994). Adolescents with chronic conditions and their families: The transition to adult services. In S. L. Hostler (Ed.), *Family-centered care: An approach to implementation.* Charlottesville, VA: The University of Virginia.

Blum, R. W. (1995). Transition to adult health care: Setting the stage. *Journal of Adolescent Health, 17,* 3–5.

Blum, R. W. (1997). Sexual health contraceptive needs of adolescents with chronic conditions. *Archives of Pediatric and Adolescent Medicine, 151,* 290–297.

Blum, R. W., & Geber, G. (1992). Chronically ill youth. In E. R. McAnarney, R. E. Kreipe, D. P. Orr, & G. D. Comerci (Eds.), *Textbook of adolescent medicine* (pp. 222–228). Philadelphia: W. B. Saunders.

Blum, R. W., Resnick, M. D., Nelson, R., & St. Germaine, A. (1991). Family and peer issues among adolescents with spine bifida and cerebral palsy. *Pediatrics, 88,* 280–285.

Bradley, V. J., Ashbaugh, J. W., & Blaney, B. C. (1994). *Creating individual supports for people with developmental disabilities.* Baltimore: Brookes.

Cappelli, M., MacDonald, N. E., & McGrath, P. L. (1989). Assessment of readiness to transfer to adult care for adolescents with cystic fibrosis. *CAC, 18,* 218–221.

Cox, A. W., & Shannon, P. (1997). *Youth speak out about their health.* Richmond, VA: Virginia Department of Health.

Denniston, S., & Enlow, C. (1995). *Making choices: A journal workbook for teens and young adults with spina bifida that provides opportunities for making choices about their lives.* Louisville, KY: Spina Bifida Association of Kentucky's Transition to Independence Project.

Edelman, A. (1995). Maximizing success: Transition planning for education after high school for young adults with chronic illness. *Information from HEATH,15*(1), 1–3.

Farley, T., Vines, C., McCluer, S., Stefans, V., & Hunter, J. (1994). Secondary disabilities in Arkansans with spina bifida. *European Journal of Surgery, 40,* 21–31.

Haas, M. B. (Ed.). (1993). *The school nurse's source book of individualized healthcare plans.* North Branch, MN: Sunrise River Press.

Halpern, A. S. (1994). The transition of youth with disabilities to adult life: A position statement of the Division on Career Development and Transition, The Council for Exceptional Children. *Career Development for Exceptional Individuals, 17,* 115–124.

Hardin, P. (1995a). *Becoming the me I want to be: A guide for youth with spina bifida and their parents.* Louisville, KY: Spina Bifida Association of Kentucky's Transition to Independence Project.

Hardin, P. (1995b). *Building skills: A guide for parents and professionals working with young people who have spina bifida.* Louisville, KY: Spina Bifida Association of Kentucky's Transition to Independence Project.

Hostler, S. L., Gressard, R. P., Hassler, C. R., & Linden, P. G. (1989). Adolescent autonomy project: Transition skills for adolescents with physical disabilities. *CAC, 18,* 12–18.

Igoe, J. B. (1975). The school nurse practitioner. *Nursing Outlook, 23,* 381–384.

Igoe, J. B. (1980). Summary of statement on school nurses working with handicapped children. *Journal of School Health, 50*(5), 287.

Igoe, J. B. (1994). School nursing. *Nursing Clinics of North America, 29*(3), 443–458.

Igoe, J. B., & Speers, S. E. (1992). The community health nurse in the schools. In M. Stanhope & J. Lancaster (Eds.), *Community health nursing: Process and practice for promoting health* (pp. 707–730). St. Louis, MO: Mosby-Yearbook.

Johnson, C. P. (1996). Transition in adolescents with disabilities. In A. Capute & P. Accardo (Eds.), *Developmental disabilities in infancy and childhood* (2nd ed.) (pp. 549–570). Baltimore: Brookes.

Kelly, A. (1995). The primary care provider's role in caring for young people with chronic illness. *Journal of Adolescent Health, 17,* 32–36.

Lollar, D. J. (Ed.). (1994). *Preventing secondary conditions associated with spina bifida or cerebral palsy.* Washington, DC: Spina Bifida Association of America.

Magyary, D., & Brandt, P. (1996). A school-based self-management program for youth with chronic health conditions and their parents. *Canadian Journal of Nursing Research, 28*(4), 57–77.

Maternal and Child Health Improvement Projects. (1996). *Application guidance for preparing for adolescent transitions.* Washington, DC: U.S. Department of Health and Human Services.

McManus, M. A., Newacheck. P. W., & Greaney, A. M. (1990). Young adults with special health care needs: Prevalence, severity, and access to health services. *Pediatrics, 86,* 674–682.

Meeropol, E. (1991). One of the gang: Sexual development of adolescents with physical disabilities. *Journal of Pediatric Nursing, 4,* 243–249.

Meleis, A. I. (1975). Role insufficiency and role supplementation: A conceptual framework. *Nursing Research, 24,* 264–271.

National Association of School Nurses. (1996). *Issue brief: School nurses and the Individuals with Disabilities Education Act (IDEA).* Scarborough, ME: Author.

National Center for Youth with Disabilities. (1993). *Teenagers at risk: A national perspective of state level services for adolescents with chronic illness or disability.* Minneapolis, MN: Author.

National Center for Youth with Disabilities. (1996). *Transitions from child to adult health care services: A national survey.* Minneapolis, MN: Author.

Nelson, R. P. (1991). Access to health care: The necessity of partnerships. In E. Eklund (Ed.), *Health care for youth and adults with developmental disabilities: Policies and partnerships* (pp. 51-56). Silver Spring, MD: American Association of University Affiliated Programs.

Nosek, M. A. (1995). Sexual abuse of women with physical disabilities. *Physical Medicine and Rehabilitation: State of the Art Reviews, 9*(2), 487–501.

Nosek, M. A., Howland, C. A., Young, M. E., Georgiou, D., Rintala, D. H., Foley, C. C., Bennett, J. L., & Smith, Q. (1994). Wellness models and sexuality among women with physical disabilities. *Journal of Applied Rehabilitation Counseling, 25*(1), 50–58.

Patrick, D. L., Richardson, M., Starks, H. E., & Rose, M. A. (1994). A framework for promoting the health of people with disabilities. In D. Lollar (Ed.), *Preventing secondary conditions associated with spina bifida or cerebral palsy: proceedings and recommendations of a symposium* (pp. 3–16). Washington, DC: Spina Bifida Association of America.

Peterson, P. M., Rauen, K. K., Brown, J., & Cole, J. (1994). Spina bifida: The transition into adulthood begins in infancy. *Rehabilitation Nursing, 19*(4), 229–238.

Pless, I. D., Feeley, N., Gottlieb, L., Rowat, K., Dougherty, G., & Willard, B. (1994). A randomized trial of a nursing intervention to promote the adjustment of children with chronic physical disorders. *Pediatrics, 94,* 70–75.

Proctor, S. T., Lordi, S. L., & Zaiger, D. S. (1993). *School nursing practice: Roles and standards.* Scarborough, ME: National Association of School Nurses.

Russell, M. T., Reinbold, J., & Maltby, H. J. (1996). Transferring to adult health care: Experiences of adolescents with cystic fibrosis. *Journal of Pediatric Nursing, 11*(4), 262-268.

Santilli, N. (Ed.). (1996). *Managing seizures disorders.* Landover, MD: Lippincott-Ravin.

Sawin, K. J. (1983). Assisting the adolescent with disabilities through a college health program. *Nursing Clinics of North America, 18*(2), 257–274.

Sawin, K. J. (1998). Health care concerns for women with chronic illness and disability. In E. Youngkin & M. Davis (Eds.), *Women's health: A primary care clinical guide* (2nd ed.) (pp. 697–719). East Norwalk, CT: Appleton & Lange.

Sawin, K. J., & Marshall, J. (1992). Developmental competence in adolescents with an acquired disability. *Rehabilitation Nursing Research Journal, 1,* 41–50.

Sawin, K. J., & Metzger, S. (1996). The experience of living with epilepsy from an adolescent and parent's perspective. *Epelilepsia, 37*(5), 86.

Sawin, K. J., Pellock, J., & Metzger, S. (1998). *Factors associated with developmental competence in adolescents with epilepsy.* Paper presented at the 12th Annual Conference of the Southern Nursing Research Society, Ft. Worth, TX.

Schumacher, K. L., & Meleis, A. I. (1994). Transitions: A central concept in nursing. *IMAGE: Journal of Nursing Scholarship, 26*(2), 119–127.

Sobsey, D. (1994). *Violence and abuse.* Baltimore: Brookes.

Snyder, A. A. (Ed.). (1991). *Implementation guide for the standards of school nursing practice.* Kent, OH: American School Health Association.

Spencer, A., Fife, R., & Rabinovich, C. (1995). The school experience of children with arthritis: Coping in the 1990s and transition into adulthood. *Pediatric Clinics of North America, 42*(5), 1285–1298.

Suris, J. C., Resnick, M. D., Cassuto, N., & Blum, R. W. (1996). Sexual behavior of adolescents with chronic disease and disability. *Journal of Adolescent Health, 19*(2), 124–131.

U. S. Department of Health and Human Services, Maternal and Child Health Bureau. (1992). *Moving on: Transition from child-centered to adult health care for youth with disabilities.* Washington, DC: Author.

Wehman, P. (1992). *Life beyond the classroom: Transition strategies for young people with disabilities.* Baltimore: Brookes.

Wold, S. J. (1981). *School nursing: A framework for practice.* North Branch, MN: Sunrise River Press.

Woodfill, M. M., & Beyrer, M. K. (1991). *The role of the nurse in the school setting: A historical perspective.* Kent, OH: American School Health Association.

Younger, J. B. (1991). A theory of mastery. *Advances in Nursing Science, 14*(1), 76–89.

C H A P T E R

SCHOOL SOCIAL WORK

Martha Markward

P. David Kurtz

The real purpose of our existence is not to make a living, but to make a life—a worthy, well-rounded, useful life.

—Anonymous

Society is challenged to meet the needs of persons with disabilities in transition from school to work or postsecondary education. The Human Services Institute (1985) reported that approximately 300,000 youths with disabilities leave high school each year, and the majority of them are faced with unemployment and underemployment. Apolloni, Feichtner, and West (1991) noted that 67% of all Americans with disabilities between the ages of 16 and 64 do not work; of the 33% who do work, 75% work only part time. Specialized vocational training, cooperative education, and other school-based programs serve only about 25% of America's youth (Apolloni, Feichtner, & West, 1991).

The absence of transition programs for so many young people brings into question the extent to which youth with disabilities have access to support services in the school to postschool transition. With that question in mind, this chapter examines the extent to which social work can contribute to transition planning and programming for youth with disabilities. The fourfold purpose of the chapter is to describe the discipline of social work, discuss the relationship between school social work and transition, identify challenges social workers must accept in becoming involved in the transition experience, and present a vision of the future that includes social work in transition planning and programming.

The Discipline of Social Work: A Frame of Reference

The frame of reference for considering social work involvement in the transition of individuals with disabilities is in understanding social work as a discipline. That understanding is contingent on knowledge of the mission, purposes, and values of social work, as well as on the focus, roles, and skills of social work practitioners. Within the discipline of social work, knowledge of school social work as a specialized field of practice, as well as information about transition-related policies, programs, and services, also take on salience in considering social work involvement in the transition of youths with disabilities.

Mission, Purposes, and Values of Social Work

The National Association of Social Workers (NASW) noted that the primary mission of social work is "to enhance human well-being and help meet basic human needs, with particular attention to the needs of the vulnerable, oppressed, and poor people" (Hepworth, Rooney, & Larson, 1997, p. 4). By comparison, the Council on Social Work Education (CSWE), the organization that accredits undergraduate and graduate programs, describes the social work profession as "committed to the enhancement of human well-being and to the alleviation of poverty and oppression" (Hepworth et al., 1997, p. 4). Within the context of this commitment, CSWE suggests that social work has four main purposes.

The first purpose of social work is the promotion, restoration, maintenance, and enhancement of social functioning of individuals, families, groups, organizations, and communities by helping them accomplish tasks, prevent and alleviate distress, and use resources. A second purpose is the planning, formulation, and implementation of social policies, services, resources, and programs needed to meet basic human needs and support the development of human capacities. A third purpose is the pursuit of policies, services, resources, and programs through organizational or administrative advocacy and social or political action to empower groups at risk and to promote social and economic justice. The fourth and last purpose of social work is the development and testing of professional knowledge and skills related to these programs.

With those purposes in mind, social work professionals also adhere to five values when working with clients. According to Hepworth, Rooney, and Larsen (1997), those values are (a) regard for individual worth and dignity, as well as relationships advanced by mutual participation, acceptance, confidentiality, honesty, and responsible handling of conflict; (b) respect for the individual's right to make independent decisions and to participate actively in the helping process; (c) commitment to assisting clients obtain needed resources; (d) make social institutions more humane and responsive to human needs; and (e) respect for and acceptance of the unique characteristics of diverse populations. Within the context of adhering to those five values, social workers focus on interactions between individuals and their environments.

Focus, Roles, and Skills of Social Work

Many experts agree that the focus of social work is on the interactions between individuals and their environments (Compton & Galaway, 1994; Hepworth et al., 1997; McMahon, 1990; Pincus & Minahan, 1983; Sheafor, Horejsi, & Horejsi, 1988). Gordon (1965) noted the emphasis on individualizing the person-in-situation complex to achieve the best match between each person and the environment, in which either person-behavior or environmental situation may deviate widely from the typical or normative. Similarly, Bartlett (1970) emphasized social functioning as the relation between the coping activity of people and the demands on them in the environment. This focus suggests that social work practitioners must have knowledge of human behavior, social welfare policy, research, and practice methods to take on a variety of roles.

Lister (1987) noted that social work roles include direct service provider, system linkage, system developer, system maintenance, and researcher/research consumer. *Direct service* provision involves social workers in individual casework, marital/family therapy, group work, or educator/disseminator of information. *Systems linkage* requires social workers to take on either a broker, case manager/coordinator, mediator/arbitrator, or client advocate role. *Systems development* means that social workers must know how to create effective and efficient programs. *Systems maintenance* requires social workers to act as organizational analyst, facilitator/expediter, team member, or consultant/consultee. Last, as a researcher/research consumer, social workers evaluate practice and program effectiveness.

Bisno (1969) proposed that social workers need to know what change strategies to use and how to use them. Most educators and practitioners agree that social workers must have skill in using the problem-solving method (Compton & Galaway, 1994; Hepworth et al., 1997). The problem-solving method describes a change process that requires social workers to have skills in the areas of assessment/diagnosis, planning, intervention, evaluation, and follow-up. In using this method at all levels of practice, social workers define problems independent of intervention models and then select the most appropriate, effective model of intervention.

Several researchers (Rapp, 1992; Saleeby, 1992; Weick, 1992) have emphasized the strengths, rather than the deficit, perspective on social work practice. The strengths perspective is guided by several notions. These notions include (a) respect for client strengths, (b) clients have many strengths, (c) client motivation is contingent on fostering client strengths, (d) the social worker is a collaborator with the client, (e) the victim mindset is avoided, and (f) the environment is full of resources. This perspective rests on ideas about empowerment (Rappaport, 1990), membership (Walzer, 1983), regeneration and healing from within (Dossey, 1989; Gazzaniga, 1988), synergy (Freire, 1993; Heineman-Piper, 1989; Katz, 1984), dialogue or collaboration (Friedman, 1985; Rappaport, 1990), and suspension of disbelief (Rooney, 1988).

Empowerment is the notion that people have power within themselves. *Membership* is the belief that everyone needs a communal place and identity. *Regeneration* suggests that individuals have great healing powers within themselves. *Synergy* results when resources are created from human activity and intentions. *Collaboration* occurs when relationships are formed. Finally, *suspension of disbelief* means that what people say must be believed rather than disbelieved in the here and now.

With these core ideas in mind, the three assumptions that underlie the strengths perspective create a new agenda for social work practice (Weick, 1992). First, every person has inherent power that can be recognized as life force. Second, power (from within oneself) is a potent form of knowledge that can guide personal and social transformation. Third, people are more likely to act on strengths when their positive capacities are supported. Within the context of these assumptions, many in the profession find the strengths perspective to be more consistent with social work's mission, purposes, and values than is the deficit problem-solving perspective.

Social Work and Transition

To understand the relationship between social work and transition, one must be familiar with school social work, including its history, models of practice, and changes that have occurred in this specialized field of practice. It is also necessary for one to know how school social workers are involved in the lives of youth with special needs. Last, it is important to examine the policies that give impetus to social work involvement in transition planning and programming.

School Social Work

Allen-Meares, Washington, and Welsh (1996) noted that at the turn of the century school social work grew out of the belief of settlement workers that it was necessary for them to know the teachers of children who came to the settlement houses. In this context, settlement house workers linked home and school. By the 1920s, the role of these "visiting teachers" had expanded. The school was viewed as a strategic center of child welfare work, linking children and their families with resources they needed to learn and grow (Allen-Meares et al., 1996, p. 27). The values of social work can be applied to school social work in the following way (see Allen-Meares, Washington, & Welsh, 1996, p. 71):

- Each pupil is valued as an individual regardless of any unique characteristic.

- Each pupil should be allowed to share in the learning process and to learn.

- Individual differences should be recognized; intervention should be aimed at supporting pupils' educational goals.

- Each child, regardless of race and socioeconomic characteristics, has a right to equal treatment in the school.

Between 1920 and 1960, school social workers moved away from a focus on social change (environment) and toward a focus on social casework (individual). By the 1970s, school social workers once again focused on targeting a variety of problems in the school, and in the 1980s, they began to focus on particular groups of pupils who were experiencing problems, such as leaving school early and teen pregnancy. Over time, several models of school social work have been identified.

Sarri and Maple (1972) identified the traditional clinical, school change, social interaction, and community–school models of practice. Costin (1975) developed the school–community model and emphasized the importance of assessment as well as teaming. Respectively, those models focus on (a) the social and emotional problems of individual children and their parents; (b) the school as a client, and its policies and practices; (c) deprived or disadvantaged communities; (d) the reciprocal influences of individuals and groups; and last, (e) system changes, as well as the complexity of interactions in the school-community-pupil system.

More recently, Monkman (1996) noted that school social workers must develop networks of relationships. In doing so, they are more likely to be brokers, teachers, advocates, facilitators, managers, mediators, consultants, collaborators, and policy initiators than traditional clinicians. Freeman and Pennekamp (1988) posited that school systems should empower social workers to connect with professionals outside the school setting. Dryfoos (1994) also noted that social services provided by professionals outside the school should be linked to services provided by professionals in schools.

School social workers must now focus on interventions with children and youth that involve changes in school, community, and family necessary to achieve student-related goals. Many experts believe that school social workers must use a transactional perspective to view the child, family, and school staff as part of the change process rather than as resistant to change. In particular, Germain and Gitterman (1996) proposed that school social work must now be concerned with the life transitions of individuals, the lack of responsiveness of environments to individual needs, and communication or relationship difficulties.

Transition-Related School Social Work Activities

Several experts have identified the need for support services, student/parent involvement, and interagency linkage in transition programs (Allen-Meares, Washington, & Welsh, 1996; Halpern, 1994; Sarkees-Wircenski & Wircenski, 1994). Allen-Meares et al. conceded that "much work and thought needs to be given to the development of transitional programs [by school social workers], such as when students move from elementary to secondary education, as well as from secondary to postsecondary education and/or work" (p. 132). Nonetheless, school social workers are involved in a number of transition-related activities.

Collaboration/Teaming

Social workers collaborate with others in schools (Buchweitz, 1993; Curtis, Curtis, & Graden, 1988; Dupper, 1993; Furr, 1993; Gibelman, 1993; Harold & Harold, 1991; Pope, Campbell, & Kurtz, 1992). Gibelman (1993) contended that, during this time of service cutbacks, school social work professionals must work closely and cooperatively with other support service personnel, especially counselors and psychologists. Moreover, Buchweitz (1993) noted the importance of school social workers having interchangeable roles in working with other professionals to better serve children and youth with emotional disabilities. School social workers team with school psychologists, school counselors, and school nurses to enhance the functioning of children and youth and their families.

School social workers are involved in collaborations that address issues related to curriculum and program development. Based on findings that young women in a vocational education track are more negatively impacted across a number of outcome measures than those in the academic track, Furr (1993) recommended that school social workers facilitate interactions among teachers, administrators, and vocational students to share this information and work to improve the situation. Dupper (1993) suggested that school social workers collaborate with others to develop dropout prevention programs by focusing on the ecosystems of children or youth, early problem identification/intervention, and the factors that contribute to their problem. In some states, such as Illinois, school social workers are members of formal diagnostic or assessment teams that are comprised of a school psychologist, an occupational therapist, a speech–language specialist, and teachers.

Assessment/Diagnostics

Social workers gather data for the purpose of determining a student's eligibility for special services by completing a social developmental study (SDS) and by administering a measure of adaptive behavior to gain insights into a child's background and development. They then share their findings during the multidisciplinary conference (MDC), which may result in social work service being written into the individual educational program (IEP) as a "related" service. By contrast, school social workers in Georgia are not involved formally in the assessment process that determines a child's eligibility for special services, but on occasion, they attend the MDCs.

Several authors have highlighted the role of school social workers in the assessment of problems experienced by children and youth (Drisko, 1993; Pryor, 1996; Sands, 1994; Ziesemer & Marcoux, 1992). Ziesemer and Marcoux (1992) stressed the salience of social work involvement in early screening so that children can be included in programs that meet their needs. Drisko (1993) noted that social workers can help special educators and vocational educators assess the connection between behavior and feelings in the learning process, as well as the amount of time students are productive in the special education classroom and their functioning in the classroom group. Sands (1994) found that school social workers can assess the extent to which parents clearly understand the technical terms professionals use to communicate about a child's difficulties.

Pryor (1996) proposed that school social workers take leadership in assessing family–school relationships. As such, Pryor suggests techniques for doing this, which include (a) informal observation and discussion; (b) examination of preexisting data; (c) review places, policies, and programs; (d) focus group discussion; (e) mailed survey; (f) survey at school; (g) telephone survey; and (h) radio call-in. With respect to the number of students who begin the transition from school to work in the marketplace, Markward (1991) suggested that social workers should attend to the family-school-work connection as well.

School social workers often become involved in the assessment of special needs problems very early in a child's life. As a member of the assessment team, the school social worker comes to know many children and youth with disabilities and their families over time, even when social work services are not a related service in the IEP. As members of the assessment team, social workers are involved in reevaluating each special student's educational plan every three years; as such, they have considerable access to working with students' families over time.

Information about a student's ability to adapt in particular environments takes on salience in the student's school to postschool transition. At the time of a student's final reevaluation for special education eligibility prior to graduation from high school, even school social workers who are members of assessment teams typically pay little attention to students' adaptive behavior, especially as it relates to successful school to postschool transition. Unfortunately, few school social workers address in any substantive way the career development of these young people, despite the fact that they may have worked the students and their families for many years.

Committee/Organizational Work

School social workers sit on committees and become involved with particular organizations to affect change on behalf of children and youth (Bailey, 1992; Dupper, 1993; Raines, 1996; Streeter & Franklin, 1993). Bailey (1992) noted that some school social workers are involved in community meetings, as well as in conducting action research, in an attempt to affect change that impacts positively on particular groups of children and youth. Social workers can play a key role in site-based management, a collaborative decision-making process that occurs within the local educational agency (Streeter & Franklin, 1993). Social workers, along with parents, teachers, and students, are involved in establishing school policy that impacts on students in a particular school. Specifically, Raines (1996) proposed that school social workers educate teachers and other professionals about special education policies, as well as about students' disabilities.

In Georgia, school social workers are involved in organizational work within the context of the State's Family Connection Initiative. The initiative is a mechanism for ensuring that agencies and organizations are linked and professionals collaborate. Georgia's Family Connection initiative requires that agencies collaborate to receive block grant funding at the state level. As a result of this initiative, many school social workers sit on community-based committees and become involved with community-based organizations that provide services to youth with disabilities. For example, school social workers in Gwinnett County, Georgia are actively involved in the School-Based Resource Center, a community-based, Family Connection-funded program that focuses on school readiness and adjustment of children, as well as their families.

Linkage/Networking

Network building requires that school social workers coordinate resources, as well as integrate services, both inside and outside the school (Bennett, DeLuca, & Allen, 1996; Berrick & Duerr, 1996; Streeter & Franklin, 1993). In building networks, social workers must be especially knowledgeable of both positive and negative informal social networks of students and families in the community. Germain (1996) notes that social workers must have the ability to comprehend and conceptualize relationships between a client and multiple services, as well as among various school, agency, and community persons. Melaville and Blank (1993) contend that social workers in schools must work with community professionals to have an impact on social concerns.

By comparison, Berrick and Duerr (1996) point out that social workers from outside the school must pay particular attention to delivering effective services to students at all levels. This is problematic within the context that mental health professionals often provide traditional clinical casework services that focus on the problems within the individual, and teachers often perceive that professionals outside the school do not understand students' functioning in the school setting. Nonetheless, funding initiatives in many states, such as the P-16 Initiative in Georgia, require that communities and universities link services to enhance the aspirations of minority youth, many of whom have disabilities.

Specifically, Bennett, DeLuca, and Allen (1996) emphasize the importance of networks and linkages in working with families of children with disabilities. These researchers found that it is important to connect families with needed services that are already in existence, such as self-help groups that exist for parents of children who are learning disabled or have attention-deficit/hyperactivity disorder (ADHD). Markward (1998) notes that young adults with ADHD may lose jobs or employment opportunities because they are unable to organize work activities or are unable to handle distraction in the workplace. Social workers and others can play a critical role in helping non-ADHD family members understand the behavior of the ADHD family member.

Self-Advocacy

Several studies demonstrate the salience of self-advocacy among college students with learning disabilities (Hicks-Coolick, 1997; Hicks-Coolick & Kurtz, 1997). Hicks-Coolick and Kurtz (1997) found that successful college students with learning disabilities were highly motivated, had sound academic preparation, and were self-advocates. Hicks-Coolick (1997) found that problem solving and knowledge of the learning disability predicted self-advocacy among college students with learning disabilities. Other studies (Carpenter-Aeby & Kurtz, 1997;

Kurtz & Tandy, 1995) demonstrated the usefulness of using the narrative approach and portfolio development in working with clients and their families (Farr, 1994; Kingore, 1993; Koretz, 1992; Porter, 1995; Seely, 1994).

Parent Involvement/Home–School Relations

Parent involvement is a primary focus of many school social workers (Chavkin & Brown, 1992; Constable, 1992; Dupper, 1993; Grief, 1993; Page, 1993; Segal, 1992). Within the context that school is a community of families and educators, Constable (1992) noted that school social workers help remove obstacles that prevent parents from being involved in their children's schooling, such as cultural misunderstanding and lack of communication about a child's behavior at school. Social workers remain challenged to engage many parents who most needed to be involved in their child's learning, specifically parents of older ADHD students who had taken in much negative feedback from school personnel over the years.

Many high school personnel discourage parent involvement because they expect students to be responsible for themselves. This mindset is particularly problematic when one considers that many adolescents and young adults with disabilities are far more socially and emotionally immature than their age would indicate. Moreover, Markward (1992a) noted that the "home-school-work" relationship is important to consider with respect to high school students who work. The relationship may be especially important for youth with "invisible" disabilities who work while attending high school at a time when they are trying to detach from an "LD" (learning disability) label. These students are unlikely to ask for or receive the support in the workplace to acquire the personal and social responsibility they need to be competent workers (Markward, 1992b).

Challenges of Social Work in Transition Planning

Clearly, the mission, purposes, and values of social work are consistent with the emphasis on quality of life in the transition experience of young people with disabilities (Halpern, 1994), especially when one considers that the profession is moving toward using a strengths rather than deficit perspective. Specifically, school social workers are routinely involved in transition-related activities, including collaboration/teaming, assessment, community or organizational work, linkage or networking, parent involvement, and work with students. Even though experts on transition planning support the involvement of social workers in the process (Clark & Kolstoe, 1994; Wehman, 1996), this involvement brings challenges with it both from within and outside the profession.

Challenges from Within the Social Work Profession

The first challenge from within the profession is the territorialism in which many social workers engage. For example, social work professionals outside the school sometimes view their colleagues in schools as too generalist in their orientation. In contrast, school social workers sometimes view social workers and other helping professionals in agencies outside the school as lacking the knowledge about schools to provide appropriate services to students on campus.

The second challenge is that many school social workers view the use of services outside the school as a threat to their jobs and, in many cases, it is. In some situations, decision makers in schools perceive that it is cheaper for them to contract for services outside the school than to hire their own helping professionals. Freeman and Pennekamp (1988) proposed that, if schools empowered school social workers to coordinate, manage, and facilitate services, they could better address the life transitions of students and the unresponsiveness of environments to the needs of students in transition.

A third challenge is that most school social workers focus on the problems of students in elementary schools as a means of early intervention and prevention rather than the problems of students in high school. Moreover, Markward (1993) found that, at the secondary level, school social workers tend to provide clinical casework more frequently than any other type of service. Interestingly, Markward, Vonk, and Arnold (1998) note that social workers in postsecondary educational settings are likely to be involved in career counseling.

Challenges from Outside the Social Work Profession

The major challenge to social workers from outside the profession is acceptance into transition planning. Social work was designated a related service in the Education for All Handicapped Children Act (EHA) passed in 1975. Still, many vocational and special educators underutilize this service or do not recognize the contributions that social workers could make in transition planning for youth with disabilities. This seems salient in light of the fact that social workers have expertise in several areas of transition planning.

In fact, at the core of most educational service redesigns are better coordination of services and collaboration among professionals in the various education, health, and social services systems. With this in mind, Pennekamp (1992) questioned why restructuring documents and reform debates fail to acknowledge the skills of those best trained and most experienced in home-school-community collaboration—the school social workers, psychologists, nurses, and counselors. As noted earlier, school social workers and school nurses have consistently been involved in home—school linkage since the turn of the century.

With the budget constraints in many school districts, school administrators believe that community systems integrate services for students and their families as well or better than in-house professionals—and for less money. Pennekamp (1992) argued that this shift would likely separate education from human services and diminish the likelihood that the whole child or family would be at the center of service provision. This argument takes on significance when one considers that it took the passage of the EHA to ensure that school-based services were provided to children and youths with disabilities. Historically, community service providers have had little understanding of or commitment to youths with disabilities acquiring adult competence in living, working, and citizenship.

A related challenge to social workers who want to be involved in transition planning and programming is the problem of large caseloads. By comparison, Illinois and Michigan have many more school social workers than does Georgia. For example, Torres (1996) noted that Georgia had 206 school social workers, whereas Illinois had 1,349. Moreover, the number of school social workers in Georgia is disproportionately small in comparison to the number of school counselors (Swafford, Hooks, Markward, & Golde, 1998). Even though few school districts include social work as a related service in the IEP of students, the most recent amendments to the EHA emphasized its importance in transition planning.

Decredentializing presents another challenge to social workers becoming involved with transition planning. Although successful planning requires input from the most qualified personnel available, those personnel are the most expensive. The trend in managed care is to hire the least expensive service provider, regardless of credentials. In Georgia's state prekindergarten program, the family service coordinators have historically held a master's degree in social work (MSW); the criterion for this position is now a high school diploma. The danger is that decredentializing will result in poorly qualified people working on complex tasks such as transition planning.

A Vision of Social Work Involvement in Transition Planning

The vision of social work involvement in transition planning is one in which social workers and others use a strengths approach to enhance the preparation curriculum, transition planning, and postschool follow-up for young people with disabilities (Kochhar & West, 1995). In order for students to attain a substantial improvement in postschool adjustment and quality of life, experts suggest that transition planning must focus on basic academic knowledge or skills and functional life skills for everyday living.

Clark (1990) defined functional curriculum as "instructional content that focuses on the concepts and skills needed by students . . . in order to achieve life adjustment. These concepts and skills are individually determined through functional assessment and are targeted for current and future needs" (p. 3). Literature on this topic universally speaks of the transitional process as being different for different kinds of students and of the importance of students and families having a significant voice in all three phases of the process (Dybwad & Bersani, 1996; Edgar, 1987; Halpern, 1996).

The challenge is how can social workers enable students to maximize their potential as they move into becoming young adults? Poertner and Ronnau (1992) proposed a disability model of practice that has utility for social workers involved in the school to postschool transition of youth with disabilities. The value of this model is that it incorporates seven principles that seem quite consistent with the tenets set forth by transition experts (Poertner & Ronnau, 1992, p. 115). These principles can provide all professionals involved in transition planning and programming with a set of common guidelines for practice:

- The disability is only one of the youth's characteristics; the individual and the disability are not one and the same.
- Youth with disabilities have abilities/strengths.
- Youth with disabilities can learn and grow.
- Youth with disabilities are the primary informants on how they experience the disabilities.
- A youth with a disability should be part of the mainstream rather than outside it.
- Society should make reasonable accommodations for youth with disabilities.
- Families are primary caregivers.

The Disability Is Only One Characteristic

The vision is one in which former students who are now young adults are living in the community as happy, self-reliant, and productive individuals. What one sees is not much different from what one sees when one looks at a group of nondisabled young people—smiling, sad, excited, or concerned faces; people working, playing, reading, watching television, sleeping, or eating. The vision is one in which individuals with disabilities have had the opportunity to build on characteristics apart from their disability. Each person is living his or her life to its full potential.

School social workers often see the youth's home environment and hear about the youth's activities in the home, neighborhood, and community; they know what characteristics contribute to a youth's positive feelings about himself or herself. Social workers can ascertain from youth with disabilities themselves what traits or characteristics apart from their disability account for their resilience each day. For example, what enables a nonsighted student to make it through the day on a college campus? Among the abilities that college-bound students need are good language and communication skills, high motivation, a positive attitude toward learning, an understanding of the disability, and problem-solving skills (Hicks-Coolick, 1997; Hicks-Coolick & Kurtz, 1997; Vogel and Adelman, 1990).

Youth with Disabilities Have Abilities

Social workers, other professionals, and youth with disabilities can collaborate in identifying the abilities of youth with disabilities. In education, there has been considerable experimentation with and writing about the use of portfolios to assess students' academic performance, enrich classroom subjects, facilitate the training of teachers, and measure program outcomes (Farr, 1994; Kingore, 1993; Koretz, 1992; Porter, 1995; Seely, 1994). Portfolios have also been used to prepare adults for employment (Bernhard, Cole, & Ryan, 1993) and to facilitate the mainstreaming of a student with a disability (Karoly & Franklin, 1996).

The overall purpose of portfolio use in working with students who have disabilities is to illustrate their in-school and out-of-school experiences and hopefully create a healthier picture of themselves. Portfolios enable students to (a) realistically externalize problems that do not derive from their disabilities; (b) establish an organized record of school or work activities; (c) review reflectively their experiences with significant others; (d) narrate their growing sense of self, particularly as an advocate; (e) promote a link between current educational experiences and future postschool lives; and (f) document successes and create résumés to present at IEP meeting or to employers, landlords, and human service providers.

For example, Carpenter-Aeby and Kurtz (1997) described a situation in which a social worker in an alternative school setting made extensive use of portfolios to assist chronically disruptive students to make successful transitions back to the sending school. The study illustrated how the social worker and other school personnel used a multisystem intervention in preparing students for the transition. The social worker provided a variety of counseling services to both students and their families, brokered and coordinated community services and resources, and monitored the activities to provide cohesion during the transition. Throughout the process, the portfolio, which built on the student's self-perceptions of abilities, served as the focal point and framework for ongoing assessment and intervention by all professionals.

Youth with Disabilities Can Learn and Grow

Social workers pay particular attention to self-advocacy as a way for young people with disabilities to learn and grow. Self-advocacy is a *process* of "learning to speak up and ask for what you need . . . taking charge of your life . . . being more independent . . . building self-confidence" (Carpenter, 1986, p. 2). Self-advocacy may be a version of what Dewey (1938) promoted when he stated, "The purpose of education is to allow each individual to come into full possession of his or her personal power" (p. 23), which is very consistent with respect for self-determination (Richmond, 1922). Becoming a self-advocate is not simply a matter of acquiring a set of predetermined skills or increasing one's knowledge; rather, one must be able to experience a sense of growing independence (Dewey, 1938).

In order for students to advocate for themselves, at a minimum it seems necessary that they develop a sense of themselves as advocates, *and* that the climate in the home, school, work, and community supports and reinforces students' self-advocacy efforts. Significant others in the social environments of youth must treat the youth as resources throughout the entire transitional process, which means that professionals must let go of the attitude that they know what is best for youth and replace it with the attitude of genuine respect toward the youth's strengths and abilities (Lofquist, 1992). With this attitude, professionals can work with youth as partners, giving them a significant voice, enabling them to play key roles in decision making, and allowing them to create transition goals and solutions.

Developing a portfolio is an excellent way for youth with disabilities to learn. The process puts the students in touch with new and alternative ways of seeing themselves as whole people in relation to the disability, an essential dimension in becoming a self-advocate. The process entails accumulating course work, certificates, art work, essays, stories, and other artifacts, as well as working with social workers, teachers, counselors, and parents to construct the product. This process may very well result in the student becoming a problem-solving person who is ready to speak for herself or himself at the IEP conference and making the school to postschool transition.

Youth Are Primary Informants about Disability Experience

Despite the lack of empirical evidence to support the use of the narrative approach as an effective intervention, school social workers find the approach quite useful in assessing situations. Based on social constructivist theory which posits that perceptions form the basis of one's social reality, the major assumption under-girding the narrative approach is that all people have stories of their life experiences, which are more than simply the mirroring of life. Metaphorically speaking, people live their lives by stories and in narrative, and according to White (1993), the narrative serves to interpret and give meaning to life experiences and, insofar as behavior is prefigured by meaning making, stories shape actions.

The dominant story of college students with disabilities is often disempowering and pathologizing (Hicks-Coolick & Kurtz, 1997). The stories of some youth are filled with themes of personal limitations and accounts of adults attending to their needs. In using the narrative approach as a means of eliciting valuable information, social workers ask students and families curious questions to bring forth alternative stories that result in students reframing a negative situation into a positive one. This approach has the added benefit of allowing students and family members to be experts on their own lives and experiences.

Youth with A Disability Should Be Part of Society

Poertner and Ronnau (1992) contend that the ultimate goal of most treatment programs is for the youth with an emotional disability to become a "content, secure, productive member of society" (p. 117). Unfortunately, these authors note that many programs cut youth with emotional difficulties off from peers and normal community living. Many youth who are behaviorally or emotionally disordered leave school early because they have been excluded from the mainstream of school for many years. In 1994, Georgia passed legislation that provided state funding for alternative schools to accommodate students who are determined to be chronically disruptive.

At a time when the trend in the nation is to give state and local educational agencies more latitude in making decisions about how resources are allocated and for whom, social advocacy by social workers, psychologists, school nurses, and counselors, as well as special and vocational educators is warranted. Clearly, students who are excluded from or pushed out of school will not receive the transition services they deserve. Generally, all those who work with youth who have disabilities must advocate for youth in systems that are exclusionary.

Social workers can facilitate community involvement in transition planning. It is helpful for community human service agencies and other community resources, such as business and church representatives, to take notice of each student in transition and participate in exploring options for postschool life. Moreover, it is imperative that there is a goodness of fit between young adults with disabilities and community resources; with different disabilities, there are different needs for various community services and accommodations.

School social workers are in a unique position to broker and coordinate much involvement of community service providers. They are the school personnel who routinely work outside the school buildings in the homes, neighborhoods, and communities of students, as well as meet with human service colleagues in their offices and board rooms of their respective agencies or organizations. School social workers are regularly called upon to make home visits, attend conferences, and participate in community planning meetings.

Within this context, social workers may serve on transition councils (Clark & Kolstoe, 1994). They may also be involved in human service collaboratives, which may have a specific focus, such as homelessness or child maltreatment, or a more general focus. Collaboratives often are comprised of consumers, service providers, religious leaders, interested citizens, business persons, and government officials. The mission of a collaborative is to strengthen community responses to the needs of its citizens and coordinate services.

As such, a collaborative can serve as an excellent platform for making the needs of young adults with disabilities known to segments of the community. At the same time, a collaborative strengthens the linkage between school and community in the process of examining ways the community can be responsive to their needs. A collaborative also would provide a forum for young adults with disabilities to have a voice in community affairs and an arena for self-advocacy regarding those matters that directly affect them.

Society Should Accommodate Youth with Disabilities

Social workers can be particularly helpful in advocating for youth with disabilities in their transition from school to work or postsecondary education. Even though the Americans with Disabilities Act (ADA) of 1990 is a powerful piece of legislation that protects the civil rights of individuals with disabilities, most of those individuals need professionals who can help them take advantage of it. For many of society's youth, including early school leavers or youth with disabilities, the work experience in high school *is* their transition from school to work. Transition specialists can take steps to enhance it, perhaps through community collaboratives. In a society in which so many high school youth work, school social workers, as well as counselors and educators, must begin to link the home, school, and workplace to truly understand the school to postschool transition (Markward, 1991, 1992a, 1992b).

Families Are the Primary Caregivers

Given that school social workers have historically linked families with schools, they can share their expertise in this area by working with other professionals to meet objectives in transition planning. Social workers have considerable expertise in family-centered practice. In fact, the University of Georgia offers family-centered practice as a primary concentration of study for students working toward the MSW.

Before youth with disabilities can learn self-advocacy, their parents and families must first see themselves as resources and self-advocates. The narrative approach may also be especially useful as a means of assessing the extent to which parents have a sense of themselves as problem solvers and as knowledgeable about their child's disability, specifically its impact on the cognitive, affective, and behavioral domains of functioning. School social workers are in a unique position to work with psychologists, guidance counselors, teachers, and others to build on parents' resources and strengths.

Social workers are also challenged to advocate in the community for families of youth with disabilities. Accepting this challenge is often problematic in light of the fact that society expects high school students with mild to moderate disabilities to accept responsibility for themselves in the absence of parents. Despite this expectation, the school to postschool transition of youth with disabilities can be very unsettling for parents and families, even for those whose children are without disabilities. Social workers can be instrumental in establishing support or self-help groups for parents whose adolescents and young adults are in transition from school to work or postsecondary education.

In addition, social workers can work with counselors and others to educate the parents and families of youth with disabilities about career development and vocational options. At the minimum, parents could be educated about the workplace of those students who work while attending high school. It is essential that social workers view parents as "experts" and learn about the perceptions that form the basis of their social reality. Professionals might involve parents in empowerment research that engages them in investigating phenomena that are pertinent to the school to postschool transition of their adolescents and young adults with disabilities. In this process, professionals and parents together could develop transition programs that are meaningful to youth with disabilities and their parents.

The following case illustrates what happens when a social worker uses only several of the seven principles to guide transition planning.

 ## Tony

Tony began receiving special services in fourth grade for a learning disability that affected his learning in areas that required reading, such as social studies. In completing a measure of adaptive behavior with Tony and his parents, the social worker was able to validate to teachers, parents, and other school personnel Tony's strengths, especially his sensitivity, kindness, and gentleness. In light of the fact that the social worker discovered through a home visit that Tony was mechanically inclined, she asked Tony's teachers and parents to use reading material related to this area of interest. When Tony was in sixth grade, the social worker, special education teacher, assistant principal, and counselor gave Tony many leadership tasks to enhance his assertiveness and problem-solving capability. During middle school, the social worker facilitated a group that allowed Tony to be the primary informant about his life and disability, which resulted in his participation in IEP conferences. Unfortunately, the social worker failed to facilitate community involvement with Tony, even though the social worker was in an ideal position to link home, school, and community. Little was done by school personnel at the secondary level to ensure that society accommodate Tony's needs. Even though Tony's mother remained interested in and concerned about her son's future, neither the social worker nor other school personnel, including special and vocational education teachers, became actively involved in planning for Tony's transition from school to work. In the latter part of his freshman year in high school, Tony indicated that he no longer wanted to receive special services. By the middle of his sophomore year, Tony failed in school and associated with peers who used drugs and alcohol. He subsequently dropped out of school.

Final Thoughts

There is a growing challenge to meet the needs of persons with disabilities in transition from school to work or postsecondary education. Social workers teaming with educators and persons from the community can contribute to transitional planning and programming for young people with disabilities. Social workers can facilitate the transition process by performing important roles and providing essential services, such as collaborating with school personnel and community members, conducting various types of assessment (especially personality assessment), working with families, and keeping abreast of policies and laws.

Paulo Freire's (1993) writings related to empowerment education are informative in pointing to the importance of the role of community in enabling people to develop new beliefs in their ability to influence their personal and social spheres. A critical question he poses is, does education socialize people to be objects and accept their limited roles within the status quo, or does it encourage people to be actors in their own lives and in society? Social workers can play critical roles in helping youth with disabilities and their parents to be actors in and experts on their own lives.

References

Allen-Meares, P., Washington, R., & Welsh, B. (1996). *Social work services in schools* (2nd ed.). Needham Heights, MA: Allyn & Bacon.

Apolloni, T., Feichtner, S., & West, L. (1991). Learners and workers in the year 2001. *Journal for Vocational Special Needs Education, 14*(1), 5–10.

Bailey, D. (1992). Organizational change in a public school system: The synergism of two approaches. *Social Work in Education, 14*(2), 94–105.

Bartlett, H. (1970). *The common base of social work practice.* New York: National Association of Social Workers.

Bennett, T., DeLuca, D., & Allen, R. (1996). Families of children with disabilities: Positive adaptation across the life cycle. *Social Work in Education, 18*(1), 31–41.

Bernhard, G., Cole, D., & Ryan, C. (1993). Improving career decision making with adults: Use of the portfolio. *Journal of Employment Counseling, 30*(2), 67–73.

Berrick, J., & Duerr, M. (1996). Maintaining positive school relationships: The role of the social worker vis-a-vis full-service schools. *Social Work in Education, 18*(1), 53–57.

Bisno, H. (1969). A theoretical framework for teaching social work methods and skills with particular reference to undergraduate social welfare education. *Journal of Education for Social Work, 5*(2), 5–17.

Buchweitz, S. (1993). Birchwood: An exemplary educational program for students with emotional disabilities. *Social Work in Education, 15*(4), 241–246.

Carpenter, W. (1986). *Self advocacy for persons with learning disabilities.* Minneapolis, MN: Cognitive Learning Consultants.

Carpenter-Aeby, T., & Kurtz, D. (1997). *The portfolio as a strength-based intervention to empower chronically disruptive students in an alternative school.* Unpublished manuscript.

Chavkin, N., & Brown, K. (1992). School social workers building a multiethnic family-school-community partnership. *Social Work in Education, 14*(3), 160–164.

Clark, G. (1990). *Functional curriculum strategies.* Topeka, KS: Kansas State Department of Education.

Clark, G., & Kolstoe, O. (1994). *Career development and transition education for adolescents with disabilities* (2nd ed.). Needham Heights, MA: Allyn & Bacon.

Compton, B., & Galaway, B. (1994). *Social work process* (5th ed.). Pacific Grove, CA: Brooks/Coles Publishing.

Constable, R. (1992). The new reform and the school social worker. *Social Work in Education, 14*(2), 106–113.

Costin, L. (1975). School social work practice: A new model. *Social Work, 20*(21), 135–139.

Curtis, M., Curtis, V., & Graden, J. (1988). Prevention and early intervention through intervention assistance programs. *School Psychology International, 9,* 257–263.

Dewey, J. (1938). *Experience and education.* New York: Collier.

Dossey, L. (1989). *Recovering the soul: A scientific and spiritual search.* New York: Bantam Books.

Drisko, J. (1993). Special education teacher consultation: A student-focused, skill-helping approach. *Social Work in Education, 15*(1), 19–28.

Dryfoos, J. (1994). *Full-service schools: A revolution in health and social services for children, youth, and families.* San Francisco: Jossey-Bass.

Dupper, D. (1993). Preventing school dropouts: Guidelines for school social work practice. *Social Work in Education, 15*(3), 141–150.

Dybwad, G., & Bersani, H., Jr. (Eds.) (1996). *New voices: Self-advocacy by people with disabilities*. Cambridge, MA: Brookline Books.

Edgar, E. (1987). Secondary programs for special education: Are many of them justifiable? *Exceptional Children, 53,* 264–270.

Farr, R. (1994). *Portfolio and performance assessments: Helping students evaluate their progress as readers and writers*. Fort Worth, TX: Harcourt Brace.

Freeman, E., & Pennekamp, M. (1988). *Social work practice: Toward a child, family, school, community perspective*. Springfield, IL: Charles C. Thomas.

Freire, P. (1993). *Pedagogy of the oppressed*. New York: Continuum.

Friedman, M. (1985). *The healing dialogue in psychotherapy*. Northvale, NJ: Jason Aronson.

Furr, A. (1993). Curriculum tracking: A new arena for school social work. *Social Work in Education, 15*(1), 35–43.

Gazzaniga, M. (1988). *Mind matters*. Boston: Houghton Mifflin.

Germain, C. (1996). An ecological perspective on social work in the schools. In R. Constable, J. Flynn, & S. McDonald (Eds.), *School social work: Practice and research perspectives* (3rd ed.) (pp. 26–37). Chicago: Lyceum.

Germain, C., & Gitterman, A. (1996). *The life model of social work practice*. New York: Columbia University Press.

Gibelman, M. (1993). School social workers, counselors, and psychologists in collaboration: A shared agenda. *Social Work in Education, 15*(1), 47.

Gordon, W. (1965). Knowledge and value: Their distinction and relationship in clarifying social work practice. *Social Work, 10*(4), 32–39.

Grief, G. (1993). A school-based support group for urban African American parents. *Social Work in Education, 15*(3), 133–139.

Halpern, A. (1994). The transition of youth with disabilities to adult life: A position statement of the Division on Career Development and Transition, The Council for Exceptional Children. *Career Development for Exceptional Individuals, 17,* 115–124.

Halpern, A. (1996). The transition of youth with disabilities to adult life. In J. Patton & G. Blalock (Eds.), *Transition and students with learning disabilities*. Austin, TX: PRO-ED.

Harold, N., & Harold, R. (1991). School-based health clinics: A vehicle for social work intervention. *Social Work in Education, 13*(3), 185–195.

Heineman-Piper, M. (1985). The future of social work research. *Social Work Research and Abstracts, 21*(4), 3–11.

Hepworth, D., Rooney, R., & Larson, J. (1997). *Direct social work practice: Theory and Skills* (5th ed.). Pacific Grove, CA: Brooks/Cole Publishing.

Hicks-Coolick, A. (1997). *Self-advocacy model for college students with learning disabilities*. Unpublished doctoral dissertation, University of Georgia, Athens.

Hicks-Coolick, A., & Kurtz, D. (1997). Preparing students with learning disabilities for success in postsecondary education: Needs and services. *Social Work in Education, 19*(1), 31–42.

Human Services Institute. (1985). *Summary of data on handicapped children and youth*. Washington, DC: U.S. Department of Education.

Karoly, J., & Franklin, C. (1996). Using portfolios to assess students' academic strengths: A case study. *Social Work in Education, 18*(3), 178–186.

Katz, R. (1984). Empowerment and synergy: Expanding the community healing resources. In J. Rappaport, C. Swift, & R. Hess (Eds.), *Studies in empowerment: Steps toward understanding and action*. New York: Haworth.

Kingore, B. (1993). *Portfolios: Enriching and assessing all students, identifying the gifted grades K–6*. Des Moines, IA: Leadership Publishers.

Kochhar, C., & West, L. (1995). Future directions for federal legislation affecting transition services for individuals with special needs. *Journal of Vocational Special Needs Education, 17*(3), 85–93.

Koretz, D. (1992). *The Vermont portfolio assessment program: Interim report on implementation and impact, 1991–1992 school year*. Los Angeles: National Center for Research.

Kurtz, D., & Tandy, C. (1995). Narrative family interventions. In A. Kilpatrick & T. Holland (Eds.), *Working with Families: An integrative model by level of functioning*. Needham Heights, MA: Allyn & Bacon.

Lister, L. (1987). Contemporary direct practice roles. *Social Work, 32*, 384–391.

Lofquist, W. (1992). *The technology of prevention workbook*. Tucson, AZ: Associates for Youth Development.

Markward, M. (1991). The socialization of youths in the workplace: Implications for school social work. *Social Work in Education, 13*(4), 236–247.

Markward, M. (1992a). Involvement of workplace superiors in the lives of youths who work. *International Journal of Adolescence and Youth, 4*(1), 19–32.

Markward, M. (1992b). Agreement between young subordinates and managers about personal and social practices in the workplace. *Human Resource Quarterly, 3*(3), 273–286.

Markward, M. (1993). The relative effectiveness of social work practice in a school-community partnership: An illuminative evaluation. *Journal of Early Child Development and Care, 86*, 105–121.

Markward, M. (1998). Psychosocial treatment of attention deficit/hyperactivity disorder. In B. Thyer & J. Wodarski (Eds.), *Handbook of empirical social work practice: Volume 1, Mental Disorders* (pp. 55–74). New York: Wiley.

Markward, M., Vonk, E., & Arnold, E. (1998). *Social work practice in postsecondary education: Two case studies*. Manuscript submitted for publication.

McMahon, M. (1990). *The general method of social work practice: A problem solving approach* (2nd ed.). Englewood Cliffs, NJ: Prentice-Hall.

Melaville, A., & Blank, M. (1993). *Together we can: A guide for crafting a profamily system of education and human services*. Washington, DC: U.S. Department of Health and Human Services Office.

Monkman, M. (1996). The characteristic focus of the social worker in the public schools. In R. Constable, J. Flynn, & S. McDonald (Eds.), *School social work: Practice and research perspectives* (3rd ed.) (pp. 38–56). Chicago: Lyceum.

Page, M. (1993). Teacher and parent beliefs about problem behaviors of preschoolers: The role of the school social worker. *Social Work in Education, 15*(1), 6–18.

Pennekamp, M. (1992). Toward school-linked and school-based human services for children and families. *Social Work in Education, 14*(2), 125–130.

Pincus, A., & Minahan, A. (1983). *Social work practice: Model and method*. Itasca, IL: F.E. Peacock.

Poertner, J., & Ronnau, J. (1992). A strengths approach to children with emotional disabilities. In D. Saleeby (Ed.), *The strengths perspective in social work practice* (pp. 111–121). New York: Longman.

Pope, L., Campbell, M., & Kurtz, P. (1992). Hostage crisis: A school-based interdisciplinary approach to posttraumatic stress disorder. *Social Work in Education, 14*(4), 227–233.

Porter, C. (1995). *The portfolio as a learning strategy.* Portsmouth, NH: Boyton/Cook.

Pryor, C. (1996). Techniques for assessing family-school connections. *Social Work in Education, 18*(2), 85–94.

Raines, J. (1996). Appropriate versus least restrictive: Educational policies and students with disabilities. *Social Work in Education, 18*(2), 113–127.

Rapp, C. (1992). The strengths perspective of case management with persons suffering from severe mental illness. In D. Saleeby (Ed.), *The strengths perspective in social work practice* (pp. 45–58). New York: Longman.

Rappaport, J. (1990). Research methods and the empowerment social agenda. In P. Tolan, C. Keys, F. Chertak, and L. Jason (Eds.), *Researching community psychology* (pp. 51–63). Washington, DC: American Psychological Association.

Richmond, M. (1922). *What is casework?* New York: Russell Sage Foundation.

Rooney, R. (1998, March). Socialization strategies for involuntary clients. *Social Casework, 69,* 131–140.

Saleeby, D. (Ed.). (1992). *The strengths perspective in social work.* New York: Longman.

Sands, R. (1994). A comparison of interprofessional and team-parent talk of an interdisciplinary team. *Social Work in Education, 16*(4), 207–219.

Sarkees-Wircenski, M., & Wircenski, J. (1994). Transition planning: Developing a career portfolio for students with disabilities. *Career Development for Exceptional Individuals, 17*(2), 203–214.

Sarri, R., & Maple, F. (Eds.). (1972). *The school in the community.* Washington, DC: National Association of Social Workers.

Seely, E. (1994). *Portfolio assessment.* Westminster, CA: Teacher Created Materials.

Segal, E. (1992). Multineed children in the social services system. *Social Work in Education, 14*(3), 190–198.

Sheafor, B., Horejsi, C., & Horejsi, G. (1988). *Techniques and guidelines for social work practice.* Needham Heights, MA: Allyn & Bacon.

Streeter, C., & Franklin, C. (1993). Site-based management in public education: Opportunities and challenges for school social workers. *Social Work in Education, 15*(2), 71–81.

Swafford, L., Hooks, K., Markward, M., & Golde, M. (1998). *Perspectives of school social workers and school counselors on the frequency and importance of tasks.* Manuscript submitted for publication.

Vogel, S., & Adelman, P. (1990). Intervention effectiveness at the postsecondary level for the learning disabled. In T. Scrugg & B. Wong (Eds.), *Intervention research in learning disabilities* (pp. 329–344). New York: Springer-Verlag.

Walzer, M. (1983). *Spheres of justice.* New York: Basic Books.

Wehman, P. (1996). *Life beyond the classroom: Transition services for young people with disabilities.* Baltimore: Brookes.

Weick, A. (1992). Building a strengths perspective for social work. In D. Saleeby (Ed.), *The strengths perspective in social work practice* (pp. 18–26). New York: Longman.

White, M. (1993). Deconstruction and therapy. In S. Gilligan & R. Price (Eds.), *Therapeutic conversations* (pp. 22–61). New York: Norton.

Ziesemer, C., & Marcoux, L. (1992). Academic and emotional needs of homeless students. *Social Work in Education, 14*(2), 77–85.

CHAPTER

COUNSELING

Katherine O. Synatschk

The power of the right vision attracts commitment and energizes people, creates meaning in workers' lives, establishes a standard of excellence, and bridges the present and the future.

—Burt Nanus (1995)

Involving all students in the transition process and providing all students with the skills to make the transition to a successful life seems to be the critical element in the mission statements of most of the school districts and state education agencies in the United States. For example, the mission of the public education system in Texas is "to ensure that all Texas children have access to a quality education that enables them to achieve their potential and fully participate now and in the future in the social, economic, and educational opportunities of our state and nation" (S. 1, 1995). Likewise, the mission of the Austin Independent School District (AISD) is "to educate all our students for productive, successful lives" (AISD, 1996).

Today, students grow up with all of the normal challenges of coping with everyday problems. The changing labor market, an extended life expectancy, the expectation of life-long learning, divorce, single-parent families, blended families, teenage suicide, and peer and family pressures are some of the societal changes and needs that adolescents face today. Added to these issues are the concerns of children who have a disability that requires special support or attention, who have been abused or neglected, who are frustrated with the cycle of personal and academic failure, who are substance abusers, who engage in sexual activity, who feel worthless, and who are homeless. All of these issues have a substantial impact on students and their personal, social, career, and educational development.

Schools must respond by providing support for all students to learn effectively. To be responsive to continuing societal and individual changes as well as to calls for reform, educators must look to reforming the entire educational enterprise, including counseling in the schools. School counseling reform requires a reconceptualization of counseling from the ancillary, crisis-oriented service that has been known in the past to a comprehensive program firmly grounded in principles of human growth and development. Such a reconceptualization of school counseling requires that the counseling program become an equal partner with the instructional program.

Social pressures and the emphasis on educational student support have refocused the emphasis of school counseling from individual student response and crisis intervention to a proactive program that is comprehensive in scope and developmental in nature. This has resulted in the development of new models for programs and delivery systems. The intent of this chapter is to describe the discipline of school counseling, to discuss the Comprehensive Developmental Guidance model, and to focus on the programmatic contributions counselors operating within this model can provide to the successful transition process for all students, including those with disabilities.

Historical Overview of School Counseling

The history of school counseling can be traced to several trends and events which occurred in the United States during the latter half of the 18th century. The introduction of the more humane care of "mentally disturbed" patients and the application of scientific methods in studying human behavior was especially influential. By the turn of the century, there was a greater awareness of how people learned and of the influence that one's environment had on the development of a person. Noted philosophers and educators, such as John Dewey, emphasized the importance of the student in the educational process (Dewey, 1990).

Guidance and counseling emerged in the 1920s for the primary purpose of assisting students with occupational selection and placement. In the 1930s, an attempt was made to organize guidance in the school setting, and educational, vocational, and personal-social services were identified as the three main components of the counseling process (Campbell, 1932). At that time, three different delivery models emerged which emphasized the counseling service, the counseling process, and the duties of the counselor (American School Counselor Association [ASCA], 1997). These became the philosophical underpinning for guidance services in the schools. The emphasis was on the role of school counselor, rather than on the program and the services delivered (Gysbers & Henderson, 1994).

The National Defense Education Act of 1958 (NDEA) increased federal funds for education to assist the United States in regaining the competitive edge in the race for space. NDEA funds were also used to increase the number of secondary school counselors who were required to have expertise in college admissions and the therapeutic skills to support the student in resolving personal problems that might be a barrier to academic success. The intent was to increase the number of students aspiring to attend college. This emphasis on postsecondary opportunities and individual personal support refocused guidance and counseling as available to college bound students and for those with personal problems. This resulted in the majority of high school and junior high school students receiving minimal, if any, services from school counselors. The expansion of the guidance provision in NDEA in the early 1960s and Gilbert Wrenn's book, *The Counselor in a Changing World* (1962), significantly impacted school counseling programs. Wrenn asserted that the primary emphasis in counseling students should be placed on their individual, developmental needs, in contrast to the remedial needs and the crisis situations in their lives. Schools were encouraged to provide developmental counseling programs, particularly at the elementary level. Later, the Elementary and Secondary Education Act of 1965 (Titles I and III) provided more support for elementary school guidance. The federal government also continued its influence through such programs as the Manpower Development and Training Act, Job Corps, Youth Opportunity Centers, and Employment Services.

Thus, as characterized by Mitchell and Gysbers (1980), the first few years of school guidance (1900–1920) might be viewed as a time when occupational selection and placement was emphasized, followed by a focus on school adjustment (1930–1960), and then personal development (1960 to present). Now counseling is changing again. New themes are emerging that continue to transcend traditional approaches (Terrill, 1990). Many of the nation's problems can be addressed through prevention and early intervention. The demands of a multicultural society and the need for an educated and caring citizenship will affect the direction of educators as they seek to prevent the loss of human potential and provide for the total development of the nation's youth. There will be an increased focus on learning effectiveness and efficiency and the goal of educating responsible and productive citizens who have a global consciousness. This is the age of the developmental school counselor. Table 8.1 describes the background, training, and competencies for professional school counselors.

Table 8.1
Who Is the School Counselor?

Background and Training Required:

1. Education and Training of School Counselors
   - At the minimum a master's degree in counseling or a related field that includes coursework in individual and group counseling skills, assessment techniques, career development theory, and ethical and legal issues. Counselors should be state-licensed or certified by an independent credentialing body such as the National Board for Certified Counselors. Passing a knowledge-based examination is required by many states and credentialing bodies.
2. Experience
   - Teaching experience, usually three years in most states; supervised counseling experience.
3. Skills
   - Conceptual, interpersonal, and social skills required for position performance; technical skills of guidance, counseling, consultation, referral, coordination, program development, and test interpretation.
4. Knowledge
   - Developmental characteristics of the age group served; school system goals and policies; ethical and legal standards of the profession; guidance program goals and objectives.
5. Personal
   - Interest in and caring for children; belief in the value of education; ability to initiate programs and activities; emotional stability and good physical health.

School Counselor Roles:

1. Guidance
   - Teach developmental guidance curriculum.
   - Assist teachers in teaching guidance-related curriculum.
   - Guide individual and groups of students through the development of educational career plans.
2. Counseling
   - Counsel individual students.
   - Counsel small groups.
   - Use accepted theories and techniques appropriate to school counseling.
3. Consultation
   - Consult with parents, teachers, administrators, and other relevant individuals to enhance their work with students.
4. Coordination
   - Coordinate with school and community personnel to bring together resources for students.
   - Use an effective referral process for assisting students and others to use special programs and services.
5. Assessment
   - Participate in the planning and evaluation of the district/school group standardized testing program.
   - Interpret test and other appraisal results appropriately.
   - Use other sources of student data appropriately for assessment purposes.

(continues)

Table 8.1 *Continued*

---

6. Program Management
   - Plan, implement, and evaluate the campus comprehensive guidance program.
   - Supervise activities of guidance program support personnel.
7. Professionalism
   - Adhere to ethical, legal, and professional standards.
   - Adhere to district policies, regulations, and procedures.

At all levels, school counselors apply these competencies within the district's Comprehensive Guidance Program as follows:

---

1. Guidance Curriculum:	guidance and consultation
2. Individual Planning System:	guidance, consultation, and assessment
3. Responsive Services:	counseling, consultation, coordination, and assessment
4. System Support:	program management and professionalism

Note. Adapted from *Leading and Managing Your School Guidance Program Staff* (351–352), by P. Henderson and N. C. Gysbers, 1998, Alexandria, VA: American Counseling Association.

Trends in School Counseling

Since the 1980s, Gysbers and Henderson (1994) and Myrick (1989, 1993) have written extensively about redesigning school counseling programs into a comprehensive developmental format. Recently, the ASCA (1997) has adopted a new definition of school counseling:

> Counseling is a process of helping people by assisting them in making decisions and changing behavior. School counselors work with all students, school staff, families, and members of the community as an integral part of the education program. School counseling programs promote school success through a focus on academic achievement, prevention and intervention activities, advocacy and social/emotional and career development. (p. 3)

The Developmental Approach

Integral to the Comprehensive Developmental Guidance model is the developmental approach. Drawing upon the works of Havighurst (1953), Piaget (1970), Erikson (1963), Kohlberg and Turiel (1971), Super and Bohn (1970), and others, the developmental approach views development as a patterned, orderly, and distinct process that affects everyone. These researchers agreed that development is affected by cultural forces and events that take place in a person's life. These researchers suggested that achievement of developmental tasks at one stage of life influenced success with tasks in later stages. It was further assumed that individuals who failed to learn developmental tasks at particular periods of life were almost certain to have difficulty with later tasks, to experience disapproval and rejection from society, and to be frustrated and unhappy (Myrick, 1993). One inevitable conclusion was that if students were taught to master certain tasks and skills that coincided with the different stages, perhaps learning lifelong skills and attitudes, then they were more likely to feel a sense of control and success in their lives (Myrick, 1993). The developmental approach, then, is an attempt to identify certain life skills and experiences that students need to have in school and when preparing for adulthood.

In the developmental approach, students have an opportunity to learn more about themselves and others in *advance* of problem moments in their lives. They learn interpersonal skills before they have an interpersonal crisis. If a crisis situation does happen, they can draw upon their skills to work themselves out of their problem. The developmental perspective recognizes that every student needs sound emotional and social skills to achieve optimum benefit from the educational program. There is a commitment to individual uniqueness and the maximum development in three major areas: academic, career, and personal/social (ASCA, 1990).

Definition of the School Counseling Program

A Comprehensive Developmental Guidance program is based on the developmental approach and is systematic in nature, sequential, clearly defined, and accountable. It is jointly founded upon developmental psychology, educational philosophy, and counseling methodology (ASCA, 1990). The program is proactive and preventive in its focus and assists students in acquiring and using lifelong learning skills. More specifically, school counseling programs include strategies to enhance academics, provide career awareness, develop employment readiness, encourage self-awareness, foster interpersonal communication skills, and impart life success skills for *all* students (Gysbers & Henderson, 1994).

The school counseling program has characteristics similar to other educational programs, including a scope and sequence, student competencies, activities and processes to assist students in achieving these competencies, professionally credentialed personnel, materials and resources, and accountability methods. Comprehensive Developmental Guidance programs are an integral part of each school's total educational program and are developed by design, focusing on needs, interests, and issues related to the various stages of student growth. There are objectives, activities, special services, and expected outcomes, with an emphasis on helping students to learn more effectively and efficiently. Some assurances are provided as part of a comprehensive guidance and counseling program. Table 8.2 delineates these program assurances.

Table 8.2
Assurances Provided by the Comprehensive
Developmental School Counseling Program

For effective implementation of the Comprehensive Developmental Guidance program to occur, certain assurances must be provided by the program. The counseling program:

- serves equally all students, parents, teachers, and other recipients regardless of gender, race, ethnicity, cultural background, sexual orientation, disability, socioeconomic status, learning ability level, or language.
- guarantees the student access to the counselor and the counselor access to the student.
- helps develop and protect a student's individuality.
- helps students function effectively with others in the school, home, and community.
- helps all students develop competencies at all educational levels.
- assists students in their personal, social, career, and educational development.
- provides consultation and coordination services to the teachers, parents, administrators, and others who work with students.
- provides developmental as well as preventive and remedial services.
- is both an integral part of and an independent component of the total educational program.
- is continuously refined through systematic planning, designing, implementation, and evaluation.

Note. Adapted from *Comprehensive Developmental Guidance and Counseling: Framework for Program Implementation* (p. F-4), by K. O. Synatschk, 1998, Austin, TX: Austin Independent School District.

Four Delivery System Components

Comprehensive Developmental Guidance programs organize resources to meet priority needs of students through four delivery system components: Guidance Curriculum, Individual Planning, Responsive Services, and System Support (Gysbers & Henderson, 1994; Texas Education Agency [TEA], 1997). The Comprehensive Developmental Guidance program is composed of these four components, without duties and activities added that do not meet these categories.

Guidance Curriculum

An organized curriculum forms the foundation of the Comprehensive Developmental Guidance program. Based upon developmental stages, tasks, skills, and learning conditions, the guidance curriculum is a planned effort to promote and enhance student learning through the three broad and interrelated areas of student development. Each of these areas of student development encompasses a variety of desired student learning competencies, which in turn are comprised of specific knowledge, attitudes, and skills. The three areas of student development are academic development, career development, and personal/social development (ASCA, 1997).

Recognizing that all children do not develop in a linear fashion according to a certain timetable, there is intentional overlapping among grade levels. The school counseling program reflects the progression of student development throughout the pre-K through grade 12 experience. It is understood that mastery of basic skills facilitates the mastery of higher-order skills in each area of development.

The school counselor uses a variety of strategies, activities, delivery methods, and resources to promote the desired student development. These processes may include large group presentations such as career nights or class meetings, classroom guidance activities, small group presentations, training, or assisting teachers in the teaching of the guidance curriculum. The school counselor's responsibilities include the design, organization, implementation, and coordination of the program (Myrick, 1993).

Individual Planning

The activities of the individual planning components are designed for *all* students and are intended to assist them in the development and implementation of their personal/social, educational, and career plans. These activities are designed to help students understand and monitor their growth and development and take action on their next steps educationally or vocationally.

The activities in this component are often focused on the creation of an *Individual Academic-Career Plan* (AISD, 1995) or a similar individually focused educational plan. The activities in this component are delivered in large group, small group, and individual settings, and include the processes of advisement, assessment, and placement.

Responsive Services

This component provides special help to students who are facing problems that interfere with their healthy personal/social, career, or educational development. It includes the provision of preventive responses to students who are about to make unhealthy or inappropriate choices. Remedial interventions also are provided for students who have already made unwise choices or have not coped well with problem situations. The processes may include individual counseling, small group counseling, consultation with staff, parents, mentors, and referrals.

System Support

This component has two parts: (a) activities necessary to support the other three components; and (b) activities implemented by guidance staff that support other educational programs. Support that the guidance staff provides to other programs includes (a) the system-related aspects of the individual planning activities (e.g., student course selection); (b) linkage with other instructional areas such as special education, career education, English, social studies, and mathematics programs; and (c) guidance-related administrative assignments. The processes may include program management, consultation, public relations, and professional development.

Six Basic Counselor Interventions

The comprehensive school counseling program also integrates academic, career and personal/social development. Six interventions are necessary in an effective school counseling program: (a) individual and small group counseling, (b) consultation, (c) coordination, (d) case management, (e) guidance, and (f) program evaluation development.

Individual and Small Group Counseling

In individual counseling, the counselor conducts a personal and private interaction with a student in which they work together on a problem or topic of interest. A face-to-face, one-to-one meeting with a counselor provides a student maximum privacy in which to freely explore ideas, feelings, and behaviors. School counselors exhibit trust and information, always considering actions in terms of the rights, integrity, and welfare of students. Counselors are obligated by law and ethical standards to report and to refer a case when a person's welfare is in jeopardy. It is the counselor's duty to inform an individual of the conditions and limitations under which assistance may be provided. Individual counseling generally addresses the specific concerns of targeted students with identified needs. In small group counseling, a counselor works with two or more students together. Group size generally ranges from five to eight members. Group discussions may be relatively unstructured or may be based on structured learning activities. Group members have an opportunity to learn from each other. They can share ideas, give and receive feedback, increase their awareness, gain new knowledge, practice skills, and think about their goals and actions. Group discussions may be problem-centered, where attention is given to particular concerns or problems. Discussions may be growth-centered, where general topics are related to personal and academic development.

Consultation

The counselor as a consultant primarily helps parents and teachers to be more effective in working with others. Consultation helps parents and teachers think through problems and concerns, acquire more knowledge and skill, and become more objective and self-confident. This intervention can take place in individual or group conferences, or through professional development activities and parent educational classes. The consultation provides information and skills to parents or guardians, teachers, and the community to assist them in helping students in academic, career, and personal/social development. Consultation may be delivered individually or in small or large groups. Consultation is an essential part of developmental school counseling (Myrick, 1993). Wrenn (1962) emphasized its importance in his historic report.

Coordination

Counselors serve as a liaison between teachers, parents, support personnel, and community resources to facilitate successful student development. As student advocates, school counselors seek equitable access to programs and services for all students (ASCA, 1997).

Case Management

In case management, counselors provide the necessary monitoring of an individual student's progress toward achieving success in academic, career, and personal/social areas.

Guidance

Counselors developmentally and sequentially provide information, knowledge, and skills through academic, career, and personal/social development. This is often delivered through large group meetings, which offer the best opportunity to provide guidance to the largest number of students in a school (ASCA, 1997). Large group work involves cooperative learning methods, in which the larger group is divided into smaller working groups under the supervision of a counselor or teacher. The guidance and counseling curriculum, composed of organized objectives and activities, is delivered by teachers or counselors in classrooms or advisory groups (Gysbers & Henderson, 1994). Counselors develop and present special guidance units which give attention to particular developmental issues or areas of concern in their respective schools. They may partner with teachers and other members of the school community to deliver part of the guidance and counseling curriculum (Myrick, 1993).

Program Evaluation and Development

Counselors continually assess the needs of their students, evaluate their programs, and make changes in the school counseling program to meet the current, identified needs of students (Gysbers & Henderson, 1994).

Program Resource Allocation

The Comprehensive Developmental Guidance model has a two-fold purpose: (a) the acquisition of specific skills needed to facilitate the development of all students, and (b) the provision of high priority preventive and remedial interventions to assist students dealing with immediate, problematic concerns (Gysbers & Henderson, 1994). Because counselors focus on reaching all students, a different model is implied than the crisis-oriented model typical of past school counseling services.

Barriers to Appropriate Resource Allocation

Because school counseling has, for many years, been viewed as a counselor-clinical-services model rather than as a defined program (Gysbers & Henderson, 1994), counseling in the schools has been described as a list of duties and activities. Counselors want to respond to new needs and expectations but experience tremendous role conflict with existing duties:

> The range of counselor responsibilities and functions vary not only among school districts but among schools in the same district. The school principal is predominant in determining the daily routine of counselors and, while citing the support their principals provide them, many counselors bemoaned the plethora of administrative tasks they are called upon to perform. Without standard position descriptions, counselors "fill vacuums" with the result that counselors are expected to do "too much for too many." (Commission on Precollege Guidance and Counseling, 1986, p. 38)

Current organizational patterns of guidance in many schools are still based on this ancillary services concept loosely grouped around broad role and function statements. This condition contributes to the practice of having counselors do many inappropriate tasks because such tasks can be justified as being of service to someone. Consequently, counselors' time is spent on indirect services rather than on programs that directly impact students.

Many authors (Gysbers & Henderson, 1994; Johnson & Whitfield, 1991; Myrick, 1993) recommend assessing the current guidance program time allocations as a first step in implementing the Comprehensive Developmental Guidance model. Using the four components of the model, counselors are asked to quantify the time they devote to each component. A fifth category of nonguidance activities is added to allow calculation of time spent on those "services" that do not fit into the four components. One such program time-allocation study was

Table 8.3
Counselor Time Use

School Level	Direct Services				Indirect Services		
	Guidance Curriculum	Individual Planning	Responsive Services	Total Direct Services	System Support	Non-guidance Activities	Total Indirect Services
Elementary School	10.1%	10.0%	33.0%	53.1%	28.8%	18.1%	46.9%
Middle School	2.8%	17.9%	27.8%	48.5%	19.8%	31.6%	51.4%
High School	2.4%	32.0%	20.7%	55.1%	20.3%	24.5%	44.8%
All Levels	6.8%	16.1%	29.4%	52.3%	24.9%	22.8%	47.7%

Note. From *Comprehensive Developmental Guidance and Counseling: Framework for Program Implementation* (p. F-18), by K. O. Synatschk, 1998, Austin, TX: Austin Independent School District. Reprinted with permission.

undertaken over a one-year period by a school district. Counselors compiled a time log noting amount of time spent in activities related to each component and the nonguidance activities category. The results of the analysis of time resources allocation are shown in Table 8.3.

As is clear from the data, allocations of counselor time to direct services for students ranged from 48.5% to 55.1%. Most authors who describe comprehensive developmental guidance and counseling programs advocate at least a 75:25 ratio of direct to indirect services, with a number supporting 85:15 or less (Texas Education Agency, 1997). To the extent that this school district presents a typical picture of guidance and counseling time allocations in this country, school counselors and program leaders face quite a challenge in making the transition from the ancillary services concept of guidance, with a wide variety of tasks involved, to a comprehensive program.

Because the school counselor's duties need to be limited to program delivery and direct counseling services, inappropriate noncounseling tasks and appropriate school counseling program tasks need to be articulated so that appropriate tasks can be supported and inappropriate tasks can be shifted to another staff person or eliminated altogether. Table 8.4 lists these appropriate and inappropriate school counseling tasks.

A Parsimonious Approach to Program Resource Allocation

Myrick (1993) advocated a parsimonious approach to the delivery of the school counseling program. Resources are limited and require systematic allocation if all students' needs are to be met. Figure 8.1 illustrates the concept of allocating the largest portion of resources to the largest portion of the population. Classroom guidance is the first strategy that can be used in bring about a change in the attitudes, skills, and knowledge of students. The classroom setting provides the best avenue in which to reach the largest number of students with the skills and competencies included in the guidance curriculum. Some students, however, may not respond to this large-scale, preventive approach. Those students for whom large group guidance is not sufficient might be targeted for small group counseling. This smaller population receives less in terms of counselor resources but the focus is specific and intensive. Likewise, if a student does not respond to small group counseling, then individual counseling might be in order. If individual counseling is ineffective, then a referral might be made to another counselor or agency. The sequence of moving from large group guidance to an outside agency referral provides a systematic approach to interventions and services. There is a continual evaluation of delivery methods so that individuals are evaluated for participation in group approaches and small groups are examined for

Table 8.4
Sample Appropriate and Inappropriate School Counseling Tasks

Appropriate school counseling program tasks:	*Inappropriate nonschool counseling program tasks:*
• individual student academic program planning • interpreting cognitive, aptitude, and achievement tests • counseling students who are tardy or absent • collaborating with teachers to present guidance curriculum lessons • counseling students who have disciplinary problems • counseling students about appropriate school dress • analyzing grade point averages in relationship to achievement • interpreting student records • providing teachers with suggestions for better management of study halls • ensuring that student records are maintained as per state and federal regulations • assisting the school principal with identifying and resolving student issues, needs, and problems	• registration and scheduling of all new students • administering cognitive, aptitude, and achievement tests • responsibility for signing excuses for students who are tardy or absent • teaching classes when teachers are absent • performing disciplinary actions • sending inappropriately dressed students home • computing grade point averages • maintaining student records • supervising study halls • clerical record keeping • assisting with duties in the principal's office

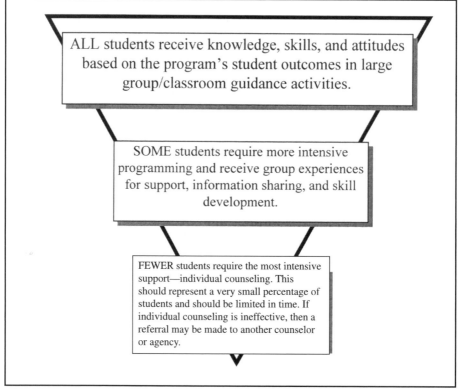

Figure 8.1. Comprehensive Guidance Program resource allocation. *Note.* Adapted from *Comprehensive Developmental Guidance and Counseling: Framework for Program Implementation* (F-10), by K. O. Synatschk, 1998, Austin, TX: Austin Independent School District.

inclusion in classroom-size group presentations. Following this model, the guidance and counseling needs of all students, from at-risk to gifted, can be met.

Most school counselors agree that their skills, time, and energy should be focused on direct services to students (ASCA, 1997). School counseling programs and the role of the school counselor should be determined by the educational, career, and personal development needs of students. The Comprehensive Developmental Guidance program places the counselor in a key position to identify the issues that impact on student learning and achievement.

Collaboration in the School Counseling Program

The school counselor is not the counseling program. Indeed, the school counselor and the school counseling program use a collaborative model as their foundation. Counselors do not work alone; all educators play a role in creating an environment which promotes the achievement of identified student goals and outcomes. The counselor facilitates the communication and establishes linkages with teaching staff, administration, families, student service personnel, agencies, businesses, and other members of the community for the benefit of students. School success depends upon the cooperation and support of the entire faculty, staff, and student services personnel. As student advocates, school counselors are committed to participate as members of the educational team. They consult and collaborate with teachers, administrators, and parents to assist students to be successful academically, vocationally, and personally.

The educational system is being challenged by the growing needs of today's students and the rising expectations of society. Some students attend school with emotional, physical, and interpersonal barriers to learning as a result of societal and other factors. However, all students require systematic support for their development. Therefore, in a comprehensive school counseling program, less emphasis is placed on crisis-oriented services. The emphasis is on development for *all* students. An effective school counseling program begins when students enter the school system and continues as they progress through the educational process. School counseling is an integral part of the total educational enterprise.

Achieving the Balance

To achieve balance among the program components, and to utilize all of the delivery methods, it is necessary to maintain a realistic counselor–student ratio that fully supports the number of staff necessary to provide a standards-based program. ASCA (1990) recommends a ratio of 1:100 (ideal) to 1:300 (maximum) in order to implement a standards-based, comprehensive school counseling program. In addition, a comprehensive developmental school counseling program is a full-time program and requires counselors to spend 75 to 80% of their time in direct contact with students.

A balanced Comprehensive Development Guidance program will provide a program of career and transition planning that spans K–12 for all students, including those with disabilities. Therefore, it is critical that professionals achieve a balanced program that can provide for all students, including those with disabilities, and one way of doing this lies in the ability of school staffs and members of the interdisciplinary teams to reallocate inappropriate duties away from the school counselor.

School Counseling Program Standards

Goals 2000, the Educate America Act of 1994, and other documents have encouraged the establishment of standards as a means for the evaluation of student growth (Council for Exceptional Children, 1994). Standards-based education has direct relevance for school counseling programs. The school counseling standards address program content and the knowledge, attitudes, and skill competencies that all students will develop as a result of participating in a school counseling program. A number of individuals, local school districts, state education agencies, and national organizations have developed frameworks for school counseling standards (ASCA, 1997; Gysbers & Henderson, 1994; TEA, 1997).

One such set of standards was developed for the students in the Austin Independent School District (AISD, 1996). The educator developed a list of standards and their accompanying student competencies by examining the literature on counseling program standards through the work of Gysbers and Henderson (1994), Myrick (1993), the ASCA (1994, 1996), the National Career Development Guidelines (NOICC, 1989), and the TEA (1997), and by incorporating the recommendations of such documents as GOALS 2000 (1994) and the Secretary's Commission on Achieving Necessary Skills (SCANS) (U.S. Department of Labor, 1991). According to the AISD (1996), students who graduate from high school having successfully completed a Comprehensive Developmental Guidance curriculum will be able to function effectively as adults in a complex, diverse, democratic society. More specifically, they will:

- demonstrate knowledge and acceptance of self to reach their fullest potential for effective functioning in a complex society.

- develop interpersonal and effective communication skills to be successful in business, family, and social situations.

- appreciate positive differences and uniqueness among people in maintaining effective relationships throughout life in our interdependent society.

- demonstrate personal responsibility recognizing the impact of individual action on one's life and on society as a whole.

- develop cooperative/collaborative interpersonal skills through conflict resolution.

- demonstrate the ability to identify problems and implement a decision making process.

- develop an appreciation of the intrinsic value of education and its importance in the fulfillment of human potential.

- evaluate the ability to achieve goals and integrate this knowledge in setting goals for the future.

- assume responsibility for self-directed learning to function effectively in a chosen career.

Strands of the Guidance Curriculum

These standards for school counseling correspond to eight strands which organize the guidance curriculum. The eight strands included (pre–K through 12) in the Comprehensive Developmental Guidance program are (1) Self-Knowledge and Acceptance, (2) Interpersonal and Communication Skills, (3) Responsible Behavior, (4) Conflict Resolution, (5) Decision Making/Problem Solving, (6) Motivation to Achieve, (7) Goal Setting, and (8) Career Planning. The strands are defined in the following list:

1. *Self-Knowledge and Acceptance*. This domain helps students learn more about their abilities, interests, and personal characteristics. Students learn to identify their strengths and the areas in which they need to improve so that true self-acceptance is possible.

2. *Interpersonal and Communication Skills*. This domain emphasizes the value of developing positive interpersonal relationships and how communication skills affect the ways in which people interact with each other. Students also learn to value differences and uniqueness among people.

3. *Responsible Behavior*. This domain assists students in developing a sense of personal responsibility for their behavior. It gives attention to how attitudes and perceptions can affect behavior, how feelings and behaviors are related to goals and consequences, and how behavior can be changed, if desired.

4. *Conflict Resolution*. The focus of this domain is nonviolent solutions to conflict situations. Students will also deal with styles of cooperative behavior, prejudice, and healthy expressions of anger.

5. *Decision Making/Problem Solving*. This domain involves learning the steps for making effective decisions and solving problems. It also involves an increased awareness of the factors that influence change and decision making, as well as helpful procedures for problem solving. There is an emphasis on responsibility and individual choice.

6. *Motivation to Achieve*. This area is designed to assist students in achieving success in school and in their adult lives. It will help them develop positive attitudes and habits that will enable them to get the most out of schooling. Students will also focus on the connections between what they are learning in school and what their future will be like.

7. *Goal Setting*. This domain is designed to help students understand the importance of setting goals for themselves and monitoring their own progress toward their goals. They will also learn to differentiate between realistic and unrealistic goals.

8. *Career Planning.* This domain helps students understand more about the world of work, increase career awareness, and do in-depth career exploration related to personal interests, values, and abilities. This domain also includes how to make effective educational plans so that students may achieve their career goals.

Each of these strands of student development encompasses a variety of desired student learning competencies, which in turn are comprised of specific knowledge, attitudes, and skills that form the foundation of the developmental school counseling program. Table 8.5 illustrates the scope of competency strands for one grade level.

Guidance Curriculum Relation to Transition

The Division on Career Development and Transition of the Council for Exceptional Children supports a life skills instruction approach when considering transition planning:

> A life skills instruction approach is a commitment to providing a set of goals, objectives, and instructional activities designed to teach concepts and skills needed to function successfully in life . . . curricular content should emphasize instruction in such areas as personal responsibility, social competence, interpersonal relationships, health (physical and mental), home living, employability, occupational awareness, job skills, recreation and leisure skills, consumer skills, and community participation. (Clark, Field, Patton, Brolin, & Sitlington, 1994, p. 126)

Organized by grade level, the guidance curriculum provides a scope and sequence of learnings for grades K–12 that can be the basis for the life skills curriculum and transition planning occurring from the earliest grade levels. Career awareness competencies, such as introducing students to the world of work, developing an appreciation for all work, and obtaining basic knowledge about clusters of different careers, are introduced developmentally throughout elementary school. The range of competencies allows for modifications for students' learning needs at various grade levels with a built in evaluation system for achievement of competencies. Appendix 8.A is a detailed illustration of guidance curriculum competencies by strand and grade level.

The implementation of the guidance curriculum at all levels for all students heightens the awareness of the staff to the transition needs of students and promotes early awareness, exploration, investigation, and planning activities that benefit students with disabilities. With this basis addressed through the compre-

Table 8.5
Sample Guidance Curriculum Expectations by Grade Level

Guidance Curriculum Domains and Expectations—Ninth Grade

Strand	*Student Competencies (all students in the ninth grade will be able to):*
Self-Knowledge and Acceptance	• explain their unique characteristics and abilities • explain that their value is not reduced as a result of criticisms or ridicule from others
Interpersonal and and Communiity Skills	• analyze how communication skills contribute toward work within a group • evaluate the importance of having friendships with peers and adults • demonstrate appropriate social skills in a variety of situations • recognize characteristics of one's own culture, background, family, and heritage in any setting
Responsible Behavior	• evaluate willingness to accept personal responsibility • analyze and describe the consequences of unacceptable or irresponsible behavior • evaluate and explain the benefits of being self-disciplined • differentiate between healthy and unhealthy solutions to problems
Conflict Resolution	• identify feelings and express them clearly and respectfully
Decision Making/ Problem Solving	• analyze how choices made now will affect lives in the future • define and prioritize personal values • analyze the importance of generating alternatives and assessing the consequences of each before making a decision
Motivation to Achieve	• describe personal learning and study skills and explain their importance • evaluate the benefits derived from learning • express positive attitudes toward work and learning • research and take advantage of opportunities for learning within the school environment and in the community • predict use of knowledge from school in future life and work
Goal Setting	• define their own unique values, interests, and capabilities • analyze how life roles, settings, and events determine preferred lifestyles
Career Planning	• analyze academic plans and experiences relevant to future education, training, and employment • demonstrate skills for locating, evaluating, and interpreting information about career opportunities

hensive guidance program, counselors and special educators can then collaborate on the achievement of more in-depth plans for students with disabilities.

Individual Planning Component

As discussed earlier, the activities of the individual planning component are provided for all students and are intended to guide students in the development and implementation of their personal, educational, and career plans. The activities help students understand and monitor their growth and development and take action on their next steps educationally or vocationally. The activities in this component are delivered either on a group or individual basis with students and parents. Teachers are often involved as advisors. This component begins to build on the skills and knowledge regarding the self, decision making, problem solving, goal setting, and career planning learned through the guidance curriculum, and applies these skills to preliminary planning decisions. Within this component, assessment data about interests, aptitudes, and work-related values are gathered and shared with students for use in their exploration and planning.

In the Austin Independent School District, an *Individual Academic-Career Plan* (IACP) (Austin ISD, 1995) is completed annually for all students in grades 6 through 12. The IACP is a long-range plan that structures the career exploration process so that students are able to connect their middle and high school courses with future goals, including college majors and skills needed to be successful in the workplace. Students' IACPs are part of a process that encourages students to make changes along the way as they acquire new interests, insights, knowledge, and skills. This basic plan facilitates students in addressing their career cluster interests, postsecondary plans, middle and high school coursework, and plans for work-based experiences and special considerations needed each year. Teachers acting as advisors contribute to the development of the IACPs in many settings. Appendix 8.B provides an example of the IACP. Moreover, the following cases offer a glimpse into the planning process from the students' perspective.

 ## Elementary School: Katie

A fifth grader at Metro Elementary, Katie has participated since kindergarten in weekly classroom sessions using the guidance curriculum to learn about herself, communicate with others, make decisions, set goals, solve problems, and plan a career.

Her favorite career planning activities were the guest speakers, career days, and field trips her class took to various business and industry sites. She also enjoyed finding out where her interests fell on some of the informal interest surveys her class completed. Each year she added new ideas to her list of what career she would like as an adult.

Now that she is in the fifth grade, she will be introduced to the process of developing an IACP in an informal way so that she is aware of educational requirements beyond the sixth grade and so that she becomes accustomed to thinking about setting goals and planning to reach those goals. She will practice with her classmates in collaborative groups the process of designing plans for each of the career clusters. She will also learn about the educational requirements associated with specific careers within those clusters. Along the way, she will talk with her parents and friends about her interests and plans.

Middle School: Joe

As an eighth grader, Joe is keenly aware that it is time to make some plans for his future. Throughout elementary and middle school, he has completed career investigation activities such as completing a report on a career of interest that included earnings, educational requirements, work descriptions, and employment trends.

Each year since sixth grade, he has completed an IACP to make the connections between his career cluster interests, career pathways, coursework in middle and high school, and postsecondary plans. It seems to him that those IACPs were probably practice runs for the one he will complete this year, which will include much more specific information for the next six years.

This year he has completed a formal interest inventory and achievement tests, discussed work-related values and abilities, and had some job shadowing experiences. On the field trips his class took, he learned as much about what he did not want to do as about what he did want to do. Now as he completes his IACP, he and his parents have a better understanding of how to design a career pathway to match his interests, talents, and goals. Selecting the right courses will be easy after using this process for several years.

High School: Matt

As a sophomore at Urbana High School, Matt is poised to enter some of the specific courses he has chosen for his career pathway some time ago. During his early years in school, he learned about career clusters, decision making, and goal setting. He has used these skills and the exploration and investigation experiences he has had to develop his IACP. He was able to define a career pathway where he has fine-tuned his interests, enhanced his employability skills, and has begun to learn some career-specific skills. He was able to include the extracurricular activities that will relate to his career pathway in his plan and his need to earn some of his school expenses.

Later, he will engage in some work-based learning experiences such as an internship and paid work. His career plans call for a college degree, so he has included plans for courses for advanced placement and to meet college entrance requirements. Matt knows that his interests may change but is confident that the planning process he has engaged in will be valuable to him in the future.

Table 8.6 illustrates the recommended planning process that follows the sequence of awareness, exploration, and planning. As noted in the cases previously described, the elementary experience is one of increasing awareness of students' interests and the world of work. Terminology and the organization of careers by clusters are taught. In middle school, students begin to explore their interests and abilities in more depth as they begin to relate current interests to possible careers. The high school experience is one of increasing

Table 8.6
Career Planning Process Student Outcomes

Grade Level	Student Outcomes
Elementary School	Awareness of: • their interests • career clusters • value of work • sources for information Fifth Graders: • explore their interests and talents in more depth • do sample plans for each of the clusters • are introduced to the IACP process
Middle School	Exploration of: • more in-depth information about careers • their interests, abilities, values • the relationship of coursework to occupations • job shadowing experiences, mentors • development of their IACP at least once a year
High School	Planning for: • opportunities to fine-tune their interests, abilities, and work-related values • opportunities to enhance their employability skills • detailed career information searches • opportunities for internships, apprenticeships, and paid employment • development of an increasingly specific and detailed IACP each year to address at least two postsecondary years

specificity in planning accompanied by real world experiences in particular career areas.

In addition to facilitating planning for all students, the individual planning component provides the avenue for participation of counselors at all levels (elementary, middle, and high school) in the multidisciplinary teams that address the transition planning, problem solving, and service needs of students with disabilities. By providing for the development of the guidance curriculum competencies, career planing process, and knowledge of postsecondary options and requirements, many of the preliminary tasks may have been completed prior to formal IEP/ITP meetings. The guidance curriculum and the individual planning process are outcome-oriented processes that align well with the required transition services listed in Section 602(30) of the IDEA. Whenever possible, all students should take advantage of the mainstream offerings as a normal course of events before pursuing specialized services. The IACP or a similar tool can be an excellent addition to the assessments and planning tools assembled. In the transition planning process, counselors are available to provide current information to parents and teachers about the postsecondary options, to recommended preparatory steps, and to help them choose the program and setting that seems to be the best match (Karge, Patton, & de la Garza, 1992; Kohler, DeStefano, Wermuth, Grayson, & McGinty, 1994; Synatschk, 1994). Counselors can help educate students and their families about the differences in postsecondary education compared with the high school setting, and can help them arrange for the necessary academic, functional, and social supports (Scott, 1996; Synatschk, 1995). Counselors are key adults who can begin to shift the responsibility for planning and decision making to the student and help students develop the self-advocacy skills that are so important for postsecondary success (Synatschk, 1994).

It is critical that the counselors' involvement focus on student advocacy, planning, and problem solving, rather than on the administrative functions needed to organize the multidisciplinary team. With the reauthorization of IDEA in 1997, it is clearer than ever that administrative functions in the process should be fulfilled by administrators. Counselors functioning within their appropriate roles will lead to more direct service delivery to students with disabilities and their families.

Maintaining the Guidance Curriculum and Individual Planning Balance

The guidance curriculum represents the competencies to be taught and the individual planning component represents the application of those competencies to planning for educational, career, and personal or social futures. Suggested time allocated for the guidance curriculum varies from level to level, with the most time spent at the elementary level and progressively less time allocated as the students move upward through the grades. Each domain, however, will be addressed to some degree at every grade level because the curriculum is designed in a sequential and developmental manner. The amount of time allocated to guidance curriculum is balanced by the amount of time devoted to the component of individual planning (see Figure 8.2), so that as the time decreases for guidance curriculum, it increases for individual planning. Note that at the middle school level, about half the time is spent teaching skills, and the other half is spent applying the skills to planning activities.

Responsive Services Component

As discussed earlier, the purpose of the responsive services component is to provide special help to students who are facing problems that interfere with their healthy personal, social, career, or educational development. This component includes the provision of preventive responses to the students who are on the brink of choosing an unhealthy or inappropriate solution to their problems or of being unable to cope with a situation. Remedial interventions are also provided for students who have already made unwise choices or who have not coped well with problem situations. This component includes such activities as individual and small group counseling, consultation with staff and parents, and referral of students and their families to other specialists or programs. According to the Comprehensive Developmental Guidance model, 30% of the total program time should be devoted to the services within this component (TEA, 1997). Based on a needs assessment of the campus, ongoing groups may be established so that they are available to meet the students' needs in a proactive way. For example, grief issues and issues of changing families are common on campuses today. An established ongoing program of support groups dealing with such issues is an effective and efficient means of meeting students' needs.

The responsive services component offers a context for the counselor to address the immediate concerns of students with disabilities and their families, both for the purpose of prevention and intervention. Relationship concerns, physical or emotional or sexual abuse, grief, substance abuse, family issues, sexuality issues, and coping with stress are some of the concerns that may be addressed in group or individual sessions. In addition, coordination with and referral to other mental health providers in the community would be helpful to students and their families in the transition process.

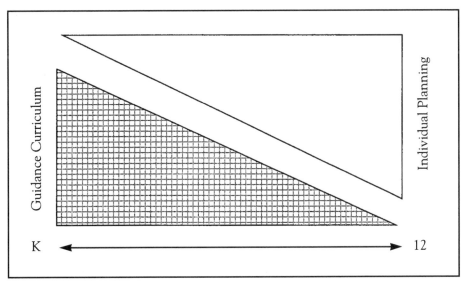

Figure 8.2. Guidance Curriculum and Individual Planning: Emphasis K–12. *Note.* From *Curriculum Design and Management Manual for Guidance Curriculum*, by Austin Independent School District, 1996, Austin, TX: Author.

System Support Component

The system support component has two parts. It includes management activities necessary to support the other three components, and activities implemented by guidance staff that support the total or other educational programs. Management activities include (a) program and staff development; (b) programs that result in budget, facilities, and appropriate policies, procedures, and guidelines; (c) research; (d) community relations; and (e) resource development. Activities that support the total educational system or other programs include consultation with teachers, efforts to enhance parental involvement in school, school improvement planning, input to policymakers, and curriculum developers on behalf of students. Though sometimes seen as a less clearly defined component, the system support component is not intended to be the "taking up slack" component that allows assigning administrative and clerical tasks to counselors. More than the criteria of being beneficial to students must be applied to the decision to assign tasks in this area. Overall, it is important to remember that services provided here, no matter how valuable, are indirect services to students and should be limited to 15% to 25% of the total program time allocation.

The system support component functions to support transition planning and transition services for students with disabilities and their families. Efforts here could include parent education programs about career planning or other concerns, consultation with special education teachers and transition coordinators, staff development to develop skills among all staff for functioning as advisors, community outreach to develop additional services and programs for students in the transition process, and assistance with coordination of postsecondary programs offering services to students with disabilities.

Assessing Outcomes of Comprehensive Developmental Guidance Efforts

Both product (student results) and process evaluation are essential in any program. Both are necessary to prove the effects of the guidance program efforts and to improve the effectiveness of strategies, techniques, and resources. Assessments will serve to document the desirable effects of the program for students. Measuring student results is similar to measuring achievement in other areas of the school curriculum and can take many forms. The sources and methods of measuring student results could include the following:

- *Standardized Instruments.* These are catalogued and described in numerous professional publications. They must, of course, match the predetermined expected results.

- *State Assessment Programs.* Data collected in these programs may be directly related to the evaluation questions being asked by counselors.

- *Locally Developed Measures.* Counselors can design measures for specific results.

- *Interviews.* Structured interviews can provide data about achievement levels and allow for further information.

- *Diaries and Journals.* Self-reporting logs can measure student activities and knowledge.

- *Checklists.* These are a convenient way to record behavior events and skills.

- *Observations.* Methods for recording observations can range from systematic observation instruments to audio or videotaping.

- *Simulations.* Simulated situations can be used to provide a stimulus for assessment items that measure students' understanding.

- *Role Playing Situations.* These can provide an opportunity for students to demonstrate behaviors.

- *Planning Forms.* A variety of forms such as the IACP can allow students to describe their plans or decision-making results.

Assessment involves analyzing the results of counseling efforts. There are three kinds of results: long range, intermediate, and immediate (Drier, Johnson, Johnson, and Whitfield, 1991). A given assessment does not necessarily assess all three kinds of results. The evaluation of long-range results may occur annually, in a scheduled sequence such as every other or every third year, or in a sequence such as one, three, five, and ten years after graduation. The content of the evaluation relates to the statement of purpose of the guidance curriculum. Intermediate results are those determined by the goals of the curriculum that are to be reached by the time the student graduates. Evaluation of goals may be accomplished in two ways. The first way is through an aggregate of data regarding the attainment of immediate goals on a yearly basis. In this type of evaluation, the students' attainment of the defined competencies is evaluated. The second and more decisive way to evaluate intermediate results is to assess students near the end of their senior year. Written surveys, interviews, review of artifacts such as career folders, résumés, student records of participation in extracurricular activities, postsecondary plans, and college acceptances can be used to determine if the students have reached the program goals. This type of senior year comprehensive evaluation is usually done on a periodic basis. Immediate results are usually stated in terms of student competencies (or performance indicators) and are measured on an ongoing basis immediately after a competency is taught. The ongoing assessment and reporting of immediate results allow counselors to maximize their time and resources to provide the best possible program for students. Immediate results are indicators that students are progressing toward the goals and long-range results of the program.

Existing Challenges

One key factor contributing to the effective and efficient transition planning and transition services for all students, especially for students with disabilities, will be the implementation of the Comprehensive Development Guidance model in all schools. However, professionals face barriers in implementing this program, including a lack of resources, resistance by teaching staffs, and a lack of administrative support.

The lack of resources that currently affects the implementation of comprehensive guidance in schools encompasses budget, materials, space, staff development, clerical, and, most of all, counselor time. Additional resources must be dedicated to the implementation of the model so that counselors are freed of the nonguidance duties they may be performing currently. The time resource can be impacted by increasing the counselor-to-student ratio and by employing others, perhaps clerical personnel, to complete some of the inappropriate tasks. Materials for guidance curriculum and the staff development to train counselors in their use are needed as well.

Resistance by teaching staff to the use of class time to focus on classroom guidance activities is a frequent barrier at all levels. Elementary and secondary teachers feel increasing pressure to help all of their students achieve academically. Often, it is difficult to convince policy makers that the affective and life-skill competencies in the guidance curriculum should be an integral part of a student's education. In addition, for the guidance curriculum to be delivered effectively to all students, counselors and teachers will have to collaborate in the teaching of the concepts and integrate them into the content area curriculum.

Lack of administrative support has been seen as a barrier to many who are implementing the Comprehensive Developmental Guidance program (Starr & Gysbers, 1992). At the building level and at the district level, it is important for administrators to support the shift from a services model to a program model for guidance and counseling because it involves changing so many of the traditional ways of doing things. Administrators need to lend verbal, policy, financial, and political support to the changes in order for these to be successful. In addition, administrators need to demonstrate creativity and ingenuity in evaluating tasks previously assigned to the counselor so that others can be designated to complete them. Administrators also need take a firm stand in demanding that all of their students, rather than a select few, achieve the competencies laid out.

A Bold Vision for the Future

The full implementation of the Comprehensive Developmental Guidance model represents the bold vision for the future of transition services—for students with disabilities as well as for those without. The comprehensive program approach is a theory-based framework to systematically organize guidance and counseling content and methodology. It is a time-management system for school counselors and others who work in the program. Based on articulated student competencies, it includes evaluation procedures that focus on the program, its personnel, and the results achieved. The implementation will be achieved by taking a team approach to guidance in the schools, and will utilize formats such as a well-developed advisory program and an individual planning tool such as the IACP. With everyone in the school taking responsibility for the achievement of guidance competencies by *all* students, students will have the skills to make them successful in their next steps educationally, vocationally, and socially.

Final Thoughts

The success of the movement to restructure school counseling to the Comprehensive Developmental Guidance model is critical to the delivery of an effective transition program for students with disabilities. In many school settings, this can mean the rethinking of every aspect of a school counseling program, from the assessment of needs, to delivery methods, and allocation of resources to ensure that all students have equitable access to services. Implementing a standards-based program requires school counselors to be willing to assume responsibility for the delivery of a quality program and to be accountable for student outcomes (ASCA, 1997). This change from a constellation of services and activities to a standards-based program represents a significant shift in thinking about the way students are supported and in the anticipated outcomes. School counselors will continue to work with students individually, in small groups, in classrooms, and in large assemblies. They will continue to provide crisis intervention and group guidance activities. School counselors will continue to support students' academic success. The standards-based Comprehensive Developmental Guidance model provides the foundation to ensure equitable access to school counseling programs for all students. Standards raise the level of expectation of the outcomes for students and make excellence in school counseling possible.

Appendix 8.A
Guidance Curriculum
Competencies by Strand

Strand I—Self-Knowledge and Acceptance

Grade	Student Competencies (all students in these grade levels will be able to):
PreK–Kindergarten	• identify some of their personal and physical traits • describe how they are like as well as different from others • recognize words that express feelings
First Grade	• verbalize a personal trait or behavior that they like about themselves • recognize that strengths and weaknesses are human characteristics • describe feelings they have in different situations
Second Grade	• identify the personal traits and characteristics that contribute to the uniqueness of each individual • be able to explain the importance of liking themselves • discuss and share feelings about themselves
Third Grade	• describe themselves accurately to classmates • analyze how they feel about their own personal characteristics • express appropriately those thoughts and feelings that are important to them
Fourth Grade	• give examples of how they are important to themselves and others • define and discuss the meaning of self concept • understand ways they manage their feelings
Fifth Grade	• specify personal characteristics and abilities that they value • explain what contributes to their feelings of self-worth • determine situations where they may express a variety of feelings and describe how they deal with those feelings
Sixth Grade	• exhibit comfort in a larger school setting which calls for more independence • identify and name their own feelings • handle their own problems or know where to get help
Seventh Grade	• recognize their own limitations and seek help when needed • express feelings in an appropriate manner • recognize adolescent physical and emotional changes
Eighth Grade	• investigate and accept their own strengths and weaknesses • describe their own uniqueness and that of others • develop and use assertiveness skills
Ninth Grade	• explain their unique characteristics and abilities • explain that their value is not reduced as a result of criticisms or ridicule from others
Tenth Grade	• analyze how characteristics and abilities develop • identify areas of personal accomplishment and achievement
Eleventh Grade	• specify characteristics and abilities they appreciate most in themselves and others

Twelfth Grade	• identify sources of personal strength or limitation
	• describe their uniqueness and develop that uniqueness
	• demonstrate that criticism may be constructive and encourage personal growth

Strand II—Interpersonal and Communication Skills/Understanding and Respect for Others/Appreciating Diversity

Grade	Student Competencies (all students in these grade levels will be able to):
PreK–Kindergarten	• identify some of their personal and physical traits
	• describe how they are like as well as different from others
	• recognize words that express feelings
First Grade	• verbalize a personal trait or behavior that they like about themselves
	• recognize that strengths and weaknesses are human characteristics
	• describe feelings they have in different situations
Second Grade	• identify the personal traits and characteristics that contribute to the uniqueness of each individual
	• explain the importance of liking themselves
	• discuss and share feelings about themselves
Third Grade	• describe themselves accurately to classmates
	• analyze how they feel about their own personal characteristics
	• express appropriately those thoughts and feelings that are important to them
Fourth Grade	• give examples of how they are important to themselves and others
	• define and discuss the meaning of self-concept
	• understand ways they manage their feelings
Fifth Grade	• specify personal characteristics and abilities that they value
	• explain what contributes to their feelings of self-worth
	• determine situations where they may express a variety of feelings and describe how they deal with those feelings
Sixth Grade	• describe the importance of communication skills in improving relationships with others
	• analyze the skills needed to make and keep friends
	• analyze the traits and behaviors admired in others
Seventh Grade	• accept and respond to compliments and criticism
	• speak respectfully to adults, peers, and members of groups different from their own
	• distinguish between the characteristics of healthy and unhealthy friendships
Eighth Grade	• practice nonverbal communication
	• evaluate the ways in which various groups are stereotyped
	• practice social skills that will help them relate in healthy personal relationships
Ninth Grade	• analyze how communication skills contribute toward work within a group
	• evaluate the importance of having friendships with peers and adults
	• demonstrate appropriate social skills in a variety of situations

Tenth Grade	• recognize characteristics of one's own culture, background, family, and heritage in any setting
	• use communication skills to help others
	• describe situations where behaviors affect others' behaviors toward them
	• maintain quality friendships with same-sex and opposite-sex individuals
	• demonstrate respect for others as individuals and accept them for their cultural heritage
Eleventh Grade	• analyze how communication skills encourage problem solving
	• assess current social and family relationships and evaluate effectiveness
	• maintain appropriate and enhancing relationships with adults and peers based on appreciation for differences and similarities in cultural heritage
Twelfth Grade	• evaluate current communication skills and assess skills needed for the future
	• understand the value of maintaining effective relationships throughout life in today's interdependent society
	• evaluate how stereotyping affects them and their relationships with others

Strand III—Responsible Behavior/Personal Responsibility

Grade	Student Competencies (all students in these grade levels will be able to):
PreK– Kindergarten	• identify rules they follow at home, school, and in the community
	• describe ways they take care of themselves
	• state positive and negative consequences of behavior
First Grade	• describe the necessity of having school, home, and community rules
	• describe the responsibilities they have at home and school
	• describe situations where they have no control, some control, or almost total control over themselves
Second Grade	• relate the impact of following rules to group effectiveness and personal success
	• describe necessary daily activities carried out by self and others
	• predict consequences for various behavior choices
Third Grade	• use knowledge of school rules and expectations when faced with choices which could interfere with learning
	• recognize that people have varying roles and describe their own roles
	• use behaviors that demonstrate respect for the feelings, property, and interests of others
Fourth Grade	• specify the differences between rights, responsibilities, and privileges
	• know their responsibilities and can be trusted to do them
	• evaluate various settings and demonstrate effective behavioral choices and self-control
Fifth Grade	• evaluate rules in home, school, and in the community
	• know their responsibilities and evaluate the effect of these responsibilities on self and others
	• analyze how growing up requires more self-control
Sixth Grade	• define their responsibilities in the school environment
	• practice asking for help from parents, teachers, and other adults without blaming others

Seventh Grade	• acknowledge that all behaviors have consequences • define their responsibilities as friends to others • recognize that they can control their own behavior, but only their own • analyze how their attitudes affect their behavior
Eighth Grade	• define their responsibilities as members of a family • describe how taking responsibility for their own behavior allows them to be in charge of their own lives • identify those behaviors in which the consequences are lifelong in nature
Ninth Grade	• evaluate willingness to accept personal responsibility • analyze and describe the consequences of unacceptable or irresponsible behavior • evaluate and explain the benefits of being self-disciplined • differentiate between healthy and unhealthy solutions to problems
Tenth Grade	• demonstrate management of environment • understand the tendency toward reciprocity of behavior between individuals • maintain self-discipline and rational behavior in dealing with emotional conflicts and stress
Eleventh Grade	• assess how avoiding responsibility hinders ability to manage environment effectively • articulate a personal theory of why people behave the way they do • distinguish between self-defeating and self-enhancing behaviors
Twelfth Grade	• assess how taking responsibility enhances their lives • accept responsibility for adhering to the goals of a selected group • recognize the degree of personal control over problems

Strand IV—Conflict Resolution

Grade	Student Competencies (all students in these grade levels will be able to):
PreK–Kindergarten	• interact with others in ways that show care and respect • identify conflicts • listen while another student describes a conflict
First Grade	• give and receive compliments • describe the elements of a conflict • identify feelings associated with conflicts
Second Grade	• encourage each other • give reasons for conflicts • brainstorm and evaluate possible solutions for conflicts
Third Grade	• predict how their behavior affects relationships • identify behaviors that make a conflict escalate or deescalate • use "I" statements
Fourth Grade	• identify "win-win," "win-lose," and "lose-lose" results of conflict • identify different points of view • demonstrate active listening skills
Fifth Grade	• become aware of issues involved with trust, neutrality, and confidentiality • describe how conflict is a normal part of life

Sixth Grade	• distinguish when to ask for help in resolving conflicts
	• apply nonviolent approaches to resolving conflicts
	• express anger without hurting themselves or others
	• evaluate how listening and talking accurately helps to resolve conflicts
Seventh Grade	• demonstrate nonviolent approaches to resolving conflicts
	• demonstrate an understanding of cooperation and cooperative behavior
	• differentiate between their own conflicts and those that belong to other people
Eighth Grade	• develop mediation skills to help others in resolving conflicts
	• recognize their own prejudices and to avoid conflicts based on prejudice
	• express their feelings directly to the person(s) involved rather than to third parties
Ninth Grade	• identify feelings and express them clearly and respectfully
Tenth Grade	• verbalize personal expectations in different situations
Eleventh Grade	• consider the point of view of others and practice empathy
Twelfth Grade	• demonstrate the ability to resolve personal conflicts and assist others through the use of mediation skills

Strand V—Decision Making/Problem Solving

Grade	Student Competencies (all students in these grade levels will be able to):
PreK–Kindergarten	• describe the choices they make in daily life
	• list alternative choices for solving problems
	• describe how they are different and the same this year
First Grade	• verbalize a personal trait or behavior that they like about themselves
	• recognize that strengths and weaknesses are human characteristics
	• describe feelings they have in different situations
Second Grade	• explain the steps in the decision-making process
	• recognize why some choices are made for them and recognize that they can accept those choices and make their own decisions when appropriate
	• describe what their major life roles are now and how they have changed or will change as they grow older
Third Grade	• explain their thought processes and feelings regarding making a decision
	• assess possible consequences of a decision before actually making the choice
	• explain strategies for feeling secure in a new group
Fourth Grade	• describe how their beliefs contribute to their decisions
	• develop a plan of action for solving problems
	• identify ways they have control over themselves and their lifestyle and evaluate intrinsic and extrinsic influences
Fifth Grade	• analyze their own skills for making personal and educational decisions
	• describe why they might want to change a decision and recognize when it is or is not possible to make that change
	• describe changes that will occur as they continue through school
Sixth Grade	• understand the steps in decision making or problem solving
	• practice generating a variety of alternatives for various problematic situations

	• gather information needed for effective decision making
Seventh Grade	• apply the decision making or problem solving skills they have learned
	• provide examples how past decisions affect present actions
	• identify probable consequences of various decisions
Eighth Grade	• expand their options by gaining more information
	• assess their own willingness to take risks and how this trait affects decisions they make
	• describe how their beliefs and values contribute to their decisions
Ninth Grade	• analyze how choices made now will affect lives in the future
	• define and prioritize values
	• analyze the importance of generating alternatives and assessing the consequences of each before making a decision
Tenth Grade	• predict some of the concerns they will have as they get older
	• describe how decisions are impacted by personal attitudes and values
	• distinguish between alternatives that involve varying degrees of risk
Eleventh Grade	• evaluate the need for flexibility in their roles and in their choices
	• analyze how values affect their decisions, actions, and lifestyles
	• analyze the consequences to self of decisions that others make
Twelfth Grade	• analyze how concerns change as situations and roles change
	• implement the decision-making process when making a decision
	• provide examples and evaluate their current ability to generate alternatives, gather information, and assess the consequences of the decisions they make

Strand VI—Motivation to Achieve

Grade	Student Competencies (all students in these grade levels will be able to):
PreK–Kindergarten	• take pride in their accomplishments
	• describe the process of learning and what they have learned
	• describe people and activities they enjoy
First Grade	• describe feelings they have when they have learned a new skill
	• describe the benefits they derive from learning
	• compare and contrast the actions of others that they may or may not appreciate
Second Grade	• describe thoughts and feelings they have while learning a new skill
	• describe the relationship between learning and effort
	• become aware of their interests and beliefs and how these motivate them to use their time
Third Grade	• explain strategies necessary to persevere when learning new tasks
	• describe study skills necessary for effective learning
	• describe strategies to balance activities in their lives
Fourth Grade	• identify their own learning style and recognize how using a variety of learning styles can improve performance
	• identify sources of school frustration and develop ways to manage it
	• give examples of and describe the importance of learning both in and out of school
Fifth Grade	• identify what motivates them to perform well

	• apply methods for using motivation and interest for the purpose of modifying weaknesses and limitations while maintaining and improving strengths
	• identify opportunities available to them in middle school
Sixth Grade	• express pride in academic achievement for themselves and others
	• explore the variety of opportunities that are available to them in middle school
	• assume responsibility for their own learning
Seventh Grade	• analyze what contributes to their feelings of competence and confidence
	• analyze the benefits they derive from learning
	• describe the attitudes necessary for success in work and learning
Eighth Grade	• summarize the high school graduation requirements
	• develop a plan for their high school years
	• predict how they will use knowledge from particular subjects in future work and work experiences
Ninth Grade	• describe personal learning and study skills and explain their importance
	• evaluate the benefits derived from learning
	• express positive attitudes toward work and learning
	• research and take advantage of opportunities for learning within the school environment and in the community
	• predict use of knowledge from school in future life and work
Tenth Grade	• evaluate personal learning and study skills and explain how they can be improved
	• analyze and evaluate motivational factors to develop academic potential
	• assume responsibility for meeting school graduation requirements
	• explain the relationship between educational achievement and career planning, training, and placement
Eleventh Grade	• predict how their developed learning and study skills can contribute to work habits in the future
	• evaluate personal accomplishments through the use of educational opportunities available in school
	• assess how feelings of competence and confidence will help in the future
Twelfth Grade	• evaluate ways they currently learn and predict how learning may change in the future
	• identify personal reasons for career selection

Strand VII—Goal Orientation/Goal Setting

Grade	Student Competencies (all students in these grade levels will be able to):
PreK–Kindergarten	• describe goals that people set
	• describe situations that will happen in the future
	• identify capabilities they have developed
First Grade	• describe goals they have set for themselves
	• describe situations desired for themselves in the future and when they would like those situations to happen
	• identify factors that enable them to reach a goal
Second Grade	• identify ways that contribute to group goals
	• recognize what they would like to accomplish when they are three years older

Third Grade	• identify factors that prevent them from reaching a goal • explain the differences between long-term and short-term goals • describe the steps in the goal setting process
Fourth Grade	• explain how environmental factors influence goals • explain the importance of goal setting • explain and define the importance of each of the steps in the goal setting process
Fifth Grade	• identify different methods of evaluating progress toward reaching goals • explain how goal setting will affect their future success • predict five goals (based on their interests and capabilities) they would like to achieve within five years
Sixth Grade	• describe the meaning of *value* and how values contribute to goal decisions • define goal setting and describe the need for it • distinguish among short, intermediate, and long-term goals
Seventh Grade	• establish goals for themselves and monitor their own progress • differentiate between realistic and unrealistic goals • set priorities in relation to goal attainment
Eighth Grade	• describe how their goals are affected by course choices • describe their vision of their preferred lifestyle and suggest goals to achieve it • consider future career plans in making educational choices
Ninth Grade	• investigate methods of evaluating progress toward goals • define their own unique values, interests, and capabilities • analyze how life roles, settings, and events determine preferred lifestyles
Tenth Grade	• compare how lifestyles differ depending on life roles, settings, and events • evaluate the importance of setting realistic goals and striving toward them
Eleventh Grade	• determine how life roles, setting, and events have influenced their current lifestyles • analyze how their values, interests, and capabilities have changed and are changing
Twelfth Grade	• assess the interactive effects of life roles, settings, and events and how these lead to a preferred lifestyle • assess their ability to achieve past goals and integrate this knowledge to set goals for the future • apply decision-making skills to personal goal setting

Strand VIII—Career Planning

Grade	Student Competencies (all students in these grade levels will be able to):
PreK–Kindergarten	• identify workers in the school setting • describe the work of family members • describe what they like to do individually and as part of a group
First Grade	• describe workers in various settings • describe different work activities and their importance • distinguish work activities in their environment done by specific people or by a group of people

Second Grade	• describe the diversity of jobs in various settings
	• define *work* and recognize that all people work
	• identify groups with which they work
Third Grade	• explain why people choose certain work activities and that those choices may change
	• describe different types of rewards obtained from work
	• describe behaviors that contribute or detract from successful group work
Fourth Grade	• define the meaning of stereotypes and indicate how stereotypes affect career choice
	• analyze how their basic study skills relate to career skills
	• explain how attitude and personal beliefs contribute to individual and group work
Fifth Grade	• compare their interests and skills to familiar jobs
	• predict how they will use knowledge from certain subjects in future life and work experiences
	• identify their own personal strengths and weaknesses and how these relate to career choices and work style
Sixth Grade	• know sources of information about jobs and careers
	• describe the importance of good work habits for school and future jobs
	• assess their own interests as these apply to career fields
Seventh Grade	• practice working in a group to accomplish a purpose
	• interact with people representing many career fields
	• assess their own aptitudes as they apply to career fields
Eighth Grade	• explore career field in which they are interested
	• apply what they have learned about themselves to career choices
	• apply what they have learned about themselves to educational choices
Ninth Grade	• analyze academic plans and experiences relevant to future education/training/employment
	• demonstrate skills for locating, evaluating, and interpreting information about career opportunities
Tenth Grade	• analyze the multiple career and educational options available to them upon completion of high school
	• determine how career concerns change as situations and roles change
Eleventh Grade	• demonstrate understanding of the need for personal and occupational flexibility in a changing world
	• explain how a changing world demands lifelong learning
Twelfth Grade	• anticipate and manage the changes experienced entering post-high-school education/training/employment
	• use decision making and goal setting to manage the post-high-school transition

Note. Adapted from *Curriculum Design and Management Manual for Guidance Curriculum,* by Austin Independent School District, 1996, Austin, TX: Author. Adapted with permission.

Appendix 8.B
Individual Academic-Career Plan (IACP) Sample Form

AUSTIN INDEPENDENT SCHOOL DISTRICT

Individual Academic-Career Plan
effective for ninth graders beginning Fall 1997 Class of 2001 and beyond

Last Name _____ First Name _____

Student ID _____ School _____

Graduation Requirements

	PLAN I		PLAN II		PLAN III
					(Same as Plan II *plus* requirements noted below)
English	4.0	☐ 1 ☐ 2 ☐ 3 ☐ 4	4.0	☐ 1 ☐ 2 ☐ 3 ☐ 4	
Social Studies	2.5	World Geo or World History U.S. History Government	3.5	World Geo and World History U.S. History Government	
Economics	0.5	☐	0.5	☐	
Mathematics	3.0	Algebra 1 Geometry Other math	3.0	Algebra 1 Geometry 2 Algebra	
Science	2.0	☐ ☐	3.0	☐ ☐ ☐	May substitute advanced math or science for 3rd year of foreign language:
Physical Ed*	1.5	☐ ☐ ☐	1.5	☐ ☐ ☐	
Health	0.5	☐	0.5	☐	
Computer Tech	1.0	☐ ☐	1.0	☐ ☐	
Fine Arts	1.0	☐ ☐	1.0	☐ ☐	
Speech	0.5	☐	0.5	☐	
Electives	5.5	(1.0 credit in W.G., W.H. or science) ☐ ☐ ☐	2.5	☐ ☐	Electives 4.5 ☐ ☐
TOTAL CREDITS	22		24		TOTAL CREDITS 26

☐ = 1/2 credit   * An additional .5 PE credit may count as .5 elective. No more than 2 credits of PE may count towards graduation.

Career Cluster: _____

Career Pathway: _____

Postsecondary Plans
☐ specialized training   ☐ 2 year college
☐ military   ☐ 4 year college

1st choice ___ 2nd choice ___

List interests, electives, pre AP courses, and extracurricular activities planned/taken in ms.

Circle high school credits earned in middle school

Algebra I   Geometry
Health   Speech
Foreign Language I
Other

TESTS
PLAN ___ PSAT ___ SAT ___ ACT ___
TAAS competency met: Writing ___ Reading ___ Math ___
Interest Inventory results ___

MIDDLE SCHOOL / POSTSECONDARY

HIGH SCHOOL PLANNING

9th		10th		11th		12th	
Fall	Spring	Fall	Spring	Fall	Spring	Fall	Spring

Other credit-earning alternatives planned (including summer school, co-enrollment, dual enrollment, Credit by Exam, correspondence courses)

Student Signature _____ Date ___ Parent/Guardian _____ Date ___ School Contact _____ Date ___

References

American School Counselor Association. (1990). *Role statement: The school counselor.* Alexandria, VA: Author.

American School Counselor Association. (1997). *The national standards for school counseling programs.* Alexandria, VA: Author.

Austin Independent School District. (1995). *Individual academic-career plan.* Austin, TX: Author.

Austin Independent School District. (1996). *Curriculum design and management manual for guidance curriculum.* Austin, TX: Author.

Campbell, M. E. (1932). *Vocational guidance committee on vocational guidance and child labor, section III: Education and training. White House Conference on Child Health and Protection.* New York: Century.

Clark, G. M., Field, S., Patton, J. R., Brolin, D. E., & Sitlington, P. L. (1994). Life skills instruction: A necessary component for all students with disabilities. A position statement of the Division on Career Development and Transition. *Career Development for Exceptional Individuals, 17,* 125–134.

Commission on Precollege Guidance and Counseling. (1986). *Keeping the options open: Recommendations.* New York: College Entrance Examination Board.

Council for Exceptional Children. (1994a). *Summary of the School-To-Work Opportunities Act.* Reston, VA: Author.

Council for Exceptional Children. (1994b). What is Goals 2000: The Educate America Act? *Teaching Exceptional Children, 27,* 78–80.

Dewey, J. (1990). *The school and society/The child and the curriculum.* Chicago: University of Chicago Press.

Drier, H. N., Johnson, C. D., Johnson, S. K., & Whitfield, E. A. (1991). Implementing the evaluation plan: Planning, forming questions, seeking answers. In S. Johnson and E. Whitfield (Eds.), *Evaluating guidance programs* (pp. 69–86). Iowa City, IA: The American College Testing Program.

Elementary and Secondary Education Act of 1965, 20 U.S.C. §7701 *et seq.*

Erickson, E.H. (1963). *Childhood and society.* New York: Norton.

Goals 2000: Educate America Act of 1994, 20 U.S.C. §5801 *et seq.*

Gysbers, N. C., & Henderson, P. (1994). *Developing and managing your school guidance program* (2nd ed.). Alexandria, VA: American Counseling Association.

Havighurst, R. J. (1953). *Human development and education.* New York: Longman.

Henderson, P., & Gysbers, N. C. (1998). *Leading and managing your school guidance program staff.* Alexandria, VA: American Counseling Association.

Individuals with Disabilities Education Act Amendments of 1997, 20 U.S.C. §1400 *et seq.*

Individuals with Disabilities Education Act of 1990, 20 U.S.C. §1400 *et seq.*

Johnson, S. K., & Whitfield, E. A. (1991). *Evaluating guidance programs.* Iowa City, IA: American College Testing Program.

Karge, B. D., Patton, P. L., & de la Garza, B. (1992). Transition services for youth with mild disabilities: Do they exist? *Career Development for Exceptional Individuals, 15,* 47–67.

Kohlberg, L., & Turiel, E. (1971). Moral development and moral education. In G.S. Lesser (Ed.), *Psychology and educational practice* (pp. 410–465). Glenview, IL: Scott, Foresman.

Kohler, P. D., DeStefano, L., Wermuth, T. R., Grayson, T. E., & McGinty, S. (1994). An analysis of exemplary transition programs: How and why are they selected? *Career Development for Exceptional Individuals, 17,* 187–201.

Mitchell, A., & Gysbers, N. C. (1980). Comprehensive school counseling and guidance programs: Planning, design, implementation, and evaluation. In *The status of guidance and counseling in the nation's schools*. Washington, DC: ACA Press.

Myrick, R. D. (1989). Developmental guidance: Practical considerations. *Elementary School Guidance and Counseling, 24*(1), 14–20.

Myrick, R. D. (1993). *Developmental guidance and counseling: A practical approach* (2nd ed.). Minneapolis, MN: Educational Media Corporation.

Nanus, B. (1995). Visionary leadership. In B. Sanders (Ed.), *Fabled service: Ordinary acts, extraordinary outcomes* (p. 11). San Diego, CA: Pfeiffer & Company.

National Defense Education Act of 1958, 20 U.S.C. §491 *et seq*.

National Occupational Information Coordinating Committee. (1989). *The national career guidance and counseling guidelines*. Washington, DC: Author.

Piaget, J. (1970). *Science of education and the psychology of the child*. New York: Onion Press.

Scott, S. (1996). Understanding colleges: An overview of college support services and programs available to clients from transition planning through graduation. *Journal of Vocational Rehabilitation, 6*, 217–230.

Starr, M., & Gysbers, N. C. (1992). *Missouri comprehensive guidance: A model for program development, implementation, and evaluation*. Jefferson City, MO: Department of Elementary and Secondary Education.

Super, D. E., & Bohn, M. J. (1970). *Occupational psychology*. Belmont, CA: Wadsworth.

Synatschk, K. O. (1994). Successful college students with learning disabilities: A cross-case analysis from a life-span developmental perspective. *Dissertation Abstracts International, 56*(01). 534B. (University Microfilms No. AAD94-15947).

Synatschk, K. O. (1995). Assessing readiness for successful college achievement in high school students with learning disabilities. *LD Forum, 20,* 17–21.

Synatschk, K. O. (1998). *Comprehensive developmental guidance and counseling: Framework for program implementation*. Austin, TX: Austin Independent School District.

Terrill, J. L. (1990). Toward the 1990s: Emerging themes in school counseling. *NASSP Bulletin, 74*(527), 84–88.

Texas Education Agency. (1997). *The comprehensive guidance program for Texas public schools: A guide for program development, Pre-K–12th Grade* (2nd ed.). Austin, TX: Author.

U.S. Department of Labor. (1991). *The secretary's commission on achieving necessary skills (SCANS)*. Washington, DC: Author.

Wrenn, C. G. (1962). *The counselors in a changing world*. Washington, DC: ACA Press.

CHAPTER

9

Leisure and Recreation

Steve A. Brannan

Leisure, recreation, and play are inherent aspects of the human experience, and are essential to health and well-being. All people, therefore, have an inalienable right to leisure and the opportunities it affords for play and recreation. Some human beings have disabilities, illnesses, or social conditions which may limit their participation in the normative structure of society. These persons have the same need for and right to leisure, recreation, and play.

—(National Therapeutic Recreation Society, 1990, as cited
in Sylvester with emphasis added, 1992, p.10)

Establishing Common Frames of Reference

The focus of this chapter is on leisure and recreation from the perspective of the discipline of special education. It is proposed that education for leisure should be an essential part of the transition process for students with disabilities, and that special educators be key facilitators of leisure education in concert with other disciplines and the parents of the students served.

Overview of the Discipline

The proposal that special educators should assume major instructional responsibility for leisure education might be considered an overlap of professional activity by certain professionals in related disciplines such as therapeutic recreation (TR) and adapted physical education (APE). These professionals represent disciplines in which traditional mission and services have been directed towards improving the physical and leisure wellness of people with disabilities. Additionally, the inclusion of leisure within transition education, which too often has focused primarily on preparation for work, is not well understood or accepted in the majority of schools providing transition services to students with disabilities.

From another viewpoint, the relevance of special education in addressing leisure and recreation has significant historical underpinnings. For example, a major precedent in support of leisure education was established years ago in general education when the Commission of the Reorganization of Secondary Education identified education for the worthy use of leisure as a major goal for the schools (National Education Association [NEA], 1918). Although general education never truly implemented such a goal for youth (with or without disabilities), the special education profession, during the last several decades, has demonstrated increased recognition of the importance of education for leisure. These efforts by the field of special education are based on the discipline's long standing mission and commitment to prepare its students in all aspects of living that are important to successful community adjustment and citizenship (Brolin, 1995; Edgar, 1987).

Perhaps more relevant than historical precedents, though, is the current awareness that special education efforts in support of transition should address the topic of leisure and recreation within an interdisciplinary framework. Such efforts are vitally needed to foster and increase ongoing communication, collaboration, and teaming among disciplines that will better ensure transition success for people with disabilities. Additionally, the impact of such collaboration is often greater when one discipline advocates for services provided by other disciplines. Recognizing the need for such advocacy, it is recommended that related disciplines (e.g., APE, TR, speech–language pathology, occupational therapy, and physical therapy) be more integrally involved with special education in the transition process serving students with disabilities in the schools.

Understanding Leisure and Recreation

A wide range of leisure-related terms are commonly used by professionals in recreation such as *leisure, leisure time, free time, discretionary time, play, avocational, recreation, leisure-time skills,* and *leisure education* (Bedini, 1993; Bedini, Bullock, & Driscoll, 1993; Dattilo & Schleien, 1994; Schleien, Meyer, Heyne, & Brandt, 1995). Special educators and APE professionals have used similar terms such as *outdoor education/recreation skills, leisure-time skills, leisure activities, lifetime sports skills, lifetime recreation skills,* and *leisure education* (or education for leisure) in their writings (Bender, Brannan, & Verhoven, 1984; Brannan, 1975; Rizzo & Davis, 1993; Sherrill, 1993; Wilcox & Bellamy, 1987). Because an understanding of leisure-related terms seems essential, a further discussion of several core terms to indicate their similarities and differences follows.

The term *leisure* seems to be the most encompassing and complex of all the terms. Dictionaries usually define leisure as being related to time free from one's obligations, but a more complete meaning of the term is provided by *American Heritage College Dictionary* (1997): "Freedom from time-consuming duties, responsibilities, or activities . . . When one has free time" (p.776). Thus, leisure might best be conceptualized in terms of two broad dimensions. First, the meaning most commonly associated with leisure is that portion of an individual's time that is not devoted to work, domestic, or other forms of required activity. Viewed in this context, leisure refers to an individual's own time, and is often referred to as free time, discretionary time, unobligated time, or leisure time. Second, the concept of leisure reflects its core or fundamental meaning—that is, leisure focuses on individuals having the freedom to choose and make voluntary decisions regarding the use of their discretionary time (Peterson & Gunn, 1984; Sylvester, 1985; 1992). Such freedom of choice enables persons to pursue leisure experiences that are more fully satisfying, enjoyable, and meaningful because they meet their own unique needs and interests. Thus, the more an activity is freely and independently chosen and experienced, the more likely it will be enjoyable, fun, fulfilling, enriching, and truly considered leisure.

The word *recreation* is closely related in meaning to leisure and even used interchangeably, but is often considered a more practical concept or term. When comparing recreation with leisure, it has been suggested that recreation operationalizes leisure (i.e., leisure in action). Typically, recreation focuses on the activities or experiences carried out during one's leisure time. Representing the special education and recreation professions, Bender et al. (1994) defined recreation as "activities or experiences conducted within leisure that are chosen voluntarily by the participant and selected because of the satisfaction or pleasure gained from them and/or their perceived personal and social values" (p. 227). TR professionals also confirm the relationship of recreation to activities: "Recreation is typically defined as an activity that people engage in for the primary reasons of enjoyment and satisfaction (e.g., swimming, table games, aerobic dance)" (Dattilo & Schleien, 1994, p. 53). In the same context, recreation means "refreshment of one's mind or body through activity that amuses or stimulates" (*American Heritage College Dictionary*, 1997, p. 1,142).

Play is another leisure-related term that has many meanings, and it is often used synonymously with recreation and leisure functioning. In infancy and early childhood, play commonly refers to the spontaneous and pleasurable behaviors with which children interact with their environment, and is a major medium through which learning and sensorimotor development occurs (Sherrill, 1986). As people move from childhood into adolescence and adulthood, the word *play* is often replaced with terms such as *playful, playfulness, recreation,* and *leisure*. When play is used to promote individual growth and development, the term *play training* in the child's early years is often replaced during later years with the term *leisure education*.

With respect to *leisure education*, there is general agreement that its purpose refers to preparing individuals to pursue their discretionary time independently and to achieve an enhanced quality of life. Lack of a prevailing definition is due, in large part, because concepts, models, and programs explaining and demonstrating leisure education are still evolving in various fields, such as TR, special education, and APE (Bedini, 1990; Brannan, 1988; Bullock & Mahon, 1997). A selection of purpose statements proposed by professionals from these disciplines is presented in Table 9.1, and these statements reflect both the common and unique concepts regarding the intent of leisure education.

Functional Use of Leisure-Related Terms

Differentiating among *leisure, recreation,* and *play* as discrete terms may not be the most functional or useful approach in promoting education for leisure with teachers, parents, students, and related disciplines. The need to employ a more functional use of these terms seems evident. Even professionals have experienced some difficulties in clearly explaining the differences among these terms.

Table 9.1
Purpose Statements of Leisure Education for People with Disabilities

1. Leisure education should prepare people with knowledge and competencies that will enable them to pursue and achieve the goal of normal recreation and leisure participation in our culture (Nesbitt, Neal, & Hillman, 1974).
2. Leisure education is a lifelong, continuous process that, in part, enables individuals to be self-determining and develops their potential for enhancing the quality of their lives (Mundy & Odum, 1979).
3. The ultimate goal of leisure education should be to facilitate self-initiated independent use of leisure time with chronologically age-appropriate recreational activities (Wehman & Schleien, 1981).
4. Leisure education includes, but is not limited to, the development of knowledge, skills, and appreciations that prepare individuals to make more independent and constructive use of their leisure time (Bender, Brannan, & Verhoven, 1984).
5. Leisure education promotes families as natural partners in person-centered leisure education that prepares students with disabilities to make self-determined leisure choices based on their individual interests and preferences (Johnson, Bullock, & Ashton-Shaeffer, 1997).

As a case in point, many of these concepts and terms are used interchangeably in the professional literature and among practitioners in various fields (Rizzo & Davis, 1993; Schleien et al., 1995). Henderson (1994) confirms there is a lack of agreement about certain leisure-related terms among professionals and citizens at large. He believes that differentiating among the terms becomes especially challenging when trying to operationalize them for use in teaching and research, and particularly when trying to help students with disabilities understand and use these concepts. From a functional and user-needs standpoint, terms such as *leisure, recreation*, and *play* should probably be considered synonymous. To support this idea, a more practical approach to leisure-related concepts is illustrated in Figure 9.1. The major terms *leisure, recreation*, and *play* each form a side of the triangle, demonstrating that they are closely interrelated and interchangeable. Inside the triangle, the words *activities, choice, enjoyment, free time, fun*, and *interests* help communicate the functional meanings of leisure, recreation, and play, and serve as their common descriptors.

Relationship of Leisure Education to Special Education and Transition

Leisure Education Accommodated in Federal Definition of Transition

With the passage in 1990 of the Individuals with Disabilities Act (IDEA) and its subsequent amendments in 1997, a broader range of life outcomes have been included in the transition process. These outcomes are to be based on the individual needs of students and include the students' participation in decisions affecting their future. Although leisure outcomes are not specifically identified in IDEA's definition of transition, elements of this legislation support these aims as part of the transition process by requiring coordinated activities to promote, in part, independent living and community participation outcomes. Preparation for leisure functioning is further accommodated in transition education because IDEA also requires that coordinated activities include instruction, community experiences, other postschool living objectives, and, when needed, the acquisition of daily living skills. Of particular significance with regard to the basic concepts underlying leisure (i.e., choice, self-determination), the array of coordinated transition activities in IDEA must be based on the individual student's needs, preferences, and interests.

A consideration of individual needs and expectations in determining needed transition services (e.g., instruction, community experiences, and interagency linkages) is required in each student's IEP/ITP. Also, under IDEA's 1997 amendments, transition service planning for such students must begin by age 14. The IEP has traditionally been based on the unique needs of students with

Figure 9.1. Functional use of leisure-related terms. Illustrates the commonalities of leisure, play, and recreation and the functional terms often used to describe their intent.

disabilities, and even though such students often have deficits in leisure skills, this area of instruction has often been neglected. Thus, IDEA's emphasis on life skill preparation, the unique needs of students, their interests and preferences, and an earlier transition process provides extensive support for incorporating leisure instruction into transition education.

Professional Organizations Identify Life-Skill Areas as Part of Transition

In recognition that a major aim of the transition process for students with disabilities is to achieve successful postschool adjustment, a wide range of life skills needs to be taught to such learners. While special educators and career/vocational educators have traditionally centered their efforts on job readiness and employment objectives, the Council for Exceptional Children (CEC) has increasingly recognized other lifelong skills as critically important in the transition process for the full range of students with disabilities.

A forward looking position on the meaning of transition has been developed for and adapted by the Division on Career Development and Transition (DCDT) of the CEC (Halpern, 1994). The DCDT position statement provided a definition of transition, helped it refocus the organization's attention on more relevant transition outcomes, and helped move the special education profession beyond the federal initiative proposals of the 1980s that conceptualized transition as a process primarily leading to employment (Will, 1983). Halpern (1994) focused on the various roles that students need to assume as adults, and in addition to employment, also addressed residential living, community participation, and personal and social relationships. Although DCDT's definition of transition ran parallel to certain concepts detailed in the 1990 IDEA legislation, there were notable additions (e.g., promoting transition during elementary and middle school years and increased student involvement in planning). This broadened perspective on transition encouraged teachers, parents, agency personnel, and students served through special education to participate in instruction and services that address various life skill areas. Thus, transition education that prepares students for the adult role of using their leisure time in a constructive manner can be inferred from the DCDT's adopted definition of transition. This is particularly true relative to improving one's personal and social relationships, because opportunities for development and learning occur most predominantly during one's leisure time.

More recently, the CEC has taken a broad-based approach to transition, conceptualizing it, in general, as a term for various educational efforts that prepare students for significant life changes, including transitioning that begins in elementary schools and continues throughout schooling. The CEC recommends to special educators, parents, and others that the traditional mind-set about transition needs to change:

> Transition is moving beyond helping students get a job. New directions include preparing students for other life goals such as social skills, independent living, community participation, transportation, and financial planning. This necessitates including new goals in the IEP. For example, if a student needs to develop better social skills, his or her IEP goals might include participation in an extracurricular activity. (CEC, 1997, p. 13)

Significant support for a broadened approach to transition education was also recently adopted by the Board of Directors, Division on Mental Retardation/Developmental Disabilities (MRDD) of the CEC. A position statement was unanimously approved by the MRDD Board in support of increased health, fitness, and wellness education for children and adults with mental retardation and other developmental disabilities. The MRDD reported that such individuals are often not afforded adequate opportunities or experiences to develop positive lifestyles, and that they should participate in educational programs that specifically promote healthy lifestyles, physical fitness, and other recreational activities

(MRDD, 1997). The programs being recommended are integral to leisure education. Although directed toward individuals with mental retardation and other developmental disabilities, the MRDD's position is equally relevant for individuals with other disabling conditions who have similar needs for healthy lifestyles.

Life Skill Models Incorporate Leisure/Recreation in Transition

Special education's efforts to promote transition education for students with disabilities in the nation's schools have been evolving from a strict focus on vocational goals to a broadened mission that prepares youth and young adults with disabilities (ages 14 to 21 and younger) for independent adjustment in their communities. Transition outcomes (i.e., desired adult functioning and competencies) for these students are also being recommended as the basis for curriculum and instruction efforts at all levels of the curriculum in special education. Extensive information on career education and life skill instructional models is now available, directed towards preparing adolescents and young adults to function successfully in postschool environments (Brolin, 1997; Cronin & Patton, 1993; Patton & Blalock, 1996; Wehman & Kregel, 1997). Many of these educational models include major curriculum areas that extend beyond the traditional career/vocational focus and address learning outcomes that will enable students to transition successfully to all major areas of adult living, including the leisure domain. As an example, Cronin and Patton (1993) recommended six major domains of adult life that are important for effective transition preparation: (1) employment/ education, (2) home and family, (3) leisure pursuits, (4) community involvement, (5) physical/emotional health, and (6) personal responsibility and relationships. Sitlington (1996) summarized approaches to transition education that also address relevant life domains:

> There is a great deal of agreement across these career education and life skills education models over the fact that maintaining a home, becoming appropriately involved in the community (including recreation and leisure activities), and experiencing satisfaction in personal and social relationships are major skills needed in adult life. (p. 51)

As a result of such efforts to identify what constitutes adequate life preparation for students with disabilities, the area of leisure is receiving increased recognition as a bonafide life skill area. A greater number of professionals are now advocating leisure as a major life domain, recommending that leisure education be more prominent in the schools, and indicating its potential to contribute positively to changes in curriculum and instruction and related transition education practices (Bedini, 1993; Bedini et al., 1993; Bradley, 1989; Brannan,

1988; Cronin & Patton, 1993; Dattilo & St. Peter, 1991; Dever, 1989; Sitling-ton, 1996).

Existing Challenges

There are numerous barriers, gaps, and issues to take into account when considering the relationship of leisure to education, specifically its connection with transition education for students who are disabled. Although not inclusive, five areas of need that pose challenges relate to (1) leisure education benefits, (2) comprehensive transition, (3) school-based leisure education, (4) interdisciplinary teaming, and (5) leisure education advocacy.

Benefits of Leisure Education not Fully Understood

Individuals with disabilities served through special education and related services have unique needs that require more individual and direct learning experiences to prepare them for all facets of community life. It is proposed that any consideration of the unique needs of such individuals should include their adjustment in all major life domains (e.g., work, domestic activity, and leisure). From this perspective, then, many such individuals need instruction (i.e., leisure education) that is targeted to improve their leisure functioning. Consequently, the primary benefit of leisure education is that children, youth, and young adults with disabilities will be equipped to take increased control of their free time (i.e., become more self-determined) and utilize it more fully and constructively in this important area of living. On a more general level, though, leisure education has potential to provide numerous benefits to students, which include (a) enhancing their growth and development during schooling, (b) preparing them to transition successfully, (c) meeting the demands of daily adult living, and of most significance (d) enabling them to achieve a more satisfying and higher quality of life.

Unfortunately, this potential is not currently being fully realized due, in large measure, to the lack of understanding by various professionals in general and special education, specialists across certain disciplines, parents, and the citizenry at large. Although the benefits of education for leisure are not new, the general recognition of their values and the implementation of their concepts in the nation's schools, homes, and communities still remain underrealized. Obviously, different strategies are needed to raise the level of appreciation, understanding, and acceptance of leisure education, and for key persons to facilitate its implementation in schooling so that students with disabilities are better prepared for transition success. Table 9.2 illustrates a wide range of positive benefits that may accrue to students with disabilities receiving leisure preparation. These benefits of leisure education are widely supported by the various professionals representing the disciplines of special education, TR, APE, and career/vocational training.

Table 9.2
Benefits of Leisure Education

1. Independence for adolescents at home, at work, and in the community is furthered through systematic leisure instruction that uses a chronologically age-appropriate curriculum, and is community-based with a focus on leisure activity skills (Wehman, Renzaglia, & Bates, 1985).
2. Collateral skill development (e.g., physical/motor, cognitive growth, personal/social, language, other academic skills) is an important outcome of planned leisure activities (Stein, 1975).
3. Inappropriate behaviors are lessened, and alternate, incompatible behaviors are achieved through leisure skill instruction using recreation activities and environments that are fun and highly motivating (Schleien, Meyer, Heyne, & Brandt, 1995).
4. Improved leisure functioning and constructive use of discretionary time is fostered through a comprehensive and interdisciplinary approach in the schools that fosters growth in leisure knowledge, skills, values, and interests (Bender, Brannan, & Verhoven, 1984).
5. Participation in leisure-related experiences in inclusive home, school, and community settings affords individuals significant opportunities for social development/skills (e.g., acceptance, friendships, models) (Schleien, Ray, & Green, 1997).
6. Significant growth in the affective domain (e.g., self-esteem, self-reliance, personal/social) is a unique outcome of participation in planned leisure programs that stress group living, fun, adventure, individual growth, and success (Brannan, Arick, & Fullerton, 1997).
7. Equipping individuals to make meaningful use of their leisure time counters forced and unfulfilling leisure periods that occur due to unemployment, underemployment, community adjustment problems, and so on (Dunn, 1996).
8. Leisure learning is interesting, motivating, and relevant because it deals with life skills and functional activities (e.g., skills related to travel, following directions, eating out) that are acquired and practiced in one's own community (Cronin, 1996).
9. Preparation for leisure when incorporated in transition education facilitates the attainment of career/vocational goals because leisure experiences are highly successful and build self-confidence (leisure focus is noncompetitive). Work and leisure use similar processes (e.g., job finding and leisure finding skills), and job opportunities can evolve from recreation activities (Kimeldorf, 1989).
10. Successful transition from school to adult living and an enriched quality of life are better achieved when leisure is included as one of the critical life skill areas in individualized educational assessment, planning, and instruction (Clark & Patton, 1997).

Comprehensive Transition Underrealized

According to Benz, Yovanoff, and Doren (1997):

> the call for stronger, more effective career guidance and planning as part of a comprehensive career education effort across elementary and secondary education has been sounded for years. Unfortunately, it still remains a low priority in public education. Our findings and those of others require that we sound the call again. (p. 163)

Although transition practices in special education have evolved over the last decade to include improved planning and services, a need still exists to expand further the concept of transition services for students with disabilities. Recent proposals by professionals in special education, career/transition education, and TR call for an expanded, lifespan model of transition that recognizes the importance of early and ongoing preparation of students with disabilities in order to achieve successful postschool adjustment (Bedini et al., 1993; Brolin, 1997; CEC, 1997; Morningstar, Turnbull, & Turnbull, 1995; Patton & Blalock, 1996).

Of particular significance, comprehensive models of transition are being recommended that have a futures orientation and that provide continuous and coordinated planning and service for individuals with disabilities from preschool through postsecondary education (Repetto & Correa, 1996). Such contemporary transition models are comprehensive in that they are *seamless* (i.e., link early childhood, elementary, middle, and secondary programs) and have a continuing student and family-centered focus. Traditionally, a missing link in transition practices has been the lack of participation by key persons (i.e., student, family, teachers, community) at elementary and middle school levels in preparing students with disabilities for postschool adjustment as adults. Repetto and Correa (1996) recommended that seamless-type transition models are needed that link all age levels of students and include the following components in delivering future-oriented services: (a) curriculum that is life-based (focus on functional knowledge and skills); (b) education in various settings (across home, school, and community settings); (c) documented transition planning (futures-oriented goals and objectives in written plans, such as Individualized Family Services Plan, IEPs, ITPs); (d) multiagency collaboration (coordination and input among various service providers); and (e) student/family focus. It is suggested that the life skill area of leisure/recreation can be effectively included in such an approach. To accomplish this task, increased efforts are needed to articulate clearly the construct of leisure education and to demonstrate its relationship to the transition planning process in school systems.

School-Based Leisure Education Inadequate

The inclusion of leisure in many transition-related curricular models indicates that it is beginning to be recognized as one of the major life domains and helps to validate its relevance as an integral part of transition education. Also, some professionals across several disciplines are advocating for a comprehensive transition approach which, if preparation for leisure is added, will help it to be more fully achieved. Still, such advocacy should not be construed as indicating that leisure education is now being effectively carried out in the nation's schools. Rather, substantial evidence suggests that there is a strong need for improved leisure education efforts with students of all disabling conditions across the school's curriculum, including students served in career/transition education programs (Bender et al., 1984; Bedini et al., 1993; Brannan, 1988; Dattilo & Schleien, 1994; Dattilo & St. Peter, 1991). This is more understandable when noting the lack of agreement in the field about what constitutes a total approach to leisure education, particularly as it relates to school programs serving students with disabilities.

A review of the leisure sections of career/transition models proposed for schools reveals a wide range of perspectives regarding education for leisure (e.g., type of learners to receive such instruction, concepts of leisure functioning, key facilitators of education, leisure activities, and related skills). As an example, leisure content and related learner competencies vary significantly across the leisure/recreation domains of many career/transition and life-skill models (Bender et al., 1984; Brolin, 1997; Cronin & Patton, 1993; Loumiet & Levack, 1991; Schleien et al., 1995; Wehman et al., 1985; Wehman & Schleien, 1981; Wilcox & Bellamy, 1987). Furthermore, the majority of leisure education models and related curriculum materials have been oriented toward adolescents and adults with moderate to severe disabilities. As a result, the need to address the total spectrum of learners with disabilities has been virtually ignored, particularly the leisure preparation of students with mild disabilities (Bedini, 1993; Brannan, 1988; Peniston, 1998; Sitlington, 1996). In order for a school-based approach to leisure education to be effective, it should address the needs of all students with disabilities, regardless of their age, disabling condition, or level of functioning. Fortunately, perspectives have recently expanded on what constitutes career/transition practices (e.g., more open to addressing major life domains, childhood through adolescence, increased student and family decision making, etc.). Still, a broadened conceptualization and a more comprehensive and substantive approach to leisure education is urgently needed. If leisure education is to be successful in the schools, its constructs must be broad-based and its outcomes clearly defined in order to meet the needs of all students who are disabled. A comprehensive leisure education model for the schools would help all disciplines involved in school-based transition services to be more effective.

Interdisciplinary Participation and Teaming Incomplete

IDEA requires professionals to provide multidisciplinary efforts in identifying and meeting the unique needs of each student with a disability. In serving such students, it is commonplace in special education to have team efforts directed towards assessment, evaluation, instructional planning, and implementation. The law requires multidisciplinary assessments and specifies that a diverse group of persons must comprise the IEP teams. Assumed in this law is that the schools will effectively utilize the expertise of needed persons, profit from their interdisciplinary efforts and, in doing so, provide more effective special education services to students.

In relation to leisure and recreation, it appears that many students served by special education are not realizing the full benefits of such teaming, namely the contributions of interdisciplinary efforts from the disciplines of APE and TR. Although instruction in physical education is defined specifically in IDEA as part of special education for students with disabilities, the reality is that appropriate physical education for such students is often missing in public schools nationwide at any level of the curriculum (National Association of State Directors of Special Education [NASDE], 1991). This is particularly disturbing when noting that a significant number of students with disabilities have marked deficits in physical fitness and motor skills that can adversely affect their life adjustment (Dattilo, 1987; Jansma & French, 1994). Increased advocacy for the use of both adapted and general physical education teachers in the education of students with disabilities is obviously needed. According to NASDE (1991), such services can improve physical fitness and motor skills, and lead to the learning of lifetime sports skills, with improved health and greater participation in community recreation or sports programs. Sherrill (1993) also reported that physical education can be a major contributor to successful transition through its focus on lifetime recreation and leisure skills.

Lack of participation of key professionals on IEP/ITP teams is also prevalent with respect to the participation of TR specialists in the public schools. This is perplexing because such professionals are also identified in IDEA, and their discipline is mentioned specifically as a related service that can make a variety of contributions to the education of students with disabilities, particularly to their leisure functioning (i.e., through provision of leisure education). The problem is due, in large measure, to the lack of leisure education programs and participation of these leisure professionals in school programs for these students (Bedini et al., 1993; Dattilo & Schleien, 1994; Dattilo & St. Peter, 1991). Evidently, the nonparticipation of TR professionals assisting students with disabilities in the schools has not changed significantly since the groundbreaking nationwide survey that found recreation as a related service to be inadequately utilized (Coyne, 1981).

In short, professionals in the disciplines of APE and TR have much to offer the total education of students with disabilities including their contributions to the transition success of such individuals. Increased advocacy from the education profession is most likely needed in order to obtain the level of participation and services (e.g., multidisciplinary teams, IEP/ITP teams, instruction, therapy) of these and related disciplines that will adequately meet the overall physical and leisure or recreation needs of students in special education.

Leadership for Leisure Education Lacking

Professionals and parents and their respective organizations need to expand their advocacy and leadership efforts if leisure education is to be fully realized for students as important to their education and successful transitioning. The recognition of this need is as true today as it was years ago when Nesbitt, Neal, and Hillman (1974) stated the following:

> It seems significant that for a number of years educational authorities unanimously accepted these principles, but the schools failed to focus attention towards developing better educated judgements about leisure among children and youth. It would appear that leisure, like the weather, is ubiquitous [unpredictable] and uncontrollable. And, like the weather, everybody talks about it, but nobody does anything about it. (p. 5)

Similar concerns have been voiced more recently by TR professionals. Bedini et al. (1993) made the observation that few leisure education programs exist in public school systems, and Dattilo and St. Peter (1991) indicated the lack of nonwork educational outcomes (i.e., leisure) in school-directed transition services. On a more positive note, vocational and special educators Clark and Patton (1997) indicated that in a recent survey at least 17 states identified leisure/recreation as one of the major domains in transition planning guides. The trend is definitely encouraging, but the number of states addressing education for leisure is still unacceptable. It is highly unlikely that students from these states have substantive leisure-related goals and objectives in their IEP/ITPs, particularly with respect to individuals who are more mildly disabled.

What are the barriers preventing implementation of leisure education in transition planning and other school programs? A special education perspective is that the lack of leisure education is linked to such preparation being viewed traditionally by educators as a low curricular priority (Brannan, 1988). Such valuing reflects a traditional approach to education that promotes the academics or basics as the primary aims of schooling. The education reform movements of the 1980s and 1990s, to a great extent, have reinforced such values with their emphasis on creating higher academic and related testing standards for students at elementary and secondary levels. In such an educational climate, nonacademic content and related learning experiences are often neglected, limited, or eliminated. As a case in point, areas of learning in education that have particular significance and potential for one's leisure time (e.g., art, music, lifetime sports, physical education, high interest electives, extracurricular activities, etc.) are often targeted first for reduction or elimination in school districts retooling their programs due to budget constraints. Such valuing can adversely affect all students, particularly students with disabilities, when so-called reform efforts pit academics against vocational and other more functional programs and educational experiences these learners vitally need for successful transition (CEC, 1997). For special education students, such priorities can adversely influence the quality of their IEP/ITPs, resulting in limited attention given to the overall life skills curriculum that includes leisure-related goals and objectives.

A Bold Vision for the Future

A School-Based Model of Leisure Education Is Essential

A holistic and school-based approach to leisure education for students with disabilities is necessary and long overdue. A proposal for such an approach under the school's leadership is represented by the Leisure Education School (LES) model in Figure 9.2. Inherent in this model are the concepts that leisure is a major life domain, that education for leisure occurs throughout schooling, and that the full range of students with disabling conditions should receive education for leisure in the schools. Thus, the LES model embraces (a) all *ages*, including early childhood, elementary, middle school, and secondary level transitions, with special focus on transition education programs serving adolescents and young adults; (b) all *disabling conditions*, as specified under current federal legislation (e.g., IDEA); and (c) all *levels of functioning*, including children, youth, and young adults who vary in performance level (e.g., students mildly to severely disabled). Such an approach facilitates transitioning at all levels of the curriculum for all students who are disabled and contributes to their potential for successful postschool adjustment. In support of the LES Model, many professionals in special education (including transition specialists), career/vocational education, TR, and APE agree with the importance of various concepts stressed in the LES model. Leisure advocates in these disciplines also agree that the concepts underlying the LES model are critically important to transition education and its primary aim to prepare students with disabilities to achieve increased independence and successful community adjustment (Bedini, 1993;

Bedini et al., 1993; Bradley, 1989; Brannan, 1981, 1988; Dattilo & St. Peter, 1991; Kimeldorf, 1989).

Major Components of the LES Model

The LES model is comprised of three major components with representative sub-components. The first major component is *leisure concepts*, which refers to the basic concepts that underlie and affect leisure functioning. Leisure concepts include the following:

1. *Awareness/Knowledge:* understanding or appreciation of leisure versus work, knowledge and utilization of resources, and leisure networking.

2. *Attitudes/Values:* oriented towards playfulness, spontaneity, and joy in leisure, responsive to own preferences, and development of one's interests.

3. *Activity Skills:* acquisition of recreation skills important for meaningful participation, exposure to a wide range of leisure activities, and skill selection and development related to interests or potential for enjoyment.

4. *Social Skills:* interpersonal/interaction skills, friendship development, verbal/nonverbal communication, and cooperation/sharing.

5. *Self-Determination Skills:* personal choice and control, decision making and self-regulation, goal setting and attainment, self-advocacy and initiative, and self-knowledge or evaluation.

The second major component of the LES is *settings*, which refers to the major environments in which leisure and related education efforts occur. Representative settings include the following:

1. *School:* Extensive leisure-related activities and learning opportunities are available through classroom and community-based instruction, physical education, lunch, playground, athletics, intramural sports, special interests groups, outdoor/environmental education, arts activities, and so on.

2. *Home:* Numerous recreation and related learning opportunities are available in the home environment for individual participation, and with family, relatives, friends, and neighbors.

3. *Community:* A wide range of recreation activities are available that are individual or group oriented, public or private agency sponsored or organized, inexpensive versus costly, and located near the community, town, and city, in outlying areas, and statewide.

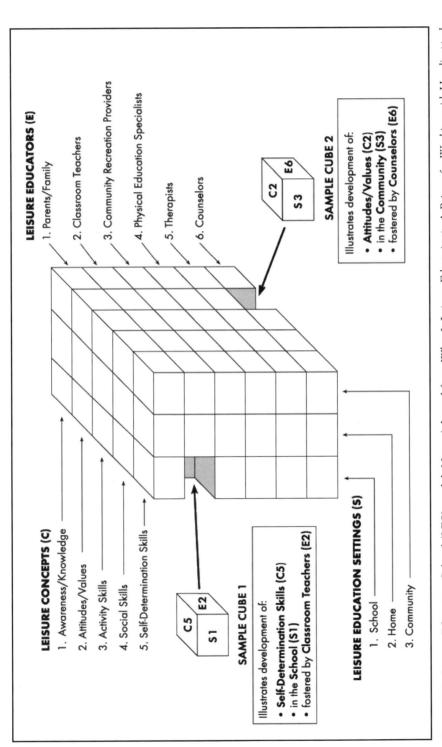

Figure 9.2. Leisure Education School (LES) model. *Note.* Adapted from *What Is Leisure Education?: A Primer for Working with Handicapped Children and Youth* (pp. 3–6), by S. Brannan, K. Chinn, and P. Verhoven, 1981, Washington, DC: Hawkins and Associates.

The third major component, *leisure educators*, refers to people who serve as important facilitators of leisure education for students with disabilities. While not an inclusive listing, the following groups play an important role in leisure education and can facilitate the leisure competence of individuals with disabilities:

1. *Parents/Family:* parents, guardians, siblings, relatives, friends, and others who play a significant personal and social role in the lives of students who are disabled.

2. *Classroom Teachers:* various special educators, paraeducators, and volunteers, as well as general educators such as early childhood specialists, elementary classroom teachers, middle/high school subject area teachers, career/vocational instructors, and so forth.

3. *Community Recreation Providers:* general park and recreation leaders, TR specialists, and recreation personnel in other public and private agencies.

4. *Physical Education Specialists:* school-based APE specialists and physical education teachers serving general education.

5. *Therapists:* speech–language pathologists, TR specialists, physical therapists, occupational therapists, music and art therapists, and so on.

6. *Counselors:* school counselors, career/guidance counselors, vocational/rehabilitation counselors, and so forth.

The LES Model Is Designed To Be Holistic

Field (1996) stated that "Models describe and simplify complex phenomena so that concepts can be applied in practical settings and make complex concepts more easily understood and, therefore, more easily applied to everyday life" (p. 65). The LES model focuses primarily on the preparation of students with disabilities. The model is intended to fill a major gap that exists relative to educators' understanding the components of leisure education, including the interrelationships of each component in promoting the successful transition of students with disabilities. It is important to note that the model need not be restricted to individuals with disabilities or to the school years; most of the concepts are relevant to individuals without disabilities and also have lifespan significance. Thus, the underlying concepts of leisure in the model are germane to both special and general education.

The holistic characteristic of the model refers to its components being both comprehensive and interdependent. The model is *comprehensive* because all designated components need to be included in order to understand and implement a total or complete program of leisure education (i.e., leisure concepts, leisure educators, leisure settings). For example, education for leisure is not solely the responsibility of the schools, but needs to be implemented in school, home, and community settings by various persons who serve an educator role (formal or informal) during the lives of children, youth, or young adults. Further, all components of the model are *interdependent* and need to interface throughout schooling in order to have the greatest impact on the leisure functioning of students with disabilities. For example, each of the leisure educators can potentially provide educational service (direct or indirect) during the entire period of schooling (from early childhood through young adulthood) to individuals with disabilities, deal with the full range of leisure concepts, and participate across the environments of school, home, and community.

The LES Model Incorporates Four Basic Principles

The first basic principle in the LES model is that leisure education is relevant to all individuals throughout their schooling. Although not illustrated in Figure 9.2, inherent in the model is that all individuals, regardless of age, type of disability, or level of functioning, need access to leisure education throughout their schooling. The model is based on the belief that all students with disabilities have potential for learning, and that appropriate instruction should be provided at all levels of the curriculum to meet the unique needs of individuals specific to their leisure functioning.

The second basic principle is that leisure education helps students improve their leisure functioning. Students need such instruction to develop awareness and understanding of leisure, appreciation and interests, skills in various types of recreation, social skills common to leisure, and skills in making and evaluating choices. These skills allow students to become more independent in their leisure and achieve a healthy leisure lifestyle. Too often, leisure education programs have been limited to skill development in recreation activities, without enough consideration to choice making, preferences, and particularly to the effective benefits of leisure participation (e.g., enjoyment, friendships, and social development) that are essential elements of a comprehensive program of instruction (Schleien et al., 1995).

The third principle is that leisure education includes an interdisciplinary team of leisure educators. Key persons from the school, home, and community can serve an ongoing role (formal or informal) as leisure educators for children, youth, and young adults with disabilities. Transition planning that includes these representatives as part of the education team is vitally important and better ensures that a comprehensive and coordinated program of leisure education will be provided to students. In promoting school-based leisure education, special and general education teachers, instructional assistants and aides, speech–language pathologists, physical education specialists (APE and general), TR specialists, occupational and physical therapists, guidance counselors, and transition specialists can all play a significant role. Special education, in particular, needs to assume a leading agency role in promoting leisure education. Special education teachers who typically guide multidisciplinary and IEP/ITP teams should provide leadership to ensure that the interdisciplinary process truly occurs as IDEA intended for purposes of assessment, planning, coordination of services, instruction, and evaluation. Particular attention should be given to the contributions of physical education specialists to leisure education (e.g., expertise in physical fitness, lifetime sports), especially because physical education is required by law to be part of specially designed instruction. Students and their parents and family members are critically important members of the team, and under IDEA, student and parent input through transition and personal futures planning activities have significant implications for the quality of leisure education that is provided. Also to be included as leisure educators and interdisciplinary team members are TR specialists, community recreation providers representing parks and recreation, and various other community agency personnel who offer innumerable leisure education services.

The fourth principle is that leisure education is implemented in school, home, and community settings. A critical cornerstone of the LES model is that special education teachers, physical education teachers, therapists, clinicians, leisure professionals, and other important facilitators are provided opportunities to collaborate or participate in the provision of leisure education to students with disabilities in school, home, and community environments (Bender et al., 1984; Dattilo & Schleien, 1994; Schleien et al., 1995). A major aim of the LES model is that teachers and other key school professionals must incorporate leisure education in their goals and curriculum to help these learners achieve a healthy leisure lifestyle. Special educators also need to provide guidance and support to parents whose efforts should complement those of the school in achieving leisure education plans that have been developed collaboratively. Furthermore, special educators need to include professionals in physical education, TR, and community recreation as essential members of the IEP team that directs and implements school-based leisure activities. These professionals need to assume a greater role (e.g., resource, consultative, instructional) in leisure education programs to more fully prepare students with disabilities for successful transition to inclusive and least restrictive recreation programs in their respective communities.

The LES model stresses the significance of the home as an environment where parents, siblings, relatives, and friends have a major influence on the leisure functioning (e.g, social skills, decision-making skills, and independence) of the individual with a disability (Johnson et al., 1997). Parents are essential team members who provide valuable input regarding their child's leisure needs and interests. In the home setting and in collaboration with professionals in the schools and community, parents and other family members play an important role in initiating, guiding, and reinforcing leisure concepts deemed important for the individual with a disability.

Extensive opportunities for participation in recreation activities also need to be made available in neighborhood and greater communitywide settings. Participation in the community involves informal (e.g., picnic at city park) and formal (e.g., organized swimming class at neighborhood pool) recreation activities. Organized recreation experiences are often led by community recreation professionals and other community agency leaders who serve an instructional and resource role. Leisure learning is furthered when such experiences are planned and undertaken in collaboration with the school and the home.

The LES model is more effectively implemented when the various leisure educators stress community-based, functional instruction. Special educators and parents have unique roles in furthering leisure skill training throughout schooling. Such preparation needs to include community-based learning experiences that incorporate recreation activities relevant to the student's home, neighborhood, and city (or town) environments. In addition to community-based instruction being more functional and motivating, generalization and reinforcement of leisure learning are facilitated in out-of-classroom settings. These are also the environments where students most often participate in desired activities that comprise their leisure time. Time for leisure, then, primarily occurs for individuals in after-school, home, and community settings during nonclassroom, nonwork, and other nonobligated time periods. When teachers, families, recreation professionals, and other key leisure educators cooperate and extend their leisure education efforts to include such settings and times, preparation is broader and has more impact on the learners. As students with disabilities transition through school, such interdisciplinary planning and collaboration better ensures they develop leisure lifestyles that will carry over into adulthood.

To help illustrate how the underlying principles of the LES model are operationalized, two case study examples of the leisure education process are presented in the following pages. The case studies provide hypothetical snapshots of two students in special education with different disabilities who receive leisure instruction as part of their IEP/ITP. In each case study, a student with either a mild or more severe disability is receiving transition education in accordance with the IDEA legislation. Principles underlying the LES model are incorporated in both case studies. In other words, the cases address various leisure concepts, include interdisciplinary participation/collaboration of persons serving as leisure educators, and demonstrate the implementation of leisure education in school, home, and community environments.

Janet

Janet is a 14-year-old student in special education who is classified with a specific learning disability. Janet is included in the general education program and receives assistance from a learning disabilities specialist who consults with her regular education teachers and provides direct instruction to Janet one period a day in the resource room. Assessments indicate that, academically, Janet has difficulty with various reading and math skills, in following directions, and also has some attention deficit problems. Her teachers have also noted that Janet has poor interpersonal skills, often appears shy and withdrawn, and seems generally uninterested in school. Her home economics (HE) teacher, however, observed different behaviors. Janet enrolled in the HE class because she likes to cook at home, so the teacher believes that this activity is of special interest and a source of enjoyment to her.

In planning an IEP/ITP meeting for Janet, the special education teacher—a learning disabilities (LD) specialist—determined the makeup of the team based on a variety of factors, including Janet's strengths, interests, and parental concerns regarding her education. The teacher extended the education team to include Janet's HE teacher, the school's vocational/ transition (V/T) coordinator, and a recreation program (RP) specialist from the city parks and recreation department. During the team meeting, Janet's parents confirmed her lack of personal/social skills, noting she has few friends and seldom initiates going places. They feel, as do several of her teachers, that Janet is self-conscious about her academic weaknesses and probably avoids activities that force her to be with other students or peers. This is also demonstrated by her nonparticipation in extracurricular activities and after-school sports. The team agreed that academic weaknesses and related social difficulties were probable causes for much of her apparent sadness and unhappy moods that have been observed by both the school staff and her parents.

The IEP/ITP team suggested building on Janet's interests and strengths (e.g., foods and cooking) through leisure-related activities she might enjoy as a means of helping improve her attitude and self-confidence. The HE teacher suggested use of a thematic unit in the class on dining out and related foods as a basis for addressing many of Janet's interests and needs. The V/T coordinator agreed to be a resource for the HE teacher, to include logistics related to bus transportation and field trips to the various types of eating establishments in the community, and to further transitioning by helping Janet (and her classmates) become aware of various food service jobs available in the area. The RP specialist suggested working with the parents to identify an appropriate cooking class offered through the community agency for Janet to consider attending. The parents agreed to support this idea and Janet, who attended part of the meeting, expressed interest in visiting various restaurants, smiled, asked questions about the cooking class, and suggested inviting a classmate or friend to take the class with her. The LD specialist agreed to meet with the HE teacher to coordinate their teaching. It was decided that, during resource room time, the LD teacher would provide needed instruction to Janet in dealing with reading directions and recipes, computing food costs and tips, and so forth.

Janet appeared to thoroughly enjoy studying about dining out in her home economics class, which included two field trips to local eating establishments. She chose to participate in a community cooking class and, when mentioned by her HE teacher at school, Janet was asked by a classmate if she might join her in attending the cooking class. Through the unit activities of eating out, Janet identified restaurants at which she may wish to dine and experience a wide variety of foods. Within a short period of time, she began to develop favorite restaurants. The school unit and cooking class enabled Janet to experience new and tasty foods, some of which she began to incorporate into her own cooking at home. Her self-confidence improved and, with parent participation, Janet chose to invite a neighborhood friend and her cooking class friend out to dinner a few times, enjoying the simple conversations, low pressure, informality, and rewarding (good food) aspects of eating out. She reported that this activity was reciprocated by both friends, who invited her out to lunch at a later time. In the school, home, and community settings, Janet learned appropriate interpersonal skills, proper etiquette skills, and a variety of academic-related skills. For example, Janet used her reading and math skills in a functional way, such as ordering from the menu, checking and calculating her bill, and figuring out how much to leave for a tip. The informal nature of dining out also afforded Janet opportunities for socialization and friendship building. The carry-over benefits of these experiences positively affected her attitude towards school and her classmates. Janet seemed happier. Of particular relevance to Janet, she began to add recipes to her cooking repertoire and became eager to try out new recipes at home and with friends. Certainly, cooking expanded as a leisure time activity for Janet, one with lifetime potential.

 ## Brian

Brian is a 17-year-old student in special education who is classified with moderate to severe mental retardation. His family rather recently moved from a more rural part of the state and Brian is now attending a city high school. His primary educational placement is in a functional life-skills program (self-contained classroom) taught by a high school trained special education (SPED) teacher and an instructional assistant. Brian also attends an adapted physical education (APE) class to meet his motor skill needs and is included in a general arts class of interest to him. He is gaining in-school work experience sweeping floors and cleaning tables in the school's cafeteria. His SPED teacher and the department's work/transition (W/T) coordinator have made direct observations and assessments of his work performance in planning for an out-of-school work placement.

Functional assessments indicate that Brian is quite verbal, has fair interpersonal skills, and is acquiring functional skills in reading, writing, and math (e.g., reads signs in school/community, pays for simple purchases and counts change, and writes his name, address and phone number). His daily living skills and mobility are improving and he is learning to use city bus transportation. The W/T coordinator and the school cafeteria manager note, however, that Brian has difficulty completing physical tasks of much duration, and his parents previously indicated some similar concerns (e.g., not wanting to finish washing the windows or raking the leaves). Recent assessments by his APE teacher reveal that Brian is not self-directed towards being active, and his physical fitness needs attention. Regarding Brian's interests, the APE teacher notes that Brian prefers going outdoors for physical education activities and seems more motivated in those settings.

In planning an IEP/ITP meeting for Brian, his SPED teacher determined the makeup of the team based on a variety of factors, including Brian's strengths, interests, and parental concerns regarding his education. The teacher extended the education team to include Brian's W/T coordinator, APE teacher, the school's vocational (VOC) instructor, and a therapeutic recreation (TR) specialist connected with the Disabled Citizens Section of the City's Parks and Recreation Program. During the team meeting, Brian's parents brought up the topic of their son being overweight and asked about school efforts in this area. They believe he spends too much of his free time at sedentary things such as watching TV and playing games on the computer. A few of his interests, though, are that he likes to go outdoors and enjoys playing with the family dog.

The IEP/ITP team agreed that Brian is progressing well in the life-skills program, but his overall health and well being need to be addressed. Brian's physical fitness and related low endurance are limiting him in terms of satisfactory job performance, participation in enjoyable physical activities, exploration of his community, and growth in social skills. The team suggested building on Brian's interests and strengths through leisure and job-related activities he might enjoy, as a means of helping him improve his overall health, interests, motivation, and performance. The SPED teacher suggested use of a thematic unit in the class on walking that would have benefit for Brian and several other students. The APE teacher agreed to collaborate with the teacher on the unit, being a resource and promoting improved fitness through walking as part of the curriculum. The VOC instructor, who heads a job club in school, suggested that Brian would profit from the interactions with general education students (and vice versa), and the class would increase his exposure to and awareness of jobs in the community. The W/T coordinator and the VOC instructor agreed to collaborate on this idea. The TR specialist suggested working with the parents and Brian to explore walking activities in the home and community that might be of interest and benefit to Brian. The parents appreciated the opportunity and Brian, who participated in much of the IEP/ITP meeting, was excited about joining a jobs club and going outdoors more and seeing different places.

Brian enjoyed the walking unit initiated by his SPED teacher. It helped equip him with knowledge and skills regarding walking (e.g., safety, appropriate dress, and environmental conditions). The unit was of high interest to Brian because it afforded him opportunities to walk and employ these skills at school, home, and in the community. The APE teacher focused on walking for fitness (e.g., techniques, breathing, extended walking times) and helped Brian learn to record his personal best times. The APE teacher also organized a school Walk-A-Thon, an inclusive event for all interested students that Brian chose to participate in and successfully complete. The job club offered Brian opportunities to learn about various jobs in the community and become more active by actually walking to and visiting a number of sites. Brian expanded his social interactions with other students (nondisabled and disabled) and acquired a new friend through a buddy system used by the VOC teacher for community study and exploration. The TR specialist arranged for a university intern in recreation to work directly with Brian and his parents relative to their interests and concerns. With Brian's approval, a plan was implemented in which he assumed major responsibility for walking the family dog in the neighborhood. This provided Brian and his pet with needed exercise, and the companionship was very therapeutic and motivating to him.

Of special significance, the variety of learning experiences involving walking incorporated in Brian's life-skills class, APE class, job class, and home pet program enabled Brian to be more physically active. He improved his physical fitness and endurance, lost some weight, and became more able and willing to participate actively at school, home, and in the community. These learning experiences helped to improve his attitude, increase his self-confidence and motivation, and expand his interests. For example, participation in his school's job club got him out into the community and heightened his interest in working at a "real" job in the community. After walking to and visiting several visiting various job sites, Brian independently visited a grocery store in his own neighborhood and inquired about a job. His W/T coordinator followed up and determined it to be a potential out-of-school job placement for Brian (e.g., duties would include paper recycling, floor sweeping, clean-up). Brian's parents have observed him finishing his chores more often and being interested in more active recreation in addition to TV. The TR specialist recently provided information to the family regarding a local Volkswalking club (noncompetitive walking for fun), and Brian is interested and asked a job club classmate to join with him. Brian seems happier, is becoming more fit, and has acquired two new friends. He has become more self-determined through walking-related activities. Of particular importance, walking is evolving into an enjoyable leisure time activity with lifetime significance for Brian.

Comprehensive Transition Should Include Preparation for Leisure

Although the case studies presented focus on federally defined ages for transition services, a seamless and comprehensive approach to transition and leisure education is being recommended. The proposed LES model illustrated in Figure 9.2 is closely aligned and can be easily incorporated with comprehensive transition proposals previously discussed for students with disabilities. Both systems stress the unique needs and interests of the student and family, and promote a life-skill, functional, and lifespan approach to curriculum and instruction. Of special significance with regard to transition planning and services, students with disabilities often demonstrate unique needs related to their leisure functioning in school, home, and community environments. Since life skill outcomes are proposed as integral to comprehensive transitioning, and education for leisure is an important life skill area, leisure preparation should be incorporated as an essential aspect of comprehensive transition practices for these students.

Table 9.3 illustrates how contemporary or seamless transition practices are more fully achieved through the inclusion of leisure education. In this table, concepts underlying comprehensive transitioning are compared with concepts basic to leisure education to help validate the importance of leisure preparation as a part of transition education. It is proposed that the LES model serve as a resource for professionals and parents who recognize leisure time as an important area of living and who want to incorporate leisure education in seamless transition practices that address all levels of schooling for students with disabilities.

General Education Needs To Incorporate Preparation for Leisure

The recommendation that professionals in special education and related disciplines include leisure education as an essential component of a broadened concept of transition preparation is incomplete without also considering the role of general education in the overall scheme. The purpose of general education long accepted by the nation's schools for all students includes building self-realization, human relationships, economic self-sufficiency, and civic responsibility. It is significant that such an encompassing purpose is realized by most people in two major areas of life activity: work and leisure. Because formal education concludes relatively early in life for most people, the overall purpose of education is achieved mainly through work and leisure activities in the community during adulthood. Although general education still falls short of its original purpose to meaningfully prepare its students to assume adult citizenship roles, opportunities to incorporate comprehensive transition now seem more feasible because of today's changing values, responsibilities, and practices affecting students with disabilities. As school-based inclusive practices become more predominant, it is envisioned that increased collaboration between special and general educators will have carryover benefits to general education and will facilitate comprehensive transition education for all students. Since the life-skill orientation of seamless transition is outcomes-based and incorporates life-skill preparation, it is also envisioned that education for leisure will also be deemed essential for both students with and without disabilities.

Recent system changes in general education already hold promise for altering curricular priorities in these directions. In serving children, youth, and young adults with disabilities, the IDEA Amendments of 1997 (P.L. 105-117) strengthen transition planning, promote greater participation of parents and

Table 9.3
Comprehensive Transition Includes Leisure Education

MAJOR CONCEPTS

Comprehensive (seamless) Transition Practices	Leisure Education School (LES) Model
The unique needs of students with disabilities determine special education services.	Improved leisure functioning (e.g., leisure time skills) is a unique need of many students with disabilities.
The focus is on the student and the family.	Students and families are involved in choices, preferences, and decision making regarding recreation and leisure preparation.
The focus is on life-based, functional curriculum.	Recreation and leisure are identified as major life-skill areas to be in the school's curriculum.
Education occurs in various inclusive settings.	Different persons serve as leisure educators in inclusive home, school, and community environments.
Written plans document desired transition outcomes.	Leisure-related goals and objectives are included in IFSP, IEPs, ITPs.
Multiagency coordination and collaboration is stressed.	Personnel representing special and regular education, vocational, adapted physical education, therapeutic recreation, and so on coordinate efforts.
Program planning and services start in early childhood and continue through age 21.	Appropriate leisure education experiences are included with children/students at preschool, elementary, middle school, secondary, and postsecondary levels.

general educators in educational planning and decisions, and increase access to the school's general curriculum for such students. Such changes should help expand transition education beyond special education to include students in general education. These changes are predicted because (a) understanding and acceptance of students with disabilities will occur as they demonstrate their individuality and gain access to the same goals and experiences as their counterparts without disabilities; (b) the expanded collaboration and understanding between parents, special educators, and general educators will help redefine what constitutes an "appropriate" education in preparing students for successful community adjustment; and (c) general educators will more likely recognize the importance of transition education (i.e., focus on major life domains) for students without disabilities when they become aware of the positive impact it has on the lives of students with disabilities.

In brief, preparation for the use of leisure time is proposed again to meet, in part, the aims of education for all students. From this perspective, both special and general education will embrace preparation for leisure, recognizing that developing a positive leisure lifestyle is as relevant for students with disabilities as for students without disabilities. In support of this point of view, a set of "mission goals" for students with and without disabilities (K–12) were developed for implementation in the nation's schools (Leisure Information Service, 1976). Subsequently, these goals were published in several works (Bender et al., 1984; Brannan, Chinn, & Verhoven, 1981). These goals of leisure education, proposed as appropriate for all students, are still relevant today and, with a few minor revisions, are presented in Table 9.4. Because the leisure education goals are presented as broadly stated student outcomes, they will need to be implemented through use of more specific aims in order to meet the needs of a wide range of learners. For example, in serving students with disabilities under IDEA, special educators, related services professionals, parents, and other leisure educators will need to use these goals as a base for developing short-term objectives or bench marks to be included in each student's IEP/ITP. Individual strengths, interests and needs, family concerns and values, resources, and other related factors will influence the degree to which students will achieve the leisure goals and objectives. Likewise, the basic set of leisure-related goals is appropriate for learners in general education, who will also accomplish them at varying levels of achievement as they transition through school. Although not an inclusive list, the leisure education goals for all students in Table 9.4 are comprehensive, support the concepts in the LES model, provide an overall framework for guiding leisure education curriculum efforts in the schools, and can be adapted to meet the individual instructional needs of students of varying ages and abilities.

Special Education Leadership Is Needed for the 21st Century

It is proposed that these changes envisioned for education will require increased advocacy if preparation for leisure is to become an integral part of the curriculum the nation's students transitioning from school to their communities in the 21st century. The merging of special education and general education through inclusionary practices holds promise for the leisure education of all students. Learners with disabilities, however, will need more direct instruction in this area of the school's curriculum if they are to become more independent and able to make the most meaningful use of their abundant leisure time. Although the call for special education leadership in promoting education for leisure has been made in prior years (Brannan, 1975; Brannan et al., 1981), the profession needs to step forward again, with a greater commitment to change and more dynamic leadership. Extended collaboration and interdisciplinary teaming with school-

Table 9.4
Leisure Education Goals for All Students

- Understand leisure as a concept encompassing discretionary time, individual choice, and personal enjoyment.
- Recognize that fuller use of discretionary time will enhance the quality of life in all areas of human endeavor.
- Appreciate the wide diversity of leisure choices and lifestyles.
- Understand the potential of leisure for both developing and responding to one's individual lifestyle.
- Recognize that appreciation of leisure experiences will be enhanced through direct exploration and participation.
- Acquire knowledge and networking skills to identify and access the wealth of leisure opportunities and resources that exist in one's family, home, school, community, state, and nation.
- Develop competency in both short- and long-term planning to ensure more effective use of one's leisure time.
- Identify and evaluate personal interests and abilities to determine participation in leisure time activities.
- Evaluate choices and performance for the various benefits derived from participating in specific leisure experiences.
- Develop a repertoire of skills necessary for participation in a variety of lifelong leisure activities.
- Understand the contributions that leisure provides for self-expression, physical, intellectual, and social development.
- Develop interests, problem-solving, and related self-determination skills to facilitate independent pursuits of leisure in home, school, and community settings.

Note. Adapted from *Leisure Education for the Handicapped: Curriculum Goals, Activities, and Resources* (p. 79), by M. Bender, S. Brannan, and P. Verhoven, 1984, Austin, TX: PRO-ED. Copyright 1994 by PRO-ED, Inc. Adapted with permission.

based related disciplines and key professionals in the community are essential to achieving improved leisure functioning for students with disabilities. Certainly, professionals in the related disciplines are needed to support special education efforts. Their various research, writings, and successful practices related to the values of leisure and recreation and leisure education efforts are long standing, well-documented, and confirm the contributions they can make to the successful transition of students (Bullock & Mahon, 1997). In moving ahead, then, special education leadership is especially needed to help overcome the lack of participation of school-based related service colleagues and community professionals in the transition process. Through fuller inclusion of such professionals and use of their expertise (e.g., IEP/ITP teams, leisure education instruction), professionals can enhance school-based transition services and programs serving students.

Fortunately, many colleagues in related disciplines also recognize the need for increased leadership and advocacy from special education and are receptive and supportive of many of the directions discussed in this chapter. Reynolds (1995) calls for special and regular educators to take on an increased advocacy role in initiating leisure education. Dattilo and St. Peter (1991) and Bedini et al. (1993), representing TR professionals, provided extensive support for instructional concepts on leisure education promoted in this chapter; their training and research efforts have resulted in complementary transition models using leisure education to prepare students with mental retardation. Dattilo and Schleien (1994) advanced the idea that special education should be the lead agency (i.e., teachers as the lead leisure educators) during the school years by promoting networking among agencies and in delivering leisure education. These authors also recommended that special education assume increased advocacy to ensure that all key players (e.g., related service professionals such as TR specialists, community recreation providers, family service providers) are more fully involved during the school years in the planning and provision of comprehensive leisure services (e.g., leisure assessment, planning, instruction, etc.).

For these changes to occur, several suggestions are proposed, with special emphasis that policy changes affecting school transition services to students with disabilities need to occur at federal, state, and local levels. The U.S. Department of Education, Office of Special Education and Rehabilitation Programs should reprioritize leisure education as a higher priority in their various research, demonstration, and training projects. Colleges and universities need to make significant improvements in their personnel preparation by infusing leisure education into their special education and transition education curriculums and methodologies. State education agencies (SEAs) need to augment their policies, procedures, and monitoring with local education agencies (LEAs) to ensure that leisure preparation is fully included in the transition process.

SEAs, in cooperation with higher education institutions, should also facilitate the provision of inservice training to LEAs regarding the importance and implementation of leisure education for all students who are disabled (mild to severe) as an integral part of transition services and programs. Likewise, LEAs need to clearly identify and integrate leisure education into their curriculums, operationalizing this life-skill area through goals, objectives, and bench marks in their special education students' IEP/ITPs. Professional organizations and their various divisions (e.g., CEC and DCDT) obviously play a major leadership role and should use multiple strategies to educate professionals and parents about leisure education and its relationship to successful transitioning. This could be accomplished through special journal issues, workshops, and conference sessions on leisure education and transition. Administrators also need to actively pursue leisure education instructional materials that are comprehensive and user friendly for special education teachers, other professionals, and parents.

Final Thoughts

Leisure and Society

Schleifer and Klein (1981) stated, "When we look at ourselves and our neighbors, we realize, again and again, that the quality of life depends as much upon the character and quality of our leisure activities and our relationships with other people as it does on our academic and vocational achievements" (p. 1). Indeed, this country is demonstrating a renewed interest in improving the quality of life for all people. Major efforts to structure and improve the qualitative aspects of living are particularly evident in the area of leisure. In contrast to previous eras, contemporary society is experiencing a value change, in which citizens are recognizing the need to reprioritize their time and more actively pursue goals that are nonvocational in nature.

Although work will continue to be a major life function for the nation's citizens, shorter work weeks, flex time and schedules, job sharing, virtual workplaces and telecommuting, earlier retirements, improved health, and increased longevity are being pursued and realized by a growing number of Americans. Surprisingly, at the same time that working conditions are affecting the stability of employment (i.e., job realignment, job downsizing), people are also electing to independently make a greater number of work or career changes during their life. Working couples, for example, are collaborating to pursue increased time off from or a change in their jobs, often choosing a job with a lower salary but with increased free time to enrich their lives (Dappen, 1997; Goldberger, 1992; Kimeldorf, 1989).

Attitudes and values toward work and leisure are definitely changing, with an increased number of people finding that time at leisure is as important as time at work. Although many people believe they are more harried and have less free time today, according to Dr. John Robinson, who headed up the "Americans Use of Time Project" at the University of Maryland, these viewpoints are more related to the ambitious schedules and lifestyles of people today that are generally more complicated than in the past. According to Robinson's research, the shortage of free time is more a matter of perception than reality. Using more objective and accurate measures of free time with individuals (e.g., time diaries vs. self-report surveys), he found that free time has actually increased and that most people work less and have more free time than they did 25 years ago (Robinson & Godbey, 1997).

Regardless of the research, there is increased evidence that a major shift is occurring in public attitudes, with more Americans seeing a need to make life changes, including reprioritizing their actual income needs. According to Chris DeMuth, President of the American Enterprise Institute, voluntary reductions in time spent at paid work have become a major social and economic phenomena for the first time in the history of Western democracies (Will, 1997). In essence, a leisure revolution might be in the making, as is evident by the increased numbers of Americans participating in recreation activities (Edginton, Jordan, DeGraaf, & Edginton, 1995). Recreation has become one of the nation's top industries, proving that an increasing number of citizens are engaged in a multitude of recreation pursuits. People are discovering that the wholesome use of their leisure time provides them with better physical and mental health and improved means for achieving greater personal fulfillment. It appears that increased leisure time is emerging as an important goal and determiner of a quality life experience for a growing number of people in the United States (Brannan, 1998; Kimeldorf, 1989).

Rededication to Successful Transitioning

One obvious implication of these value changes regarding the worth of free time and its importance to quality of life is that education for leisure is an essential aspect of transition education for the nation's students. It is recommended that leisure education be elevated and recognized as a major goal of the schools, and that its benefits be better communicated to parents and professionals in special education and general education. As previously discussed, if the successful transition to adulthood for children, youth, and young adults with disabilities is to be realized, the special education profession must assume a more dynamic leadership role. Such leadership also demands that special educators invite their colleagues in related service disciplines to participate in the transition process and collaboratively pursue creative ways for their meaningful involvement as team members. If transition outcomes are to be achieved for students with disabilities, a complete team, comprised of special educators, school-based related service disciplines, and other professionals in the community, is needed to ensure that these students develop healthy leisure lifestyles. Progressive leadership by special education also necessitates the development of closer working relationships with mainstream professionals (i.e., in general education and community recreation) because of the need to prepare students for successful adjustment in inclusive schools, neighborhoods, and the community at large. In conclusion, it seems particularly appropriate that the profession of special education rededicate itself to such leadership and, in doing so, complete the task that leaders and pioneers in physical education and recreation charged them with in the 1970s: "No professional group in America is in a better position to make this point and to advocate the development of recreation services for handicapped children and youth than are special educators" (Nesbitt et al., 1974, p. 11).

References

American Heritage college dictionary (3rd ed.). (1997). Boston: Houghton Mifflin.

Bedini, L. (1990). The status of leisure education: Implications for instruction and practice. *Therapeutic Recreation Journal, 24*(1), 40–49.

Bedini, L. (1993). Transition and integration in leisure for people with disabilities. *Parks and Recreation, 28*(11), 20–24.

Bedini, L., Bullock, C., & Driscoll, L. (1993). The effects of leisure education on factors contributing to the successful transition of students with mental retardation from school to adult life. *Therapeutic Recreation Journal, 27*(2), 70–82.

Bender, M., Brannan, S., & Verhoven, P. (1984). *Leisure education for the handicapped: Curriculum goals, activities, and resources*. Austin, TX: PRO-ED.

Benz, M., Yovanoff, P., & Doren, B. (1997). School-to-work components that predict school success for students with and without disabilities. *Exceptional Children, 63*(2), 151–165.

Bradley, C. (1989). Integrating the search for work and leisure. *Journal of Employment Counseling, 26*, 70–76.

Brannan, S. (1975). Trends and issues in leisure education for the handicapped through community education. In E. Fairchild & L. Neal (Eds.), *Common-unity in the community: A forward looking program of recreation and leisure services for the handicapped* (pp. 41–56). Eugene: University of Oregon, Center for Leisure Studies.

Brannan, S. (1981). *Explore program: Individualized instructional materials for outdoor education and recreation*. Portland, OR: Portland State University, Special Education Program.

Brannan, S. (1988). Leisure education for handicapped students: Current perspectives. In S. Pueschel (Ed.), *The young person with down syndrome: Transition from adolescence to adulthood* (pp. 93–108). Baltimore: Brookes.

Brannan, S., Arick, J., & Fullerton, A. (1997). The national camp evaluation study: A national study on the effects of specialized camps. *Camping Magazine, 70*(1), 28–31.

Brannan, S., Chinn, K., & Verhoven, P. (1981). *What is leisure education?: A primer for working with handicapped children and youth*. Washington, DC: Hawkins and Associates.

Brolin, D. (1995). *Career education: A functional life skills approach* (3rd ed.). Columbus, OH: Merrill.

Brolin, D. (1997). *Life centered career education: A competency based approach*. Reston, VA: Council for Exceptional Children.

Bullock, C., & Mahon, M. (1997). *Introduction to recreation services for people with disabilities: A person-centered approach*. Champaign, IL: Sagamore.

Clark, G., & Patton, J. (1997). *Transition planning inventory: Administrative and resource guide*. Austin, TX: PRO-ED.

Council for Exceptional Children (1997, January/February). 18th annual report affirms CEC's policy on inclusive settings. *CEC Today, 3*(7), 1–5.

Coyne, P. (1981). The status of recreation as a related service in PL 94-142. *Therapeutic Recreation Journal, 28*(1), 9–17.

Cronin, M. (1996). Life skills curricula for students with learning disabilities. In J. Patton & G. Blalock (Eds.), *Transition and students with learning disabilities* (pp. 85–112). Austin, TX: PRO-ED.

Cronin, M., & Patton, J. (1993). *Life skills instruction for all students with special needs.* Austin, TX: PRO-ED.

Dappen, A. (1997, November). The one-income family: When less means more. *Hemispheres* (United Airlines Magazine), 155–156, 158.

Dattilo, J. (1987). Recreation and leisure literature for individuals with mental retardation: Implications for outdoor recreation. *Therapeutic Recreation Journal, 21*(1), 9–17.

Dattilo, J., & Schleien, S. (1994). Understanding leisure services for individuals with mental retardation. *Mental Retardation, 32,* 53–59.

Dattilo, J., & St. Peter, S. (1991). A model for including leisure education in transition services for young adults with mental retardation. *Education and Training in Mental Retardation, 26*(4), 420–432.

Dever, R. (1989). A taxonomy of community living skills. *Exceptional Children, 55*(5), 395–404.

Dunn, C. (1996). A status report on transition planning for individuals with learning disabilities. In J. Patton & G. Blalock (Eds.), *Transition and students with learning disabilities* (pp. 19–41). Austin, TX: PRO-ED.

Edgar, E. (1987). Secondary programs in special education: Are many of them justifiable? *Exceptional Children, 53,* 555–561.

Edginton, C., Jordan, D., DeGraaf, D., & Edginton, S. (1997). *Leisure and life satisfaction: Foundation perspectives.* Dubuque, IA: Brown & Benchmark.

Field, S. (1996). Self-determination instructional strategies for youth with learning disabilities. In J. Patton & G. Blalock (Eds.), *Transition and students with learning disabilities* (pp. 61–84). Austin, TX: PRO-ED.

Goldberger, C. (1992, January). The juggling act: On family and time management in the '90s. *Sky* (Delta Airlines Magazine), 24–26.

Halpern, A. (1994). The transition of youth with disabilities to adult life: A position statement of the Division on Career Development and Transition, The Council for Exceptional Children. *Career Development for Exceptional Individuals, 17,* 115–124.

Henderson, K. (1994). An interpretive analysis of the teaching of decision-making in leisure to adolescents with mental retardation. *Therapeutic Recreation Journal, 28*(3), 133–146.

Individuals with Disabilities Act of 1990, 20 U.S.C. §1400 *et seq.*

Individuals with Disabilities Act Amendments of 1997, 20 U.S.C. §1400 *et seq.*

Jansma, P., & French, R. (1994). *Special physical education: Physical activity, sports, and recreation.* Englewood Cliffs, NJ: Prentice-Hall.

Johnson, D., Bullock, C., & Ashton-Shaeffer, C. (1997). Families and leisure: A context for learning. *Teaching Exceptional Children, 30*(2), 30–34.

Kane, M. (1991, October 15). Time crunch. *The Oregonian,* pp. D1–D2.

Kimeldorf, M. (1989). *Program guide: Pathways to work and pathways to leisure.* Bloomington, IL: Meridian Education Corporation.

Leisure Information Service. (1976). *A systems model for developing a leisure education program for handicapped children and youth K–12.* (Contract No. RFP 75-50). Washington, DC: Hawkins and Associates.

Loumiet, R., & Levack, N. (1991). *Independent living: A curriculum with adaptations for students with visual impairment. Volume III: Play and leisure*. Austin: Texas School for the Blind and Visually Impaired.

Morningstar, M., Turnbull, A., & Turnbull, H., III. (1995). What do students with disabilities tell us about the importance of family involvement in the transition from school to adult life? *Exceptional Children, 62*(3), 249–260.

MRDD. (1997). Position statement on enhancing the health and wellness of individuals with developmental disabilities. *MRDD Express, 1*, 6.

Mundy, J., & Odum, L. (1979). *Leisure education: Theory and practice*. New York: Wiley.

National Association of State Directors of Special Education. (1991). Physical education and sports: The unfulfilled promise for students with disabilities. *Liaison Bulletin, 17*(6), 1–9.

National Education Association. (1918). *Cardinal principles of secondary education*. Washington, DC: Author.

National Therapeutic Recreation Society. (1990). *Code of ethics* (revised). Alexandria, VA: National Recreation and Park Association.

Nesbitt, J., Neal, L., & Hillman, W., Jr. (1974). Recreation for exceptional children and youth. *Focus on Exceptional Children, 6*(3), 1–12.

Patton, J., & Blalock, G. (1996). *Transition and students with learning disabilities*. Austin, TX: PRO-ED.

Peniston, L. (1998). *Developing recreation skills in persons with learning disabilities*. Champaign, IL: Sagamore.

Peterson, C., & Gunn, S. (1984). *Therapeutic recreation program design*. Englewood Cliffs, NJ: Prentice-Hall.

Repetto, J., & Correa, V. (1996). Expanding views on transition. *Exceptional Children, 62*(6), 551–563.

Reynolds, R. (1995). A look toward the future in service delivery. In S. Schleien, L. Meyer, L. Heyne, & B. Brandt (Eds.), *Lifelong leisure skills and lifestyles for persons with developmental disabilities* (pp. 219–229). Baltimore: Brookes.

Rizzo, T., & Davis, W. (1993). Teaching lifetime recreation and leisure skills to individuals with disabilities. *Issues in Teacher Education, 2*(1), 27–35.

Robinson, J., & Godbey, G. (1997). *Time for life: The surprising ways Americans use their time*. University Park: Pennsylvania University Press.

Schleien, S., Meyer, L., Heyne, L., & Brandt, B. (1995). *Lifelong leisure skills and lifestyles for persons with developmental disabilities*. Baltimore: Brookes.

Schleien, S., Ray, M., & Green, F. (1997). *Community recreation and people with disabilities*. Baltimore: Brookes.

Schleifer, M., & Klein, S. (1981). Recreation and leisure: Fun begins at home. *Exceptional Parent, 2*, 1–2.

Sherrill, C. (1986). *Adapted physical education and recreation* (3rd ed.). Dubuque, IA: Brown.

Sherrill, C. (1993). *Adapted physical activity, and recreation, and sport: Crossdisciplinary and lifespan* (4th ed.). Dubuque, IA: Brown.

Sitlington, P. (1996). Transition to living: The neglected component of transition programming for individuals with learning disabilities. In J. Patton & G. Blalock (Eds.), *Transition and students with learning disabilities* (pp. 43–59). Austin, TX: PRO-ED.

Stein, J. (1975). Movement and physical activity: The foundation for the most important "R." In S. Brannan (Ed.), *Our new challenge: Recreation for the deaf-blind* (pp. 43–52). Portland, OR: Portland State University.

Sylvester, C. (1985). Freedom, leisure, and therapeutic recreation: A philosophical view. *Therapeutic Recreation Journal, 28*(1), 6–13.

Sylvester, C. (1992). Therapeutic recreation and the right to leisure. *Therapeutic Recreation Journal, 26*(2), 9–20.

Victor, J., & Swirsky, J. (1985). Meeting needs: Career education, independent living, community resources, and the family. *Exceptional Parent, 15,* 19–21.

Wehman, P., & Kregel, J. (1997). *Functional curriculum for elementary, middle, and secondary age students with special needs.* Austin, TX: PRO-ED.

Wehman, P., Renzaglia, A., & Bates, P. (1985). *Functional living skills for moderately and severely handicapped individuals.* Austin, TX: PRO-ED.

Wehman, P., & Schleien, S. (1981). *Leisure programs for handicapped persons.* Austin, TX: PRO-ED.

Wilcox, B., & Bellamy, T. (1987). *A comprehensive guide to the activities catalog: An alternative curriculum for youth and adults with severe disabilities.* Baltimore: Brookes.

Will, G. (1997, August 21). The new leisure class. *The Oregonian,* p. B12.

Will, M. (1983). *OSERS programming for the transition of youth with disabilities: Bridges from school to working life.* Washington, DC: U.S. Department of Education. (ERIC Document Reproduction Service No. ED 256 132)

C H A P T E R

ASSISTIVE TECHNOLOGY

Sherrilyn K. Fisher

*"For Americans without disabilities, technology has made things easier.
For Americans with disabilities, technology has made things possible."*

—The National Council on Disabilities (1993)

Introduction

Once upon a time, all of the accumulated knowledge of the known world was held in one place. This place was a great library created by Ptolemy I in Alexandria. Imagine—a learner who had all the knowledge of the world at his fingertips. Such endeavors were active until the 15th century, when the technology of the printing press gave rise to such an explosion of knowledge that a single library's capacity was quickly overcome. Such a vast storehouse of knowledge has never been duplicated until today; now that possibility once again exists. The creation of the World Wide Web has the potential to house all the knowledge that humans have amassed, or at least that which has been recorded in print, sound, graphics, or video. Nelson's (1965) concept of hypertext—"bridges of transclusion"—is at hand. Unlike the library of Alexandria, this knowledge is accessible though technology at any place, at any time, and by anyone, even people with disabilities.

The World Wide Web is but one example of how technology has opened up new frontiers and made things easier for many people. For people with disabilities, access to technology has made things *possible*. The Developmental Disabilities Assistance and Bill of Rights Act Amendments of 1987 (P.L. 100-146) defined three goals for all persons with disabilities: independence, productivity, and integration. In many cases, assistive technology has made achievement of these goals a reality. This chapter will explore the potential that assistive technology has for students in secondary education to accomplish those three goals as students transition—aided by technology—from school to work, to postsecondary education, and to fulfilled lives in their communities. This chapter will also look at the responsibilities of the Individual Education Plan/Individual Transition Plan (IEP/ITP) team who teach and work with the student and examine the effects of transition planning that considers assistive technology an integral part of the process. Finally, the chapter will provide a glimpse of new technologies that will move society closer to the time when people with disabilities will be fully integrated into society.

The Revolution of Assistive Technology

The use of assistive technology is a revolution that is changing the lives of people with disabilities, easing the transition from school to work and to independent living. The lines that separate assistive technology and conventional technology are becoming more and more fuzzy as technology is assimilated into the everyday lives of people. How many people can claim that they do not use technology to improve the quality of their lives or enhance efficiency and productivity? From common technology like e-mail, answering machines, VCRs, cable TV, microwaves, and digital alarm clocks, to the sophisticated technology of the Hubble telescope and DNA research, society has embraced technology.

The importance of technology has been emphasized and indeed mandated in the delivery of special education services from federal (Individuals with Disabilities Education Act of 1990 [IDEA]; Individuals with Disabilities Education Act Amendments of 1997) and state levels, as well as from professional organizations. In the spring of 1996, the Board of Directors of Council for Exceptional Children–Mental Retardation Development Disabilities (CEC–MRDD) published a position statement for review from their members which acknowledged the "critical importance of appropriate assistive technology devices and services in the lives of individuals with disabilities across cultures" (1996, p. 9)

The Revolution of Assistive Technology in Educational Practices

One reason the technology revolution is spreading so fast is because technology integration into the regular curriculum is more normal than abnormal. Children everywhere are growing up with technology as a tool to help them accomplish their goals. Some of these children are students with disabilities. With the recent reauthorization in 1997 of IDEA, inclusive environments are now and will become increasingly prevalent. Youth with disabilities are being educated in regular education classrooms that are often rich with technology. Students with disabilities need equal access, training, and the assistance of technology so they can be educated alongside their peers, transitioning successfully with their classmates from school to independence.

The use of assistive technology is one method that has allowed special education students to function in an inclusive classroom, where they can learn appropriate socials skills and have the opportunity to make friends with nondisabled peers. In this way, assistive technology lays a path for individuals with disabilities to be accepted and competitive in mainstream society as they transition naturally to employment and their adult lives. Future applications of technology hold even greater potential for full inclusion of individuals with disabilities. It has been said that technology will be the equalizer of the 21st century; in the not too distant future, robotics, muscle stimulators, replaceable body parts, and even the re-creation of brain cells will increase the quality of life and participation in all of life's events.

Along with many others (Douglas, 1995; Ludy & Blunt, 1995; Morris, 1992b; Oddone,1993; Saks , 1993; Wall, 1994), Dr. Thomas Hehir, Director of the Office of Special Education Programs at the U.S. Department of Education, feels that inclusive classrooms could not happen without the assistance of technology:

> Our assumption has to be, when we educate people with disabilities, that they will eventually become adults with full participation in society. Separating them is not going to help them reach that goal. From our perspective, the opportunities that exist with technology for children with disabilities are some of the most important things that have happened in my memory in special education. . . . We have shown as a field that kids with extensive disabilities can make it in regular classes if they have aids or devices. Kids that we didn't think capable of being mainstreamed are being included if technical supports and aids are provided. (Wall & Siegel, 1994, pp. 24–25)

This view has been strengthened by recent legislation that has not only identified assistive technology as a related service, but has included a statement that requires school districts to furnish supplementary aids and services that are to be made available in regular education classes and other education-related settings that "enable children with disabilities to be educated with their nondisabled peers to the *maximum* extent appropriate" (emphasis added) (20 U.S.C. §1401(29)). The "old" language of the Education for All Handicapped Children Act of 1975 is back.

The reasoning for such strong language is clear. A study such as one conducted by the National Council on Disabilities (Morris, 1992b) concludes that "with the assistance of technology, almost three-quarters of school-age children were able to remain in a regular classroom . . . [and] 45 percent of school-age children were able to reduce school-related services" (p. 5). Linking this information to transition outcomes (Malian & Love, 1998; U.S. Department of Education [USDOE], 1995), researchers found that students who spent a greater percentage of their school day in the general education classroom (with special education support) completed high school.

In an article in *Electronic Learning* (Wall, 1994), an educator tells of her students with learning disabilities who could not write legibly and became discouraged. However, with the help of a laptop and spell checker, these same students produced good work. The teacher noted that "they can handle the class, they can think the thoughts, but they could not get them down on paper before. . . . A keyboard and monitor unleashed a flood of words" (p. 34). In a regular education classroom, assistive technology often makes the difference between success and failure. Jacqueline Brand, the executive director of the Alliance for Technology Access, said that it is important that assistive technology be part of the whole general technology plan for the district and for each school. She elaborated that "only when the principal sees himself or herself responsible for education of all kids, will kids with disabilities get an equal education" (Wall & Siegel, 1994, p. 34). This responsibility includes appropriate technology for all children.

Overview of Assistive Technology and the Provision of Services

What is assistive technology and what does it have to do with transition? What is the promise for the combined impact of these two initiatives? These questions and others will be addressed in this chapter by examining the technology that leads to new transitions and worlds of access for young adults. As you read, it is particularly important to keep in mind the evolution of students in assuming emergent adult roles (Halpern, 1994), including employment, participating in postsecondary education, maintaining a home, becoming appropriately involved in the community, and experiencing satisfactory personal and social relationships. *A very easy way to think about assistive technology is that it includes any device that helps people with disabilities live, learn, work, and play more independently.*

Assistive technology can range from things as simple as enlarged print, Velcro fasteners and wrist and arm stabilizers, to complex solutions and devices for augmentative speech. Appropriate assistive devices become a part of what a person is—a voice, a mobility system, a way of being productive, a way of communicating—and assimilate into a persona, a part of everyday life, and the face that the world sees. So as one might imagine, the provision of the right device becomes a very sensitive and critical decision, and one that affects the quality of life for the individual.

But assistive technology goes far beyond hardware devices. The definition for assistive technology also includes eyeglasses and hearing aids that are necessary for certain students to benefit from school and participate in life's major functions (Office of Special Education Programs [OSEP], 1993; Sack, Clark, & Spellman, 1997). Assistive technology includes augmentative alternative communication (AAC)—methods of communicating that can supplement the ordinary methods of speech and handwriting (Call Centre, 1997). Augmentative communication devices support an individual's already existing speaking skills, whereas augmentative communication approaches are the primary means of communication for an individual (Flippo, Inge, & Barcus, 1995). Assistive technology also includes physical and occupational therapy devices and environment control units (ECUs). ECUs enable remote control over electronically operated appliances, allowing a person with disabilities to gain more independence. The controls can be as simple as on–off devices and as complex as "smart houses" with programmed control over all electrical appliances and systems in the home. The spectrum of assistive technology also includes related services such as evaluation, training for all involved persons, maintenance and repair, customization of a device ongoing assessment, applications, and coordinating therapies and services with assistive technology. The Technology Related Assistance for Individuals with Disabilities Act of 1988 (P.L. 100-497), known as the Tech Act, defines the term *assistive technology device* as "any item, piece of equipment, or product system, whether acquired commercially off the shelf, modified, or customized, that is used to increase, maintain, or improve functional capabilities of a child with a disability." *Assistive technology service* means any service that directly assists an individual with a disability in the selection, acquisition, or use of an assistive technology device. The term includes the following:

a. the evaluation of the needs of an individual with a disability, including a functional evaluation of the individual in the individual's customary environment;

b. purchasing, leasing, or otherwise providing for the acquisition of assistive technology devices by individuals with disabilities;

    c. selecting, designing, fitting, customizing, adapting, applying, retaining, repairing, or replacing of assistive technology devices;

    d. coordinating and using other therapies, interventions, or services with assistive technology devices, such as those associated with existing education and rehabilitiation plans and programs;

    e. training or technical assistance for an individual with disabilities or, where appropriate, the family of an individual with disabilities; and

    f. training or technical assistance for professionals (including individuals providing education or rehabilitation services), employers, or other individuals who provide services to, employ, or are otherwise substantially involved in the major life functions of individuals with disabilities.

The Tech Act first introduced, defined, and furnished guidelines for assistive technology and services in the lives of people with disabilities; its focus was to make assistive technology devices and services available to individuals with disabilities (Judith Fein National Institute on Disability and Rehabilitation Research, 1996). The Tech Act also provided the legal framework in which schools need to operate. Substantive ammendments were made to The Tech Act in 1994 (P.L. 103-218). Subsequently, IDEA further established the federal commitment to assistive technology. IDEA adopted language and definitions of the Tech Act provisions, changing only the word *individual* to *child* or *children*. Secondly, IDEA

> provides that if a child with a disability requires assistive technology devices or services, or both, in order to receive a free appropriate education, the public agency shall ensure that the assistive technology devices or services are made available to that child, either as special education, related services, or as supplementary aids and services that enable a child with a disability to be educated in regular classes. Determinations of whether a child with a disability requires assistive technology devices or services under this program must be made on an individual basis through applicable individualized education program and placement procedures. (*Federal Register*, 1991, p. 41272)

The commitment is clear. All students with disabilities (including Part C, early childhood special education, P.L. 99-457) are eligible and should be considered for assistive technology. Assistive technology is an integral part of the IEP development. The Office of Special Education Programs (OSEP) released a policy statement to that effect in a policy letter in August, 1990:

> In brief, it is impermissible under EHA-B (Education of the Handicapped Act) for public agencies (including school districts) to presumptively deny

assistive technology to a child with handicaps before a determination is made as to whether such technology is an element of a free and appropriate public education (FAPE) for that child. Thus, consideration for a child's need for assistive technology must occur on a case-by-case basis in connection with development of a child's individualized education program (IEP). (Rehabilitation Engineering and Assistive Technology Society of North America, 1992, pp. 34–35)

An even tougher stance was taken with the reauthorization of IDEA in 1997. The law now *requires* the consideration of assistive technology services for each student with a disability in IEP development. In relation to IEPs, the legislation added new requirements and expanded already existing requirements. A new section detailed what the IEP team should consider in developing each child's IEP. The new legislation stated that the IEPs should "consider whether the child requires assistive technology devices and services" (34 CFR 615 (3)(B)(v)).

When it comes to transition, two other laws come into play: the Americans with Disabilities Act of 1990 (ADA) (P.L. 101-336) and Section 504 of the Rehabilitation Act of 1973 (P.L. 93-112). Because of employment and access regulations, these laws become very important in the furnishing of services for students of transition ages and will be discussed in that context later in the chapter.

Even before the 1997 reauthorization of IDEA, it was necessary for the states and local education agencies (LEAs) to develop guidelines to assist schools as they provided assistive technology services. Though general guidelines have been written by states, specific guidelines on implementation are in varying stages of development and clarification; greater guidance is needed (Bell & Blackhurst, 1997).

Providing Services: Finding the Money

The provision of assistive technology devices and related services is not an easy accomplishment (Saks, 1993). Cost issues are obviously a challenge and seen as a two-edged sword because of the obvious benefits compared to the cost of devices (Williams, 1990). Additionally, one of the most difficult obstacles professionals face in delivering assistive technology services is keeping up with rapid changes and updating devices. There are "hidden" costs as well, including things like batteries, phone lines, space, and furniture arrangements. The initial investment, linked with training and support costs, is on an ongoing and often long-term commitment (Gardner & Edyburn, 1987).

Funding for devices may come from a variety of sources. Because cost is such an issue, districts must look at alternatives to internal funding. Some creative solutions can be found on a case-by-case basis. Community agencies, Medicaid, and private insurance are among such solutions. If the decision is to use family insurance options, as a matter of policy a professional should encourage parents to check their insurance caps and ceilings of payments. Schools, of course, cannot require parents to use private insurance (Button, 1991), but chances for getting private insurance to cover durable medical equipment (DME) will increase greatly if a prescription is written by a physician (Menlove, 1996). Also, it is important to remember that devices purchased by insurance are solely for the use of the particular individual and may not be used by others (RESNA Technical Assistance Project, 1992). Other funding ideas and resources are discussed later in the chapter.

Technology costs are not always intimidating. It is important to consider a whole range of technologies that can assist students. Many of the technologies or alternatives are neither complicated nor expensive. For instance, the following are examples of a range of alternatives for students who experience handwriting difficulties (Reed, 1997):

- Regular pencil or pen
- Pencil or pen with special grip or larger size
- Pencil or pen with special grip and special paper
- NCR copies of teacher's or peer's notes
- Typewriter/word processor/computer to keyboard instead of writing
- Word processor/computer with spell checker to improve spelling
- Computer with keyguard or support for arm to improve accuracy
- Computer with word prediction software to decrease needed keystrokes
- Single switch or other alternate way of accessing keyboard
- Voice recognition software to operate computer

These solutions are known as "low tech" devices, which are devices that are passive or simple, with few moving parts (Mann & Lane, 1991). The challenge is to match solutions to each student's need, and then to make sure the solution works within the setting. The proof is in the use of the equipment. If an expensive piece of technology is not used because it is too complicated, it obviously is not the right one for the situation. If the technology is not used because the student feels embarrassed to use it or because it does not fit into the culture of the family (Parette, 1997), it probably is not the ideal choice. If the device is not age appropriate and targeted toward acquisition of specific skills, again, it is not the right choice (Inge & Shepherd, 1995).

As noted previously, IDEA amendments requirements dictated that professionals furnish devices as needed for FAPE. The only exemption provided was for medical treatment devices. Golden (1990) compiled some medical exemption guidelines that can help professionals understand when assist devices are medical and when they are not:

1. *Expertise required:* If a medical doctor is the one who usually delivers the assistive technology, the device is probably a medical one.

2. *Intrusiveness:* Devices that are implanted surgically would most likely be medical devices.

3. *Delivery environment:* If the device can only be delivered in a hospital, it probably is considered a medical necessity.

Other criteria for a medical determination include a) the need to support life rather than to assist with a task; b) a specific prescription from a doctor; and c) what the risk, liability, and burden issues are for both student and staff.

Providing Services: Personnel Considerations

Another barrier to efficient provision or services is knowledgeable personnel. Requirements for assistive technology have come about in a relatively short period of time, with few institutes of higher education (IHEs) furnishing enough professionals trained in assistive technology. Knowing that the recent legislation requires consideration for assistive technology as part of IEP development, a case could certainly be made for having a key person in the district who could coordinate and evaluate assistive technology services, and whose task it is to keep up with the technology.

For example, even basic follow-through for student evaluation can slip by unnoticed unless someone is clearly responsible for assistive technology evaluations. In a recent case, the hearing officer held that a district had failed to conduct an evaluation of student's assistive technology needs in violation of IDEA (20 *Individuals with Disabilities Education Law Report* [IDELR] 1216, 1993). Uninformed decisions can be costly in terms of student progress, professional time, and equipment. A person who is knowledgeable about assistive technology alternatives understands that equipment. A person who is knowledgeable about assistive technology alternatives realizes that often, inexpensive low-tech devices will meet the needs of students. Sometimes these devices can be built or adapted by a creative and knowledgeable staff, making local expertise very valuable indeed.

Using existing human resources already within the system is one way that many districts have moved ahead with assistive technology. Often, speech and language practitioners and occupational or physical therapists can lead the way by forming focus groups and inservice opportunities for teachers and other involved staff. An effective and comprehensive program of assistive technology services hinges upon building ownership in the way services are delivered.

Providing Services: What Do School Districts Need To Do NOW?

The 1997 amendments to the reauthorization of IDEA were written with almost immediate implementation in mind. Therefore, districts must quickly put programs into action to assure that the benefits of assistive technology are considered in the development of the IEP. With the new requirements come new responsibilities. It seems appropriate to start by (a) raising the awareness of all staff who are involved with special education students about the issues and benefits surrounding the use of assistive technology; (b) providing access to an in-house evaluative team if at all possible; and (c) making certain that at least one member of each IEP team is knowledgeable in assistive technology. If the IEP team does decide that assistive technology is required, the IEP must include specific statements of the services, including the nature and amount of the services (Content of the Individualized Education Program, 1997). In the IEP, assistive technology can be listed several places—in transition plans and action statements, in annual and short-term goals, in related services, and in supplemental aids and services (16 *Education of Handicapped Law Reporter* 1317, 1990). Without the documentation of consideration of assistive technology, chances of services that would benefit children are reduced, while chances of violation of law are increased.

Sticky Widgets and Bytes

It is easy to get "stuck" in a myriad of issues involved in the provision of assistive technology. Several areas have been viewed as problematic and need to be addressed (Julnes & Brown, 1993b) if profesisonals are to be in compliance with the law and do the right thing for their students. The areas that need to be addressed include (a) ownership of equipment and provision for home, school, and community use; (b) training for professional personnel, students, and families; (c) determining if assistive technology is necessary for a student to receive FAPE, related services, or services in the least restrictive environment (LRE), or access to a school-sponsored program or activity on a nondiscriminatory basis; (d) developing a team-based evaluation process for assistive technology and selection of devices; and (e) furnishing services for private schools.

Devices for Home Use

If the assistive technology device is necessary to carry out IEP or transition related goals in independent living, community functioning, and so on, the student must be allowed to take the device home (Golden, 1990; OSEP, 1991). Schools cannot limit devices to school use only, but all devices do not necessarily need to be sent home. The decision needs to be based on educational, instructional, and transition activities. If a student needs a certain device to complete assignments at school, that same device is probably necessary to complete homework (Pesta, 1994). For example, a transition action statement may have been designed to develop greater functional skill in the use of some device in a community or home setting. Thus, the device needs to go home with the student, just like textbook or other school resource would be required for practice.

The school district also needs to furnish repairs, backups, and even another device for home if necessary. A school board does not have the authority to change the IEP, including access to assistive technology at home or at school (OSEP, 1991). Would we deprive a child of his voice? That is in essence what a communication device becomes—a voice. Even if the device is stolen, broken, or abused, districts must still provide the function of that equipment. School boards also may not deny home access to technology based on their insurance coverage (Morris, 1992b). In the instances where the device is furnished by another agency or funding source, the district is still responsible for maintenance of the equipment while the individual is receiving school-based services. For fiscal due diligence (a careful and thorough study of costs and benefits, both actual and hidden, as well as the return on investment of the item), schools and other providers should review their risk management policies with their insurer.

Training

Because assistive technology is such a specialized field and only recently a requirement for special education students, there are many staff who need to take a first step toward the awareness of what benefits exist for students. Awareness training can be fairly general and involves showing the staff examples of student needs and relating them to technology solutions. Once the staff sees a few examples of the potential assistive technology has to help their students, their awareness level may be raised enough to start asking questions and seek new information.

At that point, a smaller group of specifically trained staff in various areas (e.g., speech and language, technology specialists, occupational therapy, audiologist, etc.) can come together to form evaluation teams for assistive technology needs. It will be necessary in most districts to have at least one key person highly skilled in assistive technology to head up training efforts, observation, and evaluation teams. If such a professional is not available, contracted services with other districts and agencies will probably be the next best choice. Technology Assistance Centers, vendors, and university personnel also may be able to provide some of this training.

Training is the key to whether an investment in technology will pay off. This obviously not just an issue for the student, but for everyone who works with the student. All of the individuals involved (e.g., the classroom teacher, the student, the paraprofessionals, other related service providers, employers, family members) will need to be trained on specific devices. Moreover, the school is responsible for seeing that applicable training is furnished.

When training for specific devices, on-site training is key to the effective use of the hardware and software. The trainer should be one who is familiar with the regular and special education curriculum and good teaching practices (Wall, 1994). Some successful ideas on training include (a) interagency agreements to trade training and assessment expertise for other services or training in an alternative area; b) school district consortiums to share training experiences and expenses as well as expertise; c) inservicing staff using district personnel; and d) cross-training.

Institutions of higher education (IHEs) have not yet been able to furnish enough skilled professionals to meet the need in assistive technology, so most schools have had to "grow their own." Certification for specialists is available through the Rehabilitation Engineering and Assistive Technology Society of North America (RESNA) (see Appendix 10.C), and a few programs are available at the university level (e.g., the University of New Mexico). The certification process is in its infancy and is not a requirement for special education departments in public schools at this time. RESNA has established a code of ethics for its members and standards of practice for assistive technology practitioners and suppliers. Certification examination from RESNA covers areas of psychology and sociology, human anatomy, physiology, kinesiology and biomechanics, basic etiologies and pathologies, principles of learning and teaching, assessment procedures, service delivery systems and funding for assistive technology, principles of design and product development, basic product knowledge of assistive technology devices, integration of person, technology, and environment, and professional conduct (RESNA, 1997).

Training staff is not an easy accomplishment. Cost is an issue as always, with some technology experts planning anywhere from one third of the hardware investment to an equal amount of time spent training and planning compared with hardware investment. In fact, training issues are mentioned as a barrier to assistive technology implementation in several studies (Heidari, 1996; Pesta, 1994). Using and building on the expertise and technologies that are currently in place will help prioritize training needs.

Determining if a Student Really Needs Assistive Technology

The following criteria help IEP teams determine whether assistive technology should play a part in a student's education (Chambers, 1997, p. 5):

1. Is assistive technology necessary to receive FAPE?

2. Is assistive technology necessary to receive services in the least restrictive environment?

3. Are the devices and services a necessary related service?

4. If the student has assistive devices, will the student then have access to school programs and activities?

It seems reasonable that a fifth question should be asked: Is assistive technology necessary for a student to achieve employment, independent living, and social and community participation? In transition cases, it is important to note that the community and the employment environment, as well as the academic setting, must be considered. If any of the answers to these questions are yes, it is the responsibility of the school district to provide assistive technology. However, if a student who needs assistive technology is not eligible for special education, the child deserves consideration under Section 504 of the Rehabilitation Act of 1973. The modifications and adaptations would appear on the 504 accommodation plan for that particular child.

As mentioned earlier, aids for learning and functioning, such as eyeglasses and hearing aids, are considered assistive technology. If the parents do not provide eyeglasses and hearing aids and these devices are necessary to make progress on the IEP, then schools must provide them (Sack, Clark, & Spellman, 1997). There are also service organizations that can be approached for these articles. In practice, contacts to organizations on behalf of a child should be made by a school representative, such as a school nurse, classroom teacher, or counselor.

Another way of finding out if a student should receive technology services is by looking at student need related to function within a certain context. Riviere (1997) briefly described a sampling of tools and technologies that could be used by adults with learning disabilities to improve their functional capabilities in employment, education, or personal settings. In this framework, loosely adapted from Riviere, the importance of planning each technology solution is in terms of the individual's unique profile and the related function (see Table 10.1).

Items that one may not normally think of as assistive technology need to be considered as well. Such items include (a) nonmechanical and nonelectronic aids, such as a ramp to replace steps; (b) aids for daily living (cooking, bathing, dressing); (c) environmental control systems; (d) appliances, security systems, such as Call for Assistance, which is a device mounted on a wheelchair that can be activated with or without switches, or the DEUCE Environmental Central System, which provides users with access to the phone system from their immediate environment; (e) home or work site modifications including structure

Table 10.1
Examples of Assistive Technology

Needs	Devices
Organizational Skills and Memory	Personal data managers, electronic memo-minders and calendars, beepers/buzzers, alarms, tape recorders, and index cards
Auditory Management	Pressure-sensitive paper for classroom note taking, laptops, books on CD or tape, multimedia approach and tape recorders, personal (FM) listening systems, hearing aids, TTs/TDDs, vibrating alarms
Visual Processing	Large-print materials, computers with text to speech, magnified screens
Numerical Processing	Color coded columns, talking and other special feature calculators, abacus, counters, visual numerical models
Reading	Optical character recognition systems with speech synthesis, books on tape, online services, magnifying glass, ruler to read line by line
Written Language	Spell checkers, grammar checking and proofreading programs, typewriter, built-up pencil, pen holder, speech-to-text programs
Research Management	World Wide Web, telecommunications, distance learning, and sources of various services of online resources

Note. Adapted from *Assistive Technology: Meeting the Needs of Adults with Learning Disabilities* (ERIC No. Ed 401 686), by A. Riviere, 1997, Washington, DC: Academy for Educational Development and the National Institute for Literacy.

adaptations, lifestyle, and bathroom structural changes that would prevent any barriers; (f) prosthetics or orthotics (splints, braces, sitting and positioning aids); (g) accommodations to wheelchairs, bringing greater body stability; (h) trunk and head supports for reduction of pressure; (i) aids for vision, hearing, and communication; (j) mobility aids, such as scooters, vehicles, wheelchairs, walkers; and (k) vehicle modifications (Kansas Assistive Technology Project, 1993). These accommodations become particularly important as students transition from school to adult living.

The Parents Let's Unite for Kids (PLUK) Parent Training and Information Center guides parents to ask for assistive technology services when there are functions "that can be achieved by no other means." Also, the guide asks parents to request assistive technology that

> enables students to approximate a level of accomplishment which could not be achieved by any other means; provides access for participation in programs or activities which otherwise would be closed to the individual;

increases endurance or ability to persevere and complete tasks that otherwise are too laborious to be attempted on a routine basis; enables students to concentrate on learning tasks, rather than mechanical tasks; provides greater access to information; supports normal social interactions with peers and adults; supports participation in the Least Restrictive Environment (LRE). (PLUK, 1997)

As has been discussed, schools are legally obligated to provide assistive technology. Even beyond the law is the spirit of the law that begs professionals and others to implement needed assistive technology, allowing a level playing field for many people with disabilities, including students, employees, and young adults as they transition to independent living and social arenas. A framework that will help school personnel meet the intent of this law is offered by Blackhurst, Lahm, Harrison, and Chandler (in press). This framework presents a model in which the variables of external supports, functional demands, environment, context, and personal perceptions are used to explore options for technology. Selected options in turn flow into functional responses and personal changes, all within a process of evaluation and feedback. Assistive technology often is the linchpin that secures benefit from instruction and ensures that lives are lived fully and meaningfully.

Evaluating Students for Assistive Technology and Finding the Appropriate Device

The requirement from the IDEA Amendments of 1997 that school districts provide an "evaluation of the needs of the child with a disability, including a functional evaluation of the child in the child's customary environment" has established a national trend and a practical necessity to identify staff *within* the district who can become members of the assistive technology team.

A Team-Based Process

Effective evaluation for assistive technology will always demand a team-based process and decision, determined on a case-by-case basis (Hutinger, 1996). With a transdisciplinary or multidisciplanary team, each member plays an important role, contributing their own skills, talents, and unique personalities. With this type of involvement, transitions to new environments occur more smoothly for students, and a continuity of care transcends any territorial or discipline-specific entity. At the district level, the team should include (a) someone knowledgeable in the areas of special education; (b) someone knowledgeable in the area of the regular education curriculum; (c) someone knowledgeable in the area of mobility;

(d) someone knowledgeable in the area of the language, and (e) a person certified or experienced and very knowledgeable about the provision of assistive technology devices and services and programs. Other personnel recommended by Carl, Mataya, and Zabala (1994) include a school psychologist, a special education supervisor or administrator, a teacher of the visually or hearing impaired, a nurse, and a vocational counselor. At the building level, members of the decision-making team should include this core:

1. Individual and/or parents;

2. Someone knowledgeable in the area of special education;

3. Someone knowledgeable in the area of the regular education curriculum;

4. An administrator or designee (In addition, if there are needs relating to any specific related service such as speech and language or mobility, those personnel should be involved); and

5. Someone knowledgeable in the area of assistive technology, if student needs dictate.

Examples of others who could be included on the team include an audiologist, counselor, instruction assistant, physician, social worker, computer specialist, early intervention specialist, rehabilitation engineer, transition specialist, and agency representatives.

An Abilities-Driven Process

Besides being a team-based process, it is important that a comprehensive evaluation for assistive technology be abilities driven rather than device driven. In other words, the goal of an evaluation is to identify a student's communicative, motor, hearing, and visual abilities and then match these skills to appropriate technology. This approach is in sharp contrast with an evaluation model that selects a device and then seeks to teach the student skills and abilities needed in order to use the selected equipment (J. Daugherty, personal communication, August, 1996). Regarding the evaluation process for assistive technology, Daugherty felt that school personnel needed to address some initial questions. These questions can be found in Table 10.2.

There must be at least an annual review of the assistive technology needs, with reevaluations every three years. Ideally, the success of the technology interventions should be evaluated in a formative manner by a multidisciplinary team. These successes should be noted, along with progress in the IEP goals and objectives. Professionals should be aware that assistive technology should be used

Table 10.2

Questions To Ask During the Evaluation Process for Assistive Technology

1. What system or method technique is currently being used to
   • communicate?
   • to problem solving or make choices?
   • to share knowledge or products?
   • to socialize?
   • to work?
   • to acquire independent living skills?
2. What does data show about the effectiveness of the current assistive technology system (i.e., what is its present level of performance)?
3. What results are necessary that are currently not being accomplished?
4. In what settings or environments will demonstration of the skill take place?
5. What are the interests, motivations, and preferences of the individual to accomplish the skills?

Other considerations for questions might include the advantages and limitations of a device, the flexibility of the device over time, cultural demands, and what family members prefer.

to support students in the preassessment stage as well (Sack, Clark, & Spellman, 1997).

Chambers (1997) delineates several major areas that need to be considered in a team-based evaluation for assistive technology: positioning, self care, augmentative communication, environmental controls, assistive listening, visual aids, mobility, physical education, leisure, play, computer access, and computer-based instruction. Ideas for assistive technology in these areas can be found in Appendix 10.A.

Another way that one might look at assistive technology evaluation, particularly in an employment or vocational setting, is through a model of task analysis. In this method, the team looks at performance of a needed task as the key to technology selection. In other words, what is the job that needs to be done? This approach results in breaking the task down to manageable parts. Can the student do part or all of the task, or do they need services of job coach to complete the task? What devices would assist the student in getting the job done?

No matter what the method of evaluation, when at all possible, observations and evaluations for assistive technology need to take place in the setting where the technology will be used—in the school, on the job, at home, in church, and in leisure settings. A variety of factors need to be considered in each instance, including teachers or service providers, environmental conditions such as lighting and noise level, and availability of peer coaches.

An idea that is certainly worth considering is the opportunity for the potential user and the family to observe other individuals using the devices being considered (Parette, 1996). Adequate investigation of appropriate options (including visiting sites where the equipment is being used in similar situations), the learning styles of the individual, vendor and price comparisons, and consulting with other professionals will help lead to informed decision making (Rothstein & Everson, 1995). The appropriateness of the device must be reassessed as the student grows and abilities change. Reevaluation is an ongoing process; formative data need to be gathered and revisited across the many environments that a student travels. Evaluation for assistive technology should never be a "one shot" consideration. Sample forms for assistive technology evaluation are included in Appendix 10.B.

In summary, there seems to be a pattern developed from the old ways of evaluating students for assistive technology, to new ways of doing business (Carl, Mataya, & Zabala, 1994). When the trends are examined, one can see the following changes:

1. A change in philosophy of the assessment from a separate event to an ongoing process

2. A change in who conducts the assessment from a "center" outside the district, to a local team in the classroom or transition environment

3. A change in the scheduling of the assessment from once a year, or at scheduled reevaluation to a continual *process* of evaluation

4. A change in support and follow-through from a single individual's involvement to all members of the team being involved

Selecting the Right Device

The student's acceptance and use of the device is the proof of the planning. Have professionals given choices to the student and family and presented them with the strengths and weaknesses of each device? How does the device "look"? Is the device developmentally appropriate? Does the family understand and accept the device? Even though professionals feel they have made an educated selection and solution, if the device is not being used, if it is used only when prompted, or if it is not accepted in the family culture, then it is *not* the right choice. If professionals fail to consider the preferences and personal dignity of family and child, then they fail in their mission. The results could be lack of progress for the student, abandonment of the technology, and the wasting of crucial financial resources (Parette, 1997).

The plan for assistive technology must be designed for the specific needs of the individual student, not for what the school district has in stock. A student should not be evaluated for the "thing," but for the functionality that a device can provide. Professionals should keep in mind that the exact item should probably not be listed on the IEP. If listed, school districts must provide it whether or not a better or more appropriate device is invented or becomes available, if that particular item goes out for repair, or if a different interface is needed. A device that is specified by name on the IEP will be required to be available and in good working order (Golden, 1990; OSEP, 1991). Each scenario would demand a revision of the IEP; therefore, professionals should designate the provision by a *specific function* related to need, rather than the exact item. Whatever the device, it must be appropriate and a rationale must be given for its use.

Parette (1997) advocates that the team look at "domains of influence" before selecting a device. The five domains Parette notes are (1) user characteristics, (2) technology features, (3) family concerns, (4) cultural factors, and (5) service system issues (see Table 10.3). When considering this model professionals should also keep in mind the potential transition environments for a student over a life time:

1. Childhood
2. Preschool
3. Elementary School
4. Middle School
5. High School
6. Employment
7. Postsecondary Education
8. Vocational Training
9. Independent Living
10. Leisure/Social
11. Sheltered Living
12. Care Facility

Guidelines for selecting equipment need to be judged for practicality as well. Guidelines furnished by Rothstein and Everson (1995) include looking at the ease of assembly, the use and maintenance, and the device's durability and portability. Other practical questions involve the dependability, adaptability, maintenance and updating costs, and easy access to technological support. Moreover, as professionals work more and more in general education classrooms, they must ask if the device or system is compatible with the district's hardware platforms or building technology (National School Boards Association [NSBA] and OSEP, 1997). A systematic strategy for selecting assistive technology devices was designed by Inge and Shepherd (1995). The step-by-step process has a great deal of similarity to transition planning. The process involves the following steps (Inge & Shepherd, 1995):

Table 10.3

Domains of Influence To Be Considered by Assistive Technology Team Members

Issue Area	Specific Considerations
User Characteristics	• Performance levels (from assessment data) • User age • Gender • Current devices used, past experiences, and preferences • Academic and vocational aspirations • Desire for independence • Training needs and willingness to receive training • Changes in user characteristics across time
Technology Features	• Range and availability of devices • Potential to enhance user performance levels • Real cost • East of use • Comfort • Dependability • Transportability • Longevity and durability • Adaptablity • Comparability with other devices • Safety features • Availability for hands-on demonstrations • Repair considerations
Family Concerns	• Changes in activities, routines, and resources • Effect on family interaction patterns • Degree of expectations for independence
Cultural Factors	• Compatibility of device with cultural values • Extent to which device calls attention to use in social and public settings • Extent to which dependence/independence is valued • Developmental expectations for the acquisition of skills • Perception of disability
Service System Issues	• Cost • Community usage of device • Protection from theft and damage • Training

Note. From "Assistive Technology Devices and Services," by J. P. Parette, 1997, *Education and Training in Mental Retardation and Developmental Disabilities, 32*(4), p. 267–280. Copyright 1997 by the Division on Mental Retardation and Developmental Disabilities. Reprinted with permission.

1. Gathering background information;
2. Observing the student;
3. Determining the student's abilities and needs;
4. Investigating the ideal access system;
5. Proposing an access system;
6. Personalizing and maximizing the access system;
7. Setting goals for instruction and training;
8. Implementing the system; and
9. Monitoring programs and providing follow up.

The important role for family and student involvement in making technology choices cannot be overlooked. How can families who know very little about assistive technology find information? First of all, the individuals themselves need to be involved in future's planning as much as possible (Dunst, Trivette, & Deal, 1988; Meadows, 1994). One way families can help make choices is to ask for the opportunity to observe others who are using the technology (Beukelman & Mirenda, 1992). Families should ask questions about what long-term effects the technologies might have on family routines, care giving, and community activities. Questions that a family could ask about a device might be centered around (a) performance, (b) "elegance" (simplicity and efficiency), (c) ergonomics, (d) reliability, (e) safety, (f) practicality, (g) aesthetics, (h) normalization, (i) cost effectiveness, and (j) personal acceptance (PLUK, 1997). Another method is for families to talk with the technology team about the opportunity for hands-on experience with the different types of devices being considered. Family members are the only true constants in the lives of young students with disabilities; the feedback obtained from them concerning the practicality of device under consideration is invaluable. Families, after all, carry the perspective of past and future from one environment to the next environment; they alone have seen the individual in all of life's settings.

The end goal is to link transition outcomes and long-term independence. In so doing, families should look at natural and simple solutions first (Rothstein & Everson, 1995). Overuse or overreliance on devices might possibly inhibit the natural development of skills such as voice production and communication. Many types of modifications exist that do *not* require assistive technology. Solutions like color coding, peer support and tutoring, hands-on manipulatives, and environmental changes should be explored before jumping into even low-tech aides. A guide to keep in mind is that the least intrusive and the most natural solutions are first in the line of consideration.

The selection of assistive technology adaptations should never be looked upon as a "final" solution. The efficacy of the evaluative process denotes a continuity of attention throughout the transition periods of a lifetime. Just as career development is a continual process throughout one's life (Clark, Field, Patton,

Brolin, & Sitlington, 1994; Clark & Kolstoe, 1995), so too is the process of change in environments, job choices, leisure interests, and living situations. All of these factors interweave with technological advances that may change in the blink of an eye.

Furnishing Assistive Technology for Private Schools

The issue of furnishing services in private schools has been answered in reauthorization of IDEA in 1997, which stated that school districts *may* provide on-site services. These special education services include assistive technology and also extend into community placements for those students involved in transition programming. Equipment purchased for use by these students will also need to go home with them if necessary to show progress on the IEP goals. In *Zobrest v. Catalina Foothill School District*, the Circuit Court of Appeal ruled in favor of public schools providing need services to special education students attending private or parochial schools (Sack, Clark, & Spellman, 1997). With the political support of homeschooling and most recently of charter schools, the probability of funding following students—no matter where they choose to attend school—may soon make conversations about financial responsibilities a moot point. Moreover, according to a brochure put out by the Adult and Medical Services Commission of the Kansas Department of Social and Rehabilitation Services (1998), "assistive technology is provided as needed to enhance or complete other services provided to your child and belongs to your child."

Planning for Assistive Technology

Three hurdles that school districts must face in the planning for assistive technology are 1) understanding the laws which govern the furnishing of assistive technology; 2) designing programs to deliver assistive technology services; and 3) finding ways to finance the implementing of new programs.

Policies and Laws

Combining transition and assistive technology services is a complex process that involves the laws that are necessary to get assistive technology out of its developmental closet and into the hands of the people who need it most—those with disabilities. Because it is difficult for school personnel to stay informed of what employers and schools should do to meet transition/technology requirements in the framework of legal requirements, a brief synopsis is offered in this section.

Four types of legal analyses have been applied by OSEP, Office of Civil Rights (OCR), and hearing officers in determining the obligation of educational agencies to provide assistive technology devices and services. The types of legal analyses are Free and Appropriate Education (FAPE), Least Restricted Environment (LRE), Related Services, and Section 504 of the Rehabilitation Act of 1973 (Julnes & Brown, 1993a). Each type of analyses raises questions:

- *FAPE*: Is the provision of assistive technology devices or services essential for the student to receive FAPE? If so, such devices or services are legally required.

- *LRE*: Is the provision of assistive technology devices or services essential for the student to be educated in the LRE? If so, such devices or services are legally required.

- *Related Services:* Is the provision of assistive technology devices or services a necessary related service? If so, such devices or services are legally required unless it is a medically related device or a medical service.

- *Section 504*: Will the provision of assistive technology devices or services increase access to programs? If so, such devices or services are legally required.

A study by Reid (1994) reported that very few states were actively engaged in policy-related activities that would direct assistive technology services to students with disabilities. A further study by Bell and Blackhurst (in press) found that information about the delivery and evaluation of services, interagency collaboration, and interdisciplinary involvement in the delivering of assistive technology services were rarely included in state policy and guidelines for assistive technology. These researchers found that states were "more comfortable in aligning their policies closely with federal law than in providing guidance in the actual delivery and evaluation of assistive technology services" (p. 14).

Prior to the ADA, Section 504 of the Rehabilitation Act of 1973 protected people from discrimination based on their disability. These individuals were defined in the following manner:

A person having a mental or physical impairment which substantially limits one or more of a person's major life activities; has a record of a physical or mental impairment that substantially limits one or more of major life activities; or is regarded as having a physical or mental impairment that substantially limits one or more major life activities. "Major life activities" include functions such as caring for one's self, performing manual tasks, walking, seeing, hearing, speaking, breathing, learning, and work. When a condition does not substantially limit a major life activity, the individual does not qualify under Section 504.

In a school setting, a team of individuals will evaluate students who do not qualify under special education categories, but have a disability under Section 504. If the student is deemed disabled under the section, the school must develop and implement the services or accommodations. Parents must also be a part of the process. Section 504 accommodation planning is not a special education function, but a general education responsibility. Accommodations could include things like seating arrangements, tutoring, modification of free or leisure time, transportation needs, physical education adaptation or modification, study guides or organizers, assistive technology, and counseling (Kansas State Department of Education, 1997).

In the United States, people often define themselves by the type of employment they have and the work that they do; their work often is the chief way that they organize their lives, gain independence, and control their destiny (Sowers, 1995). The place work holds in American lives is certainly no different in the lives of people with disabilities. How can professionals be assured that students will be able to compete fairly as they go into the workplace?

For purposes of this chapter, case law and statutory law and how these laws affect the work environment will not be discussed in detail. However, there are also laws that assist individuals with disabilities in seeking employment. One of these laws is the ADA, which was based on the Vocational Rehabilitation Act of 1973. To qualify for consideration under these laws, a person must have an actual disability (either physical or mental) that substantially limits them in one or more major life activities, or they must be perceived to have such a disability. The employer must be informed and aware of the disability, or legal liability does not apply. Congress' intent is for strong enforcement of the ADA. Title I and Title II of the Act cover most of the employment provisions. According to the Equal Employment Opportunity Commission (EEOC):

> The ADA seeks to ensure access to equal employment opportunities based on merit. It does not guarantee equal results, establish quotas, or require preferences favoring individuals with disabilities over those without disabilities. When an individual's disability creates a barrier to employment opportunities, the ADA requires employers to consider whether reasonable accommodation could remove the barrier. (Regulation To Implement the Equal Employment Provision of the Americans with Disabilities Act, 1991)

However, if a person's disability creates significant risks of substantial harm to fellow workers, and the disability cannot be controlled by reasonable accommodations, then the protection offered by ADA does not apply. ADA requires employers to give physically impaired people the same rights as anyone else and to guarantee equal opportunity in employment, public accommodations, transportation, state and local government services, and telecommunications. Also, under the EEOC, to be qualified for a job the person must also have the "requisite skill, experience, education and other job-related requirements of the employment position" and be able "either with or without reasonable accommodation to perform the essential functions of the position" (Regulation To Implement the Equal Employment Provision of the Americans with Disabilities Act, 1991).

In Title I of the ADA, there are different types of accommodation settings that could be provided according to need. The first is in the job application process and involves making certain that discrimination does not occur in recruitment or hiring. The second is in the work environment, dealing with such things as wide versus narrow doors, job duties, and employment benefits and privileges (Parry et al., 1996). An employer should also have a discussion with the employee about identifying limitations that affect job performance, and together they should identify possible accommodations. The appropriateness and effectiveness of the accommodations should be implemented and then evaluated. The following are examples of reasonable accommodations (Parry, 1996):

- architectural or structural changes
- restructuring jobs
- modifying work schedules
- modifying exams or policies
- providing interpreters or readers
- acquiring hardware, software, or devices when necessary
- reassignment of job
- job duties
- adjusting training materials
- personal assistants
- rearranging furniture for easy access
- telephone amplifier
- job training

Many accommodations do not involve great expense (Blanck,1994; Koshakji, 1997). Free assistance to employers about accommodations that a person with disabilities might need is offered through the Job Accommodations Network (JAN). JAN also has data supporting the fact that most accommodations are not costly. Thirty percent of accommodations are actually free, and 20% cost less than $50. Most accommodations fall under $500, while 11% are more costly and involve equipment or architectural solutions. Accommodations that do not necessarily involve technology could include flexible scheduling, educating other employees about the disability, job restructuring, job training, development of work plans, providing critical feedback, and support during rough times (Parry et al., 1996) . These authors published examples of accommodations from JAN that are assisted by technology at a low cost :

- renting a headset telephone that allows an employee with cerebral palsy to write while talking ($6.10/month);

- supplying a telephone amplifier for a computer programmer with a hearing impairment ($56);

- purchasing a pressure-sensitive floor mat that signals to a blind receptionist that someone has entered the office ($50); and

- purchasing a padded wrist-rest to place under a computer keyboard to alleviate the pain of a typist with carpal tunnel syndrome ($10).

Other resources for assistive technology and transition may be found in Appendix 10.C.

As mentioned earlier, the Developmental Disabilities Assistance and Bill of Rights Act defined three goals for all persons with disabilities: independence, productivity, and integration. The legal framework as an impetus for these things to happen is in place. Thus, the challenge rests with those who have day-to-day contact with students and clients with disabilities. These professionals must encourage the incorporation of assistive technology into the practice of educators and agencies alike, as well as into the policies of employers and governmental services.

Designing a Program

A program for assistive technology should develop a process where technology will be integrated into the student's curriculum and used with continuity and effectiveness in the student's daily routines and tasks. A strong vision, undergirded with what professionals know to be best practices, will provide the basis for wise decision making. In addition, program directors will need to make sure mechanisms are in place that will support communication and collaboration between staff. As discussed previously, training is essential, along with the resources and follow-through to support it.

One way to get a program organized and in motion is to create a multidisciplinary team charged with designing and guiding services. A team designed in this manner will promote ownership, continuity, and guidance for the program. Moreover, such a team will be viewed as a grassroots organization. This team of stakeholders can perform the following tasks when creating an assistive technology program:

1. Establish the mission or basic philosophy that will guide the program;

2. Raise the knowledge of the team itself through educational readings and seminars, brown-bag lunches, workshops or conferences, and a plan to disseminate and share knowledge;

3. Design a self-study or needs assessment to determine current status of student needs and assistive technology knowledge in the district;

4. Design action, management, and implementation plans and timelines;

5. Build capacity of other staff members who are interested or may have some knowledge and expertise to contribute;

6. Design referral and evaluation process for students who may need assistive technology;

7. Assess whether current staff can meet assistive technology needs;

8. Explore ways to train staff and other service providers, ranging from basic awareness issues to intensive specific hardware and software;

9. Plan for maintenance, repair, and obsolescence;

10. Explore funding options and develop a budget for training, staffing, and hardware or software needs; and

11. Evaluate the program and processes.

Once a program has been established, this team or another team may be created to implement the recommended program. Functions that a district level team may perform in implementing the program include the following (Carl et al., 1994):

1. Reviews student's assistive technology referral information;

2. Reviews current assessment information, which may include psychoeducational, academic, developmental, speech–language, occupational therapy, and physical therapy evaluations;

3. Requests additional evaluations as necessary;

4. Conducts observations of student in classroom setting;

5. Discusses educational needs and case information with campus level team;

6. Assesses student for assistive technology;

7. Provides written recommendations to campus level team's;

8. Provides guidance/training support in implementation of the above recommendations;

9. Provides guidance in development of IEP objectives;

10. Provides information about specific devices or technology as needed;

11. Provides follow-up and technical assistance as needed;

12. Provides assistance in obtaining funding as needed;

13. Attends staffing meetings in collaboration with building level team; and

14. Attends and gives workshops on technology and trends.

The district level planning and supervisory team should work in very close collaboration with the building-level teams. Naturally, the building-level teams, who actually implement services, will be in much closer contact with the student and families and should have the final say in IEP decisions. In smaller districts, both of these teams are often combined, with just one person coordinating the program. The composition of the team was discussed earlier in the chapter.

Another way that school districts might proceed is to combine resources in a regional center concept. The BITS (Buddies in Technology Services), which is an interdistrict alliance concerned with the technology needs of students with disabilities, generated some interesting data at a planning meeting for assistive technology in a regional center concept (Fisher, Daugherty, Magrone, & Walicek, 1994). About 40 stakeholders gathered in March of 1994 to prioritize needs and ideas for such a center. They found that the center should

- be grassroots and consumer-based;

- provide "one-stop-shopping" (i.e., one contact to open doors to all types of assistive technology services that are needed);

- encourage networking, interagency collaboration;

- provide funding information and counseling available;

- provide training and trainers available to go on site;

- make certain that consumer expertise is valued and shared;

- make equipment try-out and equipment loans available; and

- raise public and professional awareness of assistive technology/disability issues.

Cost and Funding Issues

Funding issues continue to be a major problem in delivering assistive technology services to the individuals who need them. What investments are necessary in assistive technology to provide for FAPE? In selecting a device, professionals need to keep in mind that the most expensive and latest technology (or the one seen advertised) is not always the best on an individual basis. The device certainly does not need to be the "Cadillac" of all assistive technology, but it does need to meet the goal of progressing on IEP goals and of allowing the student to function in the LRE. Professionals must pay attention to the developmental age of the child in their acquisition of technology. For example, a sophisticated Sun computer workstation for a child who is 16, but who has a developmental age of 6 or 7, would obviously be excessive.

In a case from South Carolina (19 IDELR 355, 1992), the judge ruled in favor of a more expensive communication device than the school had recommended, in order for the student to receive FAPE. Cost cannot be a factor when the alternative results in denial of FAPE. The reality of today's no-frills budget dictates that professionals look carefully at the full range of technologies that might be appropriate, and then make wise choices within budgetary constraints (Nalty & Kochany, 1991). However, Parette (1997) related that once a team-based decision has been made in identifying a particular device, cost should not be a deterrent.

Because transition planning is part of the IEP process, academically related goals are not the only ones that need to be considered for assistive technology. Social functioning, independent living, and job-related activities and employment should also be considered. During transition planning, the consideration of future use of the assistive technology device should be a part of the picture. Therefore, agencies involved in transition planning may be an additional resource for funding. Making the most of what one already has involves looking at the development of a fiscally responsible program. Program development entails prioritizing needs within the budget and looking for cost savings through careful shopping. Good relationships with vendors are essential in the technology environment because of rapid changes, special pricing, and repair/maintenance issues.

Medically necessary assistive technology can be covered with Medicaid if the student is eligible. Most experts seem to feel that Medicaid funds may be accessed without parental permission (i.e., through a lawyer). The question of educational or medical designation becomes a moot point when the device is deemed necessary for a student to benefit from special education.

Another cost-saving idea for the provision of assistive technology is inter-district collaboration. A model that works in the Kansas City area is the Buddies in Technology Service (BITS) (see Appendix 10.D). In this model, the members share resources, lend equipment to try out, and arrange for collaborative training opportunities. The ability to have informal consultation and a friendly forum to trade expertise and experiences are worth the investment and time. See Appendix 10.D for an example of the BITS interdistrict agreement for assistive technology (Fisher, 1992).

Many other methods to save money can be explored. Interagency agreements can be made for borrowing, renting, or trying out equipment. Such agreements can also be used to trade training and assessment expertise for other parallel services, such as training employers, educators, parents, and so forth. Loan banks can be contacted, as well as regional assistive technology centers. Professionals may contact vocational rehabilitation and other such government agencies. They can pursue grant opportunities. Numerous organizations (e.g., Kiwanis Club, Junior League, Rotary, United Cerebral Palsy, Easter Seals, Muscular Dystrophy Association, Multiple Sclerosis Society, the United Way, etc.) can be consulted. Business partnerships could be formed that would build support in the local community. Regional Technology Assistance Projects (TAP), credit-based systems (Langton, 1990; Parette, 1991; Reeb, 1987), contracts with vendors or manufacturers revolving loan funds (Wallace, 1995), and private foundations (e.g., National Christina Foundation) can also be cost-saving ideas when providing assistive technology.

The school setting is but one of the areas that needs to be considered for assistive technology. Areas of recreation or sports, mobility, transportation, employment, and prosthetic and orthotic needs all have specific devices that can aid and assist people with disabilities. In planning for these settings, ongoing operating costs (e.g., special batteries, repair, links with other devices, etc.) need to be considered. Four mandates support the acquisition of devices across these environments and can assist with their purchase: Individual Family Services Plans (IFSP), IEPs/ITPs, Individual Written Rehabilitation Plans (IWRP), and Individual Habilitation Plans (IHP) (Kansas Assistive Technology Project, 1993). Menlove (1996) developed a funding decision tree in form of a checklist for identifying funding sources for assistive technology (see Figure 10.1). The questions that Menlove asks form a flowchart that can serve as a guide to help decision makers pinpoint alternative ways of funding devices that can be highly individualized.

Part of the planning process for transition includes vocational rehabilitation agencies. If a student or individual with disabilities qualifies for services, services that may be provided include telecommunications, sensory and other technological aids and devices, as well as individually prescribed aids and devices, which are authorized in the IWRP (Health Resource Center, 1994). Eligibility under the Rehabilitation Act of 1973 has changed considerably since its 1992 reauthorization because assistive technology has been integrated into the new

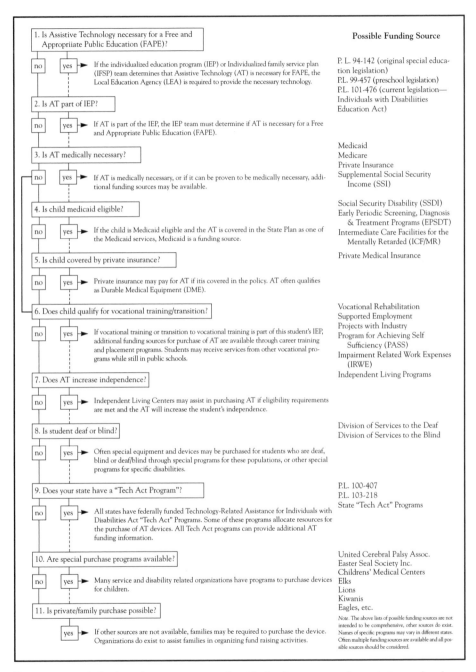

Figure 10.1. A funding decision tree to identify funding sources for assistive technology. *Note.* From "A Checklist for Identifying Funding Sources for Assistive Technology," by M. Menlove, 1996, *Teaching Exceptional Children, 28*(3), 21. Copyright 1996 by The Council for Exceptional Children. Reprinted with permission.

legislation, funding may now be available. A further note on vocational rehabilitation issues is the change from denying the existence of vocational potential to people whose employment may require much work, time, and cost
(Morris, 1992a). The 1986 reauthorization of the Rehabilitation Act prohibits
these agencies from determining lack of vocational potential without *first* considering whether the person could benefit from rehabilitation engineering
services.

Final amendments to the vocational rehabilitation regulations appeared in
the *Federal Register* on February 11, 1997 and soon went into effect. Because a
major shift in policy was delineated in these amendments, the Rehabilitation
Services Administration (RSA) issued a Policy Directive (RSA-PD-97-04) that
governs state vocational rehabilitation agencies.

This new directive requires state VR agencies to approve vocational goals
and the services to meet these goals to enable persons with disabilities to *maximize* their employment potential. This directive represents a dramatic shift in
RSA policy. RSA's 1980 policy (1505-PQ-100A) identifies "suitable employment" as the standard for determining an appropriate vocational goal for an individual with a disability. In that policy and in a 1978 policy (1505-PQ-100), RSA
described "suitable employment" as "reasonable good entry level work an individual can suitably perform" (Hager, 1998, p. 6–7).

This policy is best expressed in the following quotation from the August
1997 Policy Directive:

> The guidance provided through this Policy Directive is employment goal
> under Title I of the Act can be equated with becoming employed at *any* job.
> As indicated above the State Vocational Rehabilitation program is not
> intended solely to place individuals with disabilities in entry-level jobs, but
> rather to assist eligible individuals to obtain employment that is appropri-
> ate given their unique strengths, resources, priorities, concerns, abilities and
> capabilities. The extent to which State units should assist eligible individ-
> uals to advance in their careers through the provision of VR services depend
> upon whether the individual has achieved employment that is consistent
> with this standard (emphasis added).

The directive goes on to state that in many cases, trial work or educational
placements should be accompanied with the provision of assistive technology as
a means of overcoming a disability-related deficit. Reiterating the tone of client-
centered services, there is a provision for appeal of decisions made by the VR
agencies. The Client Assistance Program (Client Assistance Program, 1991) has
been established to protect individuals with disabilities.

As part of transition planning, it may be possible to obtain funding though
Projects with Industry (PWI) (1986) and Supported Employment (1986). The

funding sources were created to guarantee that students with disabilities have full vocational opportunities. State education agencies will have information about these programs. Additionally, Job Training Partnership Act programs can also serve students with disabilities. State rehabilitation agencies can furnish information about these programs.

If full funding is not possible from government agencies, an idea that seems to have some merit is that of the agency purchasing the assistive technology device from the school or trading services in a collaborative way in order to do what is right for the students. No matter where the funding comes from, it is important to make certain that the solution to furnishing assistive technology is a collaborative process. If parents are dissatisfied with the decision, they can ask for an independent assessment at the school district's expense. A school district's due diligence is much more cost effective than due process. The best interests of student should be at the center of every decision.

Finding the Common Ground and Making It Work

In the mid-1980s, system change initiatives sponsored by the U.S. Department of Education (USDOE) became a way of exerting influence upon and restructuring public education. Since about 1985, significant policy, interagency assistance, model demonstration, and research programs have all been used to spark best practices and implement newly passed federal requirements. Both transition and, more recently, assistive technology, have benefited from these initiatives. The mechanisms for informing schools, parents, and consumers of assistive technology have broadened the knowledge base and brought about many needed changes. However, much still needs to be accomplished.

Overcoming Problems Associated with New and Dual Implementation

The field of transition is still widely regarded as a field in its infancy. The field of assistive technology is also relatively newborn. Though transition is viewed as the culmination of the educational process for students with disabilities, only recently have requirements for transition become part of the IEP process (IDEA, 1990). Newer still is the added consideration of assistive technology in every IEP (IDEA, 1997). The unfamiliarity of the field is further compounded by rapid change and leaps in implementation, so that what was appropriate 3 years ago is "old technology" today.

The problem of intertwining the implementation of these two newly enacted requirements is complex. The complexity is heightened by lack of adequate staff with expertise in either field. IHEs have not yet participated in significant numbers to train or certify specialists in these two areas. Moreover, it is too early for public schools to benefit significantly from even minimal training that teachers may have had in transition issues or assistive technology. Many districts' staff are still at the "awareness" level of development in both these areas, but particularly so with assistive technology. The use of technological devices to assist learning still suffers from uncertainty, fear, unfamiliarity, and doubt, and tends to alienate teachers who are more comfortable with chalkboards, paper, and books. A good staff development program in assistive technology is necessary to raise the awareness and comfort level, introducing staff to what teachers and students can accomplish together through assistive technology. Training for the users, the family members, and professionals is critical to prevent "technology abandonment" (Dillard, 1989). Parette (1997) pointed out that provision for training will need to take place before, during, and after the acquisition of the device to ensure its full benefit.

For teachers who have not yet worked with assistive technology, the opportunity to include assistive technology may first be presented when a student's transition plan is created. Exploring the assistive technology concept within the transition framework is a natural development and extension of best practices, as professionals consider the next environments of functional participation in occupational awareness and exploration programs, employment, social networks, the community, and independent living (Logwood & Hadley, 1996). Each arena presents its own specific demands. For some individuals with disabilities, assistive technology may be the only way to gain full participation in life.

Similarities in Legislation and Planning

There are similarities that exist in this new legislation regarding assistive technology (IDEA, 1997) and the legislation requiring transition planning (IDEA, 1990). As seen in the years since transition planning became a required part of the IEP process, transition planning helps focus the IEP by looking at the future, whether it be in life skills instruction (Clark, Field, Patton, Brolin, & Sitlington, 1994), postsecondary education (Brinckerhoff, 1996), or in other postschool outcomes. It is the same with assistive technology, which forces glimpses into the future environments and full functioning within those environments. The requirements in transition planning for long-range services, therefore, are an optimum time to review the needs for assistive technology services or devices. Though traditionally secondary students have not accessed related services to any great extent, the reauthorization of IDEA in 1997 demanded that professionals consider these services. Transition and assistive technology are a natural fit. Looking to those future environments in which a device will be necessary directs the conversation and collaborative planning toward the supports from governmental and social agencies, school personnel, employers, and the family.

Other common ground is found in the planning processes for transition and assistive technology (Halpern, 1994). These similar planning needs include (a) student self-determination; (b) self-evaluation of present functioning; (c) identification of goals consistent with evaluations; and (d) appropriate tools, interventions, and educational experiences consistent with self-evaluations and post-school goals.

Similarities in Planning for Interagency Cooperation and Collaboration

It is at the transition planning juncture that school personnel must initiate contacts and referrals to agencies that need to be involved for the student's future education, employment, social and leisure activities, and independent living. With the family and student's dreams and ambitions as a guide, teachers, counselors, and special education staff need to draft a plan for the future that will include team members such as agencies, provision for social services, and the current employer. Action plans which assign responsibility to various members of the transition planning team and time lines for fulfilling the assignments need to be documented and carried out. For the student who requires assistive technology to carry on as normal a life as possible, these are some of the hard questions that need to be asked in the collaborative planning process with agencies:

1. Who will be responsible for purchasing new assistive technology when the student leaves school?

2. Who will be responsible for training service providers on the use of the new or existing technology?

3. Who will be responsible for the upkeep, maintenance, repair, and updates of the assistive technology?

4. Who will provide checkpoints (evaluation) to make certain that the existing assistive technology is appropriate?

5. Besides family members or the student themselves, who will become a strong advocate for the students assistive technology needs when they leave school?

In many cases, the vocational rehabilitation (VR) agency shoulders the primary burden for assuming these responsibilities. According to Lewis Golinker (1996), Director of the Assistive Technology Law Center in Ithaca, New York, age is not a criterion that VR can set for services. In fact, a VR case should begin as early as possible. For example, a case can be made for practicing for several years with some devices. Evaluative reasons alone are valid in initiating and keeping a vocational rehabilitation case open. With a professional contact, there is the potential for reevaluating current adaptations for their effectiveness and appropriateness. It is important to acquire information about expertise and resources that might be available from agencies at the IEP/ITP meeting. For example, does the local VR agency have available personnel trained in assistive technology assessment, operation, maintenance, and are they able to furnish training?

In some cases, employers will need to furnish some job accommodation and modification (ADA, 1990) that may include assistive technology, in order for the individual with a disability to have equal opportunity to work. In addition to the areas of employment, transition considerations include financial security, postsecondary education, maintaining one's own home, community involvement, and personal and social relationships, which may be the *most* important of all transition goals (Edgar, 1987; Halpern, 1994). Networks of neighbors, family, and the important relationships of friends and lovers are available for all people. Thus, social considerations, even though less traditional in transition planning, are extremely valid concerns and must be included in the overall question of needed technology.

A trend described by Saks (1993) reflects growth in collaborative arrangements between schools and agencies, which could assist with teacher training and selection of hardware and software. Schools might look to include alliances with nonprofit organizations such as the California-based Alliance for Technology Access, which has 46 assistive technology resource centers and as its mission shares information and technology resources with children and adults. The National ATA Center (see Appendix 10.C) will help identify a nearby center that can assist with identifying appropriate technology. Another project is the federally funded National Center to Improve Practice, which had a 5-year project designed to help local school systems in Newton, Massachusetts, to effectively use technology media and materials with students who have disabilities. Though easier said than done, getting communities involved in assisting and establishing projects, such as central technology centers that can circulate information and equipment throughout the state, pushes the use of assistive technology in rural areas and places where assistive technology has made few inroads. Unfortunately, federal funding for many of the state projects for assistive technology originally created with the Assistive Technology Act will be phased out starting in 2002, with all funding ceasing in 2004 (TSE, 1998).

Even though collaborative arrangements are beginning to blossom, Saks (1993) spoke of students who often had to give up computers when they graduated from high school and have not had access to the same technology that had previously given them independence. These students had been overlooked by state agencies. One reason for this might have been because the technology was not written into their transition plan. "An emphasis on lifelong learning and employment will force greater integration of services between schools and human service agencies for people with disabilities 18 years and older," Hales and Carlson suggested in an article by Saks (1993). In the same article, Patricia Corley, associate project director of the National Center to Improve Practice, said, "Some kinds of collaborative models are emerging in which state vocational rehabilitation agencies are working with schools. Perhaps together they can fund technologies to make the bridge work. People are aware of the problem and are starting to address it, but it's still a major problem. There needs to be more long-range planning and collaboration with families and state agencies" (Saks, 1993).

Another way to collaborate is cross-training on transition issues between schools, agencies, parent groups, and higher education (Guy & Schriner, 1997). Cross-training has been one of the most successful factors for change across evaluated systems change projects, helping to foster and enrich relationships between service providers and families, according to Transition Learning Networks. The involvement of collaborative training, planning, and the building of relationships such as these were among lessons learned to promote better support for student and families (Guy, Goldberg, McDonald, & Flom, 1997; Johnson & Guy).

Even as IDEA expanded IEP teams to include the students and community agencies with whom assistive services could continue, those agencies must continue the quality of life that assistive technology has brought to the lives of students while they are in school. Far-reaching and systemic changes do not come about quickly. It took nearly a decade of attention for transition policies, programs, and services to finally be included in IEP requirements (Furney, Hasazi, & DeStefano, 1997).

For agencies, employers, and other service providers to be aware of their legal responsibilities, to acquire the training necessary, to fund the assistive technology needed, and to finally put the whole thing into motion consistently and fairly will require persistent and best efforts. Practitioners must take a step beyond school, and make certain that the student retain the benefits of assistive technology as they transition to their next environments—the postsecondary education, work, independent living, and social contexts.

Similar Educational Strategies Involved in Transition and Assistive Technology

Self-Determination

Self-determination skills and strategies are essential to ensure that assistive technology benefits last throughout a lifetime. How will students know and demand what they need unless they are taught that assertiveness is a desired behavior instead of one that needs to be suppressed? Self-advocacy is a large part of what school personnel need to be teaching to prepare students for success (Field, 1996; Field, Martin, Miller, Ward, & Wehmeyer,1997; Szymanski, 1994; Ward, 1992; Wehmeyer, 1994; West & Penkowsky, 1994). IHEs also must play an important role in stressing self-determination as an important part of the curriculum for students with disabilities.

As the first generation of assistive technology users age (many who may now have many years of school services), their parents, guardians, and advocates may not be present in their lives. Moreover, as former students travel through their rapidly changing world, they need to know their rights and have the ability to make them known. Without training in self-advocacy, the potential for gains made through assistive technology may well fade away. Equipment may fall in disrepair, needs may change, job modification and adaptation may not occur, ongoing effectiveness of devices may not be assessed, and new and more advanced technologies may never reach the individual. An individual's rights and the struggle for access to technology are constant.

Much as one would like to believe that agencies, employers, and educators will always do what is necessary, in reality, one does not observe assistive technology consideration and provision as a part of everyday practice. This thread has yet to be woven into the everyday tapestry of society. Who will speak for individuals with disabilities when they leave public schools? A study by deFur, Getzel, and Kregel (1994) revealed that fewer than half of learning disabled students in the study even attended their own IEP meetings.

The concept of self-determination has often been referred to as empowerment. It is interesting to think of assistive technology and the transition process in light of the study by Lord and Farlow (1990). They found four themes that were common among people who were or considered themselves to be devalued, but who had begun to take control of their lives:

1. *Motivational trigger:* The participants all had some event or person in their life that caused them to take the first step toward control.

2. *Alteration in environment:* Most study participants had a change in venue that spurred them on.

3. *Consciousness of capacities:* As people felt more empowered, their awareness of their own capacities grew.

4. *Community involvement:* Finally, most participants mentioned that by participating in community activities they felt more empowered.

It is easy to see how assistive technology and the transition planning process could be a catalyst in each one of these life-changing events.

Similarities in Family Participation

The urgency and rationale for family participation in the planning process is a recurring theme in the both transition planning and assistive technology literature (Asselin, Todd-Allen, & deFur, 1998; Brotherson, Cook, & Parette, 1996; Love & Malian, 1997). Family involvement is perhaps the most important aspect of the selection of technology devices, because the impact and commitment is so great across *all* of the environments in which families and students interact daily and in their future. Yet, little research has been done that looks at the involvement of the family in terms of the time commitment, training, instruction, use, and overall benefits of devices (Parette, 1997). To facilitate planning with families, Inge & Shepherd (1995) have devised the following questions.

1. Do they believe that assistive technology is necessary?

2. What tasks do they want the student to accomplish or participate in with the device(s)?

3. Where does the student want to use the device(s)?

4. Do they have a gadget tolerance?

5. Do they understand how to use and maintain the proposed device?

6. If the student and family have used assistive technology devices before, what they did they like or dislike about them?

7. How and where did the student use the devices?

The relationship of the two fields of transition and assistive technology has never been more clearly and poignantly defined than in family participation in decision-making processes and in the establishment of relationships and links to services that will carry and assist the student over a lifetime.

The dreams of families who have a child with disabilities are not that much different than the dreams you and I have for our children. We want them to be able to play with other children, to go to school with them, to walk, to talk, and to grow up and have meaningful careers and happy lives. Unfortunately, many dreams are often tagged by professionals as "unrealistic, because even professionals do not have a handle on what assistive technology can do to make dreams of independence come true" (Armstrong & Jones, 1995). These authors refer to the planning process as one that must be established in a framework of team building to cooperatively "share, value and respect." Teams who work collaboratively with information about family dreams and values can prevent clinical decisions that do not make sense in families' day to day lives.

Professionals Today

Even in the 1990s people with disabilities are still not active participants in the American Dream. Young adults with disabilities are still among the poorest and most unemployed in the country (ACLU, 1997; Halpern & Benz, 1987; Love & Malian, 1997). Approximately 68% of individuals of working age who have disabilities are unemployed (Douglas, 1995). And in younger years, all too often adolescents with disabilities have found schooling too difficult, too discouraging. They drop out (Rusch & Phelps, 1987; USDOE, 1995), turn to crime, or sit unengaged at home (Edgar, 1988, 1991). People with disabilities are still seen as second class citizens, finding barriers (both attitudinal and structural) everywhere they turn. I. King Jordan, President of Gallaudet University, testifying before Congress in support of the proposed ADA, said, "There is not one disabled American alive today who has not experienced some form of discrimination. Of course, this has very serious consequences. It destroys healthy self-concepts, and it slowly erodes the human spirit. Discrimination does not belong in the lives of disabled people" (ACLU, 1997, p. 2).

Though technologies that can enrich the lives of people with disabilities exist, professionals in schools have much to learn about providing services. Professionals have just started studying the impact of assistive technology. Richard Wanderman is an example of a student who had little access to technology for much of his early school years. Wanderman talked about how his life with learning disabilities had been made successful through the use of computers. Sadly enough, Richard felt that very few school personnel "got it" enough to rework what was occurring within the curricula (Wanderman, 1997). On the difficulty of writing and the reasons that people with learning disabilities often avoid writing, Wanderman said, "When we do write with pen and paper, it's so difficult that we do it awkwardly, if at all, and we don't enjoy it. So we avoid it, and of course, don't improve. . . . It puts too much pressure on writers to have the entire thought they're trying to express . . . and get it right the first time." He went on to discuss the "elimination of dysgraphia through the keyboard," and the ease of making changes in his writing and to proofread. A "digital extension" of memory also proved helpful to him. These additions changed his life. Considering these tremendous benefits, Wanderman wondered why he spent most of his public school career without technology.

Reiterating the tone of the story above, the National Council on Disability (NCD) (1993) reported that assistive technology information did not get out to the very educational systems people who needed it most. The NCD reported that assistive technology information was fragmented and uncoordinated, difficult to find, and inconsistent. The report also said that "there is no system, public or private, uniquely devoted to the funding and goals of assistive technology to respond to the full range of unmet needs" and that "schools cannot carry the full responsibility of paying for the technology, as the child's world is much larger than his or her school hours five days a week." The study by the NCD (1993) also showed that the majority of people who might benefit from assistive technology cannot afford it and are not even aware that it exists. The report urged Congress to make changes in federal law to make it easier for consumers to get information and to be able to afford to buy assistive technology. Some of the more positive findings of the study included the following:

- Health problems decreased after using assistive technology.

- Approximately 44% of families were able to use child care or decrease the amount of parental care because of assistive technology.

- About 75% of school-age children were able to remain in regular classes, and 45% were able to reduce school-related services because of assistive technology.

- Approximately 92% of responders who held paying jobs said assistive technology helped them work faster and better, allowed them to earn more money, and made them less dependent on family members. (p. 224)

Findings like those listed above point out a very clear link between transition services and assistive technology. Both disciplines are headed toward the same adult outcomes: successful adult lives. For many young adults, the research suggests that working hand-in-hand with transition planning and assistive technology is simply the best way to get there.

A comprehensive look at the impact of assistive technology across individuals, family members, and environments has yet to be reported. Most studies have reported only the effects on individual users with specific needs, exclusive of other factors (Beukelman, Yorkston, & Dowden, 1985; Hutinger, 1994; Johnson, Baumgart, Helmstetter, & Curry, 1996; Mann & Lane, 1995; Scherer, 1993). However, a few reports suggested that family members have found reduced care demands because of assistive technology (Culp, 1987) and that they have seen their children develop more confidence, self-esteem, and independence (Parette, 1997).

Moving Forward

What do professionals in education have to say about what the future holds for the delivery of services to special education personnel? The Cosmos Corporation (1993), in cooperation with USDOE, OSEP and NSBA, conducted a 3-year project designed to (a) identify emerging issues and trends in technology; (b) investigate the evolving needs in special education; and (c) identify conditions affecting the interaction between technology and special education. The projects findings were reported in the areas of special education and technology. In sepcial education, the study found that:

1. Increasing demands on teachers will result in less time to integrate technology in the classroom;
2. The shortage of special education teachers and some related service personnel will reach crisis levels;
3. Paraprofessionals will have an increasingly important role in service delivery;
4. Increased longevity will result in expanded services for older persons with disabilities;
5. Special and regular educators will increase their collaboration; and
6. Outcomes for students with more severe disabilities will address functional life skills, rather than discrete academic skills.

In the technology, area, the study found that:

1. An uneven impact of technology will result in a greater gap between the "have and have nots;"
2. Sophisticated expert systems and other forms of artificial intelligences will find increasing application in education and training;
3. Major medical advances will result in memory recall;
4. New drugs will emerge;
5. Brain cell and tissue transplants will aid victims of retardation and head trauma;

6. Computer hardware will continue to become more portable (miniaturization) and wearable; and

7. Advances in genetic engineering will result in the eradication of some genetic disorders.

Interviews with parents, individuals with disabilities, and professionals across the country remind professionals that the major problem they face today is not primarily the research and development of new technologies, but instead the linking of already existing assistive technology solutions to the problems faced by persons with disabilities (RESNA, 1991).

Some of the practices reported by Furney, Hasazi, and DeStefano (1997) in transition practices could well be applied in the fight to keep high quality assistive technology services for the life span. One promising practice is raising awareness and buy-in to the values and belief system. This is a multifaceted approach that involves (a) caring and social responsibility and the need for community members to take care of and support one another (systemic level); (b) including students with disabilities in schools and instilling in communities the belief in the right of people to reach their potential, the right of people to have services, to really participate in life; (c) balancing initiatives with the realities of the local context; and (d) promoting responsibility and empowerment of individuals with disabilities.

Another promising practice involves following legal policies and links to several laws. This is not just a special education idea that belongs in public schools, and is often regarded as a good jump start as well as the right thing to do. Collaboration between agencies, schools, employers, and community is yet another promising practice. The hand-off approach, especially with sophisticated devices, will be much easier in a collaborative environment. An atmosphere of furnishing training, repair, vendors, adaptation and modification, materials, and general background information can prove invaluable.

The idea of building from the past to the present is an example of another promising practice. Professionals can share with communities and organizations how far the field has come, from a time when individuals with disabilities were "sentenced" to lives in institutions, nursing homes, and sheltered workshops—lives lived below potential—to a time where burgeoning technology can bring a much richer life, raise awareness and openness, and provide new opportunities for inclusion in our local communities. Finally, training or capacity building are promising practices related to transition and assistive technology. Professionals should use the human resources and leadership already available. They need to figure out ways to disseminate materials or videos. What could be more effective than showing a video to employers of an individual with a disability able to do a job using assistive technology? Or an employer sharing experiences about assistive technology successes with another employer?

Professional's success with integrating the use of assistive technology as a natural part of students' lives and their communities will be apparent by the extent to which students and young adults are participating in typical activities (Carney & Dix, 1992). The following recommendations are noted as areas of research or attention that could improve the integration and use of assistive technology to ease the transitions of individuals with disabilities across their lifetimes:

1. Studies that provide a *comprehensive* picture of the impact of assistive technology across all the domains of transitions and environments, interwoven with the effects upon families, caregivers, and service providers;

2. Certification programs for assistive technology specialists (RESNA, 1997; University of New Mexico, 1998);

3. Certification requirements for the hiring of assistive technology specialists in public schools;

4. Attention given to creative funding sources as schools and agencies struggle with assistive technology costs;

5. Guidelines for furnishing assistive technology to students with disabilities that are interpreted, supported, and enforced by state and local education agencies (Bell & Blackhurst, in press);

6. Centralized sources by local consortiums for technology information and the sharing of assistive technology devices that can be done reliably and conveniently;

7. Model for comprehensive planning for assistive technology across all of life's transitions (Brotherson & Goldstein, 1992; Parette, 1997);

8. Greater degree of collaboration between all agencies, family members, and all service providers to "examine and document perceptions and impact of assistive technology devices and services" (CEC–MRDD Board of Directors, 1996);

9. Much heavier emphasis on person- or family-centered planning and communication issues for assistive technology acquisition; and

10. Follow-up or longitudinal studies about what happens to the devices acquired by individuals in terms of updating devices, maintenance and repair, frequency of evaluations, continued appropriateness, and training needed by the individual, employers, and those who interact or furnish services.

Technologies of the Future

What looms ahead? The wildest fantasies of the 1950s could not have predicted how technology would assist people with disabilities, what with the medical advances for robotics, cloning, switches, spellers, word-prediction programs, voice-activated switches, voice-to-text and text-to-voice, and wireless technology. People who have no voices can speak. Workers who have mobility problems may choose to word at home or through telecommunications, video conferencing, e-mail, and the Internet, and they can be just as effective—if not more—than their fellow workers housed in offices.

For example, right around the corner is very sophisticated home automation, which will make independent living much less complex. Home automation will involve coding in lighting, your bath, operating curtains, entertainment, door locks, fireplaces, security, home appliances, all on one integrated and simple system. Van Hoes, owner of Radius Systems Integration in Lawrence, Kansas, believes that home automation will "be as common in homes as the automatic thermostat" (Cigard, 1997, p. 20). With voice recognition technology constantly being refined, it should not be too long before vocal commands will orchestrate homes of the future (Cigard, 1997). In fact, speech will become the major mode of human-to-computer communication, just as has been seen in science fiction for many years (Bork, 1997). Talking to a computer will be more natural than it is today and very similar to holding a conversation in the same room with another person. These innovations will remove the barrier of keyboarding for young children, those with disabilities, and those people who just cannot type.

More and more frequently, the major use of telecommunications is that of working at home. Yet, even though designed for easier, faster, and more efficient communication, telecommunications are not always accessible to people with disabilities. For example, voice mail, faxing, and remote computer use each pose unique barriers for different disabilities. As these technologies come into common use, so does the potential for inaccessibility. The good news is that there are organizations such as the Engineering Research Center on Universal Telecommunication Access, funded by the National Institute on Disability and Rehabilitation Research (see Appendix 10.C). The Center works in a collaborative way with other projects to make telecommunications accessible through six types of activities: (1) synthesizing information on issues, trends, and government policies regarding telecommunications accessibility; (2) design solutions; (3) universal design of access through computers; (4) telecommunication standards; (5) applications for independence; and (6) knowledge dissemination and utilization (Hohn, 1996).

No mention of the future of technology would be complete without mentioning the amazing power of the Internet, which has removed many of the formidable barriers relating to telecommunications that were prevalent just 4 or 5 years ago. The revolution in computers, from text to graphics, sounds, color, and movement has taken place in a startlingly fast period of time. Many tools affect job performance and provide a new freedom to workers with disabilities who either work at home or in traditional settings. But what about removing the barriers for the visually impaired? How is this being done today? Screen readers or alternatives have made advances. Screen magnification, spoken output, and Braille displays have sparked an evolution of products that can bring the screen's power to people with visual impairments as well. It is estimated that by the year 2010, 95% of all jobs will interact with computer technology in some way (Cambronne & Mundl, 1997). The 1992 reauthorization of the Rehabilitation Act of 1973, which developed guidelines for electronic and information technology and provided equal access for individuals with disabilities, made the ability to office at home instead of traditional settings an open path. Posting a résumé online, doing research and finding information about careers and new technologies are all a part of what Internet access can mean.

In another example of technological developments in our future, Joe Jacobson of MIT is working on a new way of letting people read and send information (Platt, 1997). One reason for this innovation is because some people just have trouble relating to a monitor on a desk, attached to a maze of wires. Mr. Jacobson poses this question: "What if . . . we could build a display that was so thin it seemed like paper?" Jacobson's display would mix data storage and portability, is reusable, and can send text and images from and to any digital source. The idea is an electronic book that could instantly erase and be ready for more data; an electronic book that aids multiple intelligence with a sense of touch, mapping the act of turning pages that assists people in remembering where in the text they are located. Moreover, this "book" would of course include text-to-speech ability. Imagine being able to access live and current information, research, and data from a user-friendly speaking book. For those who have mobility challenges, this kind of live and easy-to-handle information would be a very promising development.

Voice Recognition Technology (VRT) has also taken major steps. Though still in its infancy, VRT—the operation of a computer by voice—has already provided solutions to a host of barriers. VRT has become a great solution for bringing students with disabilities into inclusive classrooms. If the efficient operation of a computer could be entirely hands free and inexpensive, this would be a leap ahead for many people. Many tasks could be accomplished with this technology: networking, voice dialing, and working at home in a job such as digitally sorting and coding mail. One voice-controlled work station is part of the SuperSchool Exhibit by Ameritech. The station is Ameritech's vision of how technology can improve both the equity and the quality of education and access to jobs for people who have disabilities (Ruley, 1994). Ruley mentions a highly intelligent student with fine motor difficulty who was using a pencil to manipulate a keyboard and falling behind in college. After converting to a voice-controlled work station, the student became more successful. The ease of speaking her assignments into text instead of struggling with a letter-by-letter input made it possible for her to keep up with coursework. The process also helps dyslexic children advance more rapidly in both reading and writing, because they can "talk their ideas down" as a way of overcoming their inability to express their thoughts in written form.

An amazing study is being conducted by Theodore Berger of the University of Southern California. Berger is attempting to "unlock the brain's complex mathematical model" to bridge the gap between silicon and cerebrum (Greengard, 1997, p. 98). Berger said, "If we can speak to the brain in its own language then we begin to understand the biological basis of thought and learning." If scientists can understand the way neurons act and react in all situations, then they can go about building the technology to duplicate those functions and begin transmitting the right electrical impulses. This would give people the ability to restore physical and mental functions that were lost to strokes or trauma, epilepsy, or other disabilities. Berger's quest to build a bionic brain started with a fascinating question: "If brain tissue dies, can it be replaced with a small computer that sends the same signals . . . a bridge to restore the brain's full function?" Berger believes the team is about 5 years away from designing a brain implant for animals and about 10 to 15 years away from the first device for humans (Greengard, 1997).

Significant breakthroughs for people with disabilities also lie ahead, as described by Chriss Chinnock (1996) in *Wired* magazine. Investigators have used brain wave signals to control real-world objects. Chinnock stated that "users can play music, move computer screen cursors and interact with games, turn on appliances and even guide wheelchairs—all by controlling their brainwave patterns." It seems likely that the brain–body signals will "eventually be integrated into future human–machine interfaces, reshaping the way we interact with the world." Such interfaces may become especially important for people with disabilities in the environments of transition. Within a few years, specially tailored computer interfaces could allow disabled people to interact with their computers in ways never thought possible. In the experiments that are being conducted, brain wave signals are sensed through electrodes on the subject's head. The subjects are then trained to control through feedback the signals that their brain waves emit.

These are just a few examples of the technologies being developed. However, even with all the advances and promises that technology is bringing, many barriers are still evident. Some technology, though simple in its use and application, will remain too expensive. Some devices less costly may be too complicated and trainer-intensive to be readily used by people with disabilities. Educators, specialists, and advocates for these individuals need to stay informed and open to new technologies and to ways of teaching and guiding the transition into the 21st century. Professionals must keep in mind that the psychology is always much more difficult than the technology.

Assistive Technology Success Stories

The following cases illustrate how assistive technology has affected people with disabilities, allowing them to lead better lives and to achieve success in their schools, homes, careers, and communities.

 Mike

Mike was 17, dyslexic, and had Attention-Deficit/Hyperactivity Disorder. Mike was accepted into the DO-IT (Disabilities, Opportunities, Internetworking and Technology) program operated out of the University of Washington. Project DO-IT is funded by the National Science Foundation to retain students with disabilities into science, engineering, and mathematics academic and career programs. DO-IT also provides electronic mentoring from professionals in these fields for its participants, who are high school students with disabilities. This program allowed Mike to be accepted for who he was and to make the most of his talents through the use of assistive technology. Mike told his mother that students with disabilities had lived their "whole lives with inferior and inadequate equipment and if they can get the right technology there is nothing that can stop them in what they want to do with their lives." While in the program, people often asked Mike for his opinion and he was respected by staff. This allowed Mike to believe in himself. The responsibility that Mike learned and accepted for himself made him more responsible and gave him courage. On the way home from the university, Mike said that "he had made more friends in the past two weeks than he had in his whole life." It had always made Mike's mom's heart ache because he had never enough friends to have a birthday party. At the university, Mike celebrated his birthday with many friends for the first time (Lewis, 1994).

 Bill

Bill had a brain stem injury, which happened when a blood clot formed in the back of his neck, causing the oxygen to be cut off to his brain. This injury resulted in a total loss of muscle control, for which surgery will not help. For the past 3 years, Bill has only been able to communicate silently with his wife by lifting his left eyebrow. Until very recently, Bill spent his days looking out the window or passing time by watching television.

Things have changed with the funding of $20,000 to buy a special computer for Bill. With a computer tracking the movements of Bill's eye, the voice synthesizer says the words or phrases that Bill looks at on the screen. Before this innovation, Bill used his eye movement to indicate "Yes" or "No" as his wife pointed to hand-printed letters on a card-board sign. Bill is now using his eye movements, which are traced with infrared video to determine where he is looking to select words on the screen that the computer then pronounces. As Bill continues to practice, he is able to write notes and read, play computer games, and communicate his daily wants and needs. Bill's wife Edy says, "It could open up a whole new world for this man; he could hold a job" (Lamoy, 1997, p. B1).

 ## Anthony

Anthony, a student with cerebral palsy attending the DO-IT program at the University of Washington, was able to work for a computer factory that customizes computer systems for peoples' homes. He used a left-handed keyboard guard and a Liberator for communication (Burgstahler, 1994a, p. 6). The Liberator is a multipurpose, dedicated system used to augment communication with advanced synthesized speech, printer and computer functions (e.g., word and symbol prediction), prestoring messages, and symbol-scanning capabilities. The system can be operated by direct selection, joy sticks, head-stylus, and single switches.

 ## De' Al-Mohamed

Recreational activities are an important facet of a well-rounded life and are recognized as a major component of transition (Clark & Kolstoe, 1995; Halpern, 1988). De' Al-Mohamad, a student at the University of Missouri-Columbia, lost her vision about 3 years ago. Still, she had the best record on the university fencing team and published the fencing department newsletter. Competitive cycling, rock-climbing, and playing basketball (through the use of a goal-mounted beeper and bells inside the basketball) were among the activities she enjoyed. She used Braille and operated a computer with a speech synthesizer while majoring in human development and family studies. De' Al-Mohamad graduated and is in her first year of law school. During the summer she and four other students with vision impairment worked as legislative interns in the Missouri Senate, where most of their research was accomplished through computers and the Internet.

 ## Randy

Randy, another student scholar, talked of how his blindness caused great difficulty in obtaining information for both his academic and personal life before he was given access to a computer with speech output and the Internet. He said, "With Internet access, I have information right at my fingertips to study biology, computer science, and logical reasoning." But more importantly he added, "I have all of the information for school projects. I no longer have to get help from fellow students to do my research papers. In fact, a few have even asked me for help" (Burgstahler, 1994b).

 ## Cory

Even low-tech solutions can bring about amazing changes and independence. Cory was a young man with severe hearing impairment and in a class for students with mild mental retardation. Because of his impairment and unintelligible speech, his true abilities had been misdiagnosed. Prior to entering high school, Cory was in a self-contained classroom for Trainable Mentally Handicapped (TMH). When Cory showed up for class driving a car, the staff decided that the self-contained TMH classroom probably was not the least restrictive environment for Cory. Cory's only communication tool was his signing of a made-up language, which he used in a very primitive fashion with his family. He had little interaction with his family and did not even have a knowledge of common food names, probably because he was not allowed to eat with them. In fact, Cory got his food out of a vending machine at the school. At home, he had a room in the basement with a separate entrance. In his transition related program, Cory acquired a job at a local cafeteria. Working with job coaches and vocational rehabilitation, teachers at the Kansas School for the Deaf, and personnel at the cafeteria, the service providers were able to come up with a basic vocabulary, food names, and pictures of tasks to be done. Through funding through VR, the staff was able to obtain a TTY (a teletype machine used to communicate over the phone by typing) for Cory and obtain some supplemental security income (SSI) assistance. With these funds, a closed-caption TV and a visual alarm were purchased so that he could wake up in time for work. Cory was able to enjoy many of his meals in the cafeteria with his co-workers. As Cory grew in confidence, he began to communicate much more with his family, fellow-workers, and classmates. In fact, his classmates chose him to represent their class as class speaker on graduation night. Through the use of assistive technology, Cory spoke to a packed auditorium on his graduation night.

 ## Rich

Rich Hohn, who has polio, has broken through a wall that had literally crushed him academically. He first jumped years ahead academically with his head-stylus typing (a pointing device that aids communication by laborious selection). Later, as more advanced augmentative communication devices became available, he was able to inspire entire audiences through the use of a DynaVox. The DynaVox is a multipurpose communication system with Dec Talk synthesized speech, featuring a customizable picture symbol screen with categorized pages or layers, accessed through direct selection, single and dual switches, scanning, and joysticks. Rich now teaches art therapy to students with disabilities who can hear every instruction that Rich gives. Speaking well in front of audiences had been a 30-year-old impossible dream; now the dream has come true. Currently independent and settled in his community, Rich can do things like make calls to ask for refills, order dinner, and communicate with his wife. He often speaks in church, and demonstrates how he has overcome his disability to students and to school groups and at conferences (Hohn, 1996).

Assistive Technology, the Corporate World, and the Entertainment Industry

Assisted by technology, a wonderful partnership has been developed between medicine, the corporate world, and the entertainment industry to aid children and teenagers who are isolated and have little social development because of devastating illnesses and disabilities. Young people such as these have few opportunities to develop social networks and relationships, which are so important to transition planning and happiness. These are children who receive special education services as "other health impaired" and have a hospital/homebound special education teacher or are served in a hospital classroom.

As one provider, Sprint is one of the major players that has developed a video conferencing system along with a program called "Starbright" for students who are hospitalized long term. Steven Spielberg is a key player in this program; he lured the sponsors, donors, and media participation for this 3D virtual Eden project, which is complete with video conferencing and multiuser capabilities. Young people are able to play competitive video games, discuss common problems, establish relationships—all in real time—by means of the sophisticated technology made available in the hospital settings.

To get this project started, Lee Rosenberg, a senior vice president at William Morris Talent Agency and founder of Triad Artics, arranged a large luncheon meeting in 1993 for pediatric specialists and members of the entertainment industry, as well as representatives of companies like Broderbund and Microsoft, to find solutions to emotional and physical problems confronting critically ill children and teenagers. Eight hospitals are currently online, with more coming. Troy Aikman of the Dallas Cowboys has been instrumental in adding hospitals to the project.

An example of the benefits of the program are explained by a study conducted in a participating Los Angeles hospital, which measured the pain medication taken by children whose used Starlight Express Fun Centers (McCarthy, 1996). The participants in the study were children who could self-administer small doses of medicine by pressing a button on a pump. The study found that children not only "used less medication when using . . . the Express, but also in periods immediately before and after" (p. 237). The drop in pain medication use was between 50% and 80%. Asked about the importance of the benefits, General Norman Schwarzkopf, who headed up a campaign to raise 60 million dollars for the project, said, "I don't care whether there are measurable benefits, but as . . . far as I'm concerned, if we can cause one child to be relieved from the terrible suffering that they are going through, it's worth every nickel" (McCarthy, 1996, p. 237).

Schools and Learning in the Information Age

Technology in the information age can excite and enable its users in remarkable ways. Seven year olds can slay dark and evil forces on computer games; middle school children can graph polynomial regression; and high school students can produce movies and be part of a classroom thousands of miles away. In startling new ways, grown men can navigate the sailing ships of their dreams right from their armchair through virtual reality.

Imagine how this scenario plays our for a person with disabilities: a keyboard programmed with only the keys needed to perform tasks, or one that switches at a touch with little effort. Imagine a student who cannot talk but who suddenly can communicate with a new voice, or a teenager who thinks he or she is the only one in the world with a rare form of cancer, who can now video conference in real time with similar teenagers from all over the world. All of these possibilities now exist.

Something radical is afoot with the information age. Incredible amounts of information and communications technologies are or will soon be available. For example, it takes only 1 second for the entire *Encyclopaedia Britannica* to be sent over fiber-optic systems. People with disabilities can have equal access to this information without ever leaving their homes or classrooms, and without having to utter a sound. Moreover, physicians in far away and isolated communities can make a sophisticated, team-based diagnosis. Through the power of Tele-Medicine (a project between physicians at the University of Kansas Medical Center and the Kansas City, Kansas, School District), doctors and medical teams can communicate through video, voice, and computers with school nurses and sick or underprivileged children at their neighborhood schools to diagnose and prescribe treatment (Jones, 1996; Wheeler, 1998).

This new age has produced children and adults who expect information to be presented in many different ways. The information age produces new challenges for both regular and special educators. It is an age in which "frontal teaching" (i.e., lecturing styles, which now comprise roughly 88% of teacher activity) (Goodlad, 1993), will simply *not work*. It is a time for all educators to examine new ways to reach and teach their students, through a variety of learning styles, such as hands-on projects, multimedia devices, and student choices. It is a time when teachers need not be afraid to ask questions whose answers they do not know. It is a time for students to explore and analyze information without constraints.

What will our students coming out of information age schools know and be able to do? What will characterize educated people of the information age? Most likely, an educated person will be one who has the ability to find what is known, to think about what is discovered, to reflect upon changes, to explore, to share and debate, to question, to compare, to solve problems, and to contribute to what is known (Mecklenburger, 1993). If this defines the learner of the information age, then clearly the industrial-age school curriculum is out of date. The pedagogy of the current curriculum is nearly obsolete in terms of what students need to be doing in the future; the industrial-age school will not be adequate. In the information age, schools will be designed around the information tools available now, not the ones of the last century. Schools that have been organized around lectures, reading, and testing will instead be ones that use the tools of the information age effectively. These tools will include the traditional means of communication (e.g., pen and paper), but also cameras, graphics, recording, video editing, digital information, xerography, telecommunications, collaborative/teaming skills, assistive technology, and networking. The real power of these technological tools lies in their ability to cultivate interactivity among students and teachers who need not be in the same classroom or even on the same continent. The information age assures that the lines between community, school, and home will become fuzzy and grow dim. Learning will continue at home, in hospitals, and in far away communities through electronics. Indeed, schools may no longer be the place where most learning occurs.

In the schools of tomorrow, the mastery of material need not be the only measure of a student's education. There are many ways to get the solution or the answers needed for life's dilemmas. As students differ, so too will their ways to traverse each educational path. A student with a learning disability in writing will choose a much different path than a student gifted in writing. Technology not only gives students the flexibility to explore different paths, but gives professionals the flexibility to track these various paths, allowing each student to reach individual and desired destinations and outcomes.

The use of technology can provide efficient ways to incorporate authentic assessments, on-the-job evaluations, situational assessments, parent observations, and portfolio development. It has given professionals better ways to record, to manipulate, to display, and to review student direction and progress. It is now possible through technology to observe the process students use to make decisions, how they change their minds, and how they leap to discovery. The idea here is that teams (which include the parent and the student, along with teachers and service providers) assess how well the student has progressed and what the students should do next. In this way, education mirrors real life: Students will be allowed to work with different ages, different groups, and on different projects and ideas, just as people do in *real life*. Technology is the tool that allows professionals to view the students' education as a process, not as a subject-by-subject event. Most teachers and administrators realize that these new learning styles are much different from what they have been accustomed to. Technology enters this learning picture because it both excites and permits learners to learn individually and differently. Assistive technology allows the learner to not only have new access, but to concentrate, to pose their *own* questions, and explore their own responses to organized and good teacher-driven challenges. In this new age, teachers are the guides to islands of information that can be navigated and tied together by technology. As navigators and guides, teachers work alongside students to help shape their intuitions and to choose the right moment in which to stimulate new conceptual insights and answers. It is a horizontal way of teaching where—as in parenting—the best lessons are learned by letting go.

Technology is essential for the students, but it is just as important for teachers because it frees them from textual constraints and thus from linear boundaries. The only boundary becomes the teacher's imagination, even when teaching the Basics. This new breed of bold and brave teachers will not use curriculum that is pulled down from the shelf; they will dare to provoke questions to which there are no written answers. These risk takers will help to change the focus from how many hours or days of credits a student has, to what they can *do* and how their own particular skills have improved. These teachers' students will develop skills far refined beyond the basics, such as data synthesis, abstract thinking, and collaborative problem solving. The integration of new technologies into the curriculum will become as transparent and natural as the blackboards, microscopes, and compasses being used today.

Can teachers start viewing their schools as if they are being invented today, in their own time, and under their own protective eyes? Can they create new meaningful learning environments? Can they step back far enough to rethink the very foundations of what makes learning possible? If learning is the mission, then teachers will have to do better than the Basics. Education in the information age will incorporate technology as part of a solution to a system that needs both renewal and revitalization. In these schools of tomorrow, students with disabilities will learn and achieve alongside their peers in a seamless unitary system, accessing environments and information made possible through assistive technology. In our schools of the information age, *all* students—with classroom teachers at their sides—will travel down fresh new paths of inquiry and exploration, unearthing and using information to communicate artfully and well.

Appendix 10.A
Examples of Assistive Technology According to Need

Need	Examples of Assistive Technology
Positioning	Sidelying frames; walkers; crawling assists; floor sitters; chair inserts; adjustable chairs; wheelchairs; straps; trays; standing aides; bean bag chairs; sand bags.
Self-Care and Independent Living	Flashing alarm clock; adapted utensils; special designed toilet seats; aids for tooth brushing, washing, dressing, and grooming; clothes that open easily; robotics and electric feeders; hand controls for driving; lifts for vans.
Augmentative Communication	Symbol systems; communication boards and wallets; complex electronic communication devices (e.g., Liberator, Wolf); speech synthesizers; communication enhancement software; Kurzweil reader (translates the printed word through an optical recognition unit into a synthesized voice); speech-to-text and text-to-speech programs.
Environmental Controls	Remote control switches; adaptations of on/off switches to make equipment accessible.
Assistive Listening	Hearing aids; personal FM units; solid field FM systems; telecommunication devices for the deaf (TDDs); closed-caption TV; mild-gain hardware systems.
Visual Aids	Increasing contrast; enlarging images; making use of tactile and auditory materials; optical or electronic magnifying devices; low vision aids such as handheld spectacle mounted magnifiers or telescopes; closed circuit television read/write systems; cassette tape recordings; large-print books; Braille materials and type enhancers; computer screen reading adaptation such as enlargement; synthesized voice and refreshable Braille; scanners; optical character readers; reading machines; electronic note taking devices; Braille writers; copy enhancing in increase on contrast images; halogen or other lighting; visional stimulation devices such as light boxes; Kurzweil voice system, voice report, and voice recognition technology.
Mobility	Self-propelled walkers; manual or powered wheelchairs; powered recreational vehicles such as bikes and scooters; long white canes; electrical image sensors that

	provide information through vibration and telescopic aids; seeing-eye dogs.
Physical Education, Leisure, and Play	Drawing software; computer games; video games; computer simulations; painting with a head stick; interactive laser disks; CDs; adapted puzzles; beeping balls or goal posts; wheelchairs adapted for participation in sports; game rules in Braille or on audio cassette; balance or positional aids; swimming pool lifts; adapted sports and fitness/exercise equipment; adapted toys.
Computer Access	Input devices such as switches; expanded keyboards; mouse; trackball; touch windows; speech recognition; head positioners; keyguards; key latches; keyboard mediators (e.g., adaptive firmware card and electronic communication devices); text enlargement; synthesized speech or Braille; coordination with powered mobility, communication, and listening devices; environment control systems; environment control systems; computer-based instruction.
Curriculum Integration	Software for written expression, spelling; calculation, reading basic reason, and higher-level thinking skills; Internet for research and job-related activities.

Note. Adapted from *Has Technology Been Considered?: A Guide for IEP Teams* (pp. 1–3), by A. C. Chambers, 1997, Albuquerque, NM: CASE/TAMS Assistive Technology and Practice Group.

Appendix 10.B1
Request for Assistive Technology Services

Referral Information Packet

Student Name: _____   Date:_____

Sex: M   F   Age: _____   Date of Birth: _____   Grade: _____

School: _____   Teacher: _____

Current Placement: _____   School phone: _____

Parents: _____   Home phone: _____

Address: _____   Work phone: _____

Person(s) initiating referral: _____

Related Services Staff:

_____   _____
Name/Title   Name/Title

_____   _____
Name/Title   Name/Title

_____   _____
Name/Title   Name/Title

I. What is it that you would like to see the student doing that he or she is not doing currently?

_____

_____

Note. Adapted from *Technology for Educating All Children with Handicaps*, by TEACH Center, 1997, Shawnee Mission, KS: Shawnee Mission School District. Adapted with permission.

II. Indicate which communication system(s) the student currently uses (check all that apply):

___ change in affect (demonstrates likes and dislikes with facial expressions)
___ gestures
___ signs; how many? _____
___ few intelligible words; how many? _____
___ speech understood by familiar listeners only
___ speech understood by all
___ (nonelectronic) communication board/book

    The device uses:
    ___ representational objects   ___ symbols
    ___ photos   ___ letters/words
    ___ line drawings

___ electronic communication device

    Type: _____

    The device uses:
    ___ representational objects   ___ symbols
    ___ photos   ___ letters/words
    ___ line drawings

Describe other communication systems the student has used in the past.

_____

_____

_____

III. Indicate the type of motor response the student currently uses:

___ eye gaze   ___ extremity (which) _____
___ head movement   ___ other (describe) _____

_____

_____

Describe how student uses the above motor response.

_____

_____

IV. Check your reason(s) for referral:

___ communication
___ motor
___ other (describe) _____

_____

_____

V. Describe what the use of technology will enable the student to do. Will technology enable the student to do something new or more accurately or more quickly?

_____

_____

_____

VI. In which of the following areas do you feel the student could most benefit from assistive technology? (check all that apply)

_____ 1. Academic
           List specific skill(s): _____

           _____

           Is student at grade level? _____ yes _____ no

_____ 2. Social
           Does student interact with people in his environment?
           _____ yes (describe)   _____ no

           _____

           List reinforcers: _____

           _____

_____ 3. Recreation/Leisure
           What is of interest or pleasurable to the child?

           _____

           _____

           _____

_____ 4. Self-help/Independence
How would it benefit the student to be able to do things independently, whether at school, at home, or on the job?

_____

_____

_____

_____ 5. Vocational
Has a job setting been selected in which the student needs assistance? _____ yes (describe) _____ no

_____

_____

_____

_____ 6. Computer Use
Is the student familiar with: keyboard function _____ yes _____ no
position of letters _____ yes _____ no
The student uses:
_____ word processing _____ adapted or expanded keyboard
_____ single switch _____ software (list frequently used programs)

_____

_____

_____

_____ 7. Communication System
What would improve the student's existing communication system?

_____

_____

_____

Appendix 10.B2
Parent Information for
Assistive Technology Services

Parent Consent and Information Form

The TEACH Center (Technology for Educating All Children with Handicaps) provides services in assistive technology for Shawnee Mission School District students, staff, and parents. The TEACH program operates with a transdisciplinary team whose members integrate their areas of expertise to evaluate the unique abilities and needs of each student. Disciplines represented on the team include an occupational therapist, a speech–language pathologist, a vision and technology specialist, and educators. Working with the building staff and families of individual students, the TEACH Center team explores, implements, and evaluates technology solutions to meet the needs of students with disabilities.

Through the consultation process, one or more of the following may occur:

1. collecting data on the trial use of equipment or software;

2. training in the use of hardware of software; and

3. sharing of information regarding technology and resources.

Consent Form for a Technology Consultation

I hereby give consent for the TEACH team to provide consultation for:

_____

Student Name

_____   _____

Parent or Guardian Signature   Date

1. What is your child not doing now that you would like to see him or her doing?

_____

_____

_____

_____

2. Do you have a home computer? _____ yes _____ no

If yes, please describe: _____

_____

_____

_____

3. Describe other technology devices in use by your child.

In the home: _____

_____

_____

At school: _____

_____

_____

Note. Adapted from *Technology for Educating All Children with Handicaps,* by TEACH Center, 1997, Shawnee Mission, KS: Shawnee Mission School District. Adapted with permission.

Appendix 10.B3
Assistive Technology Evaluation Worksheet

This is a worksheet for your own use prior to initiating referral for Assistive Technology.

WHAT? 1. *What* will technology enable the student to do?
a. What communication system is currently in place?

_____

_____

b. What type of motor response does the student currently use?

_____

_____

c. Is your reason for referral communication or motor?

_____

_____

WHO? 2. *Who* will implement the technology training or evaluation? (Remember: The more individuals in the environment that support this endeavor the more successful it will be, and the more interaction between the educational team members the more successful the endeavor will be.) List the individuals committed to this referral:

_____

_____

_____

_____

WHEN? 3. *When* will the technology or the training evaluation take place? (Remember: Frequency of use is critical to success of this technology evaluation/training.) List the number of times through the day this technology will be in use:

_____

_____

_____

WHERE? 4. *Where* will the technology or the training evaluation take place? (Remember: Use across settings is critical to the success of the technology evaluation or training.) List the settings in which the technology will be used:

_____

_____

_____

HOW? 5. *How* will the success or effectiveness of the technology be assessed or evaluated? (Remember: (a) data collection is essential for decision making; (b) data collection must be in written form; and (c) data collection must be customized so that it is sensitive to the technology intervention.) Will you commit to record the data?

_____

_____

_____

Appendix 10.B4
Referral and Service Flowchart
for Assistive Technology

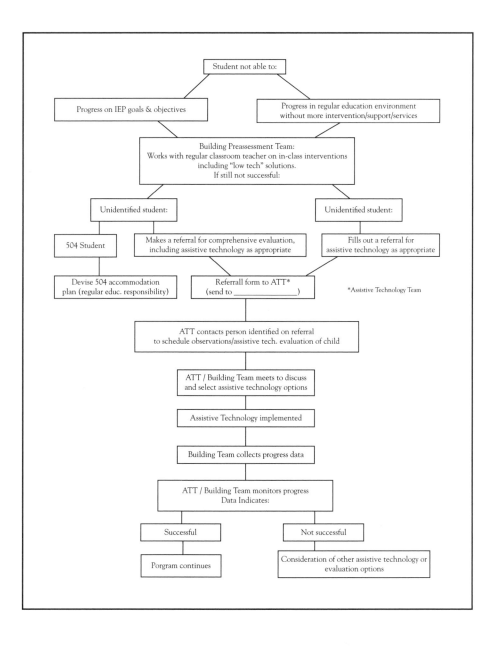

Appendix 10.C
Resource Organizations for
Assistive Technology and Transition

ATTAIN
Project Central Office
800-688-6790

ABLEDATA
Newington Children's Hospital
181 E Cedar St.
Newington, CT 06111
800-344-5405 (voice and TDD)

Alliance for Technology Access
1128 Solano Ave.
Albany, CA 94706
510-528-0747

American Speech-Language-Hearing
  Association (ASHA)
10801 Rockville Pike
Rockville, MD 20852
301-897-5700

Apple Computer
Worldwide Disability Solutions Group
20525 Mariani Ave.
Cupertino, CA 95014
408-974-7910 (voice only)

Center for Special Education Finance
American Institutes for Research
1791 Arastradero Rd.
P.O. Box 1113
Palo Alto, CA 94301
415-493-3550 (voice)
415-858-0958 (fax)
e-mail: jwolman@air-ca.org
web site:
    http://www.lists.air-dcc.org/csef_hom/

Consortium on Inclusive Schooling Prac-
  tices (CISP)
National Association of State Boards of
  Education
1012 Cameron St.
Alexandria, VA 22314
703-684-4000
703-836-2313 (fax)

DO-IT
College of Engineering/Computing and
  Communications
University of Washington
4545 15th Ave. NE
JE-25/Room 206
Seattle, WA 98195
206-685-DOIT

Equipment Exchange Network
800-437-7924
812-855-9396 (TDD)

HEATH Resource Center
800-437-7924 or 202-939-9320
e-mail: HEATH@ACE.NCHE.EDU

IBM National Support Center for Per-
  sons with Disabilities
P.O. Box 2150
Atlanta, GA 30301
800-426-2133 (voice and TDD)

Job Accommodation Network (JAN)
809 Allen Hall
P.O. Box 6123
Morgantown, WV 26506-6123
800-526-7234 (U.S. other than West Virginia; voice and TDD)
800-526-4698 (West Virginia; voice and
  TDD)
800-526-2262 (Canada; voice and TDD)

National Association of State Directors of Special Education (NASDE)
King Street Station I
1800 Diagonal Rd., Ste. 3290
Alexandria, VA 22314
703-519-3808 (voice)
703-519-7008 (TTY)
703-519-3808 (fax)

National Center to Improve Practice
Educational Development Center
55 Chapel St.
Newton, MA 02160
617-969-4529

National Christina Foundation
591 W Putnam Ave.
Greenwich, CT 06830
203-622-6000 or 800-274-7846
e-mail: ncfnasd@gteens.com

National Council on Disability
1331 F St. NW, Ste. 1050
Washington, DC 20004-1107
202-272-2004

National Information Center for Children and Youth with Disabilities
P.O. Box 1492
Washington, DC 20013
800-695-0285 (voice)
202-884-8200 (TTY)

National Institute on Deafness and Other Communication Disorders Clearinghouse
P.O. Box 37777
Washington, DC 20013-7777
800-241-1044 (voice)
800-241-1055 (TTY)

National Institute on Disability and Rehabilitation Research
c/o Macro International, Inc.
8455 Colesville Rd., Ste. 935
Silver Spring, MD 20910-3319
800-227-0216 or 301-588-9284 (voice and TTY)
301-587-1967 (fax)

National Transition Alliance for Youth with Disabilities
1875 Connecticut Ave. NW, Ste. 900
Washington, DC 20009
202-884-8181
202-884-8443 (fax)
e-mail: nta@aed.org
web site: http://www..dssc.org/nta

Rehabilitation Engineering and Assistive Technology Society of North America (RESNA) Technical Assistance Project
1700 N Moore St., Ste. 1540
Arlington, VA 22209-1903
202-857-1140 or 703-524-6686 (voice)
703-524-6639 (TTY)
703-524-6630 (fax)
web site: http://www.resna.org/resna

Technical Assistance Projects (TAPS)
(Contact the local Vocational Rehabilitation Agency)

Telecommunications for the Deaf
8719 Colesville Rd., Ste. 300
Silver Spring, MD 20910
301-589-3786 (voice)
301-589-3006 (TTY)

Trace Research and Development Center
University of Wisconsin-Madison
S-151 Waisman Center
1500 Highland Ave.
Madison, WI 53705-2280
608-262-6966 (voice)
608-262-8848 (fax)
e-mail: infor@trace.wisc.edu
web site: http://trace.wisc.edu

Appendix 10.D
Interdistrict Agreement for Instructional and Assistive Technology

<u>(Name of District)</u>

The (<u>Name of District</u>) in association with the Buddies in Technology Services (BITS) agrees to open enrollment in courses and workshops to the faculty of participating districts within the parameters of the following provisos:

1. Courses will be opened to participating districts on a "space available" option. First consideration will be given to (<u>Name of District</u>) faculty, then to administrators, and finally to support staff and classified staff.

2. A waiting list will be maintained by the district for those people from other participating districts who wish to take advantage of the class or workshop.

3. After a specified close of enrollment, interested persons from the waiting list will be notified with the option to enroll exists. Participants will be notified in the order of their original request.

4. No additional fees will be asked of enrollees other than those established by the district offering the course or workshop. The courses taken for college or university credit will have a tuition fee.

In reciprocal fashion, courses and workshops that are offered in the districts of (<u>Name of Districts</u>) will be opened to the (<u>Name of District</u>) under the same provisos.

The (<u>Name of District</u>), in association with the Buddies in Technology Services, also agrees to share specified technologies and media with special education staff under the following provisos:

1. All normal repairs would be assumed by the district owning the equipment. The recipient of the equipment would not be responsible for repair unless documented abuse of the equipment has occurred. The recipient would be responsible for loss or theft of the equipment if it occurred while the equipment was checked out to that person.

2. Directions for equipment operation and recharging will be included in each checkout. Recipients are expected to read and follow operating conditions.

3. First priority for equipment will be given to (<u>Name of District</u>) staff.

4. A waiting list will be maintained by the district for those teachers from other participating districts who wish to check out the material or eqiupment.

In addition, if our joint proposal for assistive technologies is funded, a loan bank would be established, to be operated under the following specifications:

1. The purchasing of equipment software and other resources would be a joint approval process by the administrative group (BITS).

2. Equipment and software requested for loan would be on an evaluation or training basis only. If joint requests coincide, priority for the requested item would be designated by BITS.

3. In the event that funding ceases, and no new funding source or plan of operation is secured, the loan bank's resources will be divided equally amongst the participating districts.

4. Olathe is designated as the lead agency in this proposal. The Olathe District has agreed to administer the budget, house the funded equipment, and maintain circulation responsibilities.

The (<u>Name of District</u>), in association with the Parents in Partnership with Professionals Project for Johnson & Wyandotte Co., agrees to open enrollment in courses and workshops to the faculty of participating districts within the parameters of the following provisos:

1. Courses will be opened to other districts on a "space available" option. First consideration will be given to (<u>Name of District</u>) faculty, then to administrators, and finally to support staff and classified staff.

2. A waiting list will be maintained by the district for those people from other participating districts who wish to take advantage of the class or workshop.

3. After a specified close of enrollment, interested persons from the waiting list will be notified that the option to enroll exists. Participants will be notified in the order of their original request.

4. No additional fees will be asked of enrollees other than those established by the district offering the course or workshop. The courses taken for college or university credit will have a tuition fee.

In reciprocal fashion, courses and workshops that are offered in the districts of (<u>Names of Cooperating Districts</u>) will be opened to the (<u>Name of District</u>) under the same provisos.

The undersigned agree to participate in this plan.

Signed: Date:

_____   _____
Blue Valley School District Supt.

_____   _____
Kansas City KS District Supt.

_____   _____
Olathe School District Supt.

_____   _____
Shawnee Mission District Supt.

References

American Civil Liberties Union. (1997). Disability rights. *ACLU Briefing Paper, 21*, 1–2.

Americans with Disabilities Act of 1990, 42 U.S.C. §12101 *et seq*.

Armstrong, J. S., & Jones, K. (1995). Using family dreams to develop meaningful goals involving assistive technology. *Closing the Gap, 14*(2), 1, 6.

Asselin, S. B., Todd-Allen, M., & deFur, S. (1998). Transition coordinators: Define yourselves. *Teaching Exceptional Children, 30*(3) 11–15.

Bell, J. K., & Blackhurst, A. K. (in press). National survey of state department of education assistive technology policies. *Journal of Special Education Technology*.

Beukelman, D. R., & Mirenda, P. (1992). *Augmentative and alternative communication: Management of severe communication disorders in children and adults*. Baltimore: Brookes.

Beukelman, D. R., Yorkston, K. M., & Dowden, P. A. (1985). *Communication augmentation: A casebook of clinical management*. San Diego: College Hill.

Blackhurst, E., Lahm, E., Harrison, E., & Chandler, W. (in press). *A framework for aligning technology with transition competencies*.

Blanck, P. D. (1994). Transcending Title I of the Americans with Disabilities Act: A case report on Sears, Roebuck and Co. *Mental and Physical Disabilities Law Reporter, 20*, 278–284.

Bork, A. B. (1997). The future of computers and learning. *T.H.E. Journal, 24*(11), 69–77.

Brinckerhoff, L. C. (1996). Making the transition to higher education: Opportunities for student empowerment. In J. R. Patton & G. Blalock, (Eds.), *Transition and students with learning disabilities: Facilitating the movement form school to adult life* (pp. 157–189). Austin, TX: PRO-ED.

Brotherson, M. J., Cook, C. C., & Parette, H. P. (1996). A home-centered approach to assistive technology provision for young children with disabilities. *Focus on Autism and Other Developmental Disabilities, 11*(2), 86–95.

Brotherson, M. J., & Goldstein, B. (1992). Time as a resource and constraint for parents of young children with disabilities: Implications for early intervention services. *Topics in Early Childhood Special Education, 12*, 508–527.

Burgstahler, S. (Ed.). (1994a). Anthony. *DO-IT News, 2*(2), 6. [Disabilities, Opportunities, Internetworking and Technology Project, College of Engineering/Computing and Communications, University of Washington.]

Burgstahler, S. (Ed.). (1994b). Randy. *DO-IT News, 2*(2), 3. [Disabilities, Opportunities, Internetworking and Technology Project, College of Engineering/Computing and Communications, University of Washington.]

Button, C. (1991). Policy in the making: Fast facts on individualized education programs. *Assistive Technology Quarterly: RESNA Technical Assistance Project, 1*(5), 5–6.

Call Centre. (1997). *Introduction to augmentative and alternative communication (AAC)*. Scottish National Resource and Research Centre [Online]. URL: http://call-centre.cogsci.ed.ac.uk/CALL-Research/AAC/AACIntro

Cambronne, D., & Mundl, J. (1997). Crossing the information superhighway. *Closing the Gap , 16*(2), 1.

Carl, D., Mataya, C., & Zabala, J. (1994). What's the big idea? *Assistive Technology Issues in School Settings*. Houston, TX: Region IV Educational Service Center.

Carney, J., & Dix, C. (1992). Integrating assistive technology in the classroom and community. In G. Church & S. Glennen (Eds.), *The handbook of assistive technology* (pp. 207–239). San Diego: Singular.

CEC–MRDD Board of Directors. (1996). Position statement regarding assistive technology devices and services. *MRDD Express* ,6(3), 9.

Chambers, A. C. (1997). *Has technology been considered? A guide for IEP teams*. Albuquerque, NM: CASE/TAMS.

Chinnock, C. (1996, November). Jacking In: EEG signals may be the next user interface. *Wired*, 4(11), 84.

Cigard, J. F. (1997, July/August). Homework. *Kansas City*, 20–23.

Clark, G. M., Field, S., Patton, J. R. Brolin, D. E., & Sitlington, P. L. (1994). Life skills instruction: A necessary component for all students with disabilities. A position statement of the Division on Career Development and Transition. *Career Development for Exceptional Individuals, 17*(2), 125–133.

Clark, G. M., & Kolstoe, O. P. (1995). *Career development and transition education for adolescents with disabilities* (2nd ed.). Needham Heights, MA: Allyn & Bacon.

Client Assistance Program, 29 U.S.C. §722(a)(6) (1991).

Content of the Individualized Education Program, 34 C.F.R. §300.346(a)(3) (1997).

Cosmos Update. (1993, April). *Identifying emerging trends in technology for students with disabilities*. Washington, DC: The Cosmos Corporation.

Culp, D. M. (1987). Outcome measurement: The impact of communication augmentation. *Seminars in Speech and Language, 9*, 169–184.

deFur, S., Getzel, E. E., & Kregel, J. (1994). Individual transition plans: A work in progress. *Journal of Vocational Rehabilitation, 4*, 139–145.

Developmental Disabilities Assistance and Bill of Rights Act Amendments of 1987.

Dillard, D. (1989). National study on abandonment of technology. *1989 annual report on the National Rehabilitation Hospital's Rehabilitation Engineering Center's evaluation of assistive technology*. (Cooperative Agreement No. H133E0016). Washington, DC: National Institute on Disability and Rehabilitation Research.

Douglas, R. (1995). Foreword. In K. F. Flippo, K. J. Inge, & J. M. Barcus (Eds.), *Assistive technology: A resource for school, work and community* (pp. ix–x). Baltimore: Brookes.

Dunst, C. J., Trivette, C. M., & Deal, A. G. (1988). *Enabling and empowering families: Principles and guidelines for practice*. Cambridge, MA: Brookline.

Edgar, E. (1987). Reflections on the transition initiative. In J. Repetto (Ed.), *School to work transition for handicapped youth: Perspectives on educational and economic trends* (pp. 63–70). Urbana-Chapaign: University of Illinois Office of Career Development for Special Populations.

Edgar, E. (1988). Employment as an outcome for mildly handicapped students: Current status and future directions. *Focus on Exceptional Children, 21*(1), 1–8.

Edgar, E, (1991). Providing ongoing support and making appropriate placements: An alternative to transition planning for mildly handicapped students. *Preventing School Failure, 35*(2), 36–39.

Education of Handicapped Law Report, 16, 1317 (1990, August 10).

Federal Register. (1991). p. 41272.

Federal Register. (1997, February 11). p. 6308.

Field, S. (1996). Self-determination instructional strategies for students with learning disabilities. In J. R. Patton & G. Blalock (Eds.), *Transition and students with learning disabilities: Facilitating the movement from school to adult life* (pp. 61–84). Austin, TX: PRO-ED.

Field, S., Martin, J., Miller, R., Ward, M., & Wehmeyer, M. (1997). *A practical guide to teaching self-determination*. Reston, VA: Council for Exceptional Children.

Fisher, S. (1992). *Inter-District agreement for instructional and assistive technology.* Overland Park, KS: Buddies in Technology Services (BITS).

Fisher, S., Magrone, D., Daugherty, J., & Walicek, C. (1994). *Expectations from regional technology providers.* Overland Park, KS: Buddies in Technology Services (BITS).

Flippo, K. F., Inge, K. J., & Barcus, J. M. (1995). *Assistive technology: A resource for school, work and community.* Baltimore: Brookes.

Furney, K., Hasazi, S. B., & DeStefano, L. (1997). Transition policies, practices, and promises: Lessons from three states. *Exceptional Children, 63*(3), 343–353.

Gardner, J. E., & Edyburn, D. L. (1987) . Teaching applications with exceptional individuals. In J. D. Lindsey (Ed.), *Computers and exceptional individuals* (pp. 273–310). Austin, TX: PRO-ED.

Golden, D. C. (1990). *It's the law: Now how do I do it?* Independence: Missouri Assistive Tech Project.

Golinker, L. (1996, October 16). *Special education law and related services: Medical needs and assistive technology.* Conference notes from The Kansas Association of Special Education Administrators, Lawrence, KS.

Goodlad, J. I. (1993). Technos interview. *Technos Quarterly, 2*(3), 5.

Greengard, S. (1997, February). Head start. *Wired, 5*(2) 98, 100, 102, 104–105, 217.

Guy, B., Goldberg, M., McDonald, S. E., & Flom, R. A. (1997). Potential participation in transition system change. *Career Development for Exceptional Individuals, 20*(2), 165–177.

Guy, B., & Schriner, K. (1997). Systems in transition. *Career Development for Exceptional Individuals, 20*(2), 149.

Hager, R. (1998, September). *Vocational rehabilitation (VR) agencies and assistive technology.* Proceedings of the Assistive Technology Conference, Topeka, KS.

Halpern, A. (1988). Transition: A look at the foundations. *Exceptional Children, 51,* 479–486.

Halpern, A. (1994). The transition of youth with disabilities to adult life: A position statement of the Division on Career Development and Transition, The Council for Exceptional Children. *Career Development for Exceptional Individuals, 17*(2), 115–124.

Halpern, A. S., & Benz, M. R. (1987). A statewide examination of secondary special education students with mild disabilities: Implications for the high school curriculum. *Exceptional Children, 54*(2), 122–129.

Health Resource Center. (1994). *Financial aid for students with disabilities.* Washington, DC: U.S. Department of Education.

Heidari, F. (1996). *Laboratory barriers in science, engineering and mathematics for students with disabilities.* Washington, DC: The George Washington University. (ERIC Document Reproduction Service No. EJ 527 715).

Hohn, R. (1996, October/ November). DynaVox makes my life and work easier. *Closing the Gap,*(15)4, 7.

Hutinger, P. L. (1994). *State of practice: How assistive technologies are used in educational programs of children with multiple disabilities. Final report for the U.S.D.O.E. Project, Effective use of technologies to meet educational goals of children with disabilities* (Report No. 180R10020). Macomb: Western Illinois University.

Individuals with Disabilities Education Act of 1990, 20 U.S.C. §1400 *et seq.*

Individuals with Disabilities Education Act Amendments of 1997, 20 U.S.C. §1400 *et seq.*

Individuals with Disabilities Law Report [IDELR], *19,* 355 (1992, August 22).

Individuals with Disabilities Law Report [IDELR], *20,* 1216 (1993, November 19).

Inge, K. J., & Shepherd, J. (1995). Assistive technology applications and strategies for school system personnel. In K. F. Flippo, K. J. Inge, & J. M. Barcus (Eds.), *Assistive technology: A resource for school, work and community* (133–166). Baltimore: Brookes.

Johnson D., & Guy, B. (1997). Implications of the lessons learned from a state systems change initiative on transition for youth with disabilities. *Career Development for Exceptional Individuals, 20*(2), 191–199.

Johnson, J. M., Baumgart, D., Helmstetter, E., & Curry, C.A. (1996). *Augmenting communication in natural contexts*. Baltimore: Brookes.

Jones, E. (1996, December). Cream of the crop: 10 outstanding telemedicine programs. *Telemedicine and Telehealth Networks, 2*(11), 24–41.

Judith Fein National Institute on Disability and Rehabilitation Research. (1996). A history of legislative support for assistive technology. *Journal of Special Education Technology, 13*, 1–3.

Julnes, R. E., & Brown, S. E. (1993a, July 15). The legal mandate to provide assistive technology in special education programming. *Education Law Reporter, 82*, 737–748.

Julnes, R. E., & Brown, S. E. (1993b). The legal mandate to provide assistive technology in special education programming. *WEST's Education Law Quarterly, 2*, 552–563.

Kansas Assistive Technology Project. (1993). *How to begin: A funding manual for assistive technology*. Parsons: Kansas Planning Council on Developmental Disabilities.

Kansas State Department of Education. (1997). *Kansas: A parent guide to Section 504 of the Rehabilitation Act of 1973*. Topeka, KS: Author.

Koshakji, A. (1997). *Focus on technology for the diverse workforce*. Report from the Technology for the Diverse Workforce Conference, Knoxville, TN.

Lamoy, A. (1997, January 13). It could open up a whole new world. *The Kansas City Star*, B1–B2.

Langton, A. J. (1990). Delivering assistive technology services: Challenges and realities. In A. T. Augustine (Ed.), *Proceedings of the southeast regional symposium on assistive technology* (pp. 1–9). Columbia, SC: Center for Rehabilitation Technology Services.

Lewis, R. (Ed.). (1994). Letter written to National Science Foundation by Mike's mom. *DO-IT News, 2*(2), 10. Disabilities, Opportunities, Internetworking and Technology Project, University of Washington, College of Engineering/Computing and Communications.

Logwood, M., & Hadley, F. (1996). Assistive technology in the classroom: Resources in technology. *Technology Teacher, 56*(2), 16–19.

Lord, J., & Farlow, D. M. (1990, Fall). A study of personal empowerment: Implications for health promotion. *Health Promotion*.

Love, L., & Malian, I. D. (1997). What happens to students leaving secondary special education services in Arizona?: Implications for educational program improvement and transition services. *Remedial and Special Education, 18*(5), 261–269.

Ludy, R., & Blunt, M. (1995). *Assistive technology resources building bridges for institutions of higher education*. Washington, DC: George Washington University. (ERIC Document Reproduction Service No. ED 380 016).

Malian, I. D., & Love, L. (1998). Leaving high school: An ongoing transition study. *Teaching Exceptional Children, 30*(3), 11–15.

Mann, W. C., & Lane, J. P. (1991). *Assistive technology for persons with disabilities: The role of occupational therapy*. Rockville, MD: American Occupational Therapy Association.

Mann, W. C., & Lane, J. P. (1995). *Assistive technology for persons with disabilities: The role of occupational therapy* (2nd ed.). Rockville, MD: American Occupational Therapy Association.

McCann, T. (1997, October 5). Doing it all despite disability: MU student doesn't use her blindness as an excuse. *The Kansas City Star*, B1–B2.

McCarthy, S. (1996, September) The good deed. *Wired, 4*(9), 171–175, 230–237.

Meadows, J. E. (1994). Guidelines for becoming an empowered family. *ATTAIN (Accessing Technology Through Awareness in Indiana) Fact Sheet #3*. Indianaplois: Indiana Family and Children's Social Services Administration, Division of Disability, Aging and Rehabilitative Services.

Mecklenburger, J. (1993). Two events to start a dialogue: The next generation of America's schools. *The Mecklenburger Group*. [Information letter sent out to interested individuals.]

Menlove, M. (1996). A checklist for identifying funding sources for assistive technology. *Teaching Exceptional Children, 28*(3), 20–24.

Morris, M. (1992a). Overview of the cost-benefit study on the financing of assertive technology for individuals with disabilities. *Assistive Technology Quarterly: RESNA Technical Assistance Project, 3*(3), 5–6.

Morris, M. (1992b). Policy in the making: The right to take assistive technology home from school. *Assistive Technology Quarterly: RESNA Technical Assistance Project, 3*(2), 5.

Nalty, L., & Kochany, L. (1991, Winter). Enabling technology for persons with mental retardation. *Spectrum*, 1–2, 4.

National Council on Disability. (1993). The financing of assistive technology devices and services of individuals with disabilities. *TSE, 8*(15), 224–225

National School Boards Association & the Office of Special Education Programs. (1997). *Technology for students with disabilities: A decision maker's resource guide*. Washington, DC: Author

Nelson, T. H. (1965, October 10–15). The hypertext. *1965 Congress of the International Federation for Documentation Abstracts*, 80.

Oddone, A. (1993). Integrating technology into the inclusive classroom. *Teaching Exceptional Children*.

Office of Special Education Programs (OSEP). (1990, August 10). *Letter on assistive technology to Goodman*. [Online]. URL: http://www.net/~plukmt/AT1.html#13

Office of Special Education Programs (OSEP). (1991, November 27). *Policy letter to anonymous*. [Online]. URL: http://www.ucpa.org/html/innovative/atfsc/spatnj.html

Office of Special Education Programs (OSEP). (1993, November 19). *Policy letter to ananymous*. [Online]. URL: http://www.ucpa.org/html/innovative/atfsc/spatnj.html

Parents Let's Unite for Kids (PLUK). (1997). *Family guide to assistive technology*. Billings, MT: Author.

Parry, J. (1996). *Regulation, litigation and dispute resolution under the Americans with Disabilities Act: A practitioner's guide to implementation*. Washington, DC: American Bar Association.

Parry, J., Rennert, S., & Zuckerman, D. (1996). Implementing the ADA's employment provisions. In J. Parry (Ed.), *Regulation, litigation and dispute resolution under the Americans with Disabilities Act: A practitioner's guide to implementation* (pp. 45–60). Washington, DC: American Bar Association.

Parette, J. P. (1991). The importance of technology in the education and training of persons with mental retardation. *Education and Training in Mental Retardation, 26*, 165–178.

Parette, J. P. (1996). Students who use augmentative and alternative communication (AAC) assessment and prescriptive practices for young children with disabilities: Preliminary examination of state practices. *Technology and Disability, 4*, 215–231.

Parette, J. P. (1997). Assistive technology devices and services. *Education and Training in Mental Retardation and Developmental Disabilities, 32*(4), 267–280.

Pesta, J. (1994). Assistive, adaptive, amazing technologies. *Technos, 3*(2), 10–12.

Platt, C. (1997, May). Digital ink. *Wired, 5*(5), 162–165, 208–210.

Reeb, K. G. (1987). *Private insurance reimbursement for rehabilitation equipment.* Washington, DC: Electronics Industries Foundation.

Reed, P. (1997). Wisconsin assistive technology initiative. In A.C. Chambers (Ed.), *Has technology been considered? A guide for IEP teams.* Albuquerque, MN: CASE/TAMS.

Regulation To Implement the Equal Employment Provision of the Americans with Disabilities Act, 29 C.F.R. §1630 (1991).

Rehabilitation Act of 1973, 29 U.S.C. §701 *et seq.*

Rehabilitation Act Amendments of 1986, 29 U.S.C. §701 *et seq.*

Rehabilitation Act Amendments of 1992, 29 U.S.C. §701 *et seq.*

Rehabilitation Engineering and Assistive Technology Society of North America Technical Assistance Project. (1991). *Assistive technology: A funding guide.* Washington, DC: RESNA Press.

Rehabilitation Engineering and Assistive Technology Society of North America Technical Assistance Project. (1992). *Assistive technology and the individualized education program.* Washington, DC: RESNA Press.

Rehabilitation Engineering and Assistive Technology Society of North America Technical Assistance Project. (1997). *Candidates' information bulletin* (4th ed.) [On-Line]. URL: http://www.RESNA.com

Reid, J. E. (1994). *All states survey of facilitating practices in special education.* Unpublished manuscript, Nevada Assistive Technology Collaborative, Reno.

Riviere, A. (1997). *Assistive technology: Meeting the needs of adults with learning disabilities.* Washington, DC: Academy for Educational Development and the National Institute for Literacy. (ERIC Document Reproduction Service No. ED 401 686.)

Rothstein, R., & Everson, J. M. (1995). Assistive technology for individuals with sensory impairments. In K. F. Flippo, K. J. Inge, & J. M. Barcus (Eds.), *Assistive technology: A resource for school, work and community* (pp. 105–132). Baltimore: Brookes.

Ruley, C. D. (1994, Summer). Do what I say! Voice Recognition makes major advances. *Technos, 3*(2), 15–17.

Rusch, F., & Phelps, L. (1987). Secondary special education transition from school to work: A national priority. *Exceptional Children, 53,* 487–493.

Sack, S., Clark, L., & Spellman, C. (1997). *Questions and answers for school administrators responsible for providing assistive technology devices and services to students.* Parsons: Kansas Association of Special Education Administrators and the Assistive Technology for Kansans Project.

Saks, J. B. (1993, September). Meeting student's special needs. *The Electronic School, 103*(2), 16–19.

Scherer, M. J. (1993). *Living in the state of stuck: How technology impacts the lives of people with disabilities.* Cambridge, MA: Brookline.

Sowers, J. (1995). Adaptive environments in the workplace . In K. F. Flippo, K. J. Inge, & J. M. Barcus (Eds.), *Assistive technology: A resource for school, work and community* (pp. 167–185). Baltimore: Brookes.

Szymanski, E. M. (1994). Transition: Life-span and life-space considerations for empowerment. *Exceptional Children, 60,* 401–410.

TEACH Center. (1997). *Technology for educating all children with handicaps.* Shawnee Mission, KS: Shawnee Mission School District.

Technology-Related Assistance for Individuals with Disabilities Act of 1988, 29 U.S.C. §2201 *et seq.*

Technology-Related Assistance for Individuals with Disabilities Amendments of 1994, 29 U.S.C. §2201 *et seq.*

University of New Mexico. (1998). *Research institute for assistive and training technologies* (RIATT). [Online]. URL: http://www.unm.edu/~riatt/

U.S. Department of Education. (1995). *To assure the free appropriate public education of all children with disabilities: 17th annual report to Congress on the implementation of Individuals with Disabilities Education Act.* Washington, DC: Author.

Wall , T. (1994, March). Staff development tips: Supporting inclusion with technology. *Electronic Learning, 103(7)*, 34.

Wall, T., & Siegel, J. (1994, March). All included: Inclusion of special education children in regular classrooms cannot happen without technology. *Electronic Learning, 103(7)*, 24–34.

Wallace, J. F. (1995). Creative financing of assistive technology. In K. F. Flippo, K. J. Inge, & J. M. Barcus (Eds.), *Assistive technology: A resource for school, work and community* (pp. 245–260). Baltimore: Brookes.

Wanderman, R. (1997). *How computers change the writing process for people with learning disabilities* [Online]. URL: http://www.ldonline.org

Ward, M. J. (1992). OSERS initiative on self-determination. *Interchange, 12(1)*, 1.

Wehmeyer, M. L. (1994). Perceptions of self-determination and psychological empowerment of adolescents with mental retardation. *Education and Training in Mental Retardation and Developmental Disabilities, 29(1)*, 9–21.

West, L., & Penkowsky, L. (1994). Special problems for rural youth and urban youth in transition. In A. Pautler, Jr. (Ed.), *High school to employment transition: Contemporary issues.* Ann Arbor, MI: Prakken.

Wheeler, T. (1998). Urban kids receive telemedical care at school. *Telemedicine Today, 6(2)*, 6.

Williams, R. R. (1990). Working for assistive technology systems change. *Assistive Technology Quarterly: RESNA Technical Assistance Project, 1(4)*, 1–3.

Zobrest v. Catalina Foothills Sch. Dist., 113 S. Ct. 2462 (1993).

CHAPTER

VOCATIONAL EVALUATION

Pamela J. Leconte

"There is something that is much more scarce, something finer far, something rarer than ability. It is the ability to recognize ability."

—Elbert Green Hubbard

Terms and Definitions

It is necessary to spend some time defining vocational evaluation because the term and services are so often misinterpreted or misunderstood. The term *vocational evaluation* refers to the services, methods, and practices included in the vocational assessment. Vocational evaluation represents a culminating assessment service process within a hierarchy of options. The generic term, *vocational assessment*, involves many professionals and laypersons as data collectors and can be defined simply as gathering information to make vocational and career decisions.

Vocational assessment serves as the umbrella term for several assessment options and is defined as

> a comprehensive process conducted over a period of time, usually involving a multidisciplinary team . . . with the purpose of identifying individual characteristics, education, training, and placement needs, serving as a basis for

planning an individual's educational program and which provides the individual with insight into vocational potential. (Dowd, 1993, p. 14)

Vocational assessment involves three levels of service intensity and comprehensiveness:

1. *Level I, Screening:* This usually provides a summary of existing, vocationally relevant information about an individual, and consists of data gathered from special educators or other direct service providers, informal interviews with the individual, interviews or conferences with parents or family members, and prevocational information from teachers, employers, or significant others. The information collected pertains to interest, aptitude, learning preferences, achievement information, and educational and social history from a review of cumulative records. If satisfactory conclusions cannot be made, more in-depth assessment is recommended and students participate in the next level of service to determine career goals and vocational planning.

2. *Level II, Exploration:* This involves collecting additional vocationally relevant information from administering interest inventories, learning style assessments, aptitude tests, work samples, and work experience or vocational classroom try-outs, observation of behavior, job-readiness assessment, student interviews, and teacher input. Data can be collected by teachers, direct service providers, or vocational evaluators. Determining levels of career maturity and career aspirations are included in data collection. Again, if planning cannot proceed due to insufficient information, students are referred to the most in-depth assessment process—vocational evaluation.

3. *Level III, Vocational Evaluation:* This is a comprehensive vocational assessment process which requires that additional data be collected using the following methods or activities: review of medical, psychological, educational, and social information; formal testing instruments; work samples; exploratory vocational course or job tryouts; and observation of work behavior, community-based assessments (e.g., situational assessments, on-the-job evaluations), informal teacher assessments, and others. Again, interest, career goals, learning styles, temperaments, vocational needs, aptitudes, and compatibility with various career and work attributes are identified (Leconte, 1994a, p. 37). Data are preferably collected by vocational evaluators.

Figure 11.1 depicts the flow of and various options contained in vocational evaluation services.

Vocational evaluation is further defined as

a comprehensive process that systematically uses work either real or simulated, as the focal point for assessment and vocational exploration, the pur-

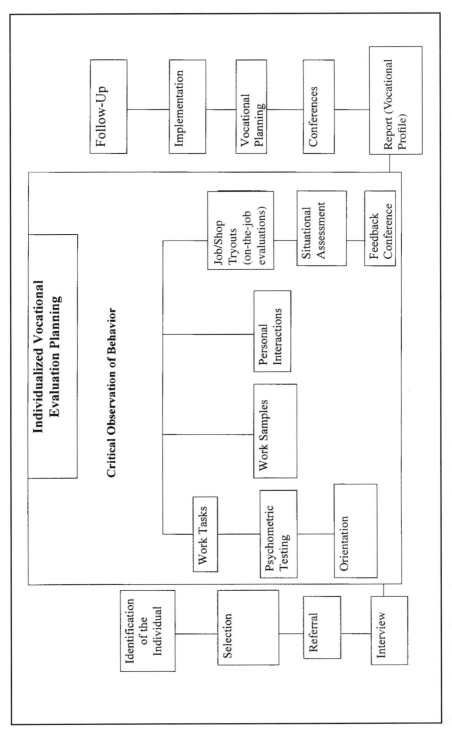

Figure 11.1. The Comprehensive vocational evaluation process.

pose of which is to assist individuals in vocational development. Vocational evaluation incorporates medical, psychological, social, vocational, educational, cultural, and economic data into the process to attain the goals of evaluation. (Dowd, 1993, p. 14)

All or a variety of assessment methods, as cited in the previous levels, are used to construct a vocational profile. The data contributions of other professionals (e.g., job trainers, psychologists, social workers, physicians, occupational therapists) are synthesized into the profile and recommendations for planning. If a school or agency provides all of the options contained in Figure 11.1 in a coordinated and systematic way, then that agency provides the third level of vocational assessment. Clearly, the completion of vocational evaluation depends upon input from many sources. Collaborative and interdisciplinary efforts are necessary to glean information from anyone involved with or concerned with the student. This information is then integrated and synthesized to ensure that the student and evaluator make realistic and feasible recommendations for future planning.

Vocational evaluation is typically conducted only one or two times in an individual's lifetime and is a time-limited service with a well-defined beginning and ending (Thomas, 1991). Many national professional associations subscribe to these categories and definitions. The Vocational Evaluation and Work Adjustment Association (VEWAA) devised the definitions to represent a building block approach to services. Screenings are needed most often and in greater numbers than are exploratory services. The information from screening forms the basis for the next exploratory assessment. The cumulative data from the first two levels can be used as starting points for the third level so as not to duplicate services. The level framework was devised as a time and cost-saving process so that the most comprehensive and costly services—vocational evaluation—are reserved for the few who need them most (VEWAA, 1975).

Stodden (1986), referring to services for secondary education, offered a clear delineation between assessment and evaluation by likening assessment and evaluation to formative and summative program evaluation terminology. He defined vocational assessment as "the collection of data/information contributing to a description of a person's performance in a career/vocational program or the world of work" (p.68). He then described "vocational evaluation as the process of reviewing/interpreting assessment information to provide meaning and significance in placement and programming decisions" (p.68). Vocational evaluation also involves utilizing data from real or simulated vocational education or work experiences.

Vocational evaluators are those professionals who coordinate and conduct both formative and summative functions. They are professionals who have special training or experience, who are eligible for certification or are "Certified in Vocational Evaluation" (CVE) (Commission on Certification of Work Adjustment and Vocational Evaluation Specialists, 1996), and who consider themselves members of the vocational evaluation profession. Some school systems call these professionals vocational assessment specialists. Vocational evaluation services are in high demand but available services are in short supply, in part because there are not enough qualified and certified professionals. Thus, many school personnel struggle to construct assessment that appropriately serves students with severe and unique needs. Vocational evaluators are able to coordinate and conduct all three levels of assessment and it is preferred that other professionals perform only the first two levels. In addition to schools, evaluators provide services in diverse settings, such as correctional institutions, hospitals, career centers, vocational rehabilitation agencies, postsecondary institutions, job training and welfare-to-work programs, worker's compensation systems, and industry.

Establishing a Common Frame of Reference

Overview of Vocational Evaluation and Assessment

Vocational assessment has been called the critical beginning point for transition planning and services (Leconte & Neubert, 1997; Rothenbacher & Leconte, 1990). A variety of professionals and laypeople can collect vocational assessment information that is relevant for assisting students in their vocational preparation, career development, and transition planning (Green, 1992; Smith et al., 1995). As the terms and definitions discussed earlier indicate, vocational assessment denotes a broad term that refers to vocationally and career-related content. The most comprehensive and intensive type of vocational assessment is vocational evaluation—the focus of this chapter. Preferably, the vocational evaluation process should be conducted by qualified vocational evaluators—professionals who are trained to collect, synthesize, and interpret complex and vocational assessment information. However, due to shortages of qualified personnel, often educators are given this responsibility.

Services for Persons with Greatest Needs

Originating as a unique and specialized human service in the 1950s and 1960s, vocational evaluation was designed as an experientially based assessment alternative to serve people with disabilities and others who faced vocational and employment challenges. The typical paper-and-pencil testing involved in most vocational assessment offerings did not yield sufficient information for career planning. People participate in vocational evaluation to acquire vocationally related self-knowledge, to learn about various vocational, employment, educational, and community options, and, finally, to make satisfactory matches between their personal attributes and various options for achieving successful employment and a desirable quality of living (Leconte, 1994a; Nadolsky, 1969). To provide meaningful services, vocational evaluators work in partnership with the students and others (e.g., teachers, parents, employers, counselors) to facilitate students' abilities to make informed choices about desired educational, vocational, and employment goals and requisite steps to achieve them (Leconte & Neubert, 1987; Thomas, 1997).

Certain components of vocational assessment have been available to secondary students since the advent of guidance counseling in schools. However, often students with disabilities were and still are excluded from even the most cursory assessment activities for several reasons. One reason frequently given for this exclusion regards the greater challenges and the greater needs these students face, along with the inadequacy of resources and personnel to address them. Experientially based vocational evaluation was created as an alternative to traditional vocational assessment services—which relied heavily on standardized testing—so that individuals with disabilities could acquire critical information about their plans and futures just as others did (Nadolsky, 1971, 1981). Since the 1970s, some school systems have provided versions of the vocational assessment levels, including vocational evaluation services for students with disabilities and other special needs (Maryland State Department of Education, 1972, 1977, 1984; Neubert, 1986). These specially designed services were initiated primarily through federal and state vocational education funds (Leconte & Neubert, 1987; Neubert, 1986). Most of these programs were modeled after services provided within vocational rehabilitation agencies. However, professionals eventually adapted and altered services to meet the unique needs of adolescents within educational—especially vocational education—contexts (Neubert, 1986).

Vocational Evaluation Is a Component of Transition Services

Many assessment strategies used for transition originate from vocational evaluation and assessment methods. In fact, some professionals are calling these adapted, newer techniques transition assessment approaches (Sitlington, Neubert, Begun, Lombard, & Leconte, 1996; Sitlington, Neubert, & Leconte, 1997). Because transition assessment is becoming a popular term and service process, some professionals fear that educators and related service personnel will lose sight of the distinct benefits and differences that distinguish broad transition goals from more focused vocational ones.

The Division on Career Development and Transition (DCDT, formerly the Division on Career Development) posits that transition assessment encompasses several types of assessment, including vocational assessment and evaluation (Sitlington et al., 1997). DCDT's stance expands an earlier position statement, which defined career assessment as including vocational assessment and evaluation (Sitlington, Brolin, Clark, & Vacanti, 1985). Although vocational evaluation and assessment can be subsumed within career and transition assessment, vocational evaluation represents finite vocational and work-oriented approaches. Individuals who participate in career development and transition processes may—or may not—need concentrated vocational evaluation services.

Vocational assessment and evaluation services differ from transition assessment. In the transition context, assessment extends beyond the vocational context and includes issues such as identifying students' support networks of family and friends (those who can help them move from one environment to another with ease), community participation activities, leisure and recreation needs, and residential living arrangements. Vocational assessment and evaluation address these areas, but they do so only regarding their relationship to and implications for career aspirations and vocational planning. Transition assessment tends to glean information primarily from "school-based, family-centered, and student-initiated activities" (Clark & Patton, 1997, p. 2), whereas vocational assessment and evaluation target information gathering within the career, vocational education, and employment realms both in school and beyond. Of course, transition assessment and vocational assessment overlap, and they both require specialized skills on the part of professionals. However, responsibility for transition assessment tends to fall to special educators or transition specialists to coordinate, while vocational evaluation is best conducted by trained specialists, such as school-related service personnel (e.g., vocational evaluators) or those who work outside the schools (e.g., personnel from vocational rehabilitation). Often, special educators and vocational educators find themselves responsible for vocational assessment, but they consistently voice concern about their lack of knowledge and skills (deFur, 1990; Stewart, 1997; Taymans & deFur, 1994).

Vocational evaluation represents intensive services that are beneficial for individuals who face the most daunting challenges (Leconte, 1994a; Nadolsky, 1971, 1981; Sitlington et al., 1997). Nadolsky (1971, 1981) and the VEWAA (1975) estimate that approximately 12% to 15% of people in special needs groups require vocational evaluation. This also holds true for secondary students, in that a small percentage require the more costly services, whereas most high school students can suffice with surveys of interests, aptitudes, teacher ratings, and interviews to identify educational and career aspirations (Nadolsky, 1981). These activities are sufficient to direct them toward achieving their goals. Others who have not clarified their dreams and goals may require expanded assessment.

Some students may not have clear ideas about their vocational futures, whereas others have vocational aspirations that are not commensurate with their skills and abilities. These students have greater needs when their disabilities and societal barriers are taken into consideration. These students make up that 12% to 15% group for whom vocational evaluation services might be necessary.

Vocational assessment as a targeted transition service has gained popularity in secondary and postsecondary schools because students with disabilities have not been well served by traditional methods. Policy makers have begun to understand that appropriate and meaningful planning cannot occur unless it is connected to individualized and holistic assessment information. The advent of transition planning as a requirement in special education law has underscored this understanding. To facilitate the transition process, policy makers have expanded mandates for preplanning assessment beyond the rehabilitation process. For decades, the Rehabilitation Act of 1973 and subsequent amendments have required vocational assessment and evaluation for development of Individualized Written Rehabilitation Plans (IWRPs). Now, many laws include an assessment process on which to construct individualized plans (e.g., Job Training Partnership Act Amendments of 1992, [P.L. 102-367]). The goal of including assessment for planning intends that students with disabilities and other special needs make the seamless transitions from school to postsecondary education, employment, and adult living.

Other laws that include assessment in some form provide resources for assessment services or support such services and activities permitted under the Individuals with Disabilities Education Act (IDEA) of 1990 (P.L. 101-476) and the recent IDEA Amendments of 1997 (P.L. 105-17). Two such statutes are the Carl D. Perkins Vocational and Applied Technology Education Act of 1990 (P.L. 101-392) and the School-to-Work Opportunities Act of 1994 (P.L. 103-239). Services allowed under these laws can work in tandem with the IDEA mandated transition planning requirements. The Americans with Disabilities Act (ADA) of 1990 (P.L. 101-336) reinforces that assessment should be equitable and appropriate for people, including students, with disabilities. Finally, policies are beginning to provide mechanisms for coordinating services in and among disciplines.

These laws establish means for interdisciplinary collaboration, particularly in assessment and transition processes. The reciprocal cross-referencing of legislation buttresses the need for interdisciplinary collaboration among special educators, vocational evaluators, and others. An example of improved interagency policy is illustrated by the "use of records" clause in the Rehabilitation Act Amendments of 1992. This clause attempts to eliminate duplication and reduce the waiting time and expense for students who are referred for vocational rehabilitation services. The Rehabilitation Amendments suggest that reassessments are not needed to gain access to rehabilitation services if students have up-to-date Individual Education Plans (IEPs), including transition objectives, which are based on *current* assessment data and documentation of their disabilities. Documentation is most likely to be accepted when it includes specific—in functional terms—strengths, needs, and preferences. The Rehabilitation Amendments also provide a presumption of benefit clause, which was devised to eliminate the extensive waiting periods that students with severe disabilities faced when trying to gain access to services. This clause allows the use of records and allows students to forego extended evaluation periods that often required extensive waiting time to schedule.

Who Provides Vocational Evaluation Services?

The DCDT (Sitlington et al., 1997) and the Interdisciplinary Council on Vocational Evaluation and Assessment (Smith et al., 1995) endorse the idea that vocational evaluation services should be provided by qualified professionals who are specially trained or experienced. Preferably, these personnel are "certified in vocational evaluation" (CVE) by the national credentialing body, the Commission on Certification of Work Adjustment and Vocational Evaluation Specialists (CCWAVES) (Leconte et al., 1993; Sitlington et al., 1997). The DCDT position also states that transition assessment responsibilities fall to a variety of interdisciplinary personnel, including students themselves, families, and others interested or involved in the students' lives. One type of professional who could oversee and conduct assessment for transition purposes is called as a "Certified Career Assessment Associate" (CCWAVES, 1997).

In 1997, CCWAVES established a second assessment certification process. This one was designed for personnel who may not have attained the same education degrees as CVEs or who may not have had the breadth or length of experience that CVEs have had. Adoption of the "Certified Career Assessment Associate" (CCAA) certification designation by state education agencies and community-based programs could help ensure that assessment personnel have met minimal competency standards and will provide more consistent high-quality services. In fact, the designation was created for these purposes and to increase the pool of professionals who can perform more in-depth assessment duties. Transition specialists who possess the necessary assessment skills could qualify for CCAA certification.

The vocational evaluation profession has evolved from several established disciplines, such as psychology, industrial engineering, and medicine (Couch, 1973; Leconte, 1994a, 1994b). These multidisciplinary origins help facilitate use of vocational evaluation services in many different settings. Because much of the original jargon and terminology remain in vocational evaluation, many trained vocational evaluators or assessment specialists feel comfortable interacting with professionals from other disciplines. For example, most evaluators discuss results of educational testing with ease and they are equally familiar using methods of time and motion studies conducted by industrial engineers.

This does not preclude the problems that vocational evaluators may experience when trying to cooperate and collaborate with others. Vocational evaluators can encounter difficulties with interdisciplinary effort at the front and back ends of the vocational evaluation process. For instance, vocational evaluators frequently feel they cannot take time to consult with referral sources, such as a special education teacher or counselor. Yet by not doing so, they are jeopardizing their findings, which will be incomplete and may be inaccurate. Often, their efforts to apply vocational evaluation findings and recommendations to other services such as transition are thwarted. For example, many vocational evaluators are not invited to or are excluded from IEP planning meetings (B. D. Busie, personal communication, 1996; I. H. Willey, personal communication, 1994; Neubert, 1986). It is left to others to interpret and connect findings to transition planning. This oversight is especially prevalent for vocational evaluators who work outside the school system.

It is fair to estimate that most local education agencies do not employ vocational evaluators, particularly ones who are trained. Thus, a large percentage of students with disabilities receive vocational evaluation services from community service agencies. Within communities, services may be purchased and provided by rehabilitation counselors, job training counselors, job development and placement specialists, or vocational evaluators. These professionals are usually employed by state–federal rehabilitation agencies, community rehabilitation programs, job training partnership services, or agencies in the developmental disability service system. These resources serve as the foundation of vocational assessment and evaluation services for young people with disabilities. However, most states do not require certification or licensure for personnel employed in these programs. This results in services of inconsistent quality. Though well meaning, these assessors sometimes jeopardize positive outcomes or feasible planning guides for students. The model situation involves a variety of people serving as data gatherers, who then relay findings to the vocational evaluator to synthesize into useful profiles and recommendations. Ideally, the data gatherers, including students, are all members of the interdisciplinary team, the members of which are responsible for transition planning and monitoring. Though the process runs more smoothly when the evaluator-coordinator is employed by the school system, such employment is not necessary if all members of the transition planning team are committed to working collaboratively.

Traditional Roles

Vocational evaluators, like school psychologists, occupational therapists, and others, "demonstrate an exclusivity of skill and practice which separates them from other rehabilitation, education, and allied health personnel" (Ayella & Leconte, 1987, p. 20). Vocational evaluators are distinguished, in part, by their integrated knowledge of occupations and work requirements, by their abilities to analyze work into elements that match personal attributes of individuals seeking work, and by their skills for "synthesizing the personal and environmental data of individuals into vocationally relevant information," (Ayella & Leconte, 1987, pp. 20–21). Knowledge of community resources and services is considered essential for evaluators because they often serve as referral and information specialists. Their need for this information arises when they have to locate more appropriate services for people who may not gain maximum benefit from vocational evaluation services at the time, or when they are researching possible postevaluation recommendations for students to pursue.

Certain perceptions by some vocational evaluators and many administrators have restricted the roles of vocational evaluators in education, rehabilitation, and transition settings. Indeed, research tends to focus on the more restricted vocational evaluator role and functions (Coffey, 1978; Green, 1992; Leahy & Wright, 1988; Taylor, Bordieri, Crimando, & Janikowski, 1993; Taylor, Bordieri, & Lee, 1993). Role and function studies have targeted direct client, consumer, or student services. It is true that evaluators spend much of their time and energy in direct student contact. Direct student services include the following:

- conducting initial interviews;

- administering and scoring tests, work samples, situational assessments, and other community-based assessments;

- conducting occupational searches with students;

- observing and recording behaviors;

- identifying learning style preferences, interests, goals, abilities, aptitudes, temperaments, levels of career development and maturity, values, attitudes, and other attributes;

- furnishing career information;

- adapting equipment and materials for students with disabilities; and

- providing feedback and interpreting results to students, referral agents (e.g., guidance counselors, teachers, psychologists), parents, and others.

Common perceptions of evaluators' roles assume that these are essential (i.e., the only) functions and that most of their time should be spent on these tasks. While these functions are critical, evaluators' roles are much more diverse and complex. Neubert's (1986) study of three school systems in Maryland found that evaluators assumed multiple roles, which extended beyond both direct student and indirect student services. Neubert found that a primary responsibility entailed advocating for students to access vocational education and ensuring that students received needed services (1986, p. 103). Evaluators even provided support assistance after students were placed in vocational education programs. Such support assistance included linking vocational education instructors with special education teachers to facilitate instructional accommodations and support, and giving instructional assistance themselves. Neubert noted that, at times, evaluators assumed related roles, such as performing administrative duties and helping with recruitment activities at vocational technical centers.

Regardless of setting, vocational evaluators spend a large portion of time performing a variety of support functions for direct student services. Though these functions often are not recorded, nearly as much time is spent on *indirect student services*. Indirect student services include the following:

- scheduling assessments;

- coordinating interviews and staffing conferences;

- researching community resources (includes site visits);

- performing training or job analyses;

- conducting labor market reviews;

- obtaining or creating assistive, adaptive devices or modifying tests, surveys, and instructions;

- reviewing student files;

- verifying information with teachers, counselors, and family members;

- researching possible recommendations;

- serving as liaisons with referral agents, teachers, counselors, and instructional support service personnel to ensure that students are linked to in-school programs and outside school services that are recommended;

- advocating and assisting with program modifications (e.g., textbooks and instructional methods in vocational education classes);

- analyzing, interpreting, and synthesizing assessment results;

- profiling and writing reports; and

- explaining results and collaboratively developing recommendations in staffing and parent conferences.

Interpreting, synthesizing, and delivering results can often be the most time-consuming tasks in an evaluator's role. Evaluators spend concentrated effort on this part of the process because the results are written and shared with others. Once results and recommendations are disseminated, they can make life-changing differences in students' lives. It is important for the evaluator to advocate so that every effort will be made to ensure that these differences are positive and desired.

Other *administrative and support services* consume large portions of vocational evaluators' time and are as essential for the success of programs and student participation as other duties. Examples of these services include the following:

- developing work tasks and work samples;

- setting up community-based assessment sites;

- investigating various disabilities and determining vocational implications;

- learning and maintaining medical knowledge regarding disabilities;

- establishing relationships for potential placement options (with employers, vocational instructors, community service professionals);

- ordering materials and upgrading assessment tools;

- performing follow-up to determine student outcomes and effectiveness of the evaluation programs;

- preparing program reports for administrators and funding agencies;

- meeting with district program coordinators to share general trends from annual data collection (e.g., reporting to a mathematics supervisor that high percentages of 9th- and 10th-grade students were unable to measure beyond 1-inch increments or could not compute fractions);

- providing orientation sessions for students, referral agents, and parents;

- educating new or potential referral agents about how to and who to refer for services;

- designing and conducting training about vocational evaluation services and how others can use them or assist with data collection;

- keeping abreast of emerging and changing laws and policies that have implications for evaluation services;

- helping to update or implement interagency cooperative agreements (e.g., between special education, career–technical education, counseling, and vocational rehabilitation);

- serving on system-wide transition advisory committees and career–technical advisory teams;

- staying informed about trends and changes in education (e.g., self-determination movement, inclusion, discipline policies);

- reviewing, evaluating, and revising program processes or methods;

- establishing linkages with other members of interdisciplinary and education teams; and

- leading or participating in planning meetings (e.g., individual education planning, individual written rehabilitation planning).

Public relations are as important to the health and survival of services as are the direct student contact services (DePoint, 1991; Ensley, 1995; Leconte, 1991; Thomas, 1997). Public relations, which encompass marketing, educating, and advocating, require that vocational evaluators be visible within schools and the community. The maxim "people won't use what they don't know about" applies here. Because vocational evaluation has not been delivered with any consistency across the country, many professionals and families are unaware of its benefits. As a result, evaluators need to devote time to marketing their services. Once students begin accessing services, others will want to participate as the benefits spread by word-of-mouth (Leconte, 1994b; Thomas, 1997). With public relations, often programs grow to the point that many maintain waiting lists.

In general, practitioners recognize the need to educate the public and promote their services at local, state, and national levels. To support such endeavors, Bowers, Schuster, and Smith (1989) promoted the development of a collaborative, national advocacy effort by creating the Interdisciplinary Council on Vocational Evaluation and Assessment. The council has fostered collaboration between 11 leading professional associations concerned with vocational assessment and evaluation since 1990 (Smith et al., 1995). These organizations include the American Occupational Therapy Association, American Rehabilitation Counseling Association, Council for Educational Diagnostic Services, Division on Career Development and Transition, National Association of Disability Evaluating Professionals, National Association of School Psychologists, National Association of Vocational Assessment in Education, National Association of Vocational Education Special Needs Personnel, National Rehabilitation Counseling Association, and Vocational Evaluation and Work Adjustment Association. The Commission on Certification of Work Adjustment and Vocational Evaluation Specialists (CCWAVES) serves an ad hoc position. The council "seeks to promote, through a unified voice, the responsible practice of vocational assessment and evaluation by encouraging advocacy, professional standards, communication, leadership, and policy development . . . [to] enhance the provision of best practice" (Smith et al., 1995). Among the council's accomplishments are a position statement which outlines core values, guiding principles, and general competencies of practice (Smith et al., 1995) and a "standards for best practice" document (Schuster & Sitlington, 1997). These represent small, beginning steps toward achieving consistent, high quality, and well-articulated services.

Ensley (1995) reported an example of public relations and advocacy within the policy realm by describing the initiative of vocational evaluators in Virginia. With the passage of the School-to-Work Opportunities Act of 1994, Virginia evaluators developed a brochure and series of meetings and public relations events to convince policy developers and state and local administrators to take advantage of requirements in the law to implement vocational assessment and evaluation services within school-to-work programming. Evaluators testified at public hearings and attended local planning meetings to advance their cause.

Such activities demonstrate that indirect and administrative activities, which support direct contact services, are as essential as direct services. Typically, minimal time is set aside for these responsibilities, and such services are not afforded the same importance as direct student services. In other words, administrators want to *see* evaluators working face to face with students. This problem has plagued effective functioning for evaluators and their programs. It is a primary reason why evaluators are often excluded from transition planning activities and meetings. Today, there is more pressure for evaluators to expand their roles to meet the needs of students in transition services. Hopefully, as other professionals, parents, and students learn the value of vocational evaluation services, more evaluators may be invited to the planning table. This may be prompted as team members begin to see gaps in the assessment information on which they are to base transition plans.

Evolving Roles

Several authors have proffered changing roles of vocational evaluators over the past decade. Leconte and Neubert (1987) described "present and emerging roles" (p.160) and placed them into the categories of assessment coordinator, profile developer, consultant, vocational liaison and advocate, and trainer/staff developer. These delineations recognized the diversity of evaluator functions. The roles were described in conjunction with vocational support instructors, who worked as team members with vocational evaluators to facilitate success of special needs students in vocational education. School evaluators partnered with support instructors to ensure that instruction was based upon assessment findings and recommendations and that sufficient assistance was provided to foster student success (Leconte & Neubert, 1987; Maryland State Department of Education, 1984; Neubert, 1994). These partnerships necessitated mutual understanding of the different professional disciplines as well as cross-disciplinary training and interdisciplinary planning. Responsibility for coordinating, developing, consulting, acting as liaisons, advocating, and training have not typically been part of the evaluator's role, but in this system it was essential for facilitating vocational education success and fostering meaningful transitions for students (Maryland State Department of Education, 1984).

Advocacy and interdisciplinary responsibilities are prevalent themes among the recommendations for role expansion by a number of vocational evaluation practitioners. For instance, Dowd (1989) emphasized the need for intensified interdisciplinary "communication, collaboration, and negotiation" for evaluators to provide maximum benefit to their clients. She described the need to work together with other professionals to improve evaluation outcomes for participants and to extend evaluation into public sectors that do not typically take advantage of services. Dowd also identified negotiation as a key skill to enhance the advocacy efforts of evaluators with employers, attorneys (Dowd, 1989), and other service providers such as occupational and physical therapists (Dowd & French, 1991).

Other professionals encouraged vocational evaluators to collaborate with employers to stimulate growth for the profession (Leconte et al., 1993; Weldon & Gibson, 1989). Since the ADA was enacted, vocational evaluators have facilitated and nurtured their employer relationships by assisting small businesses and large companies to comply with the ADA (Peterson, 1991; Thomas, Bowers, Batten, & Reed, 1993). Evaluators' knowledge of job and task analysis has helped employers identify essential functions of jobs, develop up-to-date job descriptions, design or recommend reasonable accommodations, and connect them with national resources such as the Job Accommodation Network (JAN) and ABLEDATA.

Evaluators also collaborate with rehabilitation engineers and technologists (Langton & Lown, 1995). Although rehabilitation technologists encourage vocational evaluators to acquire skills for using assistive technology in their services, they also acknowledge that often the more specialized skills or technologists and engineers are needed (Langton & Lown, 1995). Moreover, Langton and Lown claim that "determining ways to enhance the performance capabilities of individuals is one of the most important applications of rehabilitation technology in vocational evaluation" (p. 24). To accomplish this primary vocational evaluation goal, vocational evaluators, rehabilitation engineers, and technologists are collaborating increasingly as team members and are participating in training programs together (A. Noll, personal communication, September 1997). As confirmation of this type of collaboration, a team of vocational evaluators working with rehabilitation technologists at the Center for Rehabilitation Technology Services in South Carolina has developed an assistive technology guide for vocational evaluators. Interdisciplinary efforts like these enhance and augment opportunities for students who are making or planning transitions.

Another example of new and developing roles for vocational evaluators is illustrated by the diversity of responsibilities assigned to evaluators in an alternative education setting. One particular alternative setting is designed for at-risk youth who have been unsuccessful in regular school settings or who are returning from being incarcerated. Many such students have undiagnosed or untreated disabilities. Cremo (1990) identified the "changing paradigm" of vocational evaluator roles in that the skills of evaluators are used to assess programs in addition to students. Cremo gave further examples of how the evaluators' skills are being expanded beyond awareness of "community resources and career opportunities specific to geographic area" to cementing relations with the business community by serving on the Chamber of Commerce and helping businesses develop sites for community assessment. Examples of other expanded activities include developing and administering screenings to match community mentors with students, designing and coordinating career portfolio assessment, and "surveying employer needs within local economies for the development of classroom curriculum" (Cremo, 1997, p. 150).

Vocational evaluators seek and rely on information and skills provided by other professionals as well. Within school settings, they collaborate most with special educators, vocational instructors, counselors, job development and placement coordinators, and transition specialists. They retrieve and use information provided by these experts, but just as often they provide consultation. Educators and others (e.g., guidance counselors, IEP coordinators) often benefit from the skills that vocational evaluators possess, and rehabilitation counselors consult with evaluators when seeking community resource services or when trying to locate a specific service provider (S. Cooper, 1997, Y. Kranitz, 1997, personal communications). Vocational evaluators' community contacts, especially with adult service providers, are useful to transition specialists, some of whom are coordinating services between school and adult programs. To keep work samples and work processes current, vocational evaluators collaborate with secondary and postsecondary vocational instructors as well as with community trainers and employers (Leconte & Neubert, 1987; Neubert, 1986). As resources diminish, more employment specialists and community-based instructors assist evaluators by collecting job analysis, community-based assessment, and feedback from employers regarding placement and prescriptive recommendations. This sharing of assessment responsibilities requires sophisticated communication and collaboration between vocational evaluators and other personnel.

These and other collaborative and interdisciplinary functions signal a shift in the vocational evaluation field; participation in the transition services process has expedited this shift. Both vocational evaluation and transition dictate that professionals view the student holistically, in order that all perspectives are taken into account and all possible reasons for behaviors, stated interests, and goals are incorporated into planning. If evaluators and transition specialists are to trust their findings, the whole person must be assessed. Because no one person can possibly learn or know all relevant aspects of the student, professionals are dependent upon the input and feedback of professionals from other disciplines. This compels them to participate in interdisciplinary efforts and activities.

Though some evaluators and other professionals continue to operate in a restrictive multidisciplinary mode rather than in an interdisciplinary fashion, there has been significant movement toward the latter during the past few years. Those who persist in operating within the restrictive mode severely limit the accuracy and utility of vocational evaluation outcomes for students (Leconte, 1994b). Multidisciplinary practices have been distinguished from interdisciplinary ones by Petrie (1976), who stated that multidisciplinary practices mean that "everyone does his or her own thing with little or no necessity for any one participant to be aware of any other participant's work" (p. 9). Petrie, whose definition of interdisciplinary practices is similar to others' definitions (Golightly, 1987; Golin & Ducanis, 1981; Rothenbacher, 1992), describes interdisciplinary practices as those which "require more or less integration and even modification of the disciplinary subcontributions" while activity is proceeding. Petrie goes on to state that "different participants need to take into account the contributions of their colleagues to make their own contribution" (p. 9). Because vocational evaluators' roles require them to be interdisciplinary in that they interpret and synthesize all assessment results into vocational relevance, they must understand the meanings of the findings and recommendations of other interdisciplinary team members. They interpret these and synthesize them in relation to the student's goals, interests, abilities, and needs while communicating, and they verify them with the students to gain their agreement or approval.

Professionals recommend that communication and collaboration skills be included in graduate education curricula for vocational evaluators (Taylor & Pell, 1993; Thomas & Sigmon, 1989). Also, these high level skills are included in the Knowledge and Performance Areas that comprise the endorsed competencies for nationally certified evaluators (CCWAVES, 1996). A summary of these endorsed evaluator skills and competencies, which form the foundation of their professional knowledge, is presented in the next section.

Professional Competencies

Qualified vocational evaluators, meaning those trained and "certified in vocational evaluation" (CVE) and those who are eligible to take the national certification examination of CCWAVES (Leconte et al., 1993), possess specialized skills and competencies from other professionals. Vocational evaluators should possess mastery of certain skills, identified as minimum competencies of practice by CCWAVES (1996). The competencies are classified as Knowledge and Performance Areas (KPAs). The 14 KPAs are divided into four categories: Foundations of Vocational Evaluation, Planning, Standardized Testing, and Assessment Techniques. The 14 KPAs are illustrated in Table 11.1. Although other professionals possesses some training and experience in these KPAs, vocational evaluators possess all of these, with a focus on vocational and work that makes their skills specialized in the assessment arena. For instance, many guidance counselors, rehabilitation counselors, and transition personnel are trained or adept at vocational interviewing, but they may not have the time or specialized training to integrate personal preferences and abilities with available vocational options for persons with disabilities. CCWAVES and the professional associations who

Table 11.1
Knowledge and Performance Areas for Vocational Evaluators

I. Foundations of Vocational Evaluation
   A. Vocational Evaluation Process and Philosophy
   B. Occupational Information
   C. Functional Aspects of Disability

II. Planning
   A. Individualized Vocational Evaluation Planning
   B. Vocational Interviewing
   C. Vocational Report Development and Communication
   D. Modification and Accommodation Techniques

III. Standardized Testing
   A. Standardized Testing

IV. Assessment Techniques
   A. Job Analysis and Training Analysis
   B. Functional Skills Assessment
   C. Assessment of Learning and Learning Styles
   D. Situational and Community-Based Assessment
   E. Behavioral Observation
   F. Work Samples and Systems

Note. Adapted from *Standards and Procedures Manual for Certified Career Assessment Associates*, by Commission on Certification of Work Adjustment and Vocational Evaluation Specialists, 1996, Washington, DC: Author.

make up the commission require practitioners to demonstrate—through education or work experience—that they possess training and have demonstrated
competency in the KPAs. Table 11.2 illustrates the associations that make up the
commission. In addition to meeting educational and experiential criteria, evaluators must pass the national examination to gain "certified" status. Moreover,
certified vocational evaluators subscribe to the comprehensive Code of Ethics
established by CCWAVES.

These KPAs evolved from seminal role and function studies conducted on
vocational evaluators and other research that was conducted nationally (Coffey,
1978; Leahy & Wright, 1988; Taylor, Bordieri, Crimando, & Janikowski, 1993;
Taylor, Bordieri, & Lee, 1993). Though it may not seem apparent initially, the
activities included in the KPAs require various degrees of interdisciplinary communication, cooperation, collaboration, and sometimes negotiation. The "three
C's" of interdisciplinary relationships—communication, cooperation, and collaboration—could be broadened to include cross-training and courage—courage
to seek new information, to learn about different systems, to enter unknown turf,
and to persuade others to work together on behalf of the student. Interdisciplinary endeavors oblige vocational evaluators to glean raw data and interpretive
input from other professionals at the onset and during the evaluation process,

Table 11.2
Professional Associations Represented on the Commission on Certification of
Work Adjustment and Vocational Evaluation Specialists (CCWAVES)

National Organization	Number of Representatives
Vocational Evaluation and Work Adjustment Association (VEWAA)*	4
National Association of Vocational Education Special Needs Personnel (NAVESNP)	1
Division on Career Development and Transition (DCDT)	1
Council of State Administrators of Vocational Rehabilitation	1
National Association of Special Needs State Administrators	1
American Rehabilitation Association	1
The ARC: A National Organization in Mental Retardation**	1
National Association of Rehabilitation Professionals in the Private Sector	1
Total	11

*VEWAA holds four positions because its members initiated and established the Commission and certifica-
tion process and it is the only association with vocational evaluation in its primary mission.

**The ARC represents consumers with disabilities.

and later to provide outputs and interpretation of results to these same professionals and others. These outputs are designed to contribute to transition planning.

Seeking input is critical in that evaluators operate on a triangulation model of data collection. Vocational evaluators should not base their conclusions on information that is not verified. The standard rule requires that they validate any finding through at least three other methods or sources. For example, if a student expresses an aptitude for a specific occupational area, evaluators will check with parents, siblings, teachers, or others to determine if they have seen these abilities demonstrated. In addition, they can place the student on work samples or in community-based sites (including a try-out or visit to a vocational technical program) to have experts in that occupation observe the student, or they can observe his or her performance themselves. If necessary, vocational evaluators can administer an aptitude assessment (i.e., test). When all sources confirm the student's stated aptitude, the findings are verified to be accurate and thus triangulated.

Challenges to Integrating Vocational Evaluation in the Transition Process

A study by Benz, Johnson, Mikkelsen, and Lindstrom (1995) identified key barriers to interdisciplinary benefits and coordination of assessment practices. The reasons found in their study are in line with the barriers for coordinating vocational evaluation and adult services to form seamless transitions for students. They identified as main stumbling blocks the absence of "specific procedures for cross-agency coordination of assessment practices" and a failure to provide information and support related to assessment processes to students and parents (p. 137). These specific problems are familiar to practitioners. The study also cited "policy and definitional differences between agencies, failure to coordinate school assessments" with vocational rehabilitation and other assessments, and the neglect of adult service providers to use assessment data available from schools to facilitate eligibility determination (Benz et al., 1995, p.139).

The underlying problems point to challenges which professionals have faced in all settings when trying to coordinate services (Hodgkinson, 1989). Professionals have recommended for years that practitioners from various areas of expertise learn to understand all service areas and professions which intersect to meet students' needs (Golightly, 1987; Golin & Ducanis, 1981; Hodgkinson, 1989; Melaville & Blank, 1991), but in their list of team members they rarely mention vocational evaluators. Many other problems persist in the field. Often, people do not understand the nature or availability of services, particularly regarding possibilities and benefits for students. Moreover, many professionals use the terms *vocational assessment, vocational evaluation,* and *transition assessment* interchangeably, thus confusing consumers, parents, and other professionals. Professionals and the general public hold inaccurate understandings and presumptions about what specific services vocational evaluators can and cannot provide. Many expect that vocational evaluation will produce 'the answer' to their career planning questions, and this may not always be the case. Another problem is that people have difficulty gaining access to services due to inadequate number of programs, cumbersome eligibility requirements (e.g., qualifying for vocational rehabilitation), and inconsistent quality of services.

Many vocational evaluation personnel are inadequately trained largely due to a dearth of personnel preparation options and the absence of funding for training. Currently, the Rehabilitation Services Administration is the sole preservice funding source for training assistance. Many professionals lack cross or interdisciplinary preservice and in-service training. Currently, the few existing vocational evaluation graduate programs primarily involve rehabilitation counseling students in cross-training activities, with possibly one exception where the vocational evaluation program includes special education transition students. In particular, long-time professionals do not have access to retooling with regard to understanding and working with increasingly complex service systems and funding mechanisms for consumers.

Vocational evaluation services are often viewed as add-on programs or those that cannot be integrated into typical educational offerings. The view that these are separate services frequently dissuades people from including them in an array of service options. Instead, they determine that other (less expensive) assessment alternatives can suffice, thus leaving many students without any appropriate services.

Research, even in transition studies and journal articles, usually gives vocational assessment perfunctory mention, but rarely describes it or how it is implemented. Vocational evaluation services are noted even less. Usually implementation is addressed by listing or describing specific instruments and psychometric tests that are used by various programs (DeStefano & Linn, 1986; DeStefano, Linn, & Markward, 1987).

There seems to be a pervasive administrative view within different service systems, including education, that vocational evaluation does not require specialized skills and almost anyone can provide services. Because everyone has some responsibility for assessment and can contribute to vocational evaluation, it seems to be presumed that anyone can move from collecting assessment data to conducting comprehensive vocational evaluation. This attitude is evidenced by the frequent practice of moving teachers or entry-level rehabilitation and job-training employees into evaluation roles without any special training—a move that is not fair to teachers or students.

Another problem that persists in the field is the resistance from vocational evaluators or their administrators to alter or diversify their services to reflect the rapid changes in the labor market and work force. This resistance could simply be a misinterpretation of some administrators' reluctance to sink funding into refurbishing or restructuring programs. Some vocational evaluation programs continue to use limited methods and instruments in evaluation (and rely on outdated psychometric tests and commercial work sample systems), in spite of the fact that massive changes have occurred and are expected in world of work. Some professionals have created dissention by advocating the use of one approach versus the availability of an array of assessment options. The introduction of curriculum-based vocational assessment and supported employment represent two such approaches. These are very necessary and can feed into or from comprehensive vocational evaluation services, but they need not replace the more in-depth services.

The prevalent lack of freedom and latitude for evaluators to be creative also presents a challenge. The nature of their work requires that they take assessment to the community, into vocational programs, and to employment sites. However, these are viewed as costly luxuries rather than necessities for identifying how students perform in these nonschool environments. Diminishing resources are also a constant challenge. Educational and adult service agencies do not seem to participate in the "in kind" trades as universally as they could. These tradeoffs in the past have allowed JTPA to purchase equipment and add part-time personnel to existing programs. In return, JTPA clients were evaluated free of charge. More communities could share resources like those that invest in adult job training, welfare, rehabilitation dollars, equipment, or personnel in educational programs. By so doing, students and clients of adult services can access programs initiated and maintained by pooled funding. Demands on time also torment evaluators. Green (1992) noted time as a significant barrier to service delivery in his study of services in the state of Washington.

The prevalence of adhering to an outdated role definition (i.e., as providing only direct assessment services) induces vocational evaluators to foster more coordination and collaboration among disciplines (Dowd, 1989; Thomas, 1997). Another problem is that certification or licensure for professionals and standards for programs are not in place. With the possible exceptions of Virginia (which is continually threatened with deletion from state teacher certification endorsements), Ohio, and New Hampshire (McCarthy & Leconte, 1983; M. Stokes, personal communication, December 1997), most states do not require specialized professional certification of evaluators employed in education, rehabilitation, or other service systems. Nor do they provide or enforce mandated program standards. Finally, though CCWAVES, the national certification body, has existed since 1981 (CCWAVES, 1996) and representatives from secondary education (e.g., NAVESNP, DCDT) are represented on the commission (see Table 11.2), the commission has had too few resources to advocate and change policies and certification or licensure laws and policies that affect evaluators in education settings. The individual vocational evaluator faces many more challenges in trying to improve the lives of students, but in some areas of the nation, people are increasing their inclusion of evaluators in transition service provision and planning. A key to reducing the barriers that vocational evaluators face involves educating parents and other professionals that their expertise includes more than prescriptive and predictive skills and requires the sophisticated abilities of synthesis, advocacy, and interdisciplinary collaboration.

Vision for the Future: Roles for Vocational Evaluators in Transition Processes

School systems that have access to vocational evaluation services and vocational evaluators can benefit by using their unique "exclusivity of skills" (Ayella & Leconte, 1987). The expertise of vocational evaluators can help connect students, parents, special educators, and transition specialists with critical occupational information and key transition 'players' in the community. The transition successes and positive outcomes that will potentially be achieved in these schools should be documented with targeted research so that other schools will be encouraged to create or pitch in with other service agencies to employ vocational evaluators. In many states, these services are available but are underutilized, particularly within a transition context, a point made by Clark and Patton (1997) in their review of 17 state transition guides. Only one of the 17 states reported vocational evaluation as a core transition planning area out of the 22 areas identified. In addition to vocational evaluation, other vocational assessment services can prove helpful in the transition process, but current literature rarely distinguishes differences between evaluation and other types of assessment.

During the past decade, teachers have been encouraged to collect vocational information to make such matches by developing and conducting curriculum-based vocational assessment (Albright & Cobb, 1988; Stodden, Ianacone, Boone, & Bisconer, 1987; Swisher & Clark, 1991). Teachers who have experience and training to provide curriculum-based vocational assessment represent another rich source of assessment information, and for some students this type of assessment may be all they need. It is highly recommended, however, that an array of assessment options be accessible to students who are trying to make transition plans. With several options, all students needing assessment can access appropriate and equitable services. Therefore, curriculum-based assessment can serve most students and programming should be available for the various assessment levels discussed earlier in the chapter, including comprehensive vocational evaluation. Portfolio assessment seems ready-made to coincide with curriculum-based vocational assessment. However, experience demonstrates that many educators express their lack of confidence to implement curriculum-based assessment and it is too early to determine how effective portfolio assessment will be in secondary education.

Supported employment specialists and community-based teachers are using real work for assessment, usually within the context of training, job placement, or functional curriculum. They too provide an important perspective and different dimension to the overall transition process. Often the information known to employment specialists, community-based instructors, vocational, and special education teachers is not shared with others, due to awkward or cumbersome structuring of schedules and professional responsibilities. If the information they hold could be shared with a vocational evaluator, it could be integrated into vocational profiles or reports. These could then be used to furnish synthesized recommendations for inclusion in transition plans. Such a collaborative process would strengthen the transition plan, significantly lighten a transition coordinator's responsibility, and allow more time for other duties.

The vision for the future encompasses massive shifts in the use of electronic media and the Internet. Some professionals already are beginning to incorporate and even rely on career assessment sources that are available on the Internet. This is fine if these sources are integrated as supplements to the methods, techniques, and evaluator expertise already used. However, people should heed caution about supplanting existing practices and services with these sometimes free but quickly developed instruments. The vocational evaluator who keeps abreast of these developments can help ease those who are reluctant into engagement with computer and Internet use, while also advising professionals which of the many options are worth using.

The roles and responsibilities of vocational evaluators are changing. With local, state, and national leadership, the inclusion of vocational evaluators in the transition planning process could signal improved use of existing services and personnel and expanded professional options for vocational evaluators. For these changes to be effective, personnel from other professions hopefully will recognize that evaluators have detailed knowledge of work and the projected labor market, that they have expansive knowledge of community resources, and that they understand the nuances of how to access both the labor market and community services. Also, these changes will require evaluators to embrace new duties and roles while seeking to serve students engaged in transition processes. These expanded roles might include advocating for students to access certain services and coordinating a variety of assessment services in addition to providing vocational evaluation. Another expanded role might include communicating with or seeking resources within the business community, an activity which entails representing education issues at local or state chambers of commerce or economic development agencies. Finally, evaluators might work in concert with other professionals to build new partnerships and create new programs and opportunities for students in schools and communities.

Final Thoughts

Vocational evaluation has proven to be an effective intervention for improving the vocational and career outcomes of youth and adults with disabilities and special needs (Cresap, 1987; Evans, 1986; Grosser, Schmitt, & Scott, 1993; Neubert & Leconte, 1990; Thomas, Hiltenbrand, & Tibbs, 1997). Also, it represents a useful intervention for facilitating transition planning (M. Piatt, personal communication, November 1997; Taymans, Culbertson, Thomas, Duran, & Jacobs, 1991). With the exception of scattered programs in special education and more in vocational education, most school systems do not have a formal vocational evaluation process. The emphasis on transition for students with disabilities, the school-to-work educational reform for all students, and the return-to-work or welfare-to-work programs seems to justify the inclusion of trained vocational evaluators in communities.

The many programs needing assessment and evaluation services could provide them by pooling their resources to establish services and providing training for vocational evaluation personnel and those who will be using the services. The latter group includes special educators, vocational educators, counselors, transition specialists, families, students, and others. To justify investments from community partners and training commitments, evaluators must be dedicated to conducting research—especially outcome data—on their services.

To meet the needs of communities, particularly of students with disabilities who have varying transition planning and implementation requirements and goals, vocational evaluators are compelled to diversify their service offerings. Some evaluators have recognized the need to offer a range of assessment options. By diversifying they have increased the volume of people served while protecting and maintaining the quality of their comprehensive vocational evaluation services (S. Keller, personal communication, July 1997; A. Silva, personal communication, November 1997; M. Stokes, personal communication, March 1997).

Directions needed in vocational evaluation center around role and service changes, conducting research, and promoting more personnel preparation between disciplines and for vocational evaluators. Vocational evaluators are allowed to participate as equal stakeholders in the transition process for students with disabilities and others in their communities through involvement in professional interdisciplinary activities within communities and on the national level.

References

Albright, L., & Cobb, R. B. (1988). *Assessment of students with handicaps in vocational education: A curriculum-based approach.* Alexandria, VA: American Vocational Association.

Americans with Disabilities Act of 1990, 42 U.S.C. §12101 *et seq.*

Ayella, K. P., & Leconte, P. (1987). The professionalism of the vocational evaluator: Changing roles, changing responsibilities. In R. R. Fry (Ed.), *The issues papers: Third national forum on issues in vocational assessment* (pp. 19–25). Menomonie, WI: Materials Development Center, University of Wisconsin–Stout.

Benz, M. R., Johnson, D. K., Mikkelsen, K. S., & Lindstrom, L. E. (1995). Improving collaboration between schools and vocational rehabilitation: Stakeholder identified barriers and strategies. *Career Development of Exceptional Individuals, 18*(2), 133–144.

Bowers, C., Schuster, D. L., & Smith, F. G. (1989). Professional advocacy in vocational evaluation and assessment. In R. R. Fry (Ed.), *The issues papers: Fourth national forum on issues in vocational assessment* (pp. 33–39). Menomonie, WI: Materials Development Center, University of Wisconsin–Stout.

Carl D. Perkins Vocational and Applied Technology Education Act of 1990, 20 U.S.C. §2331 *et seq.*

Clark, G. M., & Patton, J. R. (1997). *Transition planning inventory: Administration and resource guide.* Austin, TX: PRO-ED.

Coffey, D. (1978). *Vocational evaluator role and function as perceived by practitioners and educators.* Menomonie, WI: Research and Training Center, University of Wisconsin–Stout.

Commission on Certification of Work Adjustment and Vocational Evaluation Specialists. (1996). *Standards and procedures manual for certification in vocational evaluation.* Washington, DC: Author.

Commission on Certification of Work Adjustment and Vocational Evaluation Specialists. (1997). *Standards and procedures manual for certified career assessment associates.* Washington, DC: Author.

Couch, R. H. (1973). The vocational evaluation and work adjustment association looks to the future. In R. E. Hardy & J. G. Cull (Eds.), *Vocational evaluation for rehabilitation services* (pp. 65–103). Springfield, IL: Charles C. Thomas.

Cremo, J. M. (1997). Alternative education and at-risk youth: Shifting the paradigm of vocational assessment. In R. R. Fry (Ed.), *The issues papers: Eighth national forum on issues in vocational assessment* (pp. 149–151). Menomonie, WI: The Rehabilitation Resource, University of Wisconsin–Stout.

Cresap, L. (1987). A study of the influence of vocational evaluation on the career progress of 268 special education high school students. In R. R. Fry (Ed.), *The issues papers: Third national forum on issues in vocational assessment* (pp. 99–101). Menomonie, WI: Materials Development Center, University of Wisconsin–Stout.

deFur, S. H. (1990). *A validation study of competencies needed for transition specialists in vocational rehabilitation, vocational education, and special education.* Unpublished doctoral dissertation, the George Washington University, Washington, DC.

DePoint, B. (1991). Enhancing your public relations: Shaping a successful marketing program. In R. R. Fry (Ed.), *The issues papers: Fifth national forum on issues in vocational assessment* (pp. 13–15). Menomonie, WI: Materials Development Center, University of Wisconsin–Stout.

Dowd, L. R. (1989). Professional contacts for evaluator's expanding roles. In R. R. Fry (Ed.), *The issues papers: Fourth national forum on issues in vocational assessment* (pp. 11–18). Menomonie, WI: Materials Development Center, University of Wisconsin–Stout.

Dowd, L. R. (1993). *Terminology used in vocational evaluation and assessment: VEWAA glossary of terms.* Menomonie, WI: Materials Development Center, University of Wisconsin–Stout.

Dowd, L., & French, A. C. (1991). Collaborative effort gets results. *Vocational Evaluation and Assessment Bulletin: Newsletter of the Collaborative Vocational Evaluation Training and Career Transition Assessment Emphases, 5*(1), 8–10.

Ensley, M. A. (1995). Vocational assessment/evaluation in the School-to-Work Opportunities Act: Virginia VEWAA's position and initiative. In R. R. Fry (Ed.), *The issues papers: Seventh national forum on issues in vocational assessment* (pp. 175–178A). Menomonie, WI: The Rehabilitation Resource, University of Wisconsin–Stout.

Evans, L. (1986). A study regarding placement and performance of students receiving vocational evaluations. In R. R. Fry (Ed.), *The issues papers: Second national forum on issues in vocational assessment* (pp. 135–138). Menomonie, WI: Materials Development Center, University of Wisconsin–Stout.

Golightly, C. J. (1987). Transdisciplinary training: A step forward in special education teacher preparation. *Teacher Education and Special Education, 10*(3), 126–130.

Golin, A. K., & Ducanis, A. J. (1981). *The interdisciplinary team.* Rockville, MD: Aspen.

Green, J. (1992). *Personnel and practices in vocational assessment for students with special needs in Washington state.* Paper presented at the Research Division of the American Vocational Association Conference, St. Louis, Missouri.

Grosser, D., Schmitt, T., & Scott, N. (1993). Follow-up: A look at long term results form school-based vocational evaluation. In R. R. Fry & W. Garner (Eds.), *The issues papers: Sixth national forum on issues in vocational assessment* (pp. 311–314). Menomonie, WI: Materials Development Center, University of Wisconsin–Stout.

Hodgkinson, H. L. (1989). *The same client: The demographics of education and service delivery systems.* Washington, DC: Institute for Educational Leadership, Center for Demographic Policy.

Individuals with Disabilities Education Act of 1990, 20 U.S.C. §1400 *et seq.*

Individuals with Disabilities Act Amendments of 1997, 20 U.S.C. §1400 *et seq.*

Job Training Partnership Act Amendments of 1992, 29 U.S.C. §1501 *et seq.*

Langton, A. J., & Lown, N. (1995). Rehabilitation technology resources and services: How well are we using them in vocational evaluation? In R. R. Fry (Ed.), *The issues papers: Seventh national forum on issues in vocational assessment* (pp. 19–26). Menomonie, WI: The Rehabilitation Resource, University of Wisconsin–Stout.

Leahy, M., & Wright, G. (1988). Professional competencies of the vocational evaluator. *Vocational Evaluation and Work Adjustment Bulletin, 21,* 127–132.

Leconte, P. J. (1991). Public relations: Taking the time to stay in business. In R. R. Fry (Ed.), *The issues papers: Fifth national forum on issues in vocational assessment* (pp. 5–12). Menomonie, WI: Material Development Center, University of Wisconsin–Stout.

Leconte, P. J. (1994a). *A perspective on vocational appraisal: Beliefs, practices, and paradigms.* Unpublished doctoral dissertation, the George Washington University, Washington, DC.

Leconte, P. J. (1994b). Vocational appraisal: Evolution from multidisciplinary origins and applications to interdisciplinary practices. *Vocational Evaluation and Work Adjustment Bulletin, 27*(4), 119–127.

Leconte, P. J., & Neubert, D. A. (1987). Vocational education for special needs students: Linking vocational assessment and support. *Diagnostique, 12,* 156–167.

Leconte, P. J., & Neubert, D. A. (1997). Vocational assessment: The kick-off point for successful transitions. *Alliance, The Newsletter of the National Transition Alliance 2*(2), 1, 3–4, 8.

Leconte, P. J., Thomas, S., Neville, D., Tunick, R., Lam, C., O'Brien, J., Herbert, J., & Holt, E. (1993). *Report from facilitated group of vocational evaluator educators.* Prepared for the National Council on Rehabilitation Education Annual Conference, Washington, DC.

Maryland State Department of Education. (1972). *Discovering people potential.* Baltimore: Division of Vocational Technical Education.

Maryland State Department of Education. (1977). *Vocational evaluation in Maryland public schools: A model guide for student assessment.* Baltimore: Division of Vocational Technical Education.

Maryland State Department of Education. (1984). *Handbook for vocational support service teams in Maryland.* Baltimore: Division of Vocational Technical Education.

McCarthy, I. H., & Leconte, P. (1983). Certification for vocational evaluators in Maryland. *NAVESNP Region I Conference Proceedings,* 57–63.

Melaville, A. I., & Blank, M. J. (1991). *What it takes: Structuring interagency partnerships to connect children and families with comprehensive services.* Washington, DC: Education and Human Services Consortium.

Nadolsky, J. M. (1969). The existential in vocational evaluation. *Journal of Rehabilitation, 35*(3), 22–24.

Nadolsky, J. M. (1971). *Development of a model for vocational evaluation of the disadvantaged: Interim report.* Auburn, AL: Department of Vocational and Adult Education, Auburn University.

Nadolsky, J. M. (1981). Vocational evaluation in the public school: Implication for further practice. *Journal for Vocational Special Needs Personnel, 3*(3), 5–9.

Neubert, D. A. (1986). Use of vocational evaluation recommendations in selected public school settings. *Career Development for Exceptional Individuals, 9*(2), 98–105.

Neubert, D. A. (1994). Vocational assessment in vocational–technical education: Barriers and facilitators to interdisciplinary services. *Vocational Evaluation and Work Adjustment Bulletin, 27*(4), 149–153.

Neubert, D. A., & Leconte, P. J. (1990). Vocational assessment: Effective intervention for meeting the vocational needs of rural youth with special needs. *Journal for Vocational Special Needs Education, 12*(2), 17–22.

Peterson, J. J. (1991). The impact of the ADA on the field of vocational evaluation. In R. R. Fry (Ed.), *The issues papers: Fifth national forum on issues in vocational assessment* (pp. 53–56). Menomonie, WI: Materials Development Center, University of Wisconsin–Stout.

Petrie, H. G. (1976). Do you see what I see? The epistemology of interdisciplinary inquiry. *Educational Researcher, 5*(2), 9–15.

Rehabilitation Act of 1973, 29 U.S.C. §701 *et seq.*

Rothenbacher, C. A. (1992). *The study of the implementation of a case management process for providing transition services to youths with special needs.* Unpublished doctoral dissertation, the George Washington University, Washington, DC.

Rothenbacher, C., & Leconte, P. J. (1990). *Vocational assessment: A guide for parents and professionals.* Washington, DC: National Information Center for Children and Youth with Handicaps.

School-to-Work Opportunities Act of 1994, P. L. 103=239.

Schuster, D., & Sitlington, P. L. (1997). Standards for best practice in vocational evaluation and assessment. In R. R. Fry (Ed.), *The issues papers: Eighth national forum on issues in vocational assessment* (pp. 1–3). Menomonie, WI: The Rehabilitation Resource, University of Wisconsin–Stout.

Sitlington, P., Brolin, D., Clark, G., & Vacanti, T. (1985). Career/vocational assessment in the public school settings: The position of the Division on Career Development. *Career Development of Exceptional Individuals, 8,* 3–6.

Sitlington, P., Neubert, D., Begun, W., Lombard, R., & Leconte, P. (1996). *Assess for success: Transition assessment.* Reston, VA: The Council for Exceptional Children.

Sitlington, P., Neubert, D., & Leconte, P. (1997). Transition assessment: The position of the Division on Career Development and Transition. *Career Development for Exceptional Individuals, 20*(1), 69–79.

Smith, F., Lombard, R., Neubert, D., Leconte, P., Rothenbacher, C., & Sitlington, P. (1995). Position statement of the interdisciplinary council on vocational evaluation and assessment. *Journal for Vocational Special Needs Education, 17,* 41–42.

Smith, F. G., & Schuster, D. L. (1993). Building consensus: The interdisciplinary council on vocational evaluation and assessment. In R. R. Fry & W. E. Garner (Eds.), *The issues papers: Sixth national forum on issues in vocational assessment* (pp. 51–56). Menomonie, WI: Material Development Center, University of Wisconsin–Stout.

Stewart, S. K. (1997). Assessment competencies for school to work transition professionals. In R. R. Fry (Ed.), *The issues papers: Eighth national forum on issues in vocational assessment* (pp.152–161). Menomonie, WI: The Rehabilitation Resource, University of Wisconsin–Stout.

Stodden, R. A., (1986). Vocational assessment: An introduction. *Career Development for Exceptional Individuals, 9*(2), 167–168.

Stodden, R. A., Ianacone, R. N., Boone, R. M., & Bisconer, S. W. (1987). *Curriculum-based vocational assessment: A guide for addressing youth with special needs.* Honolulu, HI: Centre Publications, International Education Corporation.

Swisher, J., & Clark, G. M. (1991). Curriculum-based vocational assessment of students with special needs at the middle school/junior high school levels. *Journal for Vocational Special Needs Education, 13*(3), 9–14.

Taylor, D., Bordieri, J., Crimando, W., & Janikowski, T. (1993). Job tasks and functions of vocational evaluators in three sectors of practice. *Vocational Evaluation and Work Adjustment Bulletin, 26,* 39–46.

Taylor, D., Bordieri, J., & Lee, D. (1993). Job tasks and functions of vocational evaluators: A national study. *Vocational Evaluation and Work Adjustment Bulletin, 26,* 146–154.

Taylor, D. W., & Pell, K. L. (1993). Vocational evaluation curricula in rehabilitation education. *Rehabilitation Education, 7*(3), 185–194.

Taymans, J. M., Culbertson, D., Thomas, J., Duran, R., & Jacobs, J. (1991). *Challenges in developing transition services for adolescents and young adults with learning disabilities.* Washington, DC: School of Education and Human Development, Department of Teacher Preparation and Special Education, The George Washington University.

Taymans, J. M., & deFur, S. H. (1994). Preservice and inservice professional development for school to adult life transition. In *School to work transition for youths with disabilities* (pp. 119–147), Conference papers from NIDRR Consensus Validation Conference, Arlington, VA.

Thomas, S. W. (1987). Competing in an open market place: The strategic marketing of a profession. In R. R. Fry (Ed.), *The issues papers: Third national forum on issues in vocational assessment* (pp. 71–76). Menomonie, WI: Materials Development Center, University of Wisconsin–Stout.

Thomas. S. W. (1991). *Vocational evaluation and traumatic brain injury: A procedural manual.* Menomonie, WI: Materials Development Center, University of Wisconsin–Stout.

Thomas, S. W. (1997). Three roles of the vocational evaluator. *Vocational Evaluation and Work Adjustment Bulletin, 30*(1), 9–12.

Thomas, S. W., Bowers, C., Batten, D., & Reed, B. (1993). The Americans with Disabilities Act: Resources for implementation through vocational evaluation. In R. R. Fry & W. E. Garner (Eds.), *The issues papers: Sixth national forum on issues in vocational assessment* (pp. 29–38). Menomonie, WI: Materials Development Center, University of Wisconsin–Stout.

Thomas, S., Hiltenbrand, D., & Tibbs, S. (1997). A new look at outcomes: Validating the vocational evaluation and work adjustment processes in the contemporary setting. In R. R. Fry (Ed.), *The issues papers: Eighth national forum on issues in vocational assessment* (pp. 117–126). Menomonie, WI: The Rehabilitation Resource, University of Wisconsin–Stout.

Thomas, S., & Sigmon, G. (1989). Critical content areas for graduate vocational evaluation education. *Rehabilitation Education, 3*, 35–42.

Vocational Evaluation and Work Adjustment Association. (1975). *Vocational evaluation project: Final report.* Menomonie, WI: Materials Development Center, University of Wisconsin–Stout.

Weldon, R., & Gibson, G. (1989). Redefining the client, expanding the evaluator's role. In R. R. Fry (Ed.), *The issues papers: Fourth national forum on issues in vocational assessment* (pp.7–9). Menomonie, WI: Materials Development Center, University of Wisconsin–Stout.

PART

III

SYNTHESIS

A MODEL FOR GUIDING THE TRANSITION PROCESS

Jeanne B. Repetto

Kristine Wiest Webb

If one advances confidently in the direction of their dreams, and endeavors to lead a life which they have imagined, they will meet with a success unexpected in common hours.

—Henry David Thoreau

Overview of Special Education

Nikki Taylor is a transition service provider for students with mild or moderate disabilities at Norman High School (NHS). She has been teaching for 5 years at NHS. During her college undergraduate program, Nikki had the opportunity to participate in a preservice program that offered classes in transition. The information she learned has assisted her as she guides and facilitates the transition process of her students. Her work responsibilities include preparation for classes and meetings, collaborating with school and agency personnel, and providing instruction to students. Her typical day is shown in Table 12.1.

Nikki Taylor's teaching day reflects some of the practices that have evolved over many years. How did these practices emerge? What historical events have influenced current practices in secondary special education? To provide

Table 12.1

A Typical Teaching Day for a Transition Service Provider

Time	Activity	To Do List
6:45 AM	Preparation for the day	Prepare for and complete two IEP/ITPs
7:00 AM	Meet with two content area teachers	Call parents for next week's IEP/ITPS
Period 1	Study Skills class	Consult with two Content Area teachers on study skills needed by students
Period 2	Cooperative Consultation in two content areas	Observe six students in two Content Area classes
Period 3	Career Exploration class	Prepare and organize individualized career exploration assignments
Period 4-Preparation	Prepare for IEP/ITPs, collaborate with team members including the community-based program teachers and related service providers	Contact Occupational Therapist and School Social Worker regarding two students
Lunch	Lunch with the guidance counselor to plan IEP/IEP service coordination for juniors and seniors	Assist a student in contacting a post-secondary service provider
Period 5	Language Arts class	Complete BRIGANCE Written Language Assessment
Period 6	Language Arts class	Confirm vocational rehabilitation attendance at a IEP/ITP meeting to be held next week
Period 7	Career Exploration class	Begin preparation for next week's IEP/ITP meetings
2:30 PM	Two IEP/ITP meetings	Update student progress folders

information and answers to these questions, a timeline (see Table 12.2) has been compiled to offer a snapshot of secondary/transition education. Moreover, for readers who desire comprehensive information, the history of special education is chronicled in several excellent sources, including *Introduction to Special Education: Teaching in an Age of Challenge* (Smith, 1998).

Transition is a model by which many people live their life and special education is among the many paths that operationalize the model. Life outcomes have been the core of special education from its inception, beginning with Jean-Marc-Gaspara Itard's goals for Victor, the "Wild Boy of Aveyron." Victor, a

(*Text continues on page 426*)

Table 12.2
Timeline

Time Period	Events Connected to Transition and Secondary Special Education

No Services for Individuals with Disabilities

Middle Ages	Individuals with disabilities were exiled to almshouses, prisons, and asylums. These individuals were often subject to ridicule, abuse, and even extermination. Often treated as children throughout their lives, persons with disabilities resorted to begging or demeaning work. One of the few attempts at education was provided by monks who served as job coaches and provided individualized instruction in a specific area (Clark & Kolstoe, 1995).

Recognition of Individual Freedom and Worth

Late 1700s	Both the American and French Revolutions brought attention to individual civil rights, a phenomena which may have had some influence upon the lives of individuals with disabilities (Clark & Kolstoe, 1995).
1799	In France, Itard developed five functional aims for Victor, the wild boy of Aveyron (Smith, 1998).
1800s	Although a large number of people with disabilities lived in institutions, many had learned skills that enabled them to work on farms.
Late 1800s	Although special education classes were a part of some regular schools, most individuals with disabilities received no schooling (Smith, 1998).
1900s	The principles of opportunity and proof were widespread among schools in the United States. While the opportunity to attend school existed for all people, students needed to demonstrate progress to stay in programs (Clark & Kolstoe, 1995).
1909	Carnegie units toward high school graduation were established. These units consisted of minimal requirements in English, science, mathematics and history, in addition to a variety of classes that granted units of credit (Clark & Kolstoe, 1995).

Recognition of Needed Services

1922	Council for Exceptional Children (CEC) was established.
1928	In Belgium, Descoeudres offered "mentally defective" persons instruction for employment (Kolstoe, 1996).
1943	In England, John Duncan analyzed jobs in the community and developed a systematic program that utilized concrete intelligence rather than abstract thinking (Kolstoe, 1996).

Occupational and Academic Opportunities

1941, 1943	Richard Hungerford developed step-by step strategies for teachers of people with mental retardation who were involved in occupational education. The steps provided teachers with information about teaching needle trades, service occupations, light industry, and other skilled and unskilled jobs (Clark & Kolstoe, 1995).
1945–1960	After World War II, classes for individuals with disabilities became widely available across the nation. Many people received instruction in self-contained schools or residential institutions.

(continues)

Table 12.2 *Continued*

Emergence of Work Programs

1960s   Work–study programs began to emerge and offered students with disabilities opportunities to earn enough Carnegie units for graduation. In addition to work skills, academic, personal, and social skills were incorporated into programs. Typical work study programs included (a) an introduction to work experiences in a sheltered environment, (b) an introduction to on-the-job training (OJT) as a bridge between school and work, and (c) placement for students in a secure job (Kolstoe, 1996).

1963   The Vocational Education Act of 1963 mandated that students with disabilities be included in vocational education classes; however, no funding was appropriated for this effort.

1968   Amendments to the Vocational Education Act of 1963 resulted in legislation that required 10% of funds to be earmarked for students with disabilities, and a state plan detailing this use of funds had to be filed or states would lose federal funding.

1969–1972   Efforts toward normalization were spearheaded by Nirje (1969) and Wolfensberger (1972). Normalization is providing individuals with disabilities and social and vocational opportunities that are valued and typical within a community.

Programming for Individuals with Disabilities

1970s   Following a decade of work–study programs, the 1970s was the known as the total programming decade (Meers & Towne, 1996). Career education included awareness, exploration, and preparation. Assimilation occurred in home, community, and school environments (Brolin, 1996).

1971   The U.S. Commissioner of Education, Sydney Marland, introduced the concept of career education in response to the high number of high school dropouts and the lack of preparation for life functions in young adults (Brolin, 1996; Kolstoe, 1996).

1974   The U.S. Office of Career Education was established with K. B. Hoyt serving as Director. Although the Bureau for the Education of the Handicapped (BEH) upheld the idea of career education, no separate entity was formed to establish career education within special education programs (Brolin, 1996).

1974   A study conducted by Management Analysis Center, Inc. (MAC) indicated a large number of teams, consisting of special education teachers, vocational educators, and vocational rehabilitation counselors, who planned, trained, placed, and conducted follow-up support for students with disabilities (Kolstoe, 1996).

1975   The Education of All Handicapped Children Act (1975) required special educators to focus on individuals rather than instructional programs (Kolstoe, 1996).

1976   The Division of Career Development (DCD) was established as a division of the Council for Exceptional Children (CEC) (Brolin, 1996; D'Alonzo, 1996; Kolstoe, 1996; White & Repetto, 1996). DCD unified various entities to facilitate communication and share successful strategies used in career planning for persons with disabilities (Meers & Towne, 1996).

(continues)

Table 12.2 *Continued*

1978	The University of Kansas Center for Research on Learning began publishing and distributing intervention strategies specifically designed for adolescents (Deshler, Ellis, & Lenz, 1996).
1979, 1985	The Life-Centered Career Education Model demonstrated how 22 competencies in daily living skills, personal/social skills, and occupational guidance and preparation could be integrated into secondary curricula (Brolin & Kokaska, 1997; Kokaska & Brolin, 1985).

Functional Skills for Life

1980s	During the 1980s, exemplary programs in secondary schools reflected a shift from academic to functional life skills (Squires, 1996).
1983	Madeleine Will (1983), the Assistant Secretary of the Office of Special Education and Rehabilitative Services (OSERS), used the term *transition* to describe the movement from school to adult work situations.
1985	Several studies reported poor adjustment in all areas of life among adults with disabilities (Hasazi, Gordon, & Roe, 1985; Mithaug, Horiuchi, & Fanning, 1985).
1988	Curriculum-Based Vocational Assessment (CBVA) was developed. Sitlington (1996) described CBVA as one of the most significant models that emerged out of vocational/technical education programs.

Outcomes for Individuals with Disabilities

1990s	Legislative mandates for transition services resulted in a focus on outcomes for persons with disabilities. As support systems were developed, new job descriptions emerged, including career specialists, job coaches, career coaches, vocational adjustment counselors, transition specialists, and employment specialists (Meers & Towne, 1996).
1990	The Individuals with Disabilities Education Act (IDEA) of 1990 was passed and mandated transition services by age 16 for all students with disabilities, including those students with traumatic brain injury and autism. Funds were allocated to support secondary special education.
1990	The Carl D. Perkins Vocational and Applied Technology Education Act of 1990 emphasized the transition process and assured that all individuals were assured access to quality vocational education programs.
1990	The Americans with Disabilities Act (ADA) of 1990 was passed and gave individuals with disabilities the right to access life components such as opportunities, accommodations, and transportation without discrimination.
1991	The Secretary of Labor's Commission on Achieving Necessary Skills (SCANS report) (1991) was developed by the Department of Labor. The report offered recommendations about needed job skills and training for future job seekers.
1994	The School-to-Work Opportunities Act (STWOA) of 1994 was passed. STWOA's goals included certification programs that reflected industrial standards for all students.
1997	IDEA was reauthorized and mandated that transition services begin by age 14.

young boy who probably had mental retardation and environmental deprivation, was discovered in the woods of France in 1799. Itard, Victor's teacher and a pioneer in the field of special education, developed the following objectives to enable Victor to function in the world. Note the similarity of these aims to many of the transition goals written for individuals today (Smith, 1998):

First aim: To interest him in social life.
Second aim: To awaken his nervous sensibility.
Third aim: To extend the range of his ideas.
Fourth aim: To lead him to the use of speech.
Fifth aim: To make him exercise the simplest mental operations.

The timeline represented in Table 12.2 is not all inclusive of special education and transition. Rather, it is a progressive representation of the development of transition and secondary education's movement toward offering students with disabilities the skills and supports needed to achieve life outcomes.

A Transition Model for Change:
The Lifelong Model for Choice Building

Throughout the past decade, the field of transition has become increasingly sophisticated and complex. Models representing the transition process have evolved from the three-tiered high-school-based Bridges model (Will, 1983) to a multitiered model developed by Clark and Kolstoe (1995) that expands transition services to be offered prekindergarten through adulthood and has multiple exit points to work, postschool education, and semiskilled jobs. Services provided to students have expanded to include school-based as well as business-, community-, and agency-based services (Gajar, Goodman, & McAfee, 1993). Transition service providers are coordinated through interagency councils that can represent over 10 providers (Halpern, Benz & Lindstrom, 1992). Researchers (Clark & Patton, 1997; Kohler, 1993) have identified best practices in transition and transition planning areas, including community participation, daily living, employment, money management, health, independent living, leisure, postsecondary education, social skills, mobility, and vocational training. The Individuals with Disabilities Education Act (IDEA) of 1990 (P.L. 101-476) and its 1997 Amendments (P.L. 105-17) have mandated transition planning for all students 14 or older, with an IEP in the areas of instruction, community experiences, employment, postschool adult living, daily living skills, and functional vocational evaluation (DeStefano & Wermuth 1992; National Association of State Directors of Special Education, 1997). Additionally, IDEA mandated that students should be invited to their transition IEP meeting, supporting self-determination and the research conducted in this area by Field and Hoffman (1994). Related legislation such as the School-to-Work Opportunities Act (STWOA) of 1994 (P.L. 103-239) incorporated many of the transition planning areas into programs for all students beginning no later than the 7th grade (U.S. Department of Education, 1994).

In addition to the school-related changes in transition, the business community has projected workforce needs in the year 2000 and beyond. These projections impact the competencies students need to learn. The Secretary's Commission on Achieving Necessary Skills (SCANS) (1991) identified a set of skills that workers will need to possess to be successful employees. Interestingly, the SCANS report included letters addressed to parents, educators, and employers, outlining their role in the acquisition of these skills and the importance of a collaborative effort to assist future workers to be successful. A similar study conducted in 1990 by Carnevale, Gainer, and Meltzer identified seven skill groups employers want employees to have. The seven skill groups, called Workplace Basics, are (1) Organizational Effectiveness/Leadership; (2) Interpersonal/Negotiation/Teamwork; (3) Self-Esteem/Goal-Setting Motivation/Employability–Career Development; (4) Creative Thinking/Problem Solving; (5) Communication (Listening and Oral communication); (6) Three R's (Reading, Writing, Communication); and (7) Learning to Learn.

This brief review, not meant to be all inclusive, highlights the changes in the field of transition over the past decade that have contributed to its increased complexity. As the field becomes more sophisticated, a new model of transition must evolve and must be reflective of this growing complexity. The Lifelong Model for Choice Building is offered as this new model. In this model, the term *choice building* replaces *transition* in order to focus the model on the outcome of transition planning rather than the planning itself. Transition should be outcome-oriented and the ultimate outcome is the ability to plan and prepare for making one's own choices in life. Components of previous models of transition (Brolin, 1992; Clark & Kolstoe, 1995; Halpern, 1985; Will, 1983) are present in this model, providing the foundation to build upon and address current and future changes in the field of transition. An illustration of the model is provided in Figure 12.1.

Figure 12.1 is representative of a segment of the repeated twisting pattern of a double helix. A double helix modeled from DNA is used as the framework for the Lifelong Model for Choice Building because the double helix symbolizes many of the basic principles relating to transition and choice building. These

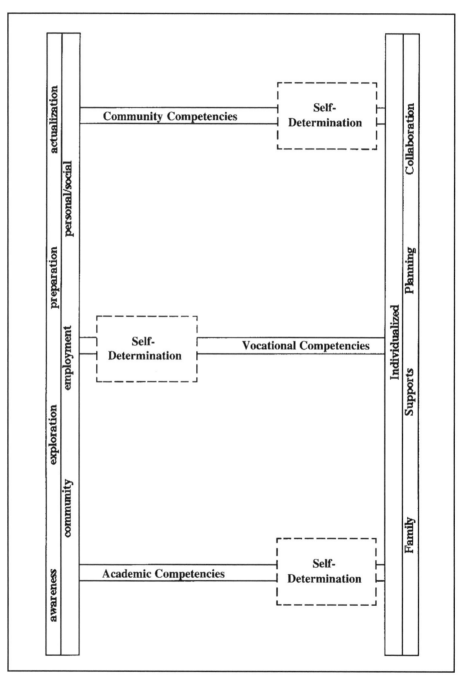

Figure 12.1. The Lifelong Model for Choice Building.

principles and their relationships to choice building are described in the following passages:

- *Nature–Nurture.* Transition planning is centered around the individual's "nature," as defined by their needs, preferences, abilities, and interests (DeStefano & Wermuth, 1992). Transition services are given to "nurture" or assist a individuals to achieve their goals.

- *Building blocks of life.* Just as DNA is the building block of life, transition planning and services form the building blocks for life choices. Through the provision of transition services, individuals receive the support and skills to achieve their goals.

- *Uniqueness.* Each person's goals and choices are unique. The choices people make form their unique construct of life, just as DNA forms their unique genetic makeup.

- *Active and ongoing.* Transition models need to be active and ongoing because people are lifelong learners, changing and making choices throughout their lives. Similarly, throughout their lives, DNA continues to be active, providing life's foundation.

- *Replicable.* As DNA replicates itself, so does the need for the skills that are learned throughout the transition process, such as self-determination, job hunting, network building, and so forth. Once learned, these skills can be applied to many situations throughout people's lives.

- *Collaboration.* DNA is made up of many building blocks working together to provide the foundation for life. In a similar manner, the provision of transition services needs to be a collaborative effort among students, families, friends, special educators, general educators, and other service providers in order to build a solid foundation for choice making.

- *Lifelong.* DNA continues to form people's genetic foundation throughout their lives. In a similar manner, people make choices and set goals throughout their lives; therefore, transition is a lifelong process that does not begin or end with one's years in school. The twist and turns in the DNA represents the convergence of transition skills and services coming together to obtain a goal.

These basic principles are operationalized through the bases and long strands of the model. The bases or rungs of the model are the essential building blocks or necessary skills needed for choice making. These skills are defined on the rungs as self-determination and community, vocational, and academic competencies. The self-determination (SD) bead allows individuals to use the competencies learned to achieve goals. It is through self-determination that individuals link the services, supports, and skills with the planning to achieve goals in specific aspects of life. For example, self-determination is the bond that allows (a) students to express their interests and needs to a Transition IEP/ITP team or (b) people to look for a new job on their company's web site and learn any necessary skills before applying for the job. In essence, self-determination then becomes the catalyst for new decisions and learning. The academic, vocational, and community competencies listed on the rungs represent the knowledge base for transitions in all aspects of life and therefore can be operationalized under the headings of community, vocational, and academic competencies. It is imperative that each of these areas of competencies is considered equally essential, though at certain times in life one area may be emphasized. It is the acquisition and application of these integrated, intertwined essential competencies that creates the ability for people to make and maintain life choices.

The sides or long strands of the model allow for, promote, and support choices. The vehicles to hold the bases intact and stable are represented on one strand through family, support services, planning, and collaboration, which are individualized to each person's needs, interest, preferences, and abilities. The other strand represents the fact that throughout life, individuals go through the stages of awareness, exploration, preparation, and actualization within their community, employment, and personal/social settings. The strands provide the vehicle to develop a unique, holistic pattern to one's life.

Applying the Model

To further explain the Lifelong Model of Choice Building, concepts will be applied to (a) the population served, (b) delivery of services, (c) planning, (d) competencies, and (e) persons or professionals involved.

Populations Served

The populations served through this model of choice building encompass all individuals; a subgroup of this group is individuals with disabilities. The authors apply this model to the population at large, but the reader may choose to apply it to any one subgroup, including individuals with disabilities, youth at risk, students who are gifted and talented, students in general education, and so on.

Delivery of Services

The delivery of services is individualized, with each person's interests, preferences, and needs determining the decisions concerning the who, what, where, how, and when of service delivery. Services are delivered anywhere a person is engaging in a goal-related activity. Accessibility to both a formal (e.g., vocational rehabilitation counselor) and informal (e.g., a neighbor) system of service delivery is crucial to the success of choice building. These services might include vocational education, cooperative consultation, situational assessment, conversations with family and friends, job shadowing, supported employment, job interviews, visits to postsecondary schools, joining a chess club or car club, taking a vacation, a bike ride, a bus ride, and so forth. Table 12.3 illustrates an example of service delivery involving many different individuals and situations.

Planning

Planning is an individual and lifelong process with repeating stages of awareness, exploration, preparation, and actualization. Central to planning is goal setting with steps (objectives) to be met in order to reach the goal. This planning could be organized or developed formally through an IEP/ITP, IWRP, or informally through personal goal setting in journals, on napkins, through conversations, or in one's own thoughts. Table 12.4 illustrates the planning process.

Table 12.3
Delivery of Services

Who	What	Where	How	When
Neighbor	Repairing a car	Neighbor's garage	Hands-on practice	Saturday morning
Vocational Rehabilitation Counselor	Situational assessment	Retail shop	Operating a cash register	Tuesday afternoon
Friends	Attending a ball game	University field	Phone conversations	Every evening for a week
Guidance Counselor and other support service personnel	Admissions	Community college	Conversation	In line during preregistration
School Nurse	Exploring health risks of certain jobs	School	Conversation and presentation	During a career exploration class
Speech and Language Therapist	Using an augmented communication device	Work, school, and community	Demonstration and guided learning	Various times throughout the week

Table 12.4
Planning

Awareness	Exploration	Preparation	Actualization
You hear about a bike trip across the country.	You gather information on the trip, bike equipment, and what kind of physical shape a participant needs to be in. You choose if you want to take the trip, taking into account financial, emotional, and physical concerns.	You sign up for the trip and get financially ready, upgrade your bike and test new equipment, and hire a physical fitness expert to help you get into good physical shape.	You ride your bike across the country without being physically, emotionally, or financially drained, and have a good time.
Your boss discusses a promotion with you.	You gather formal and informal information on the promotion and decide if you want to apply.	You talk with colleagues and co-workers about job responsibilities. You prepare for the interview.	You interview for the job.
A family friend is a carpenter and thinks that you might like to be a carpenter.	Because you just turned 14, you discuss exploring the field of carpentry in your next Transition IEP/ITP meeting.	You make a goal to gather formal and informal information on the skills and work environments of being a carpenter. You might gather information from a guidance counselor, school nurse, vocational educator, and carpenters.	You use the information you gathered to decide if your likes, interests, and abilities match this job.
You realize you are having difficulty reading and understanding classified ads.	You meet with special education teacher to explore various classes and approaches to improving your reading.	You enroll in a reading class that emphasizes functional reading.	You apply your reading skills to everyday living.

Competencies

Competencies represent levels of mastery in essential life components in the areas of community, vocational, and academics. Individuals choose to learn applicable knowledge, guided by self-determination, to obtain personal goals. For example, if a high school student chooses to become a radiologist, there are specific competencies needed to do this job. The special educator, school nurse, and guidance counselor could assist the student in determining these competencies from a much larger set of competencies in the field of medicine. Beyond competencies specific to a radiologist, there are general work skills necessary to successful employment. School guidance counselors and State Department of Labor personnel have access to listings of these competencies and can offer valuable information to students and their choice-building committees.

Persons or Professionals Involved

Throughout people's lives, they come in contact with friends, neighbors, family members, social workers, teachers, bosses, and other individuals who assist them in making and obtaining their goals. These people may be casual acquaintances or professionals whose job it is to help them. They may have located them by chance or through a formal system such as an IEP/ITP meeting. Special educators establish collaborative relationships with other professionals that may include school-based service providers, vocational educators, and personnel from postsecondary education, vocational rehabilitation, private industry, developmental services, substance abuse, mental health, blind services, and other public and private agencies. These linkages, along with friends and family, will form the foundation for individuals to build their network of support.

To further illustrate the Lifelong Model for Choice Building, Table 12.5 demonstrates the application of transition services offered to high school students with disabilities. This same type of matrix could be developed for any individuals at any stage of their lives.

The Choice-Building Team

The primary mission of the choice-building team is to support generalization of the model and its components to life outside the structure of the school system. This support is offered through assisting students to first learn the formalized school-based system of transition planning and then to generalize its components to life-integrated choice making. The key to this process is recognizing students as the core members of their choice-building teams (Blalock, 1996). Special educators teach the model to their students and provide ongoing support as students learn to negotiate and master the choice-building process.

Table 12.5
Sample High School Transition Services

Population	Service Delivery	Planning	Competencies	Persons/ Professionals Involved
Lee, age 14	Intensive support services	Lee desires to be included in community activities (volunteer work and leisure) and to participate as best he can with life at home with his family.	–Communicates with an augmentative communication device –Prepares a meal through the principle of partial participation –Volunteers at a community agency or business twice a week	–Speech therapist –Vocational rehabilitation therapist –Family members –Community agency personnel –Business personnel –Special educator –Physical therapist –Recreational and leisure therapist
Drew, age 17	Time-limited support services	Drew desires to be a registered nurse, working full-time. Drew wants to live in an apartment, have a family, and volunteer at the local fire department.	–Completes a child and family care class –Completes consumer and home-making classes –Volunteers at the local fire department –Participates in the Tech Prep program for Health	–Course instructors –Special educator –Fire department personnel –School nurse –Guidance counselor –Tech Prep teachers

Teams can be comprised of (a) people with disabilities and their families, (b) school personnel, (c) adult agency personnel, and (d) general citizens such as employers (Halpern, Benz, & Lindstrom, 1992). The specific composition of each team is based on the current and future needs and interests of the student whose transition planning is the focus of the meeting. Within these teams, special educators play an integral role because of the information they can contribute, the connections they make among other team members, and by mentoring and interacting with students.

A typical choice-building team could be comprised of the student, family members, friends, a special education teacher, a vocational teacher, a general educator, a guidance counselor, a social worker, a vocational rehabilitation counselor, a program coordinator, and a community college support service director. During the meeting each member is responsible for contributing information related to their expertise. This compilation of pertinent data contributes to successful choice building.

Implementing the Model

All the pieces to implement the Lifelong Model for Choice Building are currently available and are in place in some locations. The uniqueness of this model is that it builds on current models of transition with the addition of holistic and lifelong elements. Therefore, current school-based programs can serve as the primer to lifelong choice-building programming. Aspects of current program components and their expansion will be discussed in this section, along with currently implemented best practices.

Students

Schools need to continue teaching students to be self-advocates, because this skill will form the foundation for their ability to make and obtain choices in their lives. Students have to become skilled in making educated choices through goal setting and planning. Students need to become active and engaged participants in their IEP/ITPs and the development of their transition portfolios.

Among the current implemented best practices, Field and Hoffman (1994) have developed a model to promote self-determination. The five components of the model—know yourself, value yourself, plan, act, and experience outcomes and learn—directly apply to skills students need to become active planners in their choice building. *NEXT S.T.E.P.* (Halpern et al., 1997) assists students in becoming active members of their transition planning. It includes Transition Skills Inventories for students, teachers, and parents. Finally, the American School Counselor's Association developed a comprehensive career development portfolio called *Get a Life: Your Personal Planning Portfolio for Career Development*. This resource assists students in planning their careers beginning in the fifth grade. It includes information in four areas: self-knowledge, life roles, educational development, and career exploration and planning (American School Counselor's Association, 1992).

Systems

Agencies, communities, and schools need to continue their interagency collaboration efforts and become even more user-friendly among service providers. Further services need to be coordinated and made easily accessible to students and their families. Professionals must strive to build flexibility into programs so that students can try out and learn new skills in the community, workplace, and school. Equal value must be given to programs for all students, from those who are going to college to those students who are entering supported employment. Teachers must present competencies that are more thematic and pertinent rather than providing information in isolation.

Among the current implemented best practices, Foley and Mundschenk (1997) have suggested that both special and general educators would benefit from knowledge of each other's professional perspective. Information about strategies using collaboration, barriers to collaboration, and effective communication skills should be an integral part of preservice programs for special and general educators. Blalock (1996) proposed the collaborative building of community transition teams that will ensure a comprehensive continuum of transition services for all individuals within a community. Team roles include (a) the definition of desired transition services in the community, (b) identification of community strengths, and (c) identification of targeted needs in the community. Community transition teams may function at several levels, including IEP/ITP committees, school-based transition committees, community and regional transition teams, and state-level transition teams. Moreover, Kohler (1998) described interagency collaboration by dividing the topic into two subcategories. Collaborative frameworks focus on community teams to ensure that there are no service delivery gaps or service duplication, and setting a framework for ongoing collaborative relationships. Collaborative service delivery designed by the IEP/ITP team is a student-centered educational program that includes the mechanisms for assessing progress.

Network of Support

Professionals must be aware that all networks of support are focused on the unique interests, wants, and needs of the person with disabilities. People who can collaboratively facilitate this process may include family members, friends, employers, co-workers, school personnel, agency personnel, service providers, mentors, postsecondary personnel, and community members.

Some of the best practices include *Dare to Dream*, a publication designed as a catalyst to goal planning. In this practice, students determine the makeup of their IEP/ITP committee and personally invite committee members to attend (Bureau of Instructional Support and Community Services, 1995). Mount (1994) found that when developing transition plans for individuals with disabilities, committee members should recognize and utilize both formal (e.g., teachers, vocational rehabilitation counselor) and informal (e.g., neighbor, friend) supports in assisting the people as they achieve goals. Moreover, networks of support should focus on the planning of everyday activities. Committee members should keep in mind that services are as important as family or community connections. Networks of support consist of a group of collaborators; no single person should carry the responsibility for all activities (O'Brien, 1987).

Professionals

All professionals working with students 14 or older need to consider themselves transition specialists. They need to be aware of and able to access the complete range of transition services offered to their students. They should be coordinators of services and have the ability to collaborate with many individuals (within and outside of schools). Transition providers must possess a diverse set of skills. They must be (a) educators, (b) behavior managers, (c) leaders, (d) collaborators, (e) communicators, and (f) time managers. Teacher education programs need to be expanded to include these competencies in their programs.

Among the best practices, deFur and Taymans (1995) have validated a list of competencies needed by transition specialist in the fields of vocational rehabilitation, vocational education, and special education. The list includes skills such as (a) consultation/communication, (b) consultation/leadership; (c) individualized program planning; (d) vocational assessment integration; (e) job development, placement, and maintenance; (f) direct services; and (g) program evaluation. A national survey identified competencies needed by secondary special educators in collaborative activities (Foley & Mundschenk, 1997). The data assist professionals in the skills necessary to incorporate into preservice and in-service teacher preparation. Additionally, the data support the need to expand teacher preparation programs to include competencies in facilitating collaboration. Finally, interdisciplinary personnel preparation occurs in several university-based programs that involve individuals from regular education, special education, vocational education, social work, and vocational rehabilitation. These professionals attend the same classes, work on projects together, and intern in cross-disciplinary sites (Asselin & Cook, 1994; Repetto & Phelps, 1992).

Existing Challenges

The Lifelong Model for Choice Building represents the current state of transition services but also offers a vision of the future of transition planning. It is an indication that the future is here and should be noted. Components necessary to move towards this model are available or currently under development. It is now a matter of putting transition components all together, or perhaps simply changing one's mindset to view transition in a more holistic, regenerative, and lifelong nature.

The following components need to be addressed to aide in the implementation of the Lifelong Model for Choice Building: school programs and professional preparation.

School Programs

Secondary school settings offer many challenges to the collaborative efforts needed for successful choice building, including (a) departmental structure, (b) limited common planning time, (c) diverse roles and expertise of colleagues, and (d) increased use of community resources (Foley & Mundschenk, 1997). Beyond these systematic concerns are student-centered issues. Choice building must be centered around the desires, interests, and needs of the individual. The outcomes of the process will have more likely be attained if students, family, friends, and service providers are active members of choice-building teams. Service coordination needs to occur among agencies, schools, and communities. Finally, school curriculum needs to become more thematic, realistic, and connected to the world outside of the school.

Professional Preparation

Competencies that have been identified as necessary for secondary special educators need to be included in in-service and preservice teacher preparation programs (deFur & Taymans, 1995; Foley & Mundschenk, 1997; Repetto, 1995). Course work in special education teacher preparation programs tends to be weighted toward elementary programming (Pierce, Smith, & Clarke, 1992) and many states (31%) offer K–12 special education teacher certification (Putnam & Habanek, 1993). Both of these factors need to be reevaluated by universities and state departments of education in order to offer course work that best prepares secondary special educators. In-service programs are crucial to update the skills of educators already graduated from systems that were geared towards elementary programming. Additionally, to support collaboration across disciplines, interdisciplinary in-service and preservice programs should be encouraged. Interdisciplinary programs would offer skill updating in choice building to school administers, all teachers, employers, related service personnel, community members, and agency personnel.

Final Thoughts

The National Association of Secondary School Principals (1996), in partnership with the Carnegie Foundation for the Advancement of Teaching, published a report on the high school in the 21st century. The report set a vision for these high schools. This vision could also be the vision for the field of transition, even though such a vision would need to expanded to all grade levels and life beyond the school walls. The following is a list of the vision for high schools of the next century as described by the National Association of Secondary School Principals (1996, p. 5):

I. High school is, above all else, a learning community and each school must commit itself to expecting demonstrated academic achievement for every student in accord with standards that can stand up to national scrutiny.

II. High school must function as a transitional experience, getting each student ready for the next stage of life, whatever it may be for that individual, with the understanding that, ultimately, each person needs to earn a living.

III. High school must be a gateway to multiple options.

IV. High school must prepare each student to be a lifelong learner.

V. High school must provide an underpinning for good citizenship and for full participation in the life of a democracy.

VI. High school must play a role in the personal development of young people as social beings who have needs beyond those that are strictly academic.

VII. High school must lay a foundation for students to be able to participate comfortably in an increasing technological society.

VIII. High school must equip young people for life in a country and a world in which interdependency will link their destiny to that of others, however different those others may be from them.

IX. High school must be an institution that unabashedly advocates on behalf of young people.

Meeting the challenges listed in this report will require the engagement of school and agency personnel, community team members, employers, parents, and students. Some communities may use this list as a blueprint for systems change and long-range planning, whereas others may adopt only some components of the report. As with any systems change, these efforts are merely a step in the direction of creating schools and communities that will facilitate and support the visions of our young people. Ultimately, is that not what each of us deserve from our schools and communities?

References

American School Counselor's Association. (1992). *Get a life: Your personnel planning portfolio for career development.* Alexandria, VA: Author.

Americans with Disabilities Act of 1990, 42 U.S.C. §12101 *et seq.*

Asselin, S., & Cook, A. (1994, December). *Vocational special needs/transition specialists: The validation of competencies through teacher education follow-up.* Paper presented at the meeting of the American Vocational Association, Dallas, TX.

Blalock, G. (1996). Community transition teams as the foundation for transition services for youth with learning disabilities. In J. R. Patton & G. Blalock (Eds.), *Transition and students with learning disabilities* (pp. 213–235). Austin, TX: PRO-ED.

Brolin, D. (1993). *Life centered career education: A competency-based approach* (4th ed.). Reston, VA: Council for Exceptional Children.

Brolin, D. E. (1996). Reflections on the beginning . . . and future directions. *Career Development for Exceptional Individuals, 19* (2), 93–100.

Brolin, D. E., & Kokaska, C. J. (1979). *Career education for handicapped children and youth.* Columbus, OH: Merrill.

Bureau of Instructional Support and Community Services. (1995). *Dare to dream.* Tallahassee: Florida Department of Education.

Carl D. Perkins Vocational and Applied Technology Education Act of 1990, 20 U.S.C. §2301 *et seq.*

Carnevale, A. P., Gainer, L. J., & Meltzer, A. S. (1990). *Workplace basics: The essential skills employers want.* San Francisco: Jossey-Bass.

Clark, G. M., & Kolstoe, O. P. (1995). *Career development and transition education for adolescents with disabilities* (2nd ed.). Needham Heights, MA: Allyn & Bacon.

Clark, G., & Patton, J. (1997). *Transition planning inventory.* Austin, TX: PRO-ED.

D'Alonzo, B. J. (1996). A historical analysis of the Division on Career Development and Transition: Introspective and retrospective viewpoints. *Career Development for Exceptional Individuals, 19* (2), 121–128.

deFur, S. H., & Taymans, J. M. (1995). Competencies needed for transition specialists in vocational rehabilitation, vocational education, and special education. *Exceptional Children, 62,* 39–51.

Deshler, D. D., Ellis, E. S., & Lenz, B. K. (1996). *Teaching adolescents with learning disabilities: Strategies and methods* (2nd ed.). Denver, CO: Love.

DeStefano, L., & Wermuth, T. R. (1992). IDEA (P.L. 101-476): Defining a second generation of transition services. In F. R. Rusch, L. DeStefano, J. Chadsey-Rusch, L. A. Phelps, & E. Szymanski (Eds.), *Transition from school to adult life: Models, linkages, and policy* (pp. 537–549). Sycamore, IL: Sycamore.

Education for All Handicapped Children Act of 1975, 20 U.S.C. §1400 *et seq.*

Field, S., & Hoffman, A. (1994). Development of a model for self-determination. *Career Development for Exceptional Individuals, 17* (2), 159–169.

Foley, R. M., & Mundschenk, N. A. (1997). Collaboration activities and competencies of secondary school special educators: A national survey. *Teacher Education and Special Education, 20* (1), 47–60.

Gajar, A., Goodman, L., & McAfee, J. (1993). *Secondary schools and beyond: Transition of individuals with mild disabilities.* New York: Merrill.

Halpern, A. S. (1985). Transition: A look at the foundations. *Exceptional Children, 51,* 479–486.

Halpern, A. S. , Benz, M. R., & Lindstrom, L. E. (1992). A systems change approach to improving secondary special education and transition programs at the community level. *Career Development for Exceptional Individuals*, 15 (1), 109–120.

Halpern, A. S., Herr, C., Wolf, N., Doren, B., Johnson, M., & Lawson, J. (1997). *NEXT S.T.E.P.: Student transition and educational planning*. Austin, TX: PRO-ED.

Hasazi, S., Gordon, L., & Roe, C. (1985). Factors associated with the employment status of handicapped youth exiting high school from 1979 to 1983. *Exceptional Children*, 51, 455–469.

Individuals with Disabilities Education Act of 1990, 20 U.S.C. §1400 *et seq*.

Individuals with Disabilities Education Act Amendments of 1997, 20 U.S.C. §1400 *et seq*.

Kohler, P. D. (1993). Best practices in transition: Substantiated or implied? *Career Development for Exceptional Individuals*, 16 (2), 107–121.

Kohler, P. D. (1998). Implementing a transition perspective of education: A comprehensive approach to planning and delivering secondary education and transition services. In F. R. Rusch & J. G. Chadsey (Eds.), *Beyond high school: Transition from school to work* (pp. 179–205). Belmont, CA: Wadsworth.

Kokaska, C. J., & Brolin, D. E. (1985). *Career education for handicapped individuals* (2nd ed.). Columbus, OH: Merrill.

Kolstoe, O. P. (1996). From a perspective of forty years in the field: Retrospective and prospective. *Career Development for Exceptional Individuals*, 19 (2), 111–120.

Meers, G. D., & Towne, V. A. (1996). Relfections/projections: A review of language, legislation, and labor for the transition of students with disabilities. *Career Development for Exceptional Individuals*, 19 (2), 129–136.

Mithaug, D., Horiuchi, C., & Fanning, P. (1985). A report on the Colorado statewide follow-up survey of special education students. *Exceptional Children*, 51, 397–404.

Mount, B. (1994). Benefits and limitations of persons futures planning. In V. J. Bradley, J. W. Ashbaugh, & B. C. Blaney (Eds.), *Creating individual supports for people with developmental disabilities: A mandate for change at many levels*. Baltimore: Brookes.

National Association of Secondary School Principals. (1996). *Breaking ranks: Changing an American institution*. Reston, VA: Author.

National Association of State Directors of Special Education. (1997). *Comparison of issues: Previous Law & P.L. 105-17 (1997 IDEA Amendments)*. Alexandria, VA: Author.

Nirje, B. (1969). The normalization principle and its human management implications. In R. B. Kugel & W. Wolfensberger (Eds.), *Changing patterns in residential services for the mentally retarded* (pp. 179–195). Washington, DC: President's Committee on Mental Retardation.

O'Brien, J. (1987). A guide to life-style planning: Using *The Activities Catalog* to integrate services and natural support systems. In B. Wilcox & G. T. Bellamy (Eds.), *A comprehensive guide to* The Activities Catalog: *An alternative curriculum for youth and adults with severe disabilities*. Baltimore: Brookes.

Pierce, T. B., Smith, D. D., & Clarke, J. (1992). Special education leadership: Supply and demand revisited. *Teacher Education and Special Education*, 15(3), 175–182.

Putnam, M., & Habanek, D. (1993). A national survey of certification requirements for teachers of students with mild handicaps: State of confusion. *Teacher Education and Special Education*, 17 (2), 155–160.

Repetto, J. (1995). Curriculum beyond school walls: Implications of transition education. *Peabody Journal of Education*, 70(3), 125–140.

Repetto, J., & Phelps, A. (1992). Effective change in vocational special needs education through project-oriented leadership development. *Journal of Vocational Special Needs Education*, 15(1), 20–26.

Secretary's Commission on Achieving Necessary Skills (SCANS). (1991). *What work requires of schools: A SCANS report for America 2000.* Washington, DC: U.S. Department of Labor. (ERIC Document Reproduction Service No. ED 332 054).

Sitlington, P. L. (1996). Transition assessment: Where have we been and where should we be going? *Career Development for Exceptional Individuals, 19*(2), 159–168.

Smith, D. D. (1998). *Introduction the special education: Teaching in an age of challenge.* Needham Heights, MA: Allyn & Bacon.

Squires, S. (1996). Successful secondary special education programs: A long view. *Career Development for Exceptional Individuals, 19*(2), 137–143.

U.S. Department of Education. (1994). School-to-Work Opportunities Act of 1994 [Online]. URL: http://www.stw.ed.gov/factsht/act.htm

Vocational Education Act of 1963, 26 U.S.C.

Vocational Education Act Amendments of 1968, 26 U.S.C.

White, W. J., & Repetto, J. B. (1996). What's in a name? *Career Development for Exceptional Individuals, 19*(2), 101–110.

Will, M. (1983). *OSERS programming for the transition of youth with disabilities: Bridges from school to working life.* Washington, DC: Office of Special Education and Rehabilitative Services, U.S. Department of Education.

Wolfensberger, W. (Ed). (1972). *The principal of normalization in human services.* Toronto: National Institute on Mental Retardation.

Making the Delivery
of Transition Services
Collaborative: An Epilogue

Gary M. Clark

"I wouldn't give a fig for the simplicity on this side of complexity; I would give my right arm for the simplicity on the far side of complexity."

—Oliver Wendell Holmes

The mandate of the IDEA for local schools to be responsible for transition services planning and service delivery is clear. However, who is to deliver transition services is not always so clear. The general mandate for transition services is interpreted by many educational administrators and other educators as the unique responsibility of special education teachers or specially designated personnel who have teacher certification or the interests, training, or experience that would make a good match for the job. The job, as it has evolved since the early 1990s, requires competencies for transition services delivery that are associated not only with teaching, but also with student assessment/evaluation, collaborative consultation, behavior management/ programming, counseling and guidance, crisis intervention and creative problem solving, family coordination, social and communication skills coaching, job and employability skills coaching, health, fitness, and sexuality advising, community services linkage and coordination, and leisure and recreation brokering. Typically, certified special education teachers are expected to perform these tasks or connect students with someone who can. Some of these competencies are the general domains of the major disciplines in school-based related services: school psychology, school guidance and counseling, school social work, school nursing/health coordination, speech and language pathology, recreation therapy, vocational evaluation, assistive technology, occupational therapy, and physical therapy.

It has often been a concern that most states require demonstration of knowledge and competencies of the practitioners in a large number of occupational or trade areas but not for transition specialists. For example, it is common among states to have proficiency requirements, examinations, and licenses or certifications for barbers, cosmetologists, real estate agents, building contractors, plumbers, electricians, roofers, embalmers and funeral directors, court reporters, hearing aid dispensers, private investigators, and, of course, most medical, health, and psychological or social services professionals. Whereas teachers, and specifically special education teachers, are also among the commonly licensed or certified educational professionals in states, the transition specialist (sometimes called transition coordinator or transition counselor) is free in nearly all states to perform many nonteaching, out-of-discipline roles and tasks without any required, demonstrated competencies other than those that were required for them as special education teachers. In some states, that teacher certification could be as narrow as a specific category of special education teacher (mental retardation, learning disabilities, visual impairment, severe and multiple disabilities, etc.).

Obviously, one person needs to be a coordinator of transition services planning and delivery for every student 14 years of age and older, but it is too much to ask of untrained transition specialists to perform all the tasks they currently are being asked to perform. Many have natural talents that make them highly effective and many learn and develop transdisciplinary skills through experience. Sadly, some of that experience is learned through mistakes—mistakes on young people. This would not be the case if there were ever anyone else qualified and available to assist and help prevent or minimize mistakes. Who is there in the school setting who has the qualifications and is available to assist in the transition services delivery process? It is appropriate at this point in the development of transition services and programs in public schools that the service delivery process for transition services be examined and put into context with current middle and secondary school educational personnel roles and the school-based related services disciplines that could contribute.

The school-based related services disciplines represented in this book are the most relevant to transition services planning and delivery efforts, although some disciplines are not included that are, in fact, not only qualified but available in some school districts (e.g., music therapy or rehabilitation counseling) to assist with certain needed transition services planning and delivery. Deciding what disciplines should be included in this book and recognizing their potential contributions was simple. Saying collaboration is needed is simple. More difficult and more complex is getting special educators to "let go" and request collaboration of related services colleagues from those disciplines. Another complex challenge is getting related services professionals to take transition services delivery on as part of their responsibilities and then see the task as collaborative rather than ancillary. A third difficulty is getting administrators to see the potential in school-based related services for contributing to transition services and programs, and not only authorizing, but facilitating, collaboration.

Most individuals view the various disciplines much like they view their own families. Publicly, people acknowledge strengths and ignore or deny weaknesses, problems, or failures of the past. Privately, people are very concerned about problems and weakness, frequently minimizing strengths. People also tend to have visions of the future for their families, visions that set high expectations and standards for performance. People talk about those expectations publicly to get approval from others. People in disciplines in education and human services exhibit many of these same behaviors, some of which were described by various chapter authors in this book. As with family visions for expectations and standards, the expectations are frequently unrealistically high, at least for short-term, day-to-day evaluations.

Two ideas were made clear in the previous chapters of this book. First, the related services disciplines' representatives selected for their participation in the symposium to develop this book acknowledged that their participation in the transition process involving planning, education/training, related services delivery, and follow through was exceedingly complex for many students. Secondly, having a legal mandate, regulations, professional standards and ethics, value statements, and certifications or licensures does not guarantee quality services for students or individual professional competence in transition-related activities.

With these two perspectives as foundations for summing up a beginning dialogue between special educators and school-based related services personnel, this chapter highlights (a) the major collaboration themes that were common throughout the chapters, and (b) some barrier themes that were raised by chapter authors. This chapter also proposes or reiterates some recommendations that came out of the symposium and preparation of final versions of the chapters.

Major Collaboration Themes

The following are the major collaboration themes, that emerged from the chapters of this book.

▶ A life span perspective in transition planning and services is important.

Most disciplines involved in working with persons with disabilities realize the importance of early intervention. The federal legislative actions that mandated transition planning and services targeted the beginning (age 3) and ending (ages 14 to 21) of public school responsibilities, but did not mandate services between the ages of 3 and 14. Recommended practice is clear on the need for a seamless transition planning and service delivery from early childhood through adulthood for the many kinds of transitions people face through life.

▶ Students and their families must be empowered to give direction to life span transition processes.

Not only did the reauthorization of the IDEA strengthen the participatory roles of students and their families in the IEP/ITP process, but school-based related service disciplines commonly spoke to the positive effects of family involvement in their planning and intervention procedures. It is becoming more and more apparent that as attention is given to needs, preferences, and interests in other important performance areas other than just academic performance, families see that classroom teachers are not the sole source of knowledge or information on the student for all areas.

▶ Quality of life in all areas of life, not just employment, must be the basis for transition outcome goals.

There was unanimous agreement among the authors that quality of life in such areas as health, sexuality, personal and social communication, mobility, community participation, independence in daily living, and leisure and recreation was equally important to employment. This agreement was tremendously heartening. It appears that the broader definitions of transition services advocated by Brolin (1993), Halpern (1985, 1994), Clark and Kolstoe (1995), Wehman (1996) and many others has finally overcome the narrow focus of the early federal transition initiatives on school-to-work transitions (Will, 1984).

▶ Common humanistic values across disciplines related to service delivery for persons with disabilities provide a common language and perspective for professionals.

Values that are built into professional standards and codes of ethics communicate important messages about a discipline. Collaboration is most successful when there is a mutually held set of values that are critical to establishing trust. Special educators reading the chapters in this book will find kindred spirits among these related services discipline representatives. While there was honest reflection by the authors on their respective fields' readiness to move quickly into the transition services delivery process, several authors cited research that revealed a high percentage of field practitioners stating that transition from school to adult living is important and that they should be involved, even if they were not currently involved.

▶ Competence, training, and interest in transition services delivery are more important in determining collaborative involvement than are traditional roles or professional turf boundaries.

In most disciplines, there are many professionals who have the training and competence to perform a variety of transdisciplinary tasks but who have no interest in doing so. There are others who have all the skills but are never asked to help. The theme that came out in the authors' comments about the nature of real transdisciplinary collaboration was that committed (i.e., interested) individuals are usually willing to relinquish control or ask for assistance from someone they trust as having the competence, training, and interest to do a better job than they could themselves. In Chapter 3, Levinson and Murphy made the point that professionally competent school psychologists who are untrained in the transition process show their true professionalism and commitment, however, by seeking out the specific training that is needed to be truly competent. This notion applies to other disciplines as well.

▶ Assessments unique to school-based related services disciplines are critical in revealing a broad array of needs, preferences, and interests for transition planning.

Planning based solely on educational assessments for present level of performance is too restrictive for good transition assessment and planning. Information is needed in a wide range of transition planning areas, some of which should be conducted by professionals in other disciplines. Special education personnel may not be aware of or competent in conducting assessments in such areas as communication, social histories and environmental assessments, health and fitness, formal or functional assessments of independent living, occupational aptitudes, physical abilities, or leisure and recreational skills and interests. Collaborative transition assessment and planning may be especially appropriate in cases where students are difficult to assess because of physical, cognitive, or communication problems. From a strategy perspective of encouraging participation of related services colleagues in the transition planning process, the multidisciplinary assessment process is an ideal way of "hooking" colleagues into the lives of individual students who need them.

▶ Participation or collaboration in the transition process for an individual student may come at any point in the process, not just at a transition planning meeting.

The essence of this theme seems to be the notion that related services personnel may be trained for clinical or specialized settings, but since being brought into the process of providing comprehensive services in school-based settings, their professional competencies are used in a variety of ways: assessment, direct intervention, consultation with teachers and families, and serving as liaison between the school and nonschool service agencies. If a related service professional is going to be involved in service delivery at all, he or she should definitely be involved in some aspect of planning for that involvement. This involvement does not have to be at the IEP meeting necessarily, but can occur prior to or after the meeting. Naturally, the more a related service colleague is needed with a student in planning and delivering transition services, the more likely the involvement will increase at multiple points in time.

Major Barrier Themes

While all the authors of the chapters emphasized the positive contributions that their respective disciplines can and should be making, they also felt obliged to address some of the current barriers preventing collaborative transition efforts with special educators at the secondary level. Each of these is presented and discussed briefly in this section.

▶ Terminology, discipline cultures, and discipline perspectives present some barriers in communication within and across disciplines.

It was no surprise to symposium participants that these barriers emerged both in most chapter drafts and in participant comments. The direct ties of some disciplines' roots to the fields of medicine or psychology suggest valid reasons for unique vocabulary and philosophies of intervention that are not familiar to other colleagues in school settings. Some of the examples of discipline cultures and status stereotypes are real, others are myths. Differences between and among disciplines in the amount of training or examinations required of its licensed or certified professionals tend to add to the mystique of those disciplines. Discipline perspectives, particularly those coming out of the medical model, can also pose problems in communication in school-based settings where the medical model is frequently openly rejected.

The candid admission by several of the authors of these common barriers within their own disciplines should be informative to educators. The major implication of this is that if an educator hesitates to request assistance or collaboration from a colleague in another discipline because of preconceived notions about what "they" do, believe, or support, there is a real danger in being guilty of stereotyping that colleague as well as the discipline itself. Intradiscipline differences in values related to professional roles and responsibilities are common in education and it should not be surprising that they exist in school psychology, communication disorders, occupational therapy, social work, or any other discipline.

▶ Both research and observational data indicate that school-based related services personnel report constraints on their active collaboration in the transition process.

The three most common barriers to collaboration or participation in the transition process with secondary students with disabilities are lack of time, lack of funding, and administrative restrictions based on assigned roles or job descriptions. Anyone who has worked in schools or other public institutions or bureaucracies will recognize these as familiar complaints. The research data several authors presented indicating discrepancies between what actual job roles were and what they should be support the notion that these three barriers and others are part of the reality of current school systems. The time barrier may relate to itinerant service delivery models, emphasis on serving only the most severe cases, and emphasis on serving elementary and middle school students rather than high school students. Funding relates to any number of aspects of service delivery, but may affect caseloads and decisions related to the number of related service personnel who can or will be employed. Administrative restrictions may stem from the funding barrier, but they may also stem from a lack of understanding of student needs for transition and the kinds of competencies and skills that related services personnel could bring to transition programs and services. Limited or biased views of what transition services are can also contribute to the general category of administrative restrictions.

It was also suggested that perhaps a more basic reason for limited participation or collaboration was the simple fact of not being invited to participate in ongoing transition planning activities. Special educators should respond to this notion immediately. Certainly, the best test of whether or not there are time, funding, and administrative barriers comes after it is clear that related services professionals have been invited to participate. Secondary special education personnel engaged in transition planning and service delivery must take the initiative to seek out and invite related services colleagues, even if those colleagues

are housed in an elementary building or some administrative center away from
high school campuses.

▶ Retrenchment and decredentialing in school-based related services disciplines is an alarming trend.

In spite of strengthened provisions in the IDEA through the 1997 reauthorization for related services being an expected part of the transition services mandate, the reality of funding for local schools is that fewer people are expected to
do more work. In addition to the funding retrenchments, there are serious shortages in both educational and related services personnel, forcing state and local
education agencies to authorize employment of people who are not fully trained
or certified. Given the logic and desirability of transdisciplinary collaboration,
retrenchment and decredentialing make no sense and represent serious barriers
to the idea that well-trained, competent professionals can work together in an
increasingly complex system.

▶ Professional standards in education and related services disciplines are
inadequate to encourage and support transdisciplinary collaboration in
transition services.

The focus of this stated barrier was that disciplines vary in their current
interest in or awareness of transition services delivery. Some disciplines include
standards that do specifically relate to one or more transition services (e.g., vocational assessment in school psychology and vocational evaluation, pragmatics
communication assessment in communication disorders, coordination of human
service organizations in social work, independent living assessment and training
in occupational therapy, etc.). Other disciplines have standards that may indi-
rectly relate to one or more transition service activities, but may have no standards at all for other transition services that could be included. A troublesome
aspect of current professional standards that do refer to transition-related competency requirements is that there is inadequate accountability to see that personnel preparation programs do, in fact, ensure that those competency areas are
covered in training and the students demonstrate the competencies prior to exit
from the program. At this point, no single school-based related services discipline has standards that specifically refer to transition services responsibilities or
competency requirements, except for the field of vocational evaluation. Unfortunately, vocational evaluation is not a common school-based related service in
the vast majority of states.

▶ Current organizational structures in public education inhibit transdisciplinary transition services delivery.

The theme of a need for new paradigms for delivering transition services was one that evolved over the two and a half days of the symposium and appeared in several chapters. Participants shared their beliefs that public education and its supportive related services need to change not only the ways they approached students and their families, but also the delivery models themselves. There is no doubt that some kind of reform or restructuring will emerge over the next decade that will demand some changes in both approaches and systems. It was agreed that value systems and politics within the larger society (parents, school boards, policy makers, advocacy groups, etc.) will try to shape any recommended reforms and that current societal concerns for educational programs for students without disabilities may be counterproductive to developing creative delivery system alternatives for students with disabilities.

Recommendations for Developing and Improving Transdisciplinary Collaboration in Transition Programs and Services

The thoughtful preparation and development of the various discipline participants' chapters resulted in some interesting and challenging recommendations for their own fields as well as for all those interested in the transition process for all students with disabilities. The following recommendations come directly out of the chapters or from inferences made after reflection subsequent to the symposium reactions and comments and the final versions of the chapters:

1. Educational and school-based related services disciplines need to look at major paradigm shifts in their approach to students and families and the entire educational delivery system for students with disabilities (Chapters 2, 4, 8, and 12).

2. School-based related service disciplines should be involved in the transition process (all chapters).

3. School guidance and counseling programs should be restructured to reflect the standards underlying the Comprehensive Developmental School Counseling Model (Chapter 8).

4. The school nurse should be recognized legislatively within IDEA as a legitimate related services provider (Chapter 5).

5. School-based related services personnel need to develop strategies for active marketing of their services to policy makers and consumers of transition services (students and parents).

6. The Division on Career Development and Transition (DCDT-CEC) and professional organizations representing school-based related services should collaborate to form an Interdisciplinary Council on Transition Services modeled after the Interdisciplinary Council on Vocational Evaluation and Assessment described by Leconte in Chapter 11.

7. Higher education professional development programs in special education and disciplines offering school-based related services need to include collaboration among school personnel across disciplines in delivering transition services.

Final Thoughts

I have been involved in one form or another in the transition process of young people with disabilities for 36 years now. During that time the issue of collaborative efforts has maintained itself as a basic need, a basic premise of success, but as only a partially achieved goal. There have been identifiable periods of progress: cooperative work–study programs in the 1960s and early 70s between public school special education and state vocational rehabilitation agencies; cooperative agreements and programs between special education and vocational education in the 1970s and 1980s; collaborative teaming between general and special education and related services personnel after the implementation of the EHA; and the interagency agreements between special education, vocational rehabilitation, vocational education, and other related disability agencies at the state and local levels in the 1980s and 1990s. Despite the progress, any gathering of professionals involved in developing and implementing transition services and programs usually results in some show of concern (sometimes anger, nearly always frustration and impatience) with the continuing barriers to better collaboration. It is easy—very easy—to despair.

The very talented and able writers of this book, brought together through the symposium, have renewed my hope. They presented, both individually and as a group, a forceful, reasoned appeal to special educators, administrators, and colleagues in their own disciplines for a collaborative approach to transition services. They made strong cases for not only the potential for but also the readiness of related services disciplines as untapped sources of support for transition programs and services. They have given voice to what I think Oliver Wendell Holmes was talking about in his phrase, "the simplicity on the far side of complexity."

Transition specialists or special education teachers, who feel overwhelmed with all there is to do and the little time or knowledge to do it, need to take these writers' ideas seriously. I would be disappointed if any special educator read this book and was not given the same renewal of hope and sense of direction I experienced.

References

Brolin, D. E. (1993). *Life centered career education: A competency-based approach* (4th ed.). Reston, VA: Council for Exceptional Children.

Clark, G. M., & Kolstoe, O. P. (1995). *Career development and transition education for adolescents with disabilities* (2nd ed.). Needham Heights, MA: Allyn & Bacon.

Halpern, A. S. (1985). Transition: A look at the foundations. *Exceptional Children, 51,* 479–486.

Halpern, A. S. (1994). The transition of youth with disabilities to adult life: A position statement of the Division on Career Development and Transition, The Council for Exceptional Children. *Career Development for Exceptional Individuals, 17,* 115–124.

Wehman, P. (1996). *Life beyond the classroom: Transition services for young people with disabilities* (2nd ed.). Baltimore: Brookes.

Will, M. (1984). *OSERS programming for the transition of youth with disabilities: Bridges from school to working life.* Washington, DC: U.S. Department of Education.

Author Index

Subject Index

465

DATE DUE

OCT 3 0 2003			

GAYLORD

PRINTED IN U.S.A.